VISUAL QUICK

MW01252623

Mac OS X Lion

MARIA LANGER

Peachpit Press

Visual QuickStart Guide
Mac OS X Lion
Maria Langer

Peachpit Press
1249 Eighth Street
Berkeley, CA 94710
510/524-2178
510/524-2221 (fax)

Find us on the Web at www.peachpit.com.
To report errors, please send a note to errata@peachpit.com.
Peachpit Press is a division of Pearson Education.

Copyright © 2012 by Maria Langer

Editor: Clifford Colby
Production Coordinator: David Van Ness
Copyeditor: Clifford Colby
Technical Editors: Clifford Colby and Maria Langer
Compositors: Maria Langer and David Van Ness
Indexer: Julie Bess
Cover Design: RHDG / Riezebos Holzbaur Design Group, Peachpit Press
Interior Design: Peachpit Press
Logo Design: MINE™ www.minesf.com

Notice of Rights

Notice of Liability

Trademarks

ISBN-13: 978-0-321-78673-9
ISBN-10:   0-321-78673-4

9 8 7 6 5 4 3 2 1

Printed and bound in the United States of America

Dedication

To the Beaumont Family
of Quincy, Washington

for making me feel so welcome
in my home away from home.

Special Thanks:

To Cliff Colby, who has been working with me on *Mac OS Visual QuickStart Guides* since the dawn of time (or so it seems). A special big thanks to Cliff this year for making this old author feel *appreciated* right from the start of this project, setting a positive tone for the massive task ahead of us.

To David Van Ness, for his sharp eye and layout skills. If this book looks as great as I think it does, it's David you need to thank—not me.

To Julie Bess, for coming through yet again on another tight deadline indexing project. I know I promised her more time on my next book, but I must have meant the one *after* this one.

To Michael Rose, Debbie Ripps, and Miraz Jordan for helping me with a few screen shots that were difficult (or downright impossible) for me to get on my own.

Speaking of screen shots, to the folks at Ambrosia Software, for developing and supporting Snapz Pro X. I could not have taken the 2,000+ screen shots in this book without that great application. A big thanks to David Dunham for quickly getting me on the beta program when I was having trouble getting Snapz Pro to work with Lion.

To the Mac OS development team at Apple, for continuing to refine and improve the world's best operating system. I didn't think they could make it any better but they proved me wrong.

And to Mike, for the usual reasons.

Contents at a Glance

Table of Contents

Introduction

Mac OS X Lion—or also simply called OS X Lion—is the latest version of the computer operating system that put the phrase *graphic user interface* in everyone's vocabulary. With Mac OS, you can point, click, and drag to work with files, applications, and utilities. Because the same intuitive interface is utilized throughout the system, you'll find that a procedure that works in one program works in virtually all the others.

Using This Book

This Visual QuickStart Guide will help you learn OS X Lion by providing step-by-step instructions, plenty of illustrations, and a generous helping of tips. On these pages, you'll find everything you need to know to get up and running quickly with Mac OS X—and a lot more!

This book was designed for page flipping. Use the table of contents or index to find the topics you need help for, learn what you need to know, and get on with your work. If you're brand new to Mac OS, however, I recommend that you begin by reading at least Part I of this book. In those chapters, you'll find basic information about techniques you'll use every day with your computer.

If you're interested in information about new Mac OS X features, be sure to browse through this Introduction. It'll give you a good idea of what you can expect to see on your computer.

But Wait, There's More!

Although this book is almost 650 pages long, it doesn't cover every single aspect of using Mac OS X. You can find additional material that didn't make it into this book—including content about features that were just being announced when this book when to press—on my book support website, **www.MariasGuides.com**.

Visual QuickStart Guides are now even more visual: Building on the success of the top-selling Visual QuickStart Guide books, Peachpit now offers Video QuickStarts. As a companion to this book, Peachpit offers more than an hour of short, task-based videos that will help you master Lion's top features and techniques; instead of just reading about how to use a tool, you can watch it in action. It's a great way to learn all the basics and some of the newer or more complex features of the program. Log on to the Peachpit site at **www.peachpit.com/register** to register your book, and you'll find a free streaming sample; purchasing the rest of the material is quick and easy.

New Features in OS X Lion

Mac OS X Lion includes several brand new features, as well as a handful of interface and functionality improvements and "under-the-hood" changes to improve performance.

Here's a look at some of the new and revised features you can expect to find in OS X Lion; most of these features are covered in detail throughout the pages of this book.

TIP You can learn more about the new features of Mac OS X Lion on Apple's Web site at **www.apple.com/lion**.

Brand New Features

- **App Store** availability of Mac OS makes it easier than ever to buy and install and update OS X Lion on any computer authorized with your Apple ID.

- **Mission Control** Ⓐ combines the features of Exposé and Spaces into a single interface that makes it a snap to navigate and access open windows and applications.

Ⓐ Mission Control offers fast access to Dashboard, Spaces, Full-Screen Apps, and individual applications.

Ⓑ Launchpad displays icons for all of your installed applications in one place.

Ⓒ The Full-Screen Apps feature gives you a great, distraction-free environment for working with documents.

D AirDrop makes it very easy to share files with other Mac users within range.

E FaceTime makes it possible to see just how nervous your editor is days before a big deadline.

F The Resume feature can restore your system's applications and document window to the way they were when you shut down.

- **Launchpad B** gives you quick access to all of the applications installed on your computer and includes an uninstall feature for applications purchased from the App Store.

- **Auto Save** automatically saves your documents as you work and makes it easy to go back to a previous version of a document.

- **Versions** records the history of a document, helping you quickly revert to a previous version.

- **Full-Screen Apps C** makes it possible to fill your screen with the window(s) from just one application, removing distractions so you can work more efficiently.

- **AirDrop D** enables you to easily but securely exchange files with other AirDrop-enabled computers within rage.

- **FaceTime E** enables you to make video calls to other Intel-based Mac OS computers, iPad 2, iPhone 4, and the latest iPod touch.

- **Resume F** lets you restore an application's open windows as they were when you quit. It also works for your System, making it possible on startup to restore your work environment—open applications and documents—to the way it was when you shut down.

- **Lookup** gets Dictionary, Thesaurus, and Web information for any word you double-tap with three fingers on a Multi-Touch device.

- **Restore Partition**, which is automatically installed with OS X Lion, makes it possible to repair or reinstall Mac OS without the need for a bootable disc.

System & Finder Improvements

- About This Mac ⓖ helps you find important information about your Mac and connected storage devices.

- The Mail, Contacts & Calendars preferences pane ⓗ makes it a breeze to set up accounts for Microsoft Exchange, Gmail, Yahoo!, and AOL.

- You can show or hide the indicator lights for open applications in the Dock.

- You can change the scroll direction preferences for Multi-Touch gesture scrolling.

- You can now sort files by category, kind, application, date modified, date added, or size.

- An All My Files smart folder ⓘ makes it quick and easy to see an organized view of all the files on your Mac in one window.

- Now you can quickly create a folder full of multiple selected items using the New Folder with Selection command.

- When copying or moving a file to a location that already has a file with the same name, you now have an option to keep both files.

- The Finder now supports more gestures for Multi-Touch devices.

- Screen sharing improvements make it possible to connect to a Mac and access it while another user is connected.

- Spotlight has been improved for easier searching and the ability to search the Web.

- Auto-correction has been improved to suggest spellings before making a change.

ⓖ The About This Mac window has been redesigned.

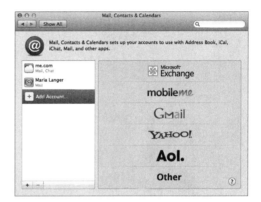

ⓗ The Mail, Contacts & Calendars preferences pane makes it easy to set up accounts from a number of services.

ⓘ The new All My Files feature makes it easy to see...well, all your files.

J Address Book now has a simpler interface.

K Mail's updated interface includes previews in the message list. (This brand new computer is sitting in a box behind me as I work. Do you think that's enough motivation to finish up quickly?)

L iCal's new Day view helps you keep on top of the things you have to do today and in the near future.

Other Improved Features

- **Address Book J** has been revised with a new, simpler interface and new or improved support for Yahoo!, FaceTime, iPhoto, instant messaging, and social network profiles.

- **Mail K** has been improved with a cleaner interface, message previews, a favorites bar, conversations, the ability to hide quoted text, and color-coded labels.

- **Safari** improvements include a new Reading List feature, navigation gestures for Multi-Touch devices, Privacy settings, and sandboxing to protect your data from malicious websites.

- **iCal L** has been revised with a new, streamlined look, day view, year view, Quick Add feature, and heat map to identify busy days.

- **Preview** improvements include at-a-glance search results, iWork and Office document support, and Smart Magnify.

- **QuickTime Player** now enables you to merge clips, rotate video, record only a portion of the screen, and share video directly to Vimeo, Flickr, FaceBook, iMovie, and Mail.

- **TextEdit** now has a formatting toolbar and other improvements to make it more functional and easy to use.

- **iChat** now supports Yahoo! Messenger and displays all of your buddies in one list.

- **Photo Booth** adds new effects, high-resolution photos, and the ability to trim video clips.

continues on next page

- **Security** preferences now include a Privacy pane where you can set options for location services and diagnostic and usage data collection.

- **FileVault** now protects your entire hard disk from unauthorized access with XTS-AES 128 encryption.

- **Time Machine** now supports local snapshots, making it possible to keep a history of your documents without an external hard disk.

- The **System Preferences** 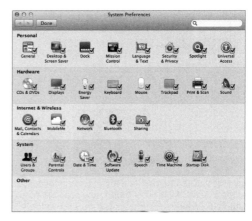 window can be customized to hide icons you don't want to see.

- **Migration Assistant**  can now import data from a Microsoft Windows PC to a Mac.

- **Accessibility** has been improved by the addition of new voices, language support, picture-in-picture zoom, Braille verbosity settings, and VoiceOver activities.

- **AppleScript** and **Automator** have been improved to offer more flexibility for automating tasks.

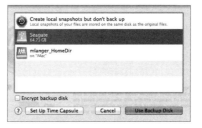

M Time Machine now offers the option of creating local snapshots.

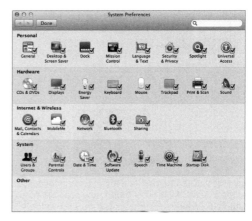

N You can toggle check boxes in this window to determine which System Preferences panes appear.

O You read right: Migration Assistant now supports migrating from a Windows PC.

Getting Started with Mac OS X

In This Part

Setting Up
Mac OS X Lion

Before you can use Mac OS X Lion, you must install it on your computer and configure it to work the way you need it to. These are two separate steps and you may not need to do both.

- If you purchased a new computer with Mac OS X Lion already installed, you won't need to install it, so you can skip the first half of this chapter. When you start your computer for the first time, it'll open the Setup Assistant to step you through the process of configuring your computer. This is discussed in the second half of this chapter.

- If you are upgrading a Mac you already own to Mac OS X Lion, you'll need to install Lion on your computer as discussed in the first half of this chapter. Once that's done, your Mac shouldn't need any additional configuration, so you can skip the second half of this chapter.

With all that in mind, this chapter covers how to install and configure OS X Lion.

In This Chapter:

Installing
Mac OS X Lion

Mac OS X's installer application handles all aspects of a Mac OS installation. When you open it, it prompts you for some information, then restarts your computer and installs the software. When the installation process is finished, the installer automatically restarts your computer from your hard disk and, if necessary, displays the Setup Assistant so you can configure Mac OS X Lion for your use.

OS X Lion is the first version of Mac OS software that Apple is making available only as an App Store download. Because of this, you'll need a few things to purchase, download, and install the software:

- **A Macintosh computer with one of the following Intel processors: Core 2 Duo, Core i3, Core i5, Core i7, or Xeon.** Older Macintosh models cannot run Lion.

- **Mac OS X Snow Leopard 10.6.7 or later.** This is the first version of OS X that supports the App Store, which you'll need to get the OS X Lion installer. If you don't have the latest version of Snow Leopard installed on your computer, you'll need to run Software Update to get it.

- **An Apple ID.** This is the same account you might already use for the App Store, iTunes Store or MobileMe. If you don't have an Apple ID, you'll need to sign up to get one; it's free.

- **An Internet connection.** Since you'll be downloading OS X Lion and the file is large, you'll want the fastest Internet connection possible.

This part of the chapter explains how to prepare for and install Mac OS X Lion.

TIP The installation instructions in this chapter assume you know basic Mac OS techniques, such as pointing, clicking, double-clicking, dragging, and selecting items from a menu. If you're brand new to the Mac and don't know any of these techniques, skip ahead to Chapter 2, which discusses Mac OS basics.

TIP If your computer is brand new and you haven't even started it yet, chances are you have OS X Lion installed. When you start your computer, it'll display the Setup Assistant. Skip ahead to the section titled "Configuring OS X Lion" on page 9.

TIP The OS X Lion installer is almost 4 GB in size and can take quite some time to download, even over a fast connection. Do not even *think* about downloading it using a dialup or mobile hotspot connection to the Internet.

TIP If you don't have a fast Internet connection, consider taking your Mac to an Apple Store or somewhere else where a fast connection is available. If that's not possible, contact Apple at 1-800-MY-APPLE for advice or assistance.

Ⓐ Choose About This Mac from the Apple menu.

Ⓑ The About This Mac window provides information about the currently installed version of Mac OS and your computer's processor, among other things.

To learn your computer's processor & Mac OS version:

1. Choose Apple > About this Mac **Ⓐ**.

2. In the About This Mac window that appears **Ⓑ**, consult the Version number and Processor information.

3. Click the window's close button to dismiss it.

TIP Remember, you need Version 10.6.7 and an Intel Core 2 Duo, Core i3, Core i5, Core i7, or Xeon processor.

To update to the latest version of Snow Leopard:

Follow the instruction in the section titled "To manually check for updates" on page 566 and "To install updates" on page 567.

TIP It's best to install *all* updates that Software Update finds.

To set up an Apple ID:

1. Click the App Store icon in the Dock to open the App Store application.

2. Follow the instructions in the section titled "To get an Apple ID" on page 177.

TIP If you already have an Apple ID, you don't need to do this.

To buy Mac OS X Lion:

1. Follow the instructions in Chapter 13 to open the App Store, sign in, and search for Mac OS X Lion.

2. Click the $29.99 buy button near the Lion icon.

3. Follow the prompts that appear to complete the purchase.

   Your computer should begin downloading OS X Lion immediately. If it does not, follow the instructions in the section titled "To download Mac OS X Lion" below to download it.

4. When the download is complete, continue following the instructions in the section titled "To install Mac OS X Lion" on page 7.

To download Mac OS X Lion:

1. If you have already purchased Lion but have either not downloaded it or want to download it again for another computer, click the Purchases button in the App Store application.

   A list of all your purchased software appears .

2. Click the Install button on the right end of the line for Mac OS X Lion.

   Your computer should begin downloading OS X Lion immediately.

3. When the download is complete, continue following the instructions in the section titled "To install Mac OS X Lion" on page 7.

TIP You can download and install OS X Lion on any Macintosh you own.

C The Purchases screen lists all App Store purchases for your Apple ID.

D The Mac OS X Lion installer icon looks like this.

Mac OS X Lion

E The first installer screen.

F The Software license agreement.

To install Mac OS X Lion:

1. Do one of the following:
   - ▸ If the Mac OS X Lion installer opened automatically after it was downloaded, skip ahead to step 2.
   - ▸ If the Mac OS Lion installer did not automatically open, double-click its icon **D**. You should find it in the Applications folder on your hard disk.

2. An Install Mac OS X window appears **E**. Click Continue.

3. A software license agreement appears next **F**. Read the contents of this dialog, click Agree, and then click Agree again in the smaller confirmation dialog that appears.

4. The next dialog indicates which hard disk Mac OS X will be installed on **G**:
   - ▸ To install on the hard disk displayed in the window **G**, click Install.
   - ▸ To install on another hard disk that's connected to your computer but not displayed, click Show All Disks. Then select the disk in the list that appears **H** and click Install.

continues on next page

G Confirm that you want to install on the displayed disk...

H ...or choose a different disk attached to your computer.

5. A password dialog appears next . Enter an administrator name and password and click OK.

6. Wait while the Mac OS X Lion installer installs the software. You should see the following processes:

   ▸ The installer prepares to install . This includes checking the downloaded file to make sure it is problem-free.

   ▸ Your computer restarts.

   ▸ The installer installs Mac OS X. This can take 30 minutes or more, depending on your computer.

   ▸ Your computer restarts again.

7. When the installation is finished, one of two things happens:

   ▸ If you are updating an existing Mac OS X installation, a Thank You message appears. Click Start Using Lion to quit the installer. If prompted, log in to go to the Finder desktop. You're finished.

   ▸ If you have installed Mac OS X on a hard disk that did not already contain a Mac OS installation, the first screen of the Setup Assistant appears. Continue following instructions in the section titled "Configuring Mac OS X Lion" on page 9.

TIP In step 3, if you click the Disagree button, you will not be able to install Mac OS X.

TIP The password dialog **I** prevents someone without administrator privileges from installing system software. This is especially important on a computer accessible to others.

TIP Software Update (page 566) may run right after installing Mac OS X Lion. If any software updates are available for your computer, a dialog with update information appears.

I Enter an administrator name and password in this dialog to continue the installation.

J The installer prepares to install Mac OS.

Configuring Mac OS X Lion

The Mac OS X Setup Assistant uses a simple question-and-answer process to get information about you and the way you use your computer. The information you provide is automatically entered in the various System Preferences panes of Mac OS X to configure your computer for Mac OS X.

TIP The Mac OS X Setup Assistant automatically opens when you first start a new computer or a computer with a new Mac OS X installation.

TIP If the Mac OS X Setup Assistant does not appear, Mac OS X is already configured. You can skip this section.

TIP Although I'm pretty good at getting screenshots for my book, I was unable to capture images of Mac OS X's Setup Assistant. Try to follow along with the text. As you'll see, the process is pretty self-explanatory.

To configure Mac OS X:

1. In the Welcome window that appears after installing Mac OS X, select the name of the country you're in. Click Continue.

2. In the Select Your Keyboard window, select a keyboard layout. Click Continue.

3. In the Select Your Wi-Fi Network window, do one of the following:

   ‣ If the network you connect to is listed, select it, enter a password if necessary, and click Continue.

   ‣ If you connect to a network or the Internet using a different method, click Other Network Options, select one of the options in the How Do You Connect? window, and click Continue.

The Mac OS X Setup Assistant may prompt you for more information. Follow the prompts.

4. In the Transfer Information to This Mac window, select one of the options and click Continue:

   ‣ **From another Mac** enables you to connect your Mac to another Mac and transfer configuration settings and data from the other Mac. If you choose this option, continue following the instructions that appear onscreen. You should be able to skip most of the rest of these steps.

   ‣ **From a Windows PC** enables you to connect your Mac to a Windows PC and transfer configuration settings and data from the PC. If you choose this option, continue following the instructions that appear onscreen. You should be able to skip most of the rest of these steps.

   ‣ **From a Time Machine or other disk** enables you to configure your Mac from a Time Machine backup or another attached disk. If you choose this option, continue following instructions that appear onscreen. You should be able to skip most of the rest of these steps.

   ‣ **Don't transfer now** does not transfer any configuration information. Continue following these steps.

5. In the Enter Your Apple ID window, if you have an Apple ID, enter it and your account password. If you don't, leave both boxes blank. Then click Continue.

6. In the Registration Information window, fill in the form. You can press Tab to move from one field to the next. When you're done, click Continue.

continues on next page

7. In the Create Your Computer Account window, fill in the form to enter information to set up your Mac OS X account:

   ▸ **Full Name** is your name.

   ▸ **Account Name** is a short version of your name used for networking. This name is also used to label your Home folder. I usually use my first initial followed by my last name: *mlanger*.

   ▸ **Password** is a password you want to use with your account.

   ▸ **Verify** is the same password you entered in the Password box.

   ▸ **Allow my Apple ID to reset this user password** enables you to reset your password on your computer if you forget it by entering your Apple ID.

   ▸ **Require password when logging in** requires that you enter your password when starting up or logging into your computer. This, in effect, disables automatic login.

   ▸ **Password Hint** is a hint that will remind you what your password is. Don't use this box to enter your password again, since it will appear when you cannot successfully log in to your account.

   When you're finished entering account information, click Continue.

8. In the Select a Picture for This Account window, choose an options:

   ▸ **Take a snapshot** enables you to use the computer's FaceTime camera to take a photo. Frame the subject—you?— in the preview window and click the Take a photo snapshot button. Your computer will beep the countdown from three and snap a photo. You can repeat this process if you don't like the results.

   ▸ **Choose from the picture library** displays Apple's library of user icons. Choose the one you like. If you don't have a FaceTime camera and this screen appears, this is the only option you'll have to select a picture for your account, although you can always use a picture from a photo file to change it later.

   When you're finished selecting a picture, click Continue.

9. The Select Time Zone window may appear. Click the world map to set your approximate location, then choose a city from the Closest City pop-up menu. Click Continue.

10. If you do not have an Internet connection, the Set Date and Time window may appear. Set the date and time and click Continue.

11. In the Thank You, window, Click Start Using Lion. If prompted, log in to go to the Finder desktop. You're finished.

TIP In step 1, if you wait long enough, you'll hear your Mac provide some instructions using its VoiceOver feature (page 371). You can also press the Esc key to get VoiceOver instructions for configuration.

TIP In step 6, if you have an Apple ID and a connection to the Internet, your contact information may already be filled in based on data stored on Apple's servers.

TIP In step 6, you can learn about Apple's privacy policy by clicking the Privacy button.

TIP When you enter your password in steps 7, it displays as bullet characters. That's why you enter it twice: so you're sure you entered what you thought you did the first time.

TIP It's a good idea to use the Password Hint field to enter a hint that makes your password impossible to forget.

2

Finder Basics

The Finder is an application that is part of Mac OS. You use the Finder's graphic user interface to open, copy, delete, list, organize, and perform other operations on computer files.

The Finder is a special application that starts when you turn on your computer and is always open while your computer is running. In fact, under normal circumstances, you cannot quit it.

This chapter provides important instructions for using the Finder and its interface elements, including the desktop, windows, menus, and Dock. It's important that you understand how to use these basic Finder techniques, since you'll use them again and again every time you work with your Mac.

In This Chapter

The Finder & Desktop

The Finder's interface includes a number of elements, most of which are illustrated here **A**.

- **Menu bar** (page 17) offers access to all the Finder's menus.

- **Window** (page 27) displays the contents of a folder or search results.

- **Icon** (page 21) represents a document, folder, application, or other file on your computer.

- **Pointer** enables you to work directly with items you see onscreen. You control the pointer with your mouse, trackpad, or other pointing device (page 13).

- **Dock** (page 38) offers quick access to applications, documents, folders, or other items you use often.

- **Desktop** is an image or colored background for the Finder.

As you work with Mac OS, you'll find that these basic Finder elements appear over and over in all applications.

Menu bar   Window   Icon   Pointer   Dock   Desktop

A Basic Finder interface elements.

A A USB Apple Mouse (left) and **B** a Bluetooth Magic Mouse (right).

C Laptops such as a MacBook Pro have a built-in trackpad.   *Trackpad*

D Apple's Magic Trackpad is a multi-touch trackpad.

The Mouse & Trackpad

Mac OS, like most graphic user interface systems, uses a mouse or trackpad as an input device to manipulate an onscreen pointer.

A **mouse** works by moving the mouse on your work surface or mouse pad. This moves the pointer on your screen. You can then press down on the mouse or use its button to click, double-click or drag. Apple computers work with a variety of mouse models, including the **Apple Mouse A** (sometimes known as the **Mighty Mouse**) and **Magic Mouse B**.

A **trackpad** works by moving your finger along the surface of the trackpad. This moves the pointer on your screen. You can then press down on the trackpad or its button to click, double-click, or drag. Apple laptop computers such as the **MacBook Pro** and **MacBook Air** have a trackpad built in **C**; Apple's **Magic Trackpad D** is another example of a trackpad that works with Mac computers.

There are several basic techniques you must know to use your computer:

- *Point* to a specific item onscreen.
- *Click* an item to select it.
- *Double-click* an item to open it.
- *Drag* to move an item or select multiple items.

In addition to these techniques, you can also use *gestures* on a *multi-touch* device such as a trackpad or Magic Mouse to work with items onscreen.

TIP You can use the Mouse and Trackpad preferences panes (pages 516 and 519) to customize the functionality of your mouse or trackpad.

To point:

1. Do one of the following:

   ▸ With a mouse, move the mouse on the work surface or mouse pad.

   ▸ With a trackpad, move the tip of one finger (usually your forefinger) on the surface of the trackpad.

   The pointer, which usually looks like an arrow , moves on your computer screen.

2. When the tip of the pointer's arrow is on the item you want to point to , stop moving it.

TIP The tip of the pointer is its "business end."

To click:

1. Point to the item you want to click.

2. Do one of the following:

   ▸ With a mouse that has a physical button, press (and release) the mouse button. (If it has two buttons, use the left button.)

   ▸ On a mouse that does not have a physical button (such as an Apple Mouse or Magic Mouse), use one finger to press (and release) the top-left corner of the mouse.

   ▸ On a trackpad with a physical button, press (and release) the button.

   ▸ On a trackpad without a physical button (such as a Magic Trackpad), use one finger to press (and release) the trackpad.

   The item you clicked becomes selected or 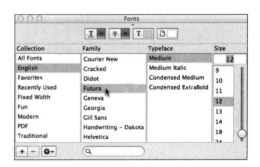.

E The pointer usually looks like an arrow pointer when you are working in the Finder.

About Stacks.pdf

F Move the pointer so the arrow's tip is on the item you want to point to.

About Stacks.pdf

G Click to select an icon...

H ...or an item in a list.

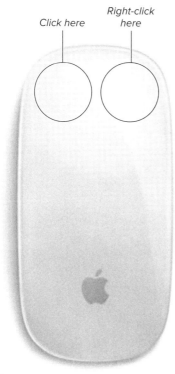

Click here   *Right-click here*

❶ "Button" locations on a Magic Mouse.

To right-click:

1. Point to the item you want to right-click.

2. Do one of the following:

   ▸ On a one-button mouse or trackpad, hold down the Control key and press (and release) the button.

   ▸ On a mouse that has two physical buttons, press (and release) the right mouse button.

   ▸ On a mouse that does not have physical buttons (such as an Apple Mouse or Magic Mouse ❶), use one finger to press (and release) the upper-right corner of the mouse.

   ▸ On a trackpad without a physical button (such as a Magic Trackpad), use two fingers to press (and release) the trackpad.

TIP **Throughout this book, when you need to right-click something, I use the phrase** *right-click*. *Click* **(page 14) refers to normal clicking with the left mouse button.**

TIP **Right-clicking is used to display contextual menus (page 18).**

TIP **If right-clicking with an Apple Mouse, Magic Mouse, or trackpad does not work as discussed here, check the settings in the Mouse (page 516) or Trackpad (page 519) preferences pane to make sure the device is configured for secondary click operations.**

To double-click:

1. Point to the item you want to double-click.

2. Click twice quickly.

   The item you double-clicked opens.

To drag:

1. Point to the item you want to drag.

2. Press the mouse button or trackpad button down, or, if the device is button-less, press where you would normally press to click.

3. While holding the button down, move the pointer. The item you are dragging moves **J**.

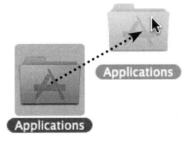

J Drag to move items such as folder icons.

To scroll:

1. Point to the item you want to scroll.

2. Do one of the following:

   ▸ On an Apple Mouse with scroll ball or other mouse with scroll wheel, roll the ball in the direction you want to scroll.

   ▸ On a Magic Mouse or multi-touch trackpad, use two fingers to "push" the content in one direction to see what lies beyond it. For example, to see the items at the bottom of a window, use two fingers in an upward sweeping motion to "push" content above it up.

TIP In previous versions of Mac OS, a window's contents moved in the opposite direction of your finger movement. Thus, to see items at the bottom of the window, you'd use two fingers to sweep down on your trackpad. Although OS X Lion scrolls in the opposite direction, you can change this behavior to work like previous versions of Mac OS by setting options in the Trackpad preferences pane (page 519).

TIP You can learn more about scrolling a window's contents on page 32.

A The menu bar offers pull-down menus.

B A submenu appears when you choose a menu option with a right-pointing triangle beside it.

C To display a pop-up menu, click it.

D A contextual menu appears when you right-click on certain items.

Menus

The Finder—and most other Mac OS applications—offers menus full of options. There are four types of menus in Mac OS X:

- A pull-down menu appears on the menu bar at the top of the screen **A**.
- A submenu appears when a menu option with a right-pointing triangle is selected **B**.
- A pop-up menu appears within a window or dialog **C**.
- A contextual menu appears when you right-click an item or hold down Control while clicking an item **D**.

Here are a few things to keep in mind about menus:

- A menu option followed by an ellipsis (...) **A B C D** display a dialog (page 172).
- A menu option that is dimmed or gray **B** cannot be chosen. Command availability varies based on what is selected.
- A menu option preceded by a check mark **A** is enabled, or "turned on."
- A menu option followed by a series of keyboard characters **A B** has a keyboard shortcut (page 20).
- Contextual menus **D** only display options that apply to the item you are pointing to.

TIP Menus and the menu bar are slightly translucent, making it possible to see the desktop picture or open windows beneath them. To keep the screenshots cleaner looking for this book, most screenshots were created with a plain white desktop.

To use a menu:

1. Point to the name of the menu .

2. Click.

   The menu opens, displaying its options **F**.

3. Point to the menu option you want **G**.

4. Click to choose the option.

   The menu disappears.

> **TIP** Mac OS X's menus are "sticky menus"—a menu opens and stays open when you click its name.

> **TIP** To close a menu without choosing an option, click outside the menu.

> **TIP** This book uses the following notation to indicate menu commands: *Menu Name* > *Submenu Name* (if necessary) > *Command Name*. For example, the instructions for choosing the My iDisk command from the iDisk submenu under the Go menu **B** would be: "choose Go > iDisk > My iDisk."

To use a contextual menu:

1. Point to the item on which you want to act.

2. Right-click or hold down the Control key and click.

   A contextual menu appears **D**.

3. Click the menu option you want.

> **TIP** Contextual menus are similar to the Action pop-up menu (page 34).

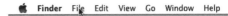

E Point to the menu name.

File		File	
New Finder Window	⌘N	New Finder Window	⌘N
New Folder	⇧⌘N	New Folder	⇧⌘N
New Folder with Selection	^⌘N	New Folder with Selection	^⌘N
New Smart Folder	⌥⌘N	New Smart Folder	⌥⌘N
New Burn Folder		New Burn Folder	
Open	⌘O	Open	⌘O
Open With	▶	Open With	▶
Print	⌘P	Print	⌘P
Close Window	⌘W	Close Window	⌘W
Get Info	⌘I	Get Info	⌘I
Compress "Applications"		Compress "Applications"	
Duplicate	⌘D	Duplicate	⌘D
Make Alias	⌘L	Make Alias	⌘L
Quick Look "Applications"	⌘Y	Quick Look "Applications"	⌘Y
Show Original	⌘R	Show Original	⌘R
Add to Sidebar	⌘T	Add to Sidebar	⌘T
Move to Trash	⌘⌫	Move to Trash	⌘⌫
Eject	⌘E	Eject	⌘E
Burn "Applications" to Disc...		Burn "Applications" to Disc...	
Find	⌘F	Find	⌘F
Label:		Label:	

F Click to display the menu.

G Click to choose the menu option you want.

TABLE 2.1 Special Character Keys

Key	Function
Enter	Enters information or "clicks" a default button.
Return	Begins a new paragraph or line or "clicks" a default button.
Tab	Advances to the next tab stop or the next item in a sequence.
Delete	Deletes a selection or the character to the left of the insertion point.
Del	Deletes a selection or the character to the right of the insertion point.
Esc	"Clicks" a Cancel button or ends the operation currently in process.

TABLE 2.2 Modifier Keys

Key	Function
Shift	Produces uppercase characters or symbols. Also works with the mouse to extend selections.
Option	Produces special characters.
Command	Accesses menu commands via keyboard shortcuts.
Control	Modifies the functions of other keys and displays contextual menus.
Fn	Switches F-keys between System and user-assigned functions.

TABLE 2.3 Dedicated Function Keys

Key	Function
Help	Displays onscreen help.
Home	Scrolls to the beginning.
End	Scrolls to the end.
Page Up	Scrolls up one page.
Page Down	Scrolls down one page.
Up, Down, Left, Right	Moves the insertion point or changes the selection.

The Keyboard

The keyboard offers another way to communicate with your computer. In addition to typing text and numbers, you can use it to choose menu commands.

There are three types of keys on a Mac OS keyboard:

- **Character keys**, such as letters, numbers, and symbols, are for typing information. Some character keys have special functions, as listed in Table 2.1.

- **Modifier keys** alter the meaning of a character key being pressed or the meaning of a mouse or trackpad action. Modifier keys are listed in Table 2.2.

- **Function keys** perform specific functions in Mac OS or an application. Dedicated function keys, which always do the same thing, are listed in Table 2.3. Function keys labeled F1 through F12 (or higher) on the keyboard—which are sometimes referred to as *F-keys*—can be assigned specific functions by applications.

TIP The key with the Apple on it is called the *Command* key—not the Apple key.

TIP On some keyboards, the Control key is labeled **Control** while on others it is labeled **Ctrl**. Throughout this book, I'll use **Control** to refer to the Control key, no matter how it might be labeled on your computer's keyboard.

TIP The Delete key does not appear on all keyboards.

To use a keyboard shortcut:

1. Hold down the modifier key(s) in the sequence. This is usually Command, but can be Option, Control, or Shift or a combination of any of these.

2. Press the letter, number, or symbol key in the sequence.

   For example, to choose the Open command, which can be found under the File menu **A**, hold down the Command key and press O.

TIP You can learn keyboard shortcuts by observing the key sequences that appear to the right of some menu commands **A**.

TIP Some commands include more than one modifier key. You must hold all modifier keys down while pressing the letter, number, or symbol key for the keyboard shortcut.

TIP Some applications refer to keyboard shortcuts as *keyboard equivalents* or *shortcut keys*.

TIP You can add or modify keyboard shortcuts for the Finder and other applications in the Keyboard preferences pane (page 512).

A When available, keyboard shortcuts appear to the right of menu commands.

TextEdit   Preview   iPhoto

A Application icons.

RTF   PDF

Letter to Cliff Flying Facts Butterfly

B Document icons often display a preview of the document's content first page.

Applications   System   Letters

C Folder icons.

Macintosh HD   mlanger   Multimedia

D Three different volume icons: hard disk, iDisk, and an external USB hard disk.

E The three faces of the Trash icon in the Dock: empty, full, and while dragging removable media.

Icons

Mac OS uses icons to graphically represent files and other items on the desktop, in the Dock, or within Finder windows:

- **Applications A** are programs you use to get work done. Chapters 11 through 18 discuss working with applications.

- **Documents B** are the files created by applications. Chapters 11 and 14 cover working with documents.

- **Folders C** are used to organize files. Chapters 3 and 6 discuss using folders.

- **Volumes D**, including hard disks, CDs, DVDs, iPods, and network disks, are used to store data. Chapter 8 covers working with volumes.

- **The Trash E**, which is in the Dock, is for discarding items you no longer want and for ejecting removable media. Using the Trash is covered on page 54.

TIP Icons can appear a number of different ways, depending on the view and view options chosen for a window. You can learn more about working with windows starting on page 27 and about window views in Chapter 4.

To select an icon:

Click the icon that you want to select.

A gray shaded box appears around the icon and its name becomes highlighted **F**.

TIP You can also select an icon in an active window by pressing the keyboard key for the first letter of the icon's name or by pressing one of the arrow keys until the icon is selected.

To deselect an icon:

Click anywhere in the window or on the desktop other than on the selected icon.

TIP If you select one icon and then click another icon, the originally selected icon is deselected and the icon you clicked becomes selected instead.

To select multiple icons by clicking:

1. Click the first icon that you want to select **F**.
2. Hold down the Command key and click another icon that you want to select **G**.
3. Repeat step 2 until all icons that you want to select have been selected.

TIP Icons that are part of a multiple selection must be in the same window.

F To select an icon, click it.

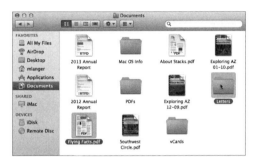

G Hold down the Command key while clicking other icons to add them to a multiple icon selection.

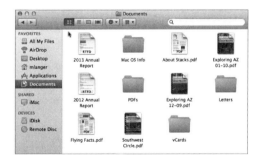

H Position the pointer above and to the left of the first icon that you want to select.

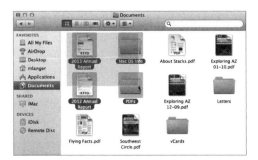

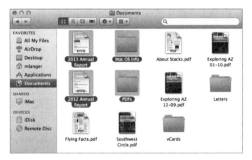

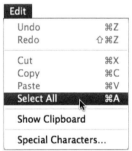

(I) Drag to draw a shaded selection box around the icons that you want to select.

(J) Release the button to complete the selection.

(K) Choose Select All from the Edit menu to select all items in the active window.

To select multiple icons by dragging:

1. Position the pointer slightly above and to the left of the first icon in the group that you want to select **(H)**.

2. Press the button, and drag diagonally across the icons you want to select.

   A shaded box appears to indicate the selection area, and the items within it become selected **(I)**.

3. When all the icons that you want to select are included in the selection area, release the button **(J)**.

TIP To select multiple icons by dragging, the icons must be adjacent.

To select all icons in a window:

Choose Edit > Select All **(K)**, or press Command-A.

All icons in the active window are selected.

To deselect one icon in a multiple selection:

Hold down the Command key while clicking the icon that you want to deselect.

The icon you clicked is deselected while the others remain selected.

To move an icon:

1. Position the pointer on the icon that you want to move.

2. Press the button and drag the icon to the new location.

   As you drag, a shadowy image of the icon moves with the pointer 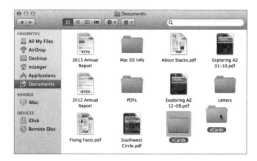 .

3. Release the button when the icon is in the desired position Ⓜ.

TIP You move icons to rearrange them in a window or on the desktop or to copy or move the items they represent to another folder or disk. Copying and moving items is discussed in Chapter 3.

TIP Your ability to reposition icons within a window is limited by the view settings for that window. For example, you cannot drag to reposition icons within windows set to list, column, or Cover Flow view. Window views are discussed in Chapter 4.

TIP You can also move multiple icons at once. First, select the icons. Then position the pointer on one of the selected icons and follow steps 2 and 3 above. All selected icons move together.

TIP To force an icon to snap to a window's invisible grid, hold down the Command key while dragging it. The grid (page 463) ensures consistent spacing between icons so your window looks neat.

Ⓛ Drag the icon to a new position.

Ⓜ Release the button to complete the move.

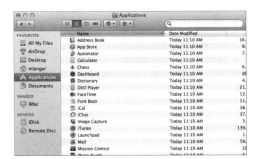

N Select the icon you want to open.

O Choose Open from the File menu.

P Here's the window in **N** with the Application folder's contents displayed.

To open an icon:

1. Select the icon you want to open **N**.

2. Choose File > Open **O**, or press Command-O.

Or:

Double-click the icon that you want to open.

TIP Only one click is necessary when opening an item in a Finder window's sidebar (page 35) or the Dock (page 38).

TIP To open a folder or disk in a new Finder window, hold down the Command key while opening it.

TIP The File menu's Open With submenu (page 149) enables you to open a document with a specific application.

Opening Icons

What happens when you open an icon depends on the type of icon you open. For example:

- Opening a disk or folder icon displays the contents of the disk or folder in the same Finder window **P**.

- Opening an application icon launches the application so that you can work with it.

- Opening a document icon launches the application that created that document and displays the document so you can view or edit it.

- Opening the Trash displays items that will be deleted when you empty the Trash.

To use enhanced icon view:

1. Point to the icon for a multiple-page document or QuickTime movie.

   Controls appear on the icon **Q** **R**.

2. Do one of the following:

   ▸ To scroll through the pages of a document in its icon, click the right arrow. The icon changes to display the next page **S**. You can use the arrows to scroll forward or backward through the pages of the document.

   ▸ To play a movie in its icon, click the arrow. The movie plays **T**. You can click again to stop movie play.

TIP Enhanced icon view works for compatible multiple-page documents or QuickTime movies that are displayed in icon, column, or **Cover Flow** view as previews.

TIP Viewing the contents of a document in enhanced icon view works best when the icon size is large (page 463) or you are viewing the icon in Cover Flow (page 67).

SouthwestCircle.pdf

Q When you point to a preview icon for a multi-page PDF file, page scrolling buttons appear.

Exploring Sedona.mp4

R When you point to a preview icon for a QuickTime movie, a play button appears.

SouthwestCircle.pdf

S Clicking the right arrow button for a document displays the next page of that document.

Exploring Sedona.mp4

T Clicking the Play button plays the movie.

Close button
Minimize button
Zoom button Toolbar Title bar Search field

Sidebar   Status bar

A A Finder window in icon view on a MacBook Air.

Column heading Scroll bars

B The same Finder window as **A**, but in list view with an Apple Mouse attached to the computer.

What's Missing?

If you've used previous versions of Mac OS, you may notice that some window elements are missing. The toolbar control and resize control are no longer part of Finder windows and scroll bar display is determined by Appearance preference settings and the type of pointing device you are using (Apple Mouse or multi-touch device). You can learn more about working with the toolbar on page 33, resizing windows on page 30, and scrolling window contents on page 31.

Windows

Mac OS makes extensive use of windows for displaying icons and other information in the Finder and documents in other applications. Two different views of a Finder window are illustrated here **A B**.

Each window includes a variety of controls you can use to manipulate it:

- The **close button** closes the window.

- The **minimize button** collapses the window to an icon in the Dock.

- The **zoom button** toggles the window's size between full size and a custom size.

- The **toolbar** displays buttons and controls for working with Finder windows.

- The **title bar** displays the window's icon and name.

- The **search field** enables you to search for files using Spotlight.

- The **sidebar** shows commonly accessed folders, volumes, and searches. The sidebar has been reconfigured for Mac OS X Lion.

- The **status bar** provides information about items in a window and space available on disk.

- **Column headings** (in list and cover flow views only) display the names of columns and let you sort by a column.

- **Scroll bars** scroll the contents of the window.

TIP By default, when you open a folder or disk icon, its contents appear in the active window. You can set Finder Preferences (page 448) to open folders in new windows.

TIP You can learn more about Finder window views in Chapter 4.

To open a new Finder window:

Choose File > New Finder Window **C**, or press Command-N.

A new Finder window appears **D**.

TIP By default, when you use the New Finder Window command, Mac OS display the All My Files window (page 106) **D**, which is new in OS X Lion. You can use Finder preferences (page 448) to specify which folder should open when you use this command.

To open a folder or volume in a new Finder window:

Hold down the Command key while opening a folder or volume icon.

A new window containing the contents of the folder or volume appears.

To close a window:

Click the window's close button **A**, or choose File > Close Window **E**, or press Command-W.

To close all open windows:

Hold down the Option key while clicking the active window's close button **A**, hold down Option while choosing File > Close All **F**, or press Option-Command-W.

TIP The Close Window/Close All commands **E F** are examples of dynamic menu items—pressing a modifier key (in this case, Option) changes the menu command from Close Window **E** to Close All **F**.

C To open a new window, choose New Finder Window from the File menu.

D By default, the All My Files window opens.

E Choose Close Window from the File menu...

F ...or hold down Option and choose Close All from the File menu.

G Use the Window menu to perform a number of tasks with open Finder windows.

H The active window appears atop all other windows. The buttons on the left end of the active window's title bar appear in color.

To activate a window:

Use one of the following techniques:

- Click anywhere in or on the window you want to activate.

- Choose the name of the window you want to activate from the list at the bottom of the Window menu **G**.

TIP Make sure the window you want to work with is active before using commands that work on the active window—such as Close Window, Select All, and View menu commands.

TIP You can distinguish between active and inactive windows by the appearance of their title bars; the buttons on the left end of an active window's title bar are in color **H**. In addition, a check mark appears beside the active window's name in the Window menu **G**.

TIP When two or more windows overlap, the active window will always be on top of the stack **H**.

TIP You can use the Cycle Through Windows command **G** or its handy shortcut, Command-`, to activate each open window, in sequence.

To bring all Finder windows to the top:

Choose Window > Bring All to Front **G**.

All open Finder windows that are not minimized are moved in front of any windows opened by other applications.

TIP Finder windows can be intermingled with other applications' windows. The Bring All to Front command gathers the windows together in the top layers. This command is useful when working with many windows from several different applications.

To move a window:

1. Position the pointer on the window's title bar **I** or status bar (if displayed).

2. Press the button and drag the window to a new location.

   As you drag, the window moves along with the pointer.

3. When the window is in the desired position, release the button.

To resize a window:

1. Do one of the following:

   ▶ To change just the height of the window, position the pointer on the top or bottom edge of the window.

   ▶ To change just the width of the window, position the pointer on the left or right edge of the window **J**.

   ▶ To change both the height and width of the window, position the pointer on a corner of the window.

   The pointer turns into a two-headed arrow that indicates which direction the edge or corner can be dragged **J**.

2. Press the button and:

   ▶ To make the window smaller, drag toward the center of the window.

   ▶ To make the window larger, drag away from the center of the window.

   As you drag, the edge or corner of the window moves with the pointer, changing the size and shape of the window **K**.

3. When the window is the desired size, release the button.

I You can move a window by dragging its title bar.

J When you position the pointer on the edge of a window, it turns into a two-headed arrow.

K Drag the window's edge or corner to resize it. This technique is brand new in OS X Lion.

① A minimized window shrinks down into an icon in the Dock.

Window	
Minimize	⌘M
Zoom	
Cycle Through Windows	⌘`
Bring All to Front	
✓ All My Files	
Applications	
◆ Documents	

① A diamond beside a window name indicates that the window has been minimized.

To minimize a window:

Use one of the following techniques:

- Click the window's minimize button **①**.
- Choose Window > Minimize **①**, or press Command-M.

The window shrinks into an icon and slips into the Dock at the bottom of the screen **①**.

TIP To minimize all Finder windows, hold down the Option key and choose Windows > Minimize All, or press Option-Command-M.

TIP You can set an option in the General preferences pane (page 486) so that double-clicking a window's title bar minimizes it.

To redisplay a minimized window:

Use one of the following techniques:

- Click the window's icon in the Dock **①**.
- Choose the window's name from the Window menu **①**.

To zoom a window:

Click the window's zoom button **①**.

Each time you click the zoom button, the window's size toggles between two sizes:

- **Standard state size** is the smallest possible size that would accommodate the window's contents and still fit on your screen.
- **User state size** is the custom size you specify by dragging a window's edge or corner.

To scroll a window's contents with the scroll bar:

Use one of the following techniques to scroll a window's contents up, down, left, or right:

- Drag a scroller along the scroll track .
- Click in the scroll track on either side of the scroller .

TIP You cannot scroll a window if all contents are already displayed.

TIP The scrollers  are *proportional*—this means that the more of a window's contents you see, the more space the scroller will take up in its scroll bar.

TIP The scroll bars  have been redesigned for OS X Lion to take up less space and appear only under certain circumstances.

TIP If you're using OS X Lion with a Multi-Touch device such as a trackpad or Magic Mouse, the scroll bars may not appear in the window. You can display them by using gestures, as discussed next, or by setting General preferences (page 486) to always display them.

To scroll a window's contents with gestures:

1. Position the pointer anywhere within the window you want to scroll.

2. On your Multi-Touch device, use two fingers to push the contents of the window up, down, left, or right.

TIP In previous versions of Mac OS, a window's contents moved in the opposite direction of your finger movement. Thus, to see items at the bottom of the window, you'd use two fingers to sweep down on your trackpad. Although OS X Lion scrolls in the opposite direction, you can change this behavior to work like previous versions of Mac OS by setting options in the Trackpad preferences pane (page 519).

Scroll bars

 Scroll bar components.   *Scroll tracks*

Back & Forward buttons
View buttons
Action pop-up menu
Arrange pop-up menu
Search field

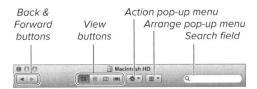

A The toolbar.

B The Action pop-up menu offer commands for working with selected items in a window.

C When the window is narrow, some toolbar items may be hidden; click the double arrow to display a menu of hidden items.

The Toolbar

The toolbar **A** offers navigation tools and view buttons within Finder windows:

- The **Back button** displays the previous window's contents.

- The **Forward button** displays the window that was showing before you clicked the Back button.

- **View buttons** (Chapter 4) enable you to change the window's view.

- The **Action pop-up menu B** offers commands for working with an open window or selected object(s) within the window.

- The **Arrange pop-up menu** (Chapter 4), which is new in OS X Lion, offers commands for arranging icons in the window.

- The **Search field** (Chapter 7) enables you to quickly search for a file.

If the window is not wide enough to show all toolbar buttons, a double arrow appears on the right side of the toolbar. Click the arrow to display a menu of missing items **C** and select the one you want.

TIP The toolbar can be customized to show the items you use most (page 469).

TIP Does the Action pop-up menu **B** look familiar? It should! It's very similar to the contextual menu shown on page 17.

To hide or display the toolbar:

Choose View > Hide Toolbar **D**, View > Show Toolbar, or press Option-Command-T.

One of two things happens:

- If the toolbar is displayed, it disappears **E**.
- If the toolbar is not displayed, it appears **A**.

TIP Options on the View menu **D** vary depending whether the toolbar is displayed or hidden.

TIP Hiding the toolbar also hides the sidebar (page 35). If the status bar (page 37) is set to display in all windows, it moves right beneath the title bar. With the toolbar and sidebar hidden, the window is smaller **E**.

To use a toolbar button:

Click the button once.

To use a toolbar pop-up menu:

1. If necessary, select the items you want to work with.
2. Click the pop-up menu to display a menu of commands.
3. Choose the command you want to use.

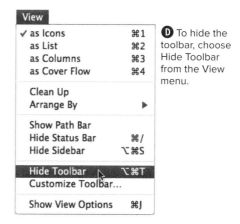

D To hide the toolbar, choose Hide Toolbar from the View menu.

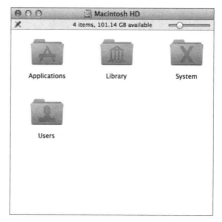

E Hiding the toolbar also hides the sidebar, making the window smaller.

A The Sidebar appears on the left side of a Finder window.

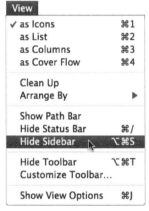

B To hide the sidebar, choose Hide Sidebar from the View menu.

C Hiding the sidebar does not hide the toolbar.

The Sidebar

The sidebar, which has been reworked for OS X Lion, appears on the left side of Finder windows **A**. It offers quick access to the items you use most.

The sidebar has three sections:

- **Favorites** displays the All My Files smart folder (page 106), AirDrop (page 404), Desktop, your Home folder (page 135), and several commonly accessed folders.

- **Shared** lists volumes available over your network (Chapter 24).

- **Devices** lists volumes that are accessible by your computer, such as your hard disk, iDisk, and optical discs (Chapter 8).

TIP You can customize the sidebar to add or remove items or change its width (page 471).

TIP When a window is resized, the size of the sidebar may also change. If the sidebar is too short to display its contents, a vertical scroll bar can appear within it.

To hide or display the sidebar:

Choose View > Hide Sidebar **B**, View > Show Sidebar, or press Option-Command-S.

One of two things happens:

- If the sidebar is displayed, it disappears **C**.

- If the sidebar is not displayed, it appears **A**.

TIP Options on the View menu **B** vary depending whether the sidebar is displayed or hidden.

TIP The toolbar (page 33) must be displayed to show the sidebar.

To use the sidebar:

Click the icon for the item you want.

One of two things happens:

- If the item is a volume or folder, the window's contents change to display the contents of the item you clicked **A**.

- If the item is an application or document, the item opens in its own window.

To show or hide sidebar sections:

1. Point to the sidebar section heading.

   A Hide **D** or Show button appears to the right of the heading in the sidebar.

2. Do one of the following:

   ▸ To hide the items in the section, click the Hide button. The section heading collapses and the items disappear from view **F**.

   ▸ To show the items in the section, click the Show button. The section expands and the items within it appear.

TIP You can customize the sidebar (page 471) to permanently remove items from it.

D When you point to a sidebar heading, a Hide or Show button appears beside it.

E Clicking the Hide button collapses the heading so the items within it no longer display in the sidebar.

A When the toolbar is displayed, the status bar appears at the bottom of the window.

B When the toolbar is hidden, the status bar appears beneath the title bar.

C The status bar displays a write-protected icon if the window's contents cannot be changed.

D To hide the status bar, choose Hide Status bar from the View menu.

E A window looks barren without a toolbar, sidebar, or status bar.

The Status Bar

The status bar is an area of a window with information about the window's contents. It can appear two different places:

- If the toolbar is displayed, the status bar appears at the bottom of the window **A**.

- If the toolbar is hidden, the status bar appears just beneath the window's title bar **B**.

What displays in the status bar depends on what is selected in the window:

- If nothing is selected, the status bar indicates how many items are in the window and how much disk space is available on that volume **A B**.

- If one or more items are selected, the status bar indicates how many items are selected and how much disk space is available on that volume.

- If the window is on a volume that cannot be written to, such as a CD, the status bar displays a write-protected icon **C**.

- The status bar also includes a slider you can use to change the size of icons in the window **A B C**.

To hide or display the status bar:

Choose View > Hide Status Bar **D**, View > Show Status Bar, or press Command-/.

One of two things happens:

- If the sidebar is displayed, it disappears **E**.

- If the sidebar is not displayed, it appears **A B**.

The Dock

The Dock **A** offers easy access to often-used applications and documents, as well as minimized windows.

TIP You can customize the Dock (page 453) to add or remove items and set a number of preferences.

To identify items in the Dock:

Point to the item.

The name of the item appears above the Dock **B**.

To open an item in the Dock:

Click the icon for the item you want to open. One of five things happens:

- If the icon is for an application that is running, the application becomes the active application.

- If the icon is for an application that is not running, it launches. Its icon in the Dock bounces so you know something is happening.

- If the icon is for a minimized window (page 31), the window is displayed.

- If the icon is for an unopened document, the document opens in the application that created it.

- If the icon is for a folder, the folder's contents appear using the Stacks feature.

TIP You can use a contextual menu for items on the Dock. Right-click on the Dock icon to display the menu **C** and choose the option you want.

A The Dock.

B Point to an icon to see what it represents.

C You can use a contextual menu on a Dock item.

A The Apple menu includes three commands for changing the work state of your computer.

B This dialog appears when you press the power key on your keyboard (if you have one) or hold down Control while pressing the Media Eject key.

Sleeping, Restarting, & Shutting Down

The Apple menu **A** offers several options that change the work state of your computer:

- **Sleep** puts the computer into a state where it uses very little power. The screen goes blank and the hard disk may stop spinning.

- **Restart** instructs the computer to shut down and immediately start back up.

- **Shut Down** closes all open documents and programs, clears memory, and cuts power to the computer.

Mac OS X Lion introduces a new feature called *Resume*, which restores your applications exactly as they were before restarting or shutting down. This means that applications that were running are automatically restarted and all open document windows reopen when your computer starts up.

TIP You can press your keyboard's power key (if it has one) or hold down the Control key while pressing the Media Eject key to display a dialog with buttons for the Restart, Sleep, and Shut Down commands **B**.

TIP Do not restart or shut down a computer by simply flicking off a power switch. Doing so prevents the computer from properly closing files, which may result in file corruption and related problems.

TIP Mac OS X includes a screen saver (page 482), which automatically starts when your computer is inactive for a while. Don't confuse the screen saver with System or display sleep—it's different.

To put your computer to sleep:

Choose Apple > Sleep **A**.

TIP Sleep mode is a good way to conserve laptop battery power without turning it off.

TIP By default, Mac OS X automatically puts a computer to sleep when it is inactive for a while. You can customize this in the Energy Saver preferences pane (page 509).

To wake a sleeping computer:

Press any keyboard key.

You may have to wait several seconds for the computer to fully wake.

TIP It's much quicker to wake a sleeping computer than to start a computer that has been shut down.

To restart your computer:

1. Choose Apple > Restart **A**.

   A dialog appears **C**.

2. To restore all applications and documents to the way they currently appear, select the Reopen windows when logging back in check box.

3. Click Restart, press Return or Enter, or simply wait until your computer restarts on its own.

To shut down your computer:

1. Choose Apple > Shut Down **A**.

   A dialog appears **D**.

2. To restore all applications and documents to the way they currently appear, select the Reopen windows when logging back in check box.

3. Click Shut Down, press Return or Enter, or simply wait until your computer shuts down on its own.

C A dialog like this appears when you choose the Restart command from the Apple menu.

D A dialog like this appears when you choose the Shut Down command from the Apple menu.

File Management Basics

If you think of your computer and its hard disk as a giant filing cabinet—one that could hold far more paper than any filing cabinet you've ever seen—you can begin to get an idea of how important it is to keep your files organized. After all, if you had a file cabinet with one giant drawer and just tossed all your files into it, how would you ever find a specific file when you need it?

In Mac OS, you use the Finder to organize and manage your files. You can:

- Rename items.

- Create folders to store related items.

- Move items stored on disk to organize them so they're easy to find and back up.

- Copy items to other disks to back them up or share them with others.

- Delete items you no longer need.

This chapter explores all of these tasks, but it starts with the basics: an overview of how Mac OS organizes its own files and provides a basic framework for organizing yours.

Mac OS X Disk Organization

Like most other computer operating systems, Mac OS X uses a *hierarchical filing system* (*HFS*) to organize and store files, including system files, applications, and documents.

The top level of the filing system is the computer level **A**, which roughly corresponds to the Devices section of the sidebar. This level shows the computer's internal hard disk, any other disks the computer is connected to (including iDisk, if you are a MobileMe member), the Network icon, and connected servers.

The next level down is the computer's hard disk level **B**. You can view this level by opening the icon with the name of your hard disk—usually *Macintosh HD*, but it can be renamed (page 48). While the contents of your hard disk may differ from what's shown here **B**, at least four folders should be the same:

- **Applications** contains Mac OS X applications that are installed for all of the computer's users.

- **System** and **Library** contain the Mac OS X system files. In general, you should not add or remove files in these folders; doing so could prevent your computer from operating properly.

- **Users** **C** contains individual folders for each of the computer's users, as well as a Shared folder. This is where the computer's users store document files.

A The top level of your computer shows all mounted disks and a Network icon.

B A typical hard disk window might look like this.

C The Users folder contains a Home folder for each user, as well as a shared folder.

By default, a Mac OS X hard disk is organized for multiple users (Chapter 10). Each user has his or her own "Home" folder, which is stored in the Users folder **C**. You can view the items inside your Home folder by opening the house icon with your user name on it on the sidebar or inside the Users folder **C**. Your Home folder is preconfigured with folders for all kinds of items you may want to store on disk **D**.

D Your Home folder is preconfigured with folders for storing a variety of item types.

TIP Unless you are an administrator, you cannot access the files in any other user's Home folder except those in the user's Public and Sites folders.

TIP If you place an item in the Shared folder inside the Users folder **C**, it can be opened by anyone who uses the computer.

Pathnames

A *path*, or *pathname*, is a kind of address for a file on disk. It includes the name of the disk on which the file resides, the names of the folders the file is stored within, and the name of the file itself. For example, the pathname for a file named *SWCircle.pdf* in the Documents folder of the mlanger folder **A** on my hard disk would be: `Macintosh HD/Users/mlanger/Documents/SWCircle.pdf`.

When entering a pathname from a specific folder, you don't have to enter the entire pathname. Instead, enter the path as it relates to the current folder. For example, the path to the above-mentioned file from the mlanger folder would be: `Documents/SWCircle.pdf`.

To indicate a specific user folder, use the tilde (~) character followed by the name of the user account. So the path to the mlanger folder would be: `~mlanger`. (You can omit the user name if you want to open your own user folder.)

To indicate the top level of your computer, use a slash (/) character. So the path to Maria Langer's MacBook Air would be: `/`.

When used as part of a longer pathname, the slash character indicates the root level of your hard disk. So `/Applications/Utilities` would indicate the Utilities folder inside the Applications folder on your hard disk.

Mac OS X offers two easy ways to learn the complete path to a specific file on your hard disk: the path bar **A**, which can be displayed at the bottom of any Finder window, and a pop-up path menu on a window's title bar **B**.

A The path bar that you can display at the bottom of a Finder window displays the complete path to a selected folder or file.

B You can also display a pop-up menu that shows all of a window's enclosing items.

Don't worry if all this sounds confusing to you. Fortunately, you don't really need to know it to use Mac OS X. It's just a good idea to be familiar with the concept of pathnames in case you run across it while working with your computer.

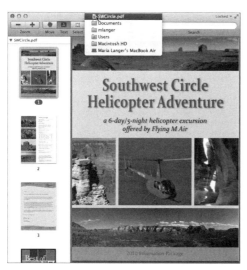

C The View menu includes a command to show (or hide) the path bar.

D You can display the path menu for a document window within an application.

To show or hide the path bar:

Choose View > Show Path Bar **C** or View > Hide Path Bar.

One of two things happens:

- If the path bar is not displayed, it appears **A**. The path bar indicates the complete path from your computer to a selected file in the window.

- If the path bar is displayed, it disappears.

TIP Options on the View menu **C** vary depending whether the path bar is displayed or hidden.

To display a window's path menu:

Hold down the Control or Command key and click the icon in a window's title bar.

A pop-up menu appears **B**. It indicates the enclosing folders, disk, and computer for the window.

TIP This technique works in the Finder as well as within most Mac OS applications that enable you to work with documents. For example, you can display the path menu for a document open in Preview **D**.

TIP You can use the path menu to open an enclosing disk or folder. Simply select its name from the menu.

The Go Menu

The Go menu ⓐ offers a quick way to open specific locations on your computer:

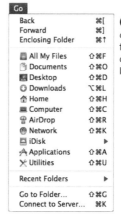

ⓐ The Go menu offers command for quickly opening specific locations.

- **Back** (Command-[) displays the contents of the folder or disk you were looking in before you viewed the current folder or disk. This command is only active if the current window has displayed the contents of more than one folder or disk.

- **Forward** (Command-]) displays the contents of the window you were viewing before you clicked the Back button. This command is only available if a window is active and if the Back button has been clicked.

- **Enclosing Folder** (Command-Up Arrow) opens the parent folder for the active window. This command is only available if a window is active and was used to display the contents of a folder.

- **All My Files** (Shift-Command-F) opens the All My Files smart folder (page 106), which is new in OS X Lion.

- **Documents** (Shift-Command-O) opens the Documents folder.

- **Desktop** (Shift-Command-D) opens your Desktop folder.

- **Downloads** (Option-Command-L) opens your downloads folder.

- **Home** (Shift-Command-H) opens your Home folder (page 42).

- **Computer** (Shift-Command-C) opens the top level window for your computer (page 42).

- **AirDrop** (Shift-Command-R) opens the AirDrop window (page 404), which is new in OS X Lion.

- **Network** (Shift-Command-K) opens the Network window (page 401).

- **iDisk** displays a submenu of options for accessing iDisk accounts and folders on Apple's MobileMe service via the Internet ⓑ.

- **Applications** (Shift-Command-A) opens the Applications folder (page 143).

- **Utilities** (Shift-Command-U) opens the Utilities folder inside the Applications folder.

- **Recent Folders** displays a submenu of recently opened folders ⓒ.

- **Go to Folder** (Shift-Command-G) lets you open any folder your computer has access to.

- **Connect to Server** (Command-K) enables you to open a server accessible via a network (page 402).

B The iDisk submenu on the Go menu offers options for opening various iDisk locations.

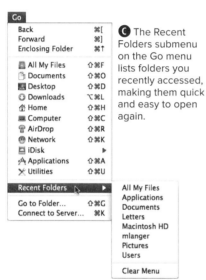

C The Recent Folders submenu on the Go menu lists folders you recently accessed, making them quick and easy to open again.

D Use the Go To Folder dialog to enter the pathname of the folder you want to open. In this example, I'm opening the Archives folder I've created within my Documents folder in my Home folder.

To open a Go menu item:

Choose the item's name from the Go menu **A** or one of its submenus **B C** or use the appropriate keyboard shortcut.

To go to a folder:

1. Choose Go > Go to Folder **A**, or press Shift-Command-G.
2. In the Go to Folder dialog that appears **D**, enter the pathname for the folder you want to open.
3. Click Go.
4. One of two things happens:
   ▶ If you entered a valid pathname, the folder opens in a Finder window.
   ▶ If you did not enter a valid pathname, an error message appears in the Go to Folder dialog. Repeat steps 2 and 3 to try again, or click Cancel to dismiss the dialog.

TIP If a window is open when you use the Go to Folder command, the Go to Folder dialog will appear as a dialog sheet attached to the window. The pathname you enter must be from that window's folder location on your hard disk.

TIP Mac OS X attempts to complete a path as you type it. Try it for yourself! Type part of a valid pathname and wait a moment. Mac OS X will complete the path with a valid pathname. (Whether it's the one you want is another story.)

TIP For OS X Lion power users: Need to open the invisible Library folder inside your Home folder? Hold down the Option key and choose Go > Library.

Icon Names

Mac OS X is very flexible when it comes to names for files, folders, and disks.

- A file or folder name can be up to 255 characters long. A disk name can be up to 27 characters long.

- A name can contain any character except a colon (:).

This flexibility makes it easy to give your files, folders, and disks names that make sense to you.

There are a few additional things to keep in mind when naming or renaming items:

- A lengthy item name may appear truncated when displayed in windows and lists.

- No two items in the same folder can have the same name.

- Because slash characters (/) are used in pathnames, it's not a good idea to use them in names. In fact, some programs (such as Microsoft Word) won't allow you to include a slash in a file name.

- In general, it's not a good idea to rename applications or their supporting documents or items in your computer's System or Library folder.

To rename an icon:

1. Click the icon to select it **A**.

2. Press Return.

   A box appears around the icon name and the name becomes selected **B**.

3. Type the new name.

   The text you type automatically overwrites the selected text **C**.

4. Press Return or Enter, or click anywhere else. The icon is renamed **D**.

A Select the icon you want to rename.

B When you press Return an edit box appears around the item name and the name is selected.

C Type in a new name.

D When you press Return the new name is saved.

TIP Note that in step 2, if the icon has a file name extension, that extension is not selected **B**. Do not change a file's extension unless you know what you're doing; making a mistake can render the file impossible to open on your computer.

TIP Not all icons can be renamed. If the edit box does not appear around an icon name in step 2, that icon cannot be renamed.

TIP You can also rename an icon in the Info window (page 94).

Letters　　　　　Images　　　　　Backup

Ⓐ Mac OS supports three kinds of folders, each with its own icon: standard folder (left), smart folder (center), and burn folder (right).

Folders

Mac OS uses folders to organize files and other folders on disk. You can create a folder, give it a name that makes sense to you, and move files and other folders into it. It's a lot like organizing paper files and folders in a file cabinet.

Mac OS X supports three different kinds of folders **Ⓐ**:

- A standard *folder* is for manually storing files on disk. You create the folder, and then move or copy items into it. Throughout this book, I use the term *folder* to refer to this kind of folder.

- A *smart folder* (page 106) works with Spotlight, Mac OS X's integrated searching feature, to automatically organize files and folders that meet specific search criteria.

- A *burn folder* (page 118) is for organizing items you want to save, or "burn," onto a CD or DVD.

This part of the book covers standard folders—the kind you'd use to organize your documents and other files. Because a folder can contain any number of files and other folders, you can easily create a filing system that works best for you.

TIP Your Home folder includes folders set up for organizing files by type. You'll find that these folders often appear as default file locations when saving specific types of files from within software applications (page 166).

TIP You can rename a folder the same way you rename any other icon (page 48).

To create a folder with the New Folder command:

1. Choose File > New Folder , or press Shift-Command-N.

   A new untitled folder appears in the active window .

2. While the edit box appears around the new folder's name , type a name for it and press Return.

To create a folder with the New Folder with Selection command:

1. Select one or more icons you want to group together into a new folder .

2. Choose File > New Folder with Selection , or press Command-Control-N.

   A new folder appears in the active window and the items that were selected are moved into it .

3. While the edit box appears around the new folder's name , type a name for it and press Return.

TIP The New Folder with Selection command is brand new in OS X Lion.

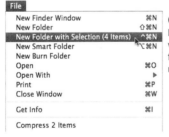

E Choose New Folder with Selection from the File menu.

B Choose New Folder from the File menu.

C A new untitled folder appears.

D Select the items you want to include in a new folder.

F A new folder appears and the items that were selected are moved into it.

Moving & Copying Items

In addition to moving icons around within a window or on the desktop (page 24), you can move or copy items to other locations on the same disk or other disks. This makes it possible to organize items into folders, make copies of items for safekeeping, and share items with others.

You can use drag and drop to move or copy an item by dragging it to a destination location:

- When you drag an item to a location on the same disk, the item is moved to that location. To force the item to be copied instead, hold down the Option key until you release the item in the destination location.

- When you drag an item to a location on another disk, the item is copied to that location. To force the item to be moved instead, hold down the Command key until you release the item in the destination location.

The next two pages provide instructions for all of these techniques, as well as instructions for duplicating items.

TIP You can move or copy more than one item at a time. Select all of the items that you want to move or copy, and then drag any one of them to the destination location.

TIP You can continue working with the Finder or any other application—even start more copy jobs—while a long copy job is in progress.

TIP You cannot move or copy items to a location that is write protected or for which you don't have write privileges (page 398).

To move or copy an item:

1. Optionally, do one of the following:

   ▸ If you want to copy the item to a location on the same disk, press and hold the Option key.

   ▸ If you want to move the item to a location on a different disk, press and hold down the Command key.

2. Drag the icon for the item that you want to move or copy as follows:

   ▸ To move or copy the item into a specific folder or volume, drag the icon onto the icon for the folder or volume. The destination icon becomes selected when the pointer moves over it **A**.

   ▸ To move or copy the item into a specific window, drag the icon into the window. A border may appear around the inside of the destination window **B**.

   Note that If the item is being copied, a green icon with a + sign inside it moves with the mouse pointer **B**.

3. Release the button (and then Option or Command key, if held down). The item is moved or copied and your Mac makes a move/copy complete sound.

> **TIP** If moving or copying takes more than a few seconds, in step 3 you may see a dialog that shows a progress bar **C**. You can click the X in that dialog to cancel the process.

> **TIP** If an item with the same name already exists in the destination location, an error message appears **D**. You have three choices: Keep Both Files moves or copies the file but renames it so it doesn't overwrite the existing file. Stop stops the move or copy. Replace replaces the original file with the one you are moving or copying.

A In this example, I'm dragging a file onto a folder icon to move it into that folder.

B In this example, I'm copying the same file into a folder window.

C You'll catch a glimpse of a dialog like this if it takes more than a few seconds to move or copy files.

D If an item with the same name already exists in the destination location, you'll see a dialog like this.

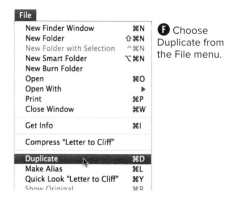

E Select the item you want to duplicate.

F Choose Duplicate from the File menu.

G A copy of the selected item appears with the original.

To duplicate an item:

1. Select the item that you want to duplicate **E**.

2. Do one of the following:
   - Choose File > Duplicate **F**, or press Command-D.
   - Hold down the Option key while dragging the item to a different place in the same window.

   A copy of the item you duplicated appears in the same location as the original. The word *copy* is appended to the file name **G**.

The Trash & Deleting Items

The Trash is a special place on your hard disk where you place items you want to delete. Items in the Trash remain there until you empty the Trash, which removes them from your disk. The Trash appears as an icon in the Dock .

The Trash icon's appearance indicates its status:

- If the Trash is empty, the Trash icon looks like an empty wire basket **A**.

- If the Trash is not empty, the Trash icon looks like a wire basket with crumpled papers in it **B**.

TIP You cannot move an item to the Trash if the item is locked (page 94) or on a write-protected disk (page 112).

To drag an item to the Trash:

1. Drag the icon for the item you want to delete to the Trash icon in the Dock.

   When the pointer moves over the Trash icon, the Trash icon becomes selected **C**.

2. Release the button.

   The item moves into the Trash.

TIP You can delete more than one item at a time. Begin by selecting all the items you want to delete, and then drag any one of them to the Trash. All items are moved to the Trash.

TIP Dragging a disk icon to the Trash does not delete or erase it. Instead, it unmounts it (page 116).

A When there's nothing in the Trash, it looks like an empty wire basket.

B When there's something in the Trash, it looks like an wire basket with crumpled papers in it.

C When you drag an item to the Trash, the Trash icon becomes selected.

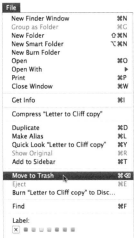

D The Move to Trash command moves selected items to the Trash.

To use the Move to Trash command:

1. Select the item that you want to delete.

2. Choose File > Move to Trash **D**, or press Command-Delete.

   The item is moved to the Trash.

TIP You can delete more than one item at a time. Begin by selecting all the items you want to delete, and then use the Move to Trash command. All items are moved to the Trash.

To drag an item out of the Trash:

1. Click the Trash icon in the Dock to open the Trash window **E**.

2. Drag the item from the Trash window to the Desktop or to another window on your hard disk.

   The item is moved from the Trash to the window you dragged it to.

To use the Put Back command:

1. Click the Trash icon in the Dock to open the Trash window **E**.

2. Select the item you want to remove from the Trash.

3. Choose File > Put Back **F**, or press Command-Delete.

   The item is moved back to where it was before you moved it to the Trash.

E Opening the Trash displays the Trash window and its contents.

F You can use the Put Back command to take selected items out of the Trash and put them back where they were before you trashed them.

To empty the Trash:

1. Use one of the following techniques:

   - Choose Finder > Empty Trash , or press Shift-Command-Delete.

   - Click the Trash icon in the Dock to open the Trash window **E** and then click the Empty button.

   - Right click the Trash icon to display a contextual menu **H** and then choose Empty Trash.

   A Trash warning dialog appears **I**.

2. Click Empty Trash to delete all items in the Trash.

TIP If you hold down the Option key while emptying the Trash, the Trash is emptied without displaying the warning dialog **I**. You can use Finder Preferences to disable the Trash warning (page 451).

To permanently remove items in the Trash from your disk:

1. Choose Finder > Secure Empty Trash **G**.

   A Trash warning dialog appears **J**.

2. Click Secure Empty Trash to permanently remove all items in the Trash.

TIP The Secure Empty Trash command makes it impossible to use special data recovery software to unerase deleted files.

TIP You may want to use the Secure Empty Trash command to erase personal files on a shared computer or a computer you plan to give away or sell.

TIP Deleting files from disk with the Secure Empty Trash command may take longer than using the Empty Trash command, especially when deleting large files.

G The Finder menu includes two commands for emptying the Trash.

H The contextual menu for the Trash includes an Empty Trash command.

I The Trash warning dialog asks you to confirm that you really do want to delete the items in the Trash.

J Using the Secure Empty Trash command displays a warning dialog like this.

Window Views

The Mac OS Finder displays the contents of your hard disk and other accessible volumes in windows. A window can show the contents of a volume or folder.

Mac OS offers several different window views that make it easy to see and work with a window's contents. For example, you can view contents as icons or hierarchical lists that can be sorted any way you like. You can even use views that include previews of document contents so you can see a document without even opening it.

In this chapter, I tell you more about how to work with Mac OS X's window views. By understanding how each view works and what features it offers, you should be able to decide which views work best for the things you need to do.

Window Views

A Finder window's contents can be displayed using four different views:

- **Icons** displays the window's contents as icons **A**. You can set the icon size and rearrange icons within the window.

- **List** displays the window's contents as a sorted list **B**. You can use disclosure triangles to hide or show folder contents.

- **Columns** displays the window's contents with a multiple-column format that shows the currently selected disk or folder and the items within it **C**. The right-most column displays a preview of a selected item.

- **Cover Flow** displays a folder's contents as preview images at the top of the window **D**. If you have a multi-touch device, you can use gestures to scroll through the preview icons.

You can switch from one view to another with the click of a button, making it easy to use any view you like for any window you're viewing. You can also set the view for each window separately.

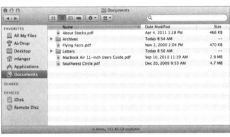

A B C D Mac OS X's four window views: icon view, list view, column view, and Cover Flow view.

E You can choose an option from the top of the View menu to change the active window's view.

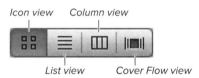

Icon view *Column view* *List view* *Cover Flow view*

F Use the View buttons on the toolbar to switch from one view to another.

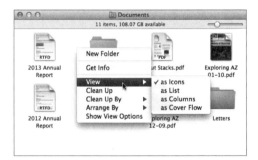

G Right-clicking in a window displays a contextual menu you can use to change the view. This is particularly handy when the toolbar is not showing.

To set a window's view:

1. If necessary, activate the window for which you want to change the view.

2. Do one of the following:

   ▸ Choose the view option you want from the View menu **E**, or press the corresponding shortcut key:
   Icon view: Command-1
   List view: Command-2
   Column view: Command-3
   Cover Flow view: Command-4

   ▸ Click the toolbar's view button for the view you want **E**. The button will appear "pushed in" when selected.

   ▸ Right-click in the window to display a contextual menu and choose the view you want from the View sub-menu **G**.

   The view of the window changes.

TIP Commands on the View menu **E** work on the active window only.

TIP A check mark appears on the View menu beside the name of the view applied to the active window **E**.

TIP If the toolbar is not showing for a window, you can choose View > **Show Toolbar**, or press Option-Command-T to display it.

Working with Icon View

Icon view displays a window's contents as icons. Unlike some other views, a window in icon view displays the contents of only one disk or folder at a time.

As discussed on page 24, icons can be dragged to reposition them in a window. You can also use commands under the View menu to align icons in the window.

TIP Chapter 2 explains the basics of working with icons in the Finder.

To clean up a window:

1. Activate the window that you want to clean up 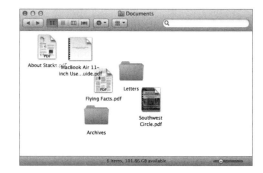.

2. Choose View > Clean Up **B**.

   The icons are moved into the nearest unoccupied space in the window's invisible grid **C**.

TIP A window's invisible grid (page 463) ensures consistent spacing between icons.

TIP You can manually position an icon in the window's invisible grid by holding down the Command key while dragging it within the window.

TIP If one or more icons in the window are selected when you display the View menu, the Clean Up command appears as Clean Up Selection. You can use this command to reposition just the selected icons in a window.

TIP You can use the new Clean Up By submenu under the View menu to neaten up a window and place icons in a specific order at the same time.

A Sometimes windows just get messy.

B You can choose the Clean Up command under the View menu...

C ...to move icons into the window's invisible grid.

Sort Column

A Click a column heading to sort by that column.

B Click the same column heading to reverse that column's sort order.

Working with List View

List view displays a window's contents in an ordered list. Items cannot be manually moved around so there's no need for a Clean Up command.

Windows displayed in list view also have a feature not found in other views: They can display the contents of folders within the window as an outline. This makes it possible to see and select the contents of more than one folder at a time.

To sort a window's contents:

Click the column heading for the column you want to sort by.

The list is sorted by that column **A**.

> **TIP** You can identify the column by which a list is sorted by its colored column heading **A**.

> **TIP** You can reverse a window's sort order by clicking the sort column's heading a second time **B**.

> **TIP** You can determine the sort direction by looking at the arrow in the sort column. When it points up, the items are sorted in ascending order **B**; when it points down, the items are sorted in descending order **A**.

> **TIP** To properly sort by size, you must turn on the Calculate all Sizes option for the window (page 466).

> **TIP** You can specify which columns should appear in a window by setting view options (page 466).

To display or hide a folder's contents in outline list view:

- To display a folder's contents, use one of the following techniques:
    - ▶ Click the right-pointing disclosure triangle beside the folder **C**.
    - ▶ Click the folder once to select it, and press Command-Right Arrow.

    The items within that folder are listed below it, slightly indented **D**.

- To hide a folder's contents, use one of the following techniques:
    - ▶ Click the down-pointing disclosure triangle beside the folder **E**.
    - ▶ Click the folder once to select it, and press Command-Left Arrow.

    The outline collapses to hide the items in the folder **D**.

TIP You can use this technique to display multiple levels of folders in the same window **F**.

Disclosure triangles

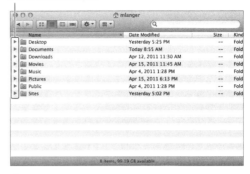

C Disclosure triangles that point to the right indicate hidden content.

Disclosure triangle

D A disclosure triangle that points down indicates displayed content. In list view, this displays folder contents as an outline.

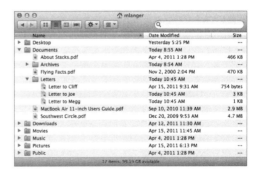

E In list view, you can display multiple levels of folders as an outline.

F Position the pointer in front of the first icon you want to select.

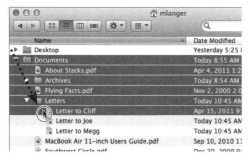

G Drag over the other icons you want to select.

H Select the first icon.

I Hold down Shift and click on the last icon.

To select multiple contiguous icons in list view:

Use one of the following techniques:

- Position the pointer in front of the first icon **F** and drag over the other icons you want to select **G**.

- Click to select the first icon **H**, hold down the Shift key, and click the last icon in the group you want to select **I**.

To select multiple noncontiguous icons in list view:

1. Click to select an icon **H**.

2. Hold down the Command key and click another icon.

   The icon is also selected **J**.

3. Repeat step 2 until all icons have been selected **K**.

To deselect icons:

Click anywhere in the window other than on an icon's line of information.

J K Command-click icons to select them.

To change a column's width:

1. Position the pointer on the line between the heading for the column whose width you want to change and the column to its right.

   The pointer turns into a vertical bar with two arrows 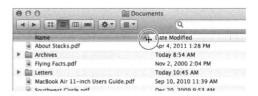.

2. Press the button down and drag:

   - To make the column narrower, drag to the left **M**.

   - To make the column wider, drag to the right.

3. When the column is displayed at the desired width, release the button.

> **TIP** If you make a column too narrow to display all of its contents, information may be truncated or condensed **M**.

To change a column's position:

1. Position the pointer on the heading for the column you want to move.

2. Press the button down and drag:

   - To move the column to the left, drag to the left **N**.

   - To move the column to the right, drag to the right.

   As you drag, the pointer turns into a grasping hand and the other columns shift to make room for the column you're dragging **N**.

3. When the column is in the desired position, release the button.

   The column changes its position **O**.

> **TIP** You cannot change the position of the Name column.

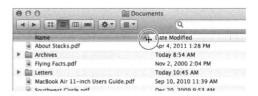

L Position the pointer on the column border.

M When you press the button down and drag, the column's width changes.

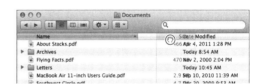

N You can drag a column heading...

O ...to change the column's position.

A Clicking a folder name in one column displays the contents of that folder in the column to its right.

B Selecting a document in column view can display a preview and additional information in the column to the right.

C Scrolling to the left moves backward through the file hierarchy to display parent folders.

Working with Column View

Column view displays the contents of a window in multiple columns. Clicking a folder in one column displays the contents of that folder in the column to its right. Clicking a document or application in a column displays a preview or information about the item in the column to its right.

To display a folder's contents:

Click the name of the folder you want to view the contents of.

The contents of the folder appear in the column to the right of the one you clicked in **A**.

To display a document preview:

Click the icon for the document you want to preview.

One of two things happens:

- If a preview for the document is available, it appears in the column to the right of the one you clicked in, along with additional information about the file **B**.

- If a preview is not available, the icon for the item appears in the column to the right of the one you clicked.

To move through the folder hierarchy:

To move through the folder hierarchy, scroll left or right in the window using the scroll bar or gestures (page 32):

- Scroll left to move backward and view parent folders **C**.

- Scroll right to move forward and view child folders.

To change column width:

1. Position the pointer on the divider between two columns or, if column scroll bars are displayed, on the handle at the bottom of the scroll bar between two columns.

   The pointer turns into a vertical line with two arrows **D** **E**.

2. Press the button down and drag:

   ▸ To make the column wider, drag to the right **F**.

   ▸ To make the column narrower, drag to the left.

3. When the column is the desired size, release the button.

To view more or fewer columns:

Change the width of the window (page 30):

   ▸ To show more columns, make the window wider **G**.

   ▸ To show fewer columns, make the window narrower.

D Position the pointer anywhere on a column border if scroll bars are not displayed...

E ...or on the column width handle at the bottom of the column if scroll bars are displayed.

F When you drag a border to the right, the column to the left of the border gets wider.

G You can view more columns by making the window wider.

Scroll bar scroller

A You can drag the scroll bar in the Cover Flow pane to flip through icons and previews.

B You can also flip through items in Cover Flow if scroll bars are not displayed.

Working with Cover Flow

Cover Flow splits the window into two panes:

- The Cover Flow pane at the top of the window displays each item in the window as an icon or a preview of its first page.

- The item list pane at the bottom of the window displays a sortable list of the items in the window.

When you select an item in the item list, its icon or preview appears in the Cover Flow pane.

You can use either pane to flip through the contents of a window to see item previews. This makes it possible to scroll through files to find one you're looking for, even if you don't know its name.

To flip through documents in Cover Flow:

Use one of the following techniques:

- If the scroll bar is displayed in the Cover Flow pane **A**, drag the scroller to the left or right to display different icons or previews.

- If you have a multi-touch device (page 13), use gestures to scroll icons and previews in the Cover Flow pane to the right or left. This works even if scroll bars are not displayed **B**.

- Click the icon or preview for an item in the Cover Flow pane.

- Press the Up Arrow or Down Arrow key to display the previous or next item.

To change the size of the Cover Flow pane:

1. Position the pointer on the resize box beneath the scroll bar in the Cover Flow pane.

   The pointer turns into a hand.

2. Press the button and drag:

   ▸ To make the Cover Flow pane smaller, drag up.

   ▸ To make the Cover Flow pane larger, drag down **C**.

   As you drag, the hand pointer seems to grasp the resize box **C** as the pane's bottom border moves.

3. When the pane is the desired size, release the button.

TIP The larger the Cover Flow pane is, the larger the icons and previews within it are **C**.

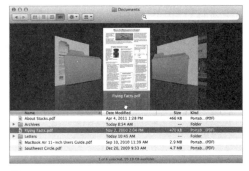

C Drag the resize handle down to make the Cover Flow pane larger, thus increasing the size of the icons and previews within it.

(A) In this example, the Documents folder is displayed in icon view and arranged by kind of file.

(B) Here's the Documents folder again, displayed in list view and arranged by kind of file.

Arranging Window Contents

In addition to moving icons and sorting lists, you can also use menu commands to arrange window icons by specific fields of information, such as kind, size, or date. Items are then grouped in the window by the arrange field you chose **(A)(B)(C)(D)**.

TIP Although previous versions of Mac OS also had the ability to arrange items by a specific field of information, OS X Lion adds the grouping feature and fine-tunes the way items are displayed in various views.

You can arrange a window's contents by nine different fields of information:

- **Name** (Control-Command-1) arranges items alphabetically by name (page 48).

- **Kind (A)(B)** (Control-Command-2) arranges items alphabetically by the kind of file.

- **Application** (Control-Command-3) arranges items alphabetically by the application that will open them (page 147).

- **Date Last Opened** (Control-Command-4) arranges items in reverse chronological order by the date they were last opened.

- **Date Added** (Control-Command-5) arranges items in reverse chronological order by the date they were added.

- **Date Modified** (Control-Command-6) arranges items in reverse chronological order by the date they were last modified.

- **Date Created** (Control-Command-7) arranges items in reverse chronological order by the date they were created.

continues on next page

- **Size** (Control-Command-8) arranges items in reverse size order. Folders have a size of 0 for this option unless you have set the window to calculate folder sizes (page 466).

- **Label** (Control-Command-9) arranges items by color-coded label (if applied; page 87).

As shown on these pages, the Arrange feature works in all window views.

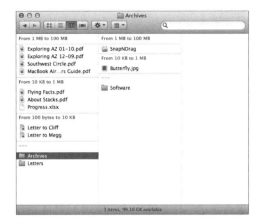

C The same Documents folder, this time in column view arranged by size.

Arranging vs. Sorting:

Although both the arranging and sorting feature put window icons in a specific order—usually the same order—there is a difference.

- *Arranging* groups items by the Arrange By option you specify. Within each group, items can also be sorted by another field. So, for example, you can arrange (and group) items by kind and, within each group, sort by creation date **A** **B**.

- *Sorting* simply sorts items by the column or sort option you specify. There's no grouping. Sorting is most often done in list or Cover Flow view by clicking a column heading (page 61), but you can also sort a window's contents by choosing a command from the Sort By submenu under the View menu (page 72).

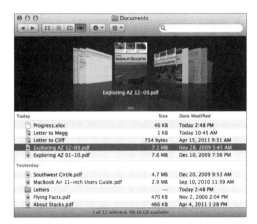

D In this example, the Documents folder is displayed in Cover Flow view and arranged by Date Last Added.

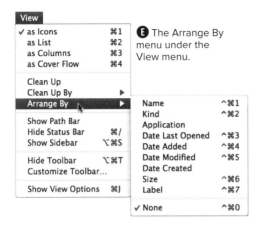

❸ The Arrange By menu under the View menu.

❻ The new Arrange menu on the toolbar.

To arrange window contents:

1. Activate the window you want to arrange.

2. Use one of the following techniques:
   - ▸ Choose a command from the Arrange By submenu under the View menu **❸**.
   - ▸ Choose a command from the Arrange pop-up menu on the window's toolbar **❻**, which is new in OS X Lion.
   - ▸ Press the appropriate keyboard shortcut (page 20).

   The icons are grouped in the window based on the Arrange By option you chose.

To remove arrangement settings from a window:

1. Activate the window you want to remove arrangement settings from.

2. Do one of the following:
   - ▸ Choose View > Arrange By > None **❸**.
   - ▸ Choose None from the Arrange pop-up menu on the window's toolbar **❻**.
   - ▸ Press Control-Command-0 (zero).

To sort and arrange a window's contents:

1. Activate the window you want to sort and arrange.

2. Follow the instructions on page 71 to remove any arrangement settings applied to the window.

3. Hold down the Option key and choose an option from the Sort By submenu under the View menu .

   The items are sorted in the order you specified.

4. Follow the instructions on page 71 to apply an arrangement option to the window.

   The items are grouped by the arrangement option and, if possible, sorted within each group by the sort option you chose in step 3.

Ⓖ Holding down the Option key turns the Arrange By submenu into a Sort By submenu.

TIP This doesn't always work. It depends on which arrangement option is selected in step 4 and whether it allows sorting. For example, you can arrange by kind and, within each group, sort by a date option Ⓑ because the kind option has distinct groups and no sorting within each group. But you cannot arrange by size and then sort by another field because within each size group, Mac OS sorts by size Ⓒ.

TIP The sort feature works just like the Keep Arranged By submenu that appeared in previous versions of Mac OS when you held down the Option key and displayed the View menu.

TIP You can also sort a window's contents by pressing one of the Sort By shortcut keys Ⓖ.

TIP In icon view, you must disable the window's sort option by choosing None from the Sort By submenu Ⓖ to be able to move icons out of their sorted positions.

5

Getting Help

Mac OS offers two basic ways to get additional information and answers to questions as you work with your computer:

- **Help Tags** identify screen items as you point to them. This help feature is supported by many (but not all) applications.

- **Help Center** provides information about using Mac OS and its applications. This feature, which has been renamed and reworked for OS X Lion, is accessible through commands on the Help menu. A great source of information, it is searchable and includes clickable links to content stored both on your Mac and online.

This chapter explains how to get help with Mac OS and applications when you need it. It also provides some tips for getting more information about your Mac, finding help, and troubleshooting problems.

In This Chapter:

Help Tags

Help Tags identify screen elements that you point to by providing information in small yellow boxes **A B C**.

Help Tags are especially useful when first using a new application. Pointing at various interface elements and reading Help Tags is a great way to start learning about how an application works.

> **TIP** Not all applications support the Help Tags feature. In addition, some applications have their own implementation of a similar feature that may work or look differently.

To use Help Tags:

Point to an item for which you want more information.

If a Help Tag is available for the item, it appears after a moment **A B C**.

> **TIP** Sometimes—but not very often—you can see an additional Help Tag if you press the Command key while a Help Tag is displayed.

A A Help Tag in a Finder window,...

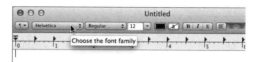

B ...in a TextEdit window,...

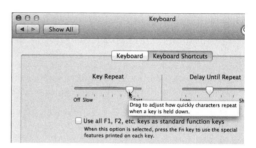

C ...and in a System Preferences pane window.

 The main Help Center window offers a table of contents with commonly used features and help topics.

Help Center

Help Center uses Mac OS X's Help Viewer to display information about Mac OS or a specific application. It includes several features that enable you to find information—and use it—quickly:

- **Main Help Center window** provides a clickable table of contents for commonly used features and help topics .

- **Search feature** enables you to search for topics containing specific words or phrases.

- **Related Topics links** enable you to move from one topic to a related topic.

- **Application links** enable you to open an application referenced by a help topic.

- **Online information links** enable you to get the latest information from Apple's website.

Help Center works for most Apple applications, as well as some Mac OS applications created by other software developers. It offers a standard interface for browsing, searching, and using help topics.

This section introduces you to Help Center and provides basic instruction for finding help when you need it. You can explore Help Center on your own to learn more about interface and features.

TIP If you are connected to the Internet when you access Help Center, the most up-to-date help information automatically appears, downloaded from Apple's servers on the Internet.

To open Help Center:

Do one of the following:

- In the Finder, choose Help > Help Center .

- In an application, choose Help > *Application Name* Help **C**.

- In a window or dialog, click a Help button **D**.

The Help Center window appears **A** **E** **F**.

> **TIP** You can only have one Help Center window open at a time. If the Help Center window is open for one application and you choose the Help command for another application, the second application's Help opens in the same window.

> **TIP** If the application does not support Help Center but has a Help option on the Help menu, that application's onscreen help will open in its own window, which may not look or work like Help center. For example, help for Microsoft Office applications opens it its own Help window.

E Opening the Help Center from within an application displays the main Help Center screen for that application.

B In the Finder, choose Help Center from the Help menu.

C In an application, the Help command starts with the name of the application.

Help button

D Some windows include a Help button.

F Clicking a Help button in a window displays the appropriate help topic for that window.

G Help Center displays groups of icons for applications that support the Help Center interface.

H Clicking the Show All link expands the group to show all applications within it.

To open help for another application from within Help Center:

1. Open the main Help Center window **A**.

2. Click the Help for all your apps link at the bottom of the window.

   A screen with groups of application icons appears **G**.

3. If necessary, click the Show all link in the top of an icon group to expand the list and display all of applications in that group **H**.

4. Click the icon for the application you want to open help for.

   The application's main Help Center screen **E**.

TIP This technique makes it possible for you to open an application's help without opening the application itself.

TIP An application may not be listed in Help Center until you've used that application or have accessed its Help window at least once.

TIP Onscreen help for applications that do not use the Mac OS Help Center interface is not accessible through this feature.

To browse help:

1. Click a link or button in a Help Center window.

   The window's contents change to view information related to the item you clicked **I**.

2. Continue clicking links or buttons to view related information **J**.

TIP Links in Help Center windows normally appear in blue type.

TIP You can backtrack through topics you have viewed by clicking the back button in the toolbar or by clicking one of the buttons in the Help Center path bar **I**.

TIP Clicking the bookmark button at the right end of the path bar **I** creates a bookmark that makes it easy to return to that topic later.

TIP To change the size of the text in Help Center window, choose Make Text Smaller or Make Text Bigger from the Action pop-up menu in the Help Center toolbar **K**.

TIP To print a help topic, choose Print from the Action pop-up menu in the Help Center toolbar **K**. (Learn more about printing in Chapter 22.)

Path bar   Bookmark button

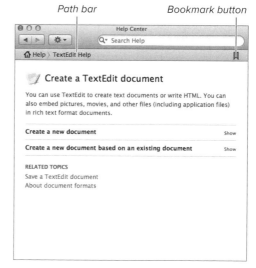

I Clicking the "Create a TextEdit Document" link in the main TextEdit Help Center window **E** displays this screen.

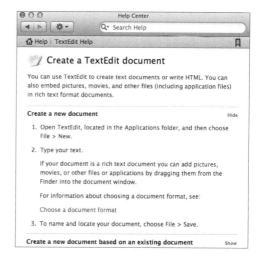

J Clicking the first Show link in the Create a TextEdit document help topic **I** expands the topic to provide detailed help information.

K The Action pop-up menu in the Help Center window.

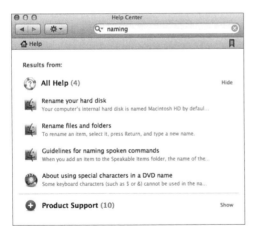

O Help Center immediately matches what you type in the Help box.

M Clicking the Rename files and folders option on the Help menu **I** or in search results **N** displays this help topic.

N A Help Center search results window.

To search help from the Help menu:

1. Click to display the Help menu.

2. In the search box, begin typing what you want to find help for.

   Help Center immediately begins listing help topics that match what you've typed so far **O**. You can continue typing, if necessary, to narrow down the search.

3. When you see the help topic you want on the menu, click it.

   Help Center displays the help topic you chose **M**.

TIP Clicking Show All Help Topics in the Help menu's search results **I** displays the Help Center window with search results displayed **N**.

To search help from the Help Center window:

1. Display any Help Center window.

2. In the search box on the toolbar, type what you want to find help for.

3. Press Return.

   A search results window with links to help topics appears **N**.

4. Click a link for the topic you want.

   Help Center displays the help topic you clicked **M**.

TIP In step 2, as you type, Mac OS will display a menu of recent search results that match what you're typing. You can click one of these to go directly to a previous search.

TIP Search results **N** can include help topics that reside on your computer as well as Support Articles that your Mac can retrieve from Apple's Product Support site if you have an Internet connection.

Help & Troubleshooting Advice

Here's some advice for learning more about your computer, getting help, and troubleshooting problems.

- **Join a Macintosh user group.** Joining a user group and attending meetings is probably the most cost-effective way to learn about your computer and get help. You can find a users' group near you by consulting the Apple User Group website, **www.apple.com/usergroups/**.

- **Attend free seminars at your local Apple Store.** You can learn more about Apple Stores and see a calendar of upcoming events at a store near you at **www.apple.com/retail/**.

- **Visit Apple's Support website.** You can find a wealth of information about your computer online. Start at **www.apple.com/support/**  and search for the information you need.

- **Visit websites that offer troubleshooting information.** MacFixIt (**reviews.cnet.com/macfixit/**), The Unofficial Apple Weblog (**www.tuaw.com**), and Mac OS X Hints (**hints.macworld.com**) are three excellent resources.

- **Visit the websites for the companies that develop the applications you use most.** A regular visit to these sites can keep you informed about updates and upgrades that can keep your software running smoothly. These sites can also provide technical support for problems you encounter while using the software. Learn the URLs for these sites by consulting the documentation that came with the software.

A Apple's support website includes a wealth of information about all Apple products—both hardware and software.

- **Read Macintosh magazines.** Several magazines, each geared toward a different level of user, can help you learn about your computer: *Macworld* (**www.macworld.com**) and *Mac|Life* (**www.maclife.com**) are two good ones. Avoid PC-centric magazines; the majority of the information they provide will not apply to your Macintosh.

- **Google the problem.** That seems like a common-sense approach to finding a solution for a problem, but it's surprising how few people do this. Enter a search phrase at **www.google.com** that describes the problem and you should come up with some search results to help guide you.

Managing Files

In This Part

Advanced Finder Techniques

In addition to the basic Finder and file management techniques covered in Chapters 2 through 4, Mac OS X offers more advanced techniques you can use to work with files:

- Use spring-loaded folders to access folders while copying or moving items.

- Apply color-coded labels to Finder items.

- Use aliases to make frequently used files easier to access without moving them.

- Quickly reopen recently used items.

- Use Quick Look to view the contents of a file or folder without opening it.

- Use the Info window to learn more about an item or set options for it.

- Compress files and folders to save disk space or minimize data transfer time.

- Undo actions you performed while working with the Finder.

This chapter covers all of these techniques.

In This Chapter:

Spring-Loaded Folders

The spring-loaded folders feature lets you move or copy items into folders deep within the file structure of a disk—without manually opening a single folder. Instead, you simply drag icons onto folders and wait as they're automatically opened. When you drop the icon into the folder you want, the item moves.

The spring-loaded folders feature works a bit differently in OS X Lion than it did in previous versions of Mac OS. Now, instead of opening each folder in a new window, folders are opened in the same window. Thus, you end up with the name number of windows open at the end of an operation as when you started. You can use the Back button on the window's toolbar to return to the window that was originally open when you began the operation.

Here are a few additional things to keep in mind:

- To use spring-loaded folders, it must be enabled in Finder preferences (page 449). This feature is normally turned on by default.

- Using spring-loaded folders requires a steady hand, good mouse or trackpad skills, and knowledge of the location of folders on your disk.

- To use spring-loaded folders to move or copy more than one item at a time, select the items first, and then drag any one of them.

- The spring-loaded folders feature is sometimes referred to as *spring-open folders*.

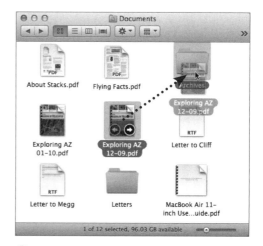

A Drag an icon onto a folder and wait...

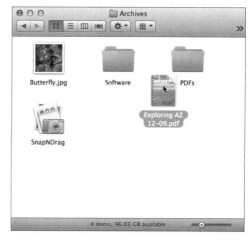

B ...until the folder opens in the same window.

TIP You can use spring-loaded folder techniques to work with folder icons (or stacks; page 292) on the Dock. So, for example, you can drag a PDF file icon from a Finder window onto the Applications stack to open the stack's window and then drop the file icon onto a compatible application to open it with that application.

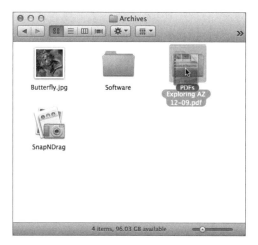

C Continue to drag the icon onto a folder in that window and wait...

D ...until that folder opens in the same window.

E When you drop the icon into a window, the item moves there.

To move an item using spring-loaded folders:

1. Drag the item you want to move onto the folder to which you want to move it **A**, but do not release the button. After a moment, the folder blinks and opens **B** in the same window.

2. Without releasing the button, repeat step 1. The destination folder becomes selected **C**, then blinks and opens **D**. Do this until you reach the final destination.

3. Release the button to place the item into the destination window **E**.

TIP In steps 1 and 2, to open a folder immediately, press the space bar while dragging an item onto it.

TIP If you open the wrong folder and want to start over, without releasing the button, move the icon away from the window. The folders you opened close, returning you to the original window.

To copy an item using spring-loaded folders:

Hold down the Option key while following the above steps.

TIP If the destination folder is on another disk, it is not necessary to hold down the Option key to copy items; they're automatically copied.

Labels

Mac OS X's Labels feature enables you to assign color-coded labels to Finder icons. You can then sort a window's contents by label or search for items based on the assigned label.

With a little imagination, labels can be a useful file management tool. For example, when I write a book and it goes through the editing process, I use labels to indicate each chapter's status. Yellow means it's a first draft, orange means it's a second draft, and green means it's final. This color-coding makes it possible for me to see a project's status just by looking inside a folder containing its files. (Imagine how good I feel when all of a book's chapter folders are green!)

TIP To sort a window's contents by label, you either need to use the **Sort By** submenu under the view menu (page 72) or, in list view, display the Labels column (page 466).

TIP You can use Finder Preferences to change the name associated with a label or its color (page 450).

A Select the icon you want to apply a label to.

B Choose a label color from the bottom of the File menu.

G In icon view, the color you chose is applied to the icon's name.

D In list view, the label color is applied to the entire line for the item.

E Choosing the X under Label on the File menu removes the label from selected icons.

To assign a label to an item:

1. In a Finder window, select the icon(s) you want to apply a label to **A**.

2. From the File menu, choose the color of the label you want to apply **B**.

   In icon view, the name of the icon is enclosed in an oval in the color you chose **C** or, in other views, the item's entire line turns the color you chose **D**.

TIP You can also assign a label to an item in its Info window (page 94).

TIP You use the same technique to change the label assigned to an item.

To remove a label from an item:

1. In a Finder window, select the icon you want to remove a label from.

2. From the File menu, choose the X beneath Label **E**.

   The label is removed.

TIP If multiple icons are selected in step 1 and different labels are applied to them, all applied labels appear selected at the bottom of the File menu. Clicking the X removes them all.

Aliases

An *alias* is a pointer to an item. You can make an alias of an item and place it anywhere on your computer. Then, when you need to open the item, just open its alias.

You can move, copy, rename, open, and delete an alias just like any other file. By putting aliases of frequently used items together where you can quickly access them—such as on your desktop or in a stacks folder (page 292) in the Dock—you make the items more accessible without actually moving them.

It's important to remember that an alias is not a copy of the item—it's a pointer. If you delete the original item, the alias will not open.

Here are a few additional things to keep in mind about aliases:

- The icon for an alias looks very much like the icon for the original item but includes a tiny arrow in the bottom-left corner.

- You can name an alias anything you like, as long as you follow Mac OS file naming guidelines (page 48). An alias's name does not need to include the word *alias*.

- The sidebar (page 35), Dock (page 38), and recent items (page 91) features all work with aliases.

Ⓐ Select an icon you want to make an alias for.

Ⓑ Choose Make Alias from the File menu.

C The alias appears with the original item.

D Choose Show Original from the File menu.

To create an alias:

1. Select the item you want to make an alias for **A**.

2. Choose File > Make Alias **B**, or press Command-L.

   The alias appears right beneath the original item **C**.

3. While the alias file's name is selected **C**, you can rename it. Just type in a new name and press Return.

4. Move the alias icon as desired to another location on disk.

TIP You can also create an alias by holding down the Command and Option keys while dragging an item's icon to a new location on disk. The alias appears in the destination.

To find an alias's original file:

1. Select the alias's icon.

2. Choose File > Show Original **D**, or press Command-R.

   A window for the folder in which the original resides opens with the original item selected.

TIP If the original item cannot be found, Mac OS displays a dialog telling you so **E**. You can learn how to fix a broken alias on the next page.

E If the original for an alias can't be found, a dialog like this appears when you look for its original or attempt to open it.

To fix a broken alias:

1. Select the alias's icon.

2. Do one of the following:

   ▸ Choose File > Show Original 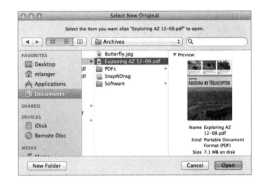, or press Command-R.

   ▸ Open the alias icon.

   A dialog appears if the original can't be found **E**.

3. Click Fix Alias.

4. Use the Select New Original dialog that appears **F** to locate and select the item that you want to use as the original for the alias.

5. Click Open.

   The item you selected is assigned to the alias.

TIP The Select New Original dialog is similar to a standard Open dialog (page 164).

TIP If you would prefer to delete a broken alias instead of fixing it, click Delete Alias in the dialog that appears when you try to open it **E**.

TIP If an alias is not broken but you want to reassign it to a new original anyway, you can click the Select New Original button in its Info window (page 94).

F Use this dialog to select a new original item for an alias.

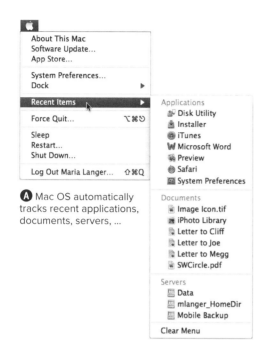

A Mac OS automatically tracks recent applications, documents, servers, ...

B ...and folders.

Recent Items

Mac OS automatically tracks the things you open. It creates submenus **A B** of the most recently opened items in four categories—applications, documents, servers, and folders—making it quick to open them again.

TIP You can specify how many recent items Mac OS X tracks in the Recent Items submenu by setting options in the General preferences pane (page 486).

To open recent items:

Do one of the following:

- To open a recently used application, document, or server, choose its name from the Recent Items submenu under the Apple menu **A**.

- To open a recently used folder, choose its name from the Recent Folders submenu under the Go menu **B**.

TIP Recent Items works with aliases (page 88); Mac OS automatically creates an alias for each item you open and stores it in a hidden folder inside your Home folder.

To clear the Recent Items or Recent Folders submenu:

Choose Apple > Recent Items > Clear Menu **A** or choose Go > Recent Folders > Clear Menu **B**.

TIP Clearing the Recent Items or Recent Folders submenu does not delete any items.

Quick Look

Quick Look makes it possible to see what's in a folder or file without actually opening it. Instead, Quick Look shows a preview of the item within a resizable Quick Look window **A** **B** **C** **D**.

TIP Quick Look is similar to enhanced icon view (page 26).

To view a file with Quick Look:

1. In a Finder window, select the item you want to view with Quick Look.

2. Choose File > Quick Look "*file name*" **E** or press Command-Y.

   A light gray, slightly translucent window appears. It displays the item's contents **A** **B** **C** or icon **D**.

TIP If you use Quick Look to view a multipage document, you can scroll through the document or click thumbnail images **B** to view its pages.

TIP If you use Quick Look to view a movie file, the movie begins playing immediately.

TIP You can open an item from the Quick Look window by clicking the Open button in the upper-right corner of the window **A** **B** **C** **D**.

To browse the Finder with Quick Look:

1. Open a Finder window for the folder you want to browse.

2. Choose File > Quick Look "*file name*" **E** or press Command-Y to open the Quick Look window.

3. Select the items you want to view with Quick Look.

   Each time a different item is selected, the Quick Look window changes to display its contents or icon **A** **B** **C** **D**.

A The Quick Look window for a Rich Text Format document created with TextEdit.

B The Quick Look window for a multi-page PDF.

C The Quick Look window for a JPG image file.

D The Quick Look window for a folder.

E One way to open Quick Look is with a command on the File menu.

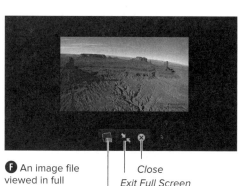

F An image file viewed in full screen mode in Quick Look.

Close
Exit Full Screen
Add to iPhoto

To switch to full screen view:

Click the Full Screen button at the top-right corner of a Quick Look window. The screen turns black and fills with the Quick View window **F**.

TIP Quick Look's full page view **E** is similar to, but not the same as, OS X Lion's new Full-Screen Apps feature (page 152). The background is black and there are no menus.

To work with full screen view:

Click one of two or three buttons that may appear at the bottom of the screen **E**:

- **Add to iPhoto** adds a displayed image to your iPhoto library. This button only appears for image files if iPhoto is installed.

- **Play/Pause** plays or pauses a displayed movie. This button only appears for movie files.

- **Exit Full Screen** closes full screen view. You can also close full screen view by pressing the Esc key.

- **Close** closes Quick Look.

TIP If the button bar disappears, move the pointer to display it again.

TIP When viewing a movie with sound, a volume slider may also appear. You can use it to change the sound level for the movie as it plays.

To close the Quick Look window:

Use one of the following techniques:

- Click the Quick Look window's close button (a tiny X in the upper-left corner).

- Choose File > Close Quick Look, or press Command-Y.

The Info Window

You can learn more about an item by opening its Info window **A** **B** **C** **D**. Depending on the type of icon (disk, folder, application, document, alias, and so on), the General information in the Info window will provide some or all of the following:

- **Kind** or type of item.
- **Size** of item or contents (folders and files only).
- **Where** item is on disk (page 44).
- **Created** date and time.
- **Modified** date and time.
- **Format** of item.
- **Capacity** of item (disks only).
- **Available** space on item (disks only).
- **Used** space on item (disks only).
- **Version** number or **Copyright** date or both (applications only).
- **Original** location on disk (aliases only; page 88).
- **Label** assigned to the item (page 86).
- **Shared folder** check box (disks and folders only) indicates whether the item is shared (page 400).
- **Stationery pad** check box (documents only) to convert the file into a stationery format file, which is like a document template.
- **Locked** check box to prevent the file from being deleted or overwritten (folders and files only).

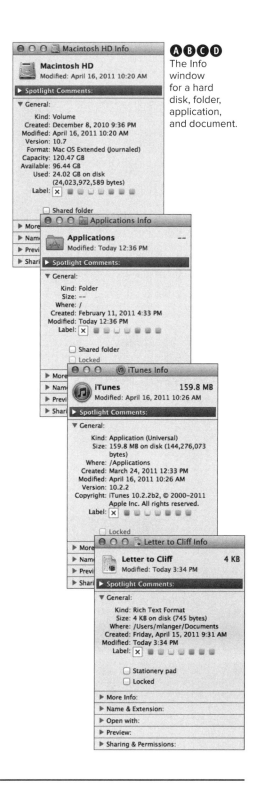

A **B** **C** **D** The Info window for a hard disk, folder, application, and document.

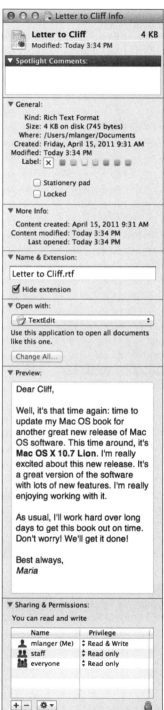

ⓔ Here's all the information you might find for a TextEdit document file.

In addition to the General category of information, the Info window offers additional categories **ⓔ**, depending on the type of item. You can click the disclosure triangle beside a category heading to display or hide the details for the category. Some of the categories include options that can be modified.

Some categories you might find in an Info window include:

- **Spotlight Comments** enable you to enter searchable comments or keywords for an item (page 96).

- **More Info** provides additional information about the file, including when the content was created and modified and when the item was last opened.

- **Name & Extension** displays an edit box you can use to change the file name (page 48) and its file name extension. A check box enables you to hide the extension in Finder windows.

- **Open with** (documents only) enables you to choose the application that should open the item and change the default application for all items of that type (page 149).

- **Preview** displays a preview for the item if one is available. Otherwise, it simply displays the item's icon.

- **Languages** (applications only; not shown in **ⓔ**) is a list of the languages built in to the application.

- **Sharing & Permissions** enables you to set file sharing permissions for the item (page 397).

TIP Changes you make in the Info window for an item are automatically saved.

To open the Info window:

1. Select the item you want to open the Info window for.

2. Choose File > Get Info **F**, or press Command-I.

   The Info window for that item appears **D** **E**.

To enter Spotlight comments in the Info window:

1. Open the Info window for the item you want to enter comments for **D** **E**.

2. If necessary, click the disclosure triangle beside Spotlight Comments near the top of the window. The window expands to show the Spotlight Comments box **E**.

3. Type your comments into the Spotlight Comments box **G**. They are automatically saved.

TIP You can use View Options to set a window's list view to display comments entered in the Info window (page 466).

To lock an application or document:

1. Open the Info window for the item you want to lock **A** **B** **C** **D** **E**.

2. Turn on the Locked check box.

TIP Locked items cannot be deleted or overwritten. They can, however, be moved.

F Choose Get Info from the File menu.

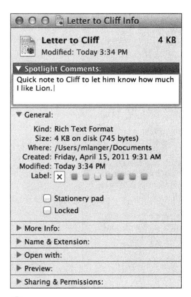

G You can type whatever you like into the Spotlight Comments box.

A Use the Compress command to compress one or more files into an archive file.

B This dialog may appear briefly as the selected item is compressed.

Documents   **Documents.zip**

C The compressed file appears in the same location as the original.

Compressing Files & Folders

Mac OS X's file compression feature enables you to create compressed copies of items that are sometimes called *archived files* or *archives*. Compressed files take up less space on disk than regular files. You may find them useful for backing up files or for sending files to others over a network or via email.

The file compression feature uses ZIP format compression, which was originally developed as a DOS and Windows PC format. As a result, document archives created with this feature are fully compatible with DOS and Windows PCs.

To compress a file or folder:

1. Select the item you want to compress.

2. Choose File > Compress "*Item Name*" **A**.

3. Wait while your computer creates the archive. If it takes more than a few seconds, a Copy status dialog may appear **B**.

   When the process is finished, the archive file appears as a .zip file in the same location as the original file **C**.

TIP You can compress multiple items at once. Select the items, then choose File > Compress *n* Items (where *n* is the number of selected items). When the archive appears, it will be named Archive.zip.

To open a compressed file:

Double-click the compressed file. The file's contents are uncompressed and appear in the same window as the compressed file.

Undoing Finder Actions

The Mac OS X Finder includes limited support for the Undo command, which can reverse the most recently completed action.

Say, for example, that you move a file from one folder to another folder. If you immediately change your mind, you can choose Edit > Undo Move of "*item name*" **A** to put the file back where it was.

TIP Don't depend on the Undo command. Unfortunately, it isn't always available **B**.

TIP The exact wording of the Undo command varies depending on the action and the item it was performed on. For example, the command shown in **A** is Undo Move of "Letter to Cliff" because the last action was to move a document icon named Letter to Cliff.

TIP The Undo command is also available (and generally more reliable) in most Mac OS applications. You'll usually find it at the top of the Edit menu (page 170).

To undo an action:

Immediately after performing an action, choose Edit > Undo "*action description*" **A**, or press Command-Z.

The action is reversed.

To redo an action:

Immediately after undoing an action, choose Edit > Redo "action description" **B**, or press Shift-Command-Z.

The action is redone—as if you never used the Undo command.

TIP Think of the Redo command as the Undo-Undo command since it undoes the Undo command.

Edit	
Undo Move of "Letter to Cliff"	⌘Z
Redo	⇧⌘Z
Cut	⌘X
Copy	⌘C
Paste	⌘V
Select All	⌘A
Show Clipboard	
Special Characters...	

A The Undo commands enables you to undo the last action you performed.

Edit	
Undo	⌘Z
Redo Move of "Letter to Cliff"	⇧⌘Z
Cut	⌘X
Copy "Letter to Cliff"	⌘C
Paste	⌘V
Select All	⌘A
Show Clipboard	
Special Characters...	

B In this example, I can redo the last thing I undid, but I can't undo anything.

Searching
for Files

Mac OS X offers a number of search features you can use to find files or folders:

- Spotlight enables you to perform a search quickly, no matter what application is active. Search results appear in a Spotlight menu or in a search results window.

- A Finder window's Search field enables you to initiate a search based on file name or content from a Finder window. Search results appear within the window.

- The Find command takes Finder searching a step further by offering additional search options, including the ability to find files based on kind, dates, labels, and size.

- Smart folders make it possible to save your search queries. Repeating a query is as easy as opening a smart folder icon.

Once you have a list of found files, opening a file is as easy as double-clicking it.

This chapter takes a closer look at the search features in Mac OS X.

In This Chapter:

The Spotlight Menu

The Spotlight menu on the far right end of the menu bar **Ⓐ** makes Finder searching always available, no matter what application is active.

To use Spotlight, click the menu, enter a search word or phrase, and wait as Spotlight lists top search results. If you see the item you want on the menu, you can click it to open it. Otherwise, you can display all search results in a Finder window, choose the one you want, or begin a new search.

TIP The types of items found and the order in which they appear in search results depends on settings in the Spotlight preferences pane (page 501).

TIP Spotlight also works within certain Mac OS X applications, such as System Preferences (page 476), as well as in standard Open (page 164) and Save (page 166) dialogs.

To find items with Spotlight:

1. Click the Spotlight icon on the far right end of the menu bar or press Command-Space Bar.

   The Spotlight search field appears in a menu **Ⓐ**.

2. Enter a search word or phrase in the search field.

   Spotlight immediately begins displaying matches for what you enter in a menu beneath the search field **Ⓑ**.

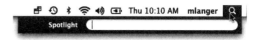

Ⓐ Click the Spotlight icon on the far right end of the menu bar to display the Spotlight search box.

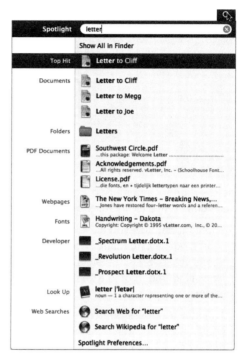

Ⓑ As you enter a search word or phrase, Spotlight immediately lists matches, sorted by kind.

 When you choose the Show All in Finder command from the Spotlight menu, it displays all search results in a Searching window.

To display all found items:

1. Follow the steps in the section titled "To find items with Spotlight" on the previous page to conduct a Spotlight search.

2. In the menu of search results ⓑ, click Show All in Finder.

   A Searching window full of search results appears ⓒ.

To open a found item:

Do one of the following:

- In the Spotlight menu of search results ⓑ, click the item you want to open.

- In the Searching window of found items ⓒ, double-click the item you want to open.

To perform a new search:

Do one of the following:

- Follow the instructions in the section titled "To find items with Spotlight" on the previous page. You may have to overwrite an existing search word or phrase with the new one.

- In the search box at the top of the Searching window ⓒ, enter a new search word or phrase.

TIP To quickly clear the contents of the search box, click the X button on the right side of the search box ⓑ ⓒ.

The Search Field

The Finder's Search field appears in the top-right corner of a Finder window's toolbar Ⓐ. You can use it to initiate a search based on item name or contents. Simply enter a word or phrase in the field, and Mac OS X displays a list of matches in the same window.

TIP A window's toolbar must be displayed (page 34) to use the Search field.

To find files with the Search field:

1. Click in the Search field of a Finder window to position the blinking insertion point there Ⓐ.

2. Enter the word or phrase you want to search for.

   As soon as you begin typing, the window turns into a Searching window. Mac OS begins displaying results Ⓑ.

3. When you finished typing press Return.

   The search results for what you typed appear in the window Ⓒ.

TIP Remember, this search feature searches by name or contents. If you're not sure of a file's name, search for some text you expect to find within it.

TIP To search based on file name only, before pressing Return in step 3, choose the Filename option in the menu beneath the search box Ⓑ.

To return to the original window:

Click the back button on the toolbar.

The search box is cleared and the window that was open when you started the search reappears.

Ⓐ The Search field appears in the toolbar on every Finder window.

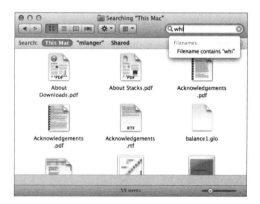

Ⓑ As you enter a search word, Mac OS immediately begins displaying search results.

Ⓒ When you finish typing the word or phrase, the final search results appear. In this example, I searched for the word *white* and found 18 items that contain that word.

A The Find command displays the Searching window with some additional options.

B You can use the attributes pop-up menu to choose types of criteria to add.

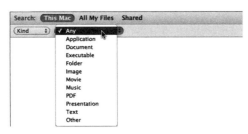

C When you choose the Kind criteria, you can select from various types of items.

D Use this pop-up menu and the options with it to set the various date-related search criteria.

The Find Command

Mac OS X's Find command also works with the Search field, but it automatically offers additional search options **A**:

- **Search locations** appear as buttons near the top of the window:

    ▸ **This Mac**, which always appears, searches your entire computer.

    ▸ "*Location name*" is the item that was selected or active when you chose the Find command.

    ▸ **Shared** is any network volumes currently accessible to your computer.

- **Criteria filters** appear in rows above the search results area. You can set options with these filters to narrow down the search results. Use an Attributes pop-up menu **B** to choose a search attribute and set up a filter:

    ▸ **Kind** is the type of items to search. Choose an option from the pop-up menu **C**.

    ▸ **Last opened date** is the date the item was last opened. You can use a pop-up menu **D** to set criteria options and set a date or date range.

    ▸ **Last modified date** is the date the item was last changed. The options are the same as Last opened date **D**.

    ▸ **Created date** is the date the item was created. The options are the same as Last opened date **D**.

continues on next page

▶ **Name** is the item's name. This tells Spotlight not to search the contents of an item to match text. If you choose this option, you can use a pop-up menu  and enter text to set criteria.

▶ **Contents** is the contents of the item. This tells Spotlight *not* to search the name of the item to match text. You can enter the search criteria in a text box.

▶ **Other** displays a dialog 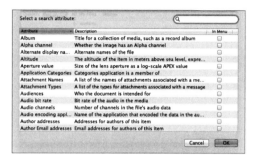 that you can use to add additional search attributes to the pop-up menu **B**. This makes it possible to search by virtually any kind of information associated with a Finder item. Turn on the check box beside each attribute you want to add.

You can add as many criteria filters as you like to fine-tune a search. Mac OS will attempt to match *all* filters—thus, the more filters you add, the fewer search results will appear.

TIP You can display criteria filters when using the Search field (page 102). Click the Add (+) button near the top of the Searching window to add a filter row.

TIP If you choose Other from the attribute pop-up menu **B** you can use the dialog **F** to turn off check boxes for search attributes you never use, thus fully customizing the menu.

E Use this pop-up menu to specify how a file name should match the criteria you enter.

F This dialog enables you to customize the Attributes pop-up menu **B**.

G Choose Find from the File menu.

To find files with the Find command:

1. If necessary, activate the Finder.

2. To search a specific location on your computer, open a Finder window for that location.

3. Choose File > Find **G**, or press Command-F.

   A Searching window appears **A**.

4. Enter a search word or phrase in the Search field.

5. Click a location button to choose one of the search locations.

6. Set up a criteria filter by choosing an option from the Attribute pop-up menu **B** and setting related criteria options **H**.

7. To add additional criteria filters, click the Add (+) button at the right end of a criteria row. Then set options in the new row that appears **I**. You can repeat this step as necessary to add as many filters as you like.

   Search results appear in the Searching window **H I** as you set search criteria.

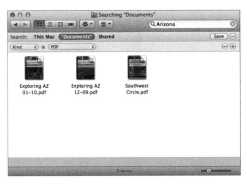

H In this example, I've entered a search word in the Search box, selected a search location, and set the Kind of file to PDF.

TIP You can perform any combination of steps 4 through 7. Each step you perform adds criteria that narrows the search results.

TIP The search results must match *all* search criteria specified in steps 4 through 7.

TIP To remove a criteria filter, click the Remove (–) button at the right end of its row.

TIP Clicking the Save button near the top of the Searching window creates a smart folder (page 106).

I In this example, I've added another criteria filter: Last opened date within last 2 days. This narrows down the search results even more.

Smart Folders

The smart folders feature takes the Find command one step further. It enables you to save search criteria as a special folder. Opening the folder automatically performs a search and displays matching items. The smart folder's contents always contain items that match search criteria, even if the files and folders on your computer change.

You can create a smart folder two ways:

- Use the New Smart Folder command under the Finder's File menu **Ⓐ** to open a New Smart Folder window **Ⓑ**, enter search criteria, and save the search.

- Click the Save button in the Searching window after performing a search you want to save and save the search.

Either way, you'll create a smart folder with an interface that looks and works just like the Searching window that appears when you use the Search field (page 102) or Find command (page 103).

When you save a search, you can choose the location in which you want the smart folder saved. Although smart folders are normally saved in the Saved Searches folder in the invisible Library folder (page 47) in your Home folder (page 42), you can save a smart folder anywhere on disk. You can also toggle a check box to automatically place a smart folder in the sidebar when you create it.

TIP The All My Files item which appears under the Go menu and, by default, in the sidebar, is actually a smart folder with its criteria predefined by Apple.

Ⓐ One way to create a smart folder is to choose New Smart Folder from the File menu.

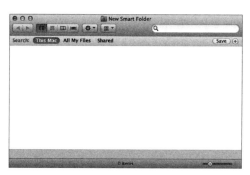

Ⓑ The New Smart Folder window looks just like the Searching window.

Ⓒ In this example, I've searched my Mac for document files opened within the past 30 days.

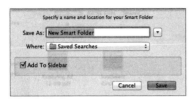

D The Save dialog might appear small, like this...

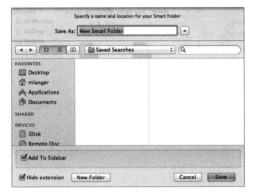

E ...or expanded, like this.

F When you save a smart folder, the name you gave it appears in its title bar when it's open. In this example, I've also added it to the sidebar, which is displayed here, too.

To create a smart folder:

1. To create a smart folder that searches a specific location on your computer, open a Finder window for that location.

2. Choose File > New Smart Folder **A**, or press Option-Command-N.

   A New Smart Folder window opens **B**.

3. Follow steps 4 through 7 on page 105 to set up search criteria for the smart folder.

   The search results appear in the window **C**.

4. Click the Save button near the top of the New Smart Folder window **C**.

   The Save dialog (page 166) appears **D** or **E**.

5. Set options in the dialog:

   ▸ **Save As** is the name of the smart folder. Give it a name that describes what the folder will contain.

   ▸ **Where** is the location in which the smart folder will be saved. You can use the Where menu **D** to choose a location or click the disclosure triangle beside the Save As box to expand the dialog **E** and choose any location on disk.

   ▸ **Add To Sidebar** instructs Mac OS X to add an alias of the folder to the sidebar **F**.

6. Click the Save button.

   The name you gave the smart folder appears in the window's title bar **F**, and the smart folder is saved for future use.

TIP If you create a smart folder by clicking the Save button in any Searching window, just follow steps 5 and 6 above.

To open a smart folder:

Do one of the following:

- If the smart folder has been added to the sidebar, click its name in the sidebar **F**.

- If the smart folder has not been added to the sidebar, open its icon **G**.

  The contents of the smart folder appear in a window **F**.

To edit a smart folder:

1. Open the smart folder you want to edit **F**.

2. Choose Show Search Criteria from the Action pop-up menu in the window's toolbar **H**.

   The search criteria you used to create the smart folder appears at the top of the window **I**

3. Make changes as desired to the search criteria.

   The search results in the window change accordingly.

4. Click the Save button.

   The changes are saved to the smart folder's definition.

To delete a smart folder:

Drag the smart folder's icon **G** to the Trash (page 54).

TIP Deleting a smart folder does not delete the contents of the smart folder. It simply deletes the search criteria that displays those contents. The original items remain on disk.

G A smart folder icon.

Recent Documents

H Choose Show Search Criteria from the Action pop-up menu in the window's toolbar.

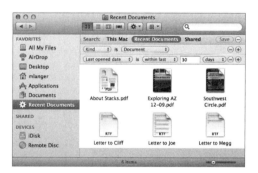

I The search criteria reappears at the top of the window so you can modify it.

A Clicking the icon for one of your search results displays the path to that item in the path bar at the bottom of the window.

B Choose Open Enclosing Folder from the File menu to open a selected item's parent folder.

C The enclosing folder opens in a new window.

Working with Search Results

No matter how you search for items, you will eventually wind up with a window full of found items **A**. Because this window is very much like any other Finder window, you can:

- Change the window's view.
- Use menu commands on any selected item in the window.
- Open an item by simply double-clicking its icon.

Here are a two other things you can do with these windows.

TIP Consult Chapters 2, 3, and 4 for more information about using the Finder and working with windows:

To see where an item resides on disk:

In the search results window, select the item.

Its location on disk appears at the bottom of the window **A**.

To open an item's parent folder:

1. In the search results window, select the item for which you want to open the parent folder.

2. Do one of the following:
   - In the directory path at the bottom of the window, double-click the folder listed to the left of the item name **A**.
   - Choose File > Open Enclosing Folder **B**, or press Command-R.

   The folder in which the item resides opens in a new window **C**.

Storage Devices & Media

As you work with your Mac, humming away under its hood is some kind of storage device—most often a hard disk—that's giving you access to the applications, documents, and other files you and your computer need to get work done. Similarly, you might use other internal and external storage devices to open, save, organize, or archive your files.

This chapter explores some of the storage device that you might use with your Mac and Mac OS X and explains how you can write data to recordable CDs and DVDs.

Storage Devices & Media

A Macintosh computer can read data from, or write data to, a wide range of storage devices and media, including (but not limited to):

- **Hard disk**—high capacity magnetic media consisting of a number of spinning disks encased with movable read/write heads. All Macs have internal hard drives.

- **Solid state drive (SSD)**—high capacity storage media that utilizes semiconductors for storage. MacBook Air computers have solid state drives; they are offered as an option on other computer models as well.

- **CD and DVD discs**—high capacity, removable optical media.

- **SD cards**—small, relatively high capacity media cards supported by many digital cameras. MacBook Pro computers released after June 2009 include an SD card reader slot.

- **Flash, or "thumb," drives**—small, relatively high capacity USB devices that are commonly used to move files from one computer to another.

- **RAID devices**—extremely high capacity magnetic storage devices, normally used in business environments for servers or backup.

- Other legacy magnetic media, including floppy disks, or diskettes, and Zip disks.

Storage devices can be:

- **Internal**—inside your computer and not easily removed. For example, all Mac models come with an internal hard disk. Most Macs also come with internal CD

TABLE 8.1 Terminology for Storage Media Capacity

Term	Abbreviation	Size
byte	byte	1 character
kilobyte	KB	1,024 bytes
megabyte	MB	1,024 KB
gigabyte	GB	1,024 MB
terabyte	TB	1,024 GB

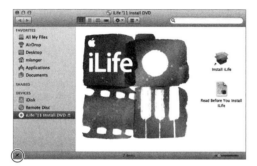

A A write-protected icon appears in the status bar for CD or DVD discs and other write-protected media.

or DVD drives; the device itself (the drive) is internal even though the media (the disc) is removable.

- **External**—attached to your computer by a cable. Most modern Mac models support FireWire and USB connections for external storage devices. Additional connection options, including Thunderbolt, is supported on Mac OS models introduced after mid 2011.

To use storage media, it must be:

- **Mounted**—inserted, attached, or otherwise accessible to your computer.

- **Formatted** or **initialized**—specially prepared for use with your computer.

Storage media capacity is specified in terms of *bytes*, *kilobytes*, *megabytes*, *gigabytes*, and *terabytes* (**Table 8.1**). Although terms for larger capacities do exist, these are the only ones you need to know—at least these days.

This chapter explains how to work with most common storage devices and media.

TIP Don't confuse storage media with memory. The term *memory* usually refers to the amount of *RAM*, or *random access memory*, in your computer, not disk space. RAM is temporary high-speed data storage space used by applications that is erased when you shut down.

TIP At a minimum, all new Macintosh computers include a hard disk; all except the MacBook Air also include a CD/DVD drive.

TIP If a disk is write-protected or locked, files cannot be saved or copied to it. A pencil with a line through it appears in the status bar (page 37) of write-protected or locked disks **A**.

TIP If your computer does not have a built-in SD card reader, you can buy a USB device that will connect to your computer and read SD cards, as well as similar types of media cards.

Mounting Disks

Mounting a disk makes it available for your computer to use. When a disk is mounted, your computer "sees" it and can access the information it contains. You must mount a disk to use it.

Mounted disks appear in the top-level window for your computer . To display this window, choose Go > Computer **B** or press Shift-Command-C (page 47).

Mounted disks may also appear on the desktop **A**, depending on how Finder preferences (page 449) are set for the display of items on the desktop.

> **TIP** To learn how to mount disks that are not specifically covered in this book, consult the documentation that came with the disk drive.

> **TIP** You mount a network volume by using the Connect to Server command under the Go menu **B** or by browsing the network and opening the disk you want to mount. You can learn more in Chapter 26.

To mount a CD or DVD disc on a computer with a slot-loading optical drive:

Insert the CD or DVD disc into the CD/DVD drive slot.

After a moment, the disc icon appears in the top-level computer window **A**.

> **CAUTION** Do not insert a mini CD or DVD disk into a slot-loading CD or DVD drive. Most Mac CD and DVD slot-loading drives do not support mini discs; inserting one can damage the drive mechanism.

A Here's a desktop and computer folder window with an internal hard disk, external hard disk, network volume, and DVD disc inserted. The Network and Remote Disc icons offer access to networked disks that are not mounted.

B You can use the Go menu to open the top-level computer folder or connect to a server.

To mount a CD or DVD disc on a computer with a tray-loading optical drive:

1. Press the Media Eject key on the keyboard to open the CD or DVD disc tray.

2. Place the CD or DVD disc in the tray or caddy, label side up.

3. Push the tray or caddy into the drive.

   After a moment, the disc icon appears in the top-level computer window Ⓐ.

TIP Although a Media Eject key appears on most Apple keyboards, it may not appear on a third-party keyboard.

To mount an external hard disk:

1. If necessary, connect the hard drive's power cord and plug it into a power outlet.

2. Connect the drive's FireWire, USB, or Thunderbolt cable to the drive and your computer.

3. If necessary, turn on the drive's power switch.

After a moment, the drive's hard disk icon should appear in the top-level computer window Ⓑ.

TIP Some external hard disk drives can draw their power from your computer via the connection interface cable. These drives do not require a power cord and do not have a power switch; you can skip steps 1 and 3.

TIP When you connect an external hard drive for the first time, a dialog may ask if you want to use the disk with Time Machine (page 125). If you don't, click Don't Use.

Unmounting & Ejecting Disks

When you *unmount* a disk, you make it unavailable for further use by the computer—until you mount it again. The disk disappears from the top-level computer window. Once a disk is unmounted, it can safely be ejected or removed.

There are several ways to unmount a disk and they work the same way, no matter what kind of disk is mounted. How the disk is removed, however, depends on the type of disk it is.

To unmount a hard disk:

Use one of the following techniques:

- Select the disk's icon and choose File > Eject "*Disc Name*" , or press Command-E.

- Click the eject button to the right of the disc name in the sidebar .

- Drag the disc's icon to the Trash. As you drag, the Trash icon turns into a rectangle with a triangle on top **C**. When the pointer moves over the Trash icon, release the button.

The disk's icon disappears from the computer window, desktop, and sidebar.

TIP You cannot unmount the startup disk.

A Use the File menu's Eject command.

B An eject button appears on the sidebar beside each item that can be unmounted.

C When you drag a disk icon to the Trash, the Trash icon changes to an eject icon.

To disconnect a hard disk:

1. Unmount the hard disk.
2. Disconnect the cable.

CAUTION Disconnecting a hard disk before it has been unmounted can cause data loss. Be sure to *always* unmount a disk before disconnecting it.

To unmount & eject an optical disc:

Use one of the following techniques:

- Select the disc's icon and choose File > Eject *"Disc Name"* **A**, or press Command-E.

- Click the eject button to the right of the disc name in the sidebar **B**.

- Drag the disc's icon to the Trash. As you drag, the Trash icon turns into a rectangle with a triangle on top **C**. When the pointer moves over the Trash icon, release the button.

- Press and hold the Media Eject key on the keyboard until the disc (or disc tray) slides out.

The disc's icon disappears from the computer window, desktop, and sidebar. Remove the disc from the drive slot or tray.

TIP Although a Media Eject key appears on most Apple keyboards, it may not appear on a third-party keyboard.

Burning CDs & DVDs

If your Macintosh includes a SuperDrive or Combo drive or you have a MacBook Air SuperDrive, you can write, or burn, files onto blank optical media. This is a good way to archive important files that you don't need on your computer's hard disk and to share files with other computer users.

The type of drive your computer has determines the type of media it can write to:

- A combo drive can write to CD-R and CD-RW discs.
- A SuperDrive may be able to write to CD-R, CD-RW, DVD-R, DVD-W, DVD-RW, DVD+R, and DVD+RW discs.

The Finder offers three ways to burn a CD or DVD:

- Select a disc or folder and use the Burn command to burn its contents to a CD or DVD.
- Create a burn folder, fill the folder with the files you want to include on the CD or DVD, and use the Burn Disc command to burn the disc.
- Insert a blank CD or DVD, name it, and then drag the icons for the files you want to include on it onto its icon. Then use the Burn Disc command to burn the CD or DVD.

On the following pages, I explain how to use all three of these techniques.

TIP Not all SuperDrives can write to DVD+RW discs. You can use System Information (page 369) to see what formats your optical drive supports.

TIP You can also burn CDs or DVDs from within iTunes and iDVD (Chapter 17) or other third-party utilities, such as Roxio Toast.

File	
New Finder Window	⌘N
New Folder	⇧⌘N
New Folder with Selection	⌃⌘N
New Smart Folder	⌥⌘N
New Burn Folder	
Open	⌘O
Open With	▶
Print	⌘P
Close Window	⌘W
Get Info	⌘I
Compress "Archives"	
Duplicate	⌘D
Make Alias	⌘L
Quick Look "Archives"	⌘Y
Show Original	⌘R
Add to Sidebar	⌘T
Move to Trash	⌘⌫
Eject	⌘E
Burn "Archives" to Disc...	
Find	⌘F
Label:	

A The File menu includes commands for creating burn folders and burning discs.

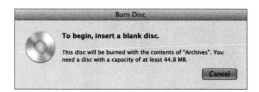

B The Burn Disc dialog instructs you to insert a disc with enough capacity for the folder or disc you want to copy to a CD or DVD.

C You can use a dialog like this to enter a name for the new disc and set a burn speed.

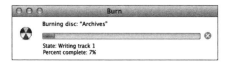

D A progress bar indicates the new disc is being prepared.

E The new disc appears in the computer window.

To burn an existing folder or disc to CD or DVD:

1. Select the folder or disc you want to copy to a CD or DVD.

2. Choose File > Burn "*Folder or disc name*" to Disc **A**.

   A Burn Disc dialog appears **B**.

3. Insert a CD or DVD in your computer.

   You may need to press the Media Eject button to open the media tray and then press it again to slide the tray and disc back into the computer.

   Another dialog appears **C**.

4. Set options as desired:

   ▸ **Disc Name** is the name you want to give the disc.

   ▸ **Burn Speed** is the speed your computer will use to burn the disc.

5. Click Burn.

   A Burn status dialog **D** appears as the disc is burned. When the dialog disappears, an icon for the CD or DVD appears in the computer window and in the Sidebar **E**. The disc is ready to use.

To burn a CD or DVD from a burn folder:

1. Choose File > New Burn Folder **A**.

   A burnable folder icon named Burn Folder appears in the active window **F**.

2. While the folder name is selected, enter a new name for the folder and press Return.

   The folder's name changes.

3. Drag the files you want to include on the new CD or DVD to the burnable folder.

   You can create regular folders inside the burnable folder to organize the files you add to it **G**.

4. When you are finished adding files, do one of the following:

   ▸ Click the Burn button near the top of the folder's window **G**.

   ▸ Select the folder icon and choose File > Burn "*Folder name*" to Disc **A**.

   A Burn Disc dialog appears.

5. Follow steps 3 through 5 in the section titled "To burn an existing folder or disc to CD or DVD on page 119.

TIP You can only create a burn folder in a window you have write permissions for.

TIP When you drag files to a burn folder, Mac OS creates aliases (page 88) to the original files. When it burns the disc, however, it copies the original files rather than the aliases to the disc.

TIP You might find a burn folder useful for periodically backing up important files. Fill a burn folder with the files you want to back up, and then burn a disc from that same burn folder every time you want to back up the files—Mac OS will automatically back up the latest versions of the files.

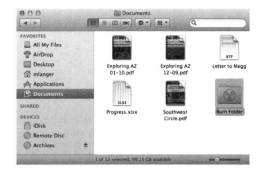

F An icon for the burn folder appears in the active window.

G The contents of a burn folder can include folders and aliases to files and folders.

Burn Folder: Keep or Delete?

When you're finished using a burn folder you can delete it or keep it:

- If you delete the burn folder, none of the original files are lost because the burn folder contains only aliases for original files.

- If you keep a burn folder, you can create new discs from it again and again in the future. Because the burn folder contains aliases rather than original files, the latest versions of the files will always be burned onto the disc.

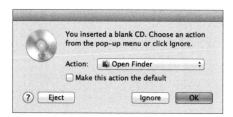

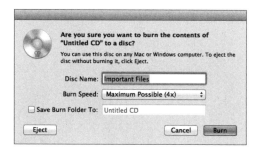

To burn files directly to a blank CD or DVD:

1. Insert a blank CD or DVD into your computer.

2. If a dialog appears **H**, make sure Open Finder is chosen from the Action pop-up menu and click OK.

   An Untitled CD or Untitled DVD icon appears on the desktop and in the Sidebar **I**.

3. If desired, rename the icon.

   The icon name is the name that will be burned onto the disc.

4. Follow steps 3 and 4 in the section titled "To burn a CD or DVD from a burn folder" on page 120.

6. In the dialog that appears **J**, set options as desired:

   ▸ **Disc Name** is the name you want to give the disc.

   ▸ **Burn Speed** is the speed your computer will use to burn the disc.

   ▸ **Save Burn Folder To** enables you to specify a name for a burn folder that will be created and saved to your computer.

7. Click Burn.

   A Burn status dialog **D** appears as the disc is burned. When the dialog disappears, the disc is ready to use.

TIP If you turn on the check box in step 6, the burn folder is saved to your desktop and a link to it appears in the sidebar. You can move the burn folder anywhere you like to save it on your computer. You can also remove it from the sidebar (page 472).

H A dialog like this appears when you insert a blank CD or DVD without being prompted to.

I The disc appears in the Sidebar as a sort of burn folder.

J A dialog like this offers the usual options, along with the ability to save the disc contents as a burn folder.

Backup & Recovery
Features

One of the most important things you can do to protect the applications and data on your computer's hard disk is to periodically back it up onto another device or media. Mac OS X includes Time Machine, an application that can automate the backup process and make it easy to restore files that have been damaged or accidentally erased.

In the event that your computer's startup disk has serious problems, OS X Lion has a new feature that can really help: the recovery partition. It makes it possible for you to get a sick Mac started and troubleshoot its problems.

This chapter looks at both of these features and provides some tips for backing up your important data files.

In This Chapter:

Backup Basics

Backing up your computer refers to the process of making copies of important files onto some other storage device or media. This makes it possible to replace damaged files with the copies you've made in advance.

Everyone has his or her own strategy for creating and maintaining backups. Here are some things to consider when formulating yours:

- **Back up often.** The more often you back up your files, the more likely you are to have an up-to-date copy of a file if you need it. It follows that the more often a file changes, the more often it should be backed up.

- **Maintain multiple backups.** If the most recent backup copy of a file is also damaged, an older backup copy might not be. If you back up important data files to CD or DVD disc, keep as many backups as practical. Be sure to label the discs with the date so you know which one is most recent.

- **Keep important backups off-site.** If your computer is destroyed by flood or fire and your backups were stored with it, you've lost everything. By keeping a backup of your important files in a different location, you add an additional level of protection.

- **Consider backing up to "the cloud."** *Cloud computing* refers to the use of computing resources accessible via the Internet. If you're a MobileMe user, you have access to "cloud" storage space through the use of iDisk. Dropbox (**www.dropbox.com**) is an example of a free service that provides secure storage for files on a remote server.

- **Automate backups whenever possible.** You're far more likely to stick to a backup strategy if it's mostly or entirely automated. Time Machine (page 125) makes this very easy to do, but there are other third-party backup solutions, including SuperDuper (**www.shirtpocket.com/SuperDuper/**) and Carbon Copy Cloner (**www.bombich.com**).

- **Consider using MobileMe to sync important data.** If you're a MobileMe user, you can use its sync feature to automatically back up your calendar, contacts, mail accounts, and other data. Although this is intended primarily for syncing this data between two or more computers or devices, it can also be used as a simple, automated backup.

It's important to note that backup files can be maintained in two formats:

- Backup software, such as that used by Time Machine, creates a single backup file and multiple incremental backup files. To restore from a single backup file like this, you need the software that created the file.

- Finder copies, whether onto external hard disks or burned onto CDs or DVDs, maintain each file as a separate file—just as it is in the Finder. This makes it easy to restore an individual file—if that's all you need—even on another computer.

TIP I use a combination of backup techniques that include Time Machine, Finder backups to hard disk and DVD disk, off-site backups to another location, and backups to both iDisk and Dropbox. Of course, not *all* of my files are backed up this way; only Time Machine backs it all up. The other files are backed up based on their importance and use.

Time Machine

Time Machine is an application that makes it easy to protect your computer's contents from loss due to accidental deletion or disk damage. It does this by keeping an up-to-date copy of everything on your Mac.

Unlike other backup software, Time Machine also remembers your system configuration on any given day, making it possible to go back in time (so to speak) to recover any of your files.

In OS X Lion, Time Machine now offers two levels of protection:

- **Local snapshots** creates hourly snapshots of all file changes and stores this information on your computer. It does not copy any files.

- **External backup** periodically backs up your computer to an external hard disk you specify.

While the new local snapshots feature does make it possible to use Time Machine without having an external hard disk attached, if your internal hard disk fails, the Time Machine backup stored as local snapshots will also be lost. On the other hand, if you use Time Machine to back up to an external hard disk, if your internal hard disk completely fails, you'll still have an external backup that can be used to restore everything to a new hard disk. In other words, the external hard disk backup option offers more protection for your files.

Time Machine's external back up is preconfigured to keep the following backups:

- Hourly backups for the past 24 hours.

- Daily backups for the past month.

- Weekly backups for all previous months until your backup disk is full.

Once you've created a Time Machine backup, you can restore individual files or, if you've created a backup on an external or networked hard disk, you can restore your entire hard disk.

Time machine consists of two components:

- The Time Machine preferences pane (page 577) enables you to configure Time Machine so it works the way you want it to.

- The Time Machine application gives you access to Time Machine's backed up data.

In this part of the chapter, I explain how to enable and use Time Machine.

TIP If you have a laptop, you might consider using Time Machine's local snapshots feature while you're traveling and the external backup feature when you're back home or in your office. This gives you some level of protection even when an external hard disk isn't available for backing up. Just set up Time Machine for both types of backups and be sure to periodically connect the external hard disk you configured for use with Time Machine when you're back at your home base.

TIP If the backup disk is not available when Time Machine needs to create a backup, it simply postpones the backup until the disk is available.

TIP What's great about Time Machine is that you can configure it to exclude certain folders from its automatic backups. This minimizes the amount of disk space needed for backups and avoids backing up files you may not need backed up. Be sure to consult the information on page 577 about the Time Machine preferences pane to learn more.

To enable Time Machine for local snapshots:

1. Choose Apple > System Preferences and click the Time Machine icon in the System Preferences window that appears.

2. In the Time Machine preferences pane **A**, click the Select Disk button.

   A window listing available disks and mounted volumes appears **B**.

3. Select Create local snapshots but don't back up.

4. Click the Use Snapshots Only button.

5. Choose System Preferences > Quit System Preferences, or press Command-Q, to close Time Machine preferences.

6. (Optional) To confirm that Time Machine is enabled for local snapshots, click the Time Machine icon on the menu bar to display the Time Machine menu **C**. The second item down should say *Local Snapshots: Enabled*.

TIP The Show Time Machine status in menu bar option must be selected in the Time Machine preferences pane **A** to display the Time Machine menu **C** in the menu bar.

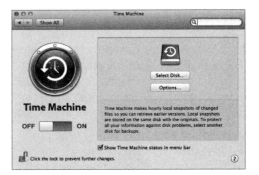

A You turn on Time Machine in the Time Machine preferences pane.

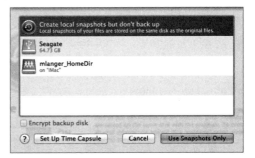

B Time Machine displays a list of options and disks that are available for backup.

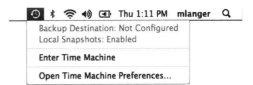

C The Time Machine status menu shows configuration options and offers access to Time Machine's features.

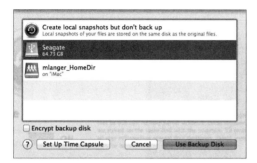

D If this dialog appears when you connect the external hard disk you want to use for backup, just click the Use as Backup Disk button.

E Choosing a hard disk in this window displays the Use Backup Disk button.

F When you enable Time Machine with an external hard disk, the hard disk's information appears in the Time Machine preferences pane.

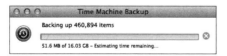

G Time Machine displays a dialog like this as it creates its first backup.

To enable Time Machine for external backup:

1. Mount an external hard disk (page 115) or network volume (page 400).

2. If a dialog asking if you want to use the disk or volume to back up with Time Machine appears **D**, click Use as Backup Disk and skip ahead to step 8.

3. Choose Apple > System Preferences and click the Time Machine icon in the System Preferences window that appears.

4. In the Time Machine preferences pane **A**, click the Select Disk button.

   A window listing available disks and mounted volumes appears **B**.

5. Select the disk you want to use as your Time Machine backup disk **E**.

6. If you want your backup encrypted, select the Encrypt backup disk check box.

7. Click the Use Backup Disk button.

   The name of the backup disk appears in the Time Machine preferences pane window **F**.

8. If necessary, click in the slider control beside On to move the slider to the On position **F**.

9. Choose System Preferences > Quit System Preferences, or press Command-Q, to close Time Machine preferences.

   Time Machine begins backing up your hard disk within two minutes of enabling it. It displays a small progress dialog **G** as it works. You can continue working with your Mac.

TIP Time Machine's first backup can take a long time. Subsequent backups are much quicker.

To restore a backed up file or folder:

1. Open the window for the disk or folder you want to restore.

2. Use one of the following techniques to open Time Machine:
   - ▶ Click the Time Machine icon in the Dock.
   - ▶ Choose Enter Time Machine from the Time Machine menu **C**.

   The window's size reduces slightly and the desktop slides away. The Time Machine interface appears **H**.

3. Navigate to the version of the window that displays the contents you want to restore. You can do this in a number of ways:
   - ▶ Click the backward or forward arrows in the lower-right corner of the screen to scroll through various versions of the window.
   - ▶ Click along the timeline on the right side of the screen **I** to go to a specific backup.
   - ▶ Click the title bar of the window version you want to see.

4. Select the item you want to restore **J**.

5. Click Restore.

   Time Machine displays an animation as it copies the file back to the folder and displays it in the Finder **K**.

TIP You can also use Time Machine in conjunction with Spotlight (Chapter 7). Perform a search for the missing item, then launch Time Machine and browse backward through search results until it appears.

H When you launch Time Machine, it begins by displaying the current window as it looks now.

I You can use the timeline on the right side of the screen to go back to a specific backup.

J When you find the item you're looking for, select it.

K When you click Restore, the file is copied to its original location.

To restore a hard disk from a Time Machine backup:

1. Insert the Mac OS X installation disc or USB flash drive that came with your computer.

2. Restart your computer while holding down the C key; you can release the key when the pointer appears onscreen.

   Your computer starts from the disc or flash drive you inserted and displays the Mac OS X installer's first screen.

3. In the window that prompts you to choose a language, select your language and click the right arrow button. (These instructions assume English.)

4. When the menu bar appears, choose Utilities > Restore System From Backup.

5. Do one of the following:

   ▸ If you are restoring from a Time Capsule (page 380) or networked hard disk, select your network from the Airport menu on the menu bar.

   ▸ If you are restoring from a Time Machine backup on an external hard disk, connect the disk and, if necessary, turn it on.

6. Read the information in the Restore Your System screen and click Continue.

   The Select a Backup Source window appears.

7. Select your Time Machine backup disk.

8. Click Continue and follow the instructions that appear onscreen to complete the restore process.

CAUTION **Restoring your computer from a Time Machine backup erases the contents of your hard disk. This cannot be undone!**

TIP **You can also initiate a Time Capsule restore from the Recovery Partition (page 130).**

Recovery Partition

Mac OS X Lion automatically creates a *recovery partition* on your computer's hard disk. This is a special area on your computer's startup disk that stores a copy of the system software and some utilities that can help you troubleshoot and repair problems. The recovery partition can also be used to reinstall Mac OS X or restore your computer from a Time Machine backup.

The recovery partition is not something for everyday use. Instead, you'd use it when you had a serious problem with your computer's startup disk—a problem that might make it impossible to start any other way. You can also use this feature to restore from a Time Machine backup or run Disk Utility.

This part of the chapter explains how to access and use the recovery partition feature of OS X Lion. Unfortunately, because of the special access required to work with these features, it is not possible to create screenshots. Follow the instructions closely and you should be able to get the job done.

To use the recovery partition:

1. Restart your computer while holding down the Option key.

   Your computer starts quickly and displays a screen with at least two options: your internal hard disk and Recovery HD.

2. Click the Recovery HD icon to select it.

3. Click the arrow beneath the Recovery HD icon to finish restarting your computer from the recovery partition.

4. In the window that prompts you to choose a language, select your lan-

guage and click the right arrow button. (These instructions assume English.)

The Mac OS X Utilities dialog appears. It offers four options:

▸ **Restore From Time Machine Backup** enables you to restore your computer's hard disk from a Time Machine backup. If you select this option, you can follow steps 5 through 8 in the section titled "To restore a hard disk from a Time Machine backup" on page 129.

▸ **Reinstall Mac OS X** reinstalls a new copy of OS X Lion. For this option to work, the Mac OS X Lion Installer must be in the Applications folder on your computer's hard disk.

▸ **Get Help Online** opens the Safari web browser (page 438) and takes you to the Apple Support website so you can search for help and trouble-shooting information. You'll need an Internet connection to do this; if you connect via Wi-Fi, be sure to choose your network from the Wi-Fi menu (page 388) on the menu bar.

▸ **Disk Utility** launches the Disk Utility application (Chapter 23) that can verify and repair permissions and disks, which might be able to resolve your problem.

5. Choose the option you want and click Continue.

6. Follow the instructions that appear onscreen or elsewhere in this book to complete the task you've selected.

TIP Starting your computer with the Option key held down is also a good way to choose a startup disk on the fly if more than one startup disk is available to your Mac.

Multiple Users

Mac OS X is designed to be a multiple-user system. This means that different individuals can log in and use a Mac OS X computer.

Each user can install his own applications, configure his own desktop, and save his own documents. User files and setup is kept private. When each user logs in to the computer with his account, he can access only the files that belong to him or are shared.

This chapter explains how to use Mac OS as a multiple user system.

TIP Using a multiple-user operating system doesn't mean that you can't keep your computer all to yourself. You can set up just one user—you.

TIP Chapter 3 provides some additional information about how Mac OS X's directory structure is set up to account for multiple users.

TIP You set up user accounts in the Users & Groups preferences pane (page 579).

In This Chapter:

Logging Out & In

If your computer is shared by multiple users, you'll probably want to log out when you're finished working. Logging out leaves the computer running but makes your account inaccessible until you log back in—thus keeping other users from accessing your files.

The Log Out command under the Apple menu  closes your account on the computer. Then, when another user wants to access the computer, all she has to do is log in to her own account and she can get right to work.

One of the new features of OS X Lion is the Finder's ability to remember your workspace when you log out and restore it to the way it was when you log back in. So, for example, suppose you had three applications and six documents open on your Mac when you log out. If you indicate that this information should be saved, when you log back in, Mac OS will automatically reopen the same applications and documents so you can continue working where you left off.

In this part of the chapter, I explain how to log out and log in. Unfortunately, the limitations of my screenshot software make it impossible for me to illustrate the login window. Follow along carefully and you should have no trouble working with what you see onscreen.

TIP If you are your computer's only user, you'll probably never use the Log Out command. (I hardly ever do.)

TIP Mac OS X's fast user switching feature (page 134) makes it quicker and easier to switch from one user account to another.

A The Log Out command is at the bottom of the Apple menu.

B A dialog like this one confirms that you really do want to log out.

To log out:

1. Choose Apple > Log Out *User Name* Ⓐ, or press Shift-Command-Q. A confirmation dialog appears Ⓑ.

2. To instruct Mac OS to remember the open documents and applications and reopen them when you log back in, make sure to select the Reopen windows when logging back in check box.

3. Click Log Out, press Return or Enter, or just wait for automatic logout.

   Your computer closes all applications and documents and then displays the login window.

TIP By default, the login window includes two buttons you can use to conserve power while the computer is idle: Sleep puts the computer to sleep and Shut Down turns the computer off. Sleep and shut down are discussed on page 39.

To log in:

1. Do one of the following:

   ▸ If the login window displays icons for user accounts, click the icon for your account.

   ▸ If the Login window displays only Name and Password boxes, enter your full or short account name in the Name box.

2. Enter your password in the Password box.

3. Click Log In.

   Your Mac OS desktop appears. If you indicated that Mac OS should reopen windows when logging back in, all windows that were open when you logged out (or shut down) open.

TIP The appearance of the login window varies depending on how the Login Options (page 588) of the Users & Groups preference pane (page 579) has been configured by the system administrator.

TIP Your user name and short name are created when your account is created, either by the Mac OS Setup Assistant (page 9) or in the Users & Groups preferences pane (page 579). You can use either name to log in.

TIP If you enter an incorrect password in step 2, the login window will shake in step 3. Try again. If you enter an incorrect password three times in a row, the login window expands to display the password hint set up for your account. It also displays this hint if you click the Forgot Password button that may appear in the login window. You set up a password hint in the Users & Groups preferences pane (page 579).

Fast User Switching

Fast user switching enables one user to log in and use the computer without another user logging out. The main benefit to this is that it's fast—hence the name.

You access the fast user switching feature from a menu that appears on the right end of the menu bar **Ⓐ**. There are a few things to keep in mind about this menu:

- The fast user switching menu is customizable, so it might not look exactly as you see it here. You can fine-tune its appearance by using commands under its Show submenu.

- An orange check icon indicates which users are logged in.

- The name of the account that appears at the top of the menu is the account currently in use.

- You can also use the menu to display the login window (page 133) or open the Users & Groups preferences pane (page 579).

TIP Fast user switching is enabled by default. However, if it has been disabled, you can enable it in Login Options (page 588) in the Users & Groups preferences pane (page 579).

To use fast user switching:

1. With the computer turned on and a user already logged in, choose a user account from the menu at the far right end of the menu bar **Ⓐ**.

2. In the login window that appears, enter the account password and click Log In.

   The screen changes (using a rotating cube graphic effect) to the account you logged in to.

Ⓐ Fast user switching puts a menu like this one on the far right end of the menu bar.

A Home folders for all users can be found in the Users folder.

B Each user's Home folder has a number of preconfigured folders for storing specific types of files.

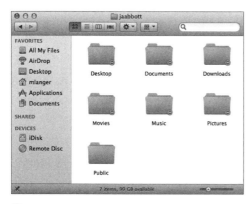

C Most folders inside another user's Home folder are locked and inaccessible to you.

The Home Folder

Mac OS X creates a Home folder for each user account in the Users folder **A**, with the user's short name as the folder name.

The icon for the folder appears as a house for the user who is currently logged in and as a regular folder for all other users. Each user's Home folder contains folders for storing his files **B**:

- **Desktop** contains all items (other than mounted disks) on the user's desktop.
- **Documents** is the default file location for document files.
- **Downloads** is the default file location for downloaded files.
- **Movies**, **Music**, and **Pictures** are for storing video, audio, and image files.
- **Sites** (which may only appear on accounts created with previous versions of Mac OS X) is for the user's Web site, which can be put online with the Web sharing feature.
- **Public** is for storing shared files.
- **Applications**, when present, is for storing applications installed by the user for his private use.
- **Library**, which is not normally visible, is maintained by Mac OS X for storing various preferences files for your account.

Although a user can open another user's Home folder, he can only open the Public (and Sites) folders within that user's Home folder; all other folders are locked **C**.

Sharing Files with Other Users

Mac OS X has three kinds of special folders that make it possible for multiple users of the same computer to share files with each other:

- The **Shared** folder in the Users folder Ⓐ offers read/write access to all users.

- The **Public** folder in each user's Home folder ⒷⒸ offers read access to all users.

- The **Drop Box** folder in each user's Public folder ⒹⒺ offers write access to all users.

Read access for a folder enables users to open files in that folder. This means that all users can open files in the Shared folder Ⓐ and individual users' Public folders ⒷⒸ. If you attempt to open a folder that you do not have read access for, Mac OS displays a dialog with an error message Ⓕ.

Write access for a folder enables users to save files into that folder. This means that all users can copy files to the Shared folder Ⓐ and individual users' Drop Box folders ⒹⒺ.

TIP Don't confuse multiple user file sharing with network file sharing. Multiple user file sharing shares files on the same computer. Network file sharing (page 400) and the new Air-Drop feature (page 404) shares files over multiple computers connected by a network.

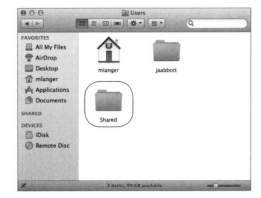

Ⓐ The Shared folder is accessible by all users.

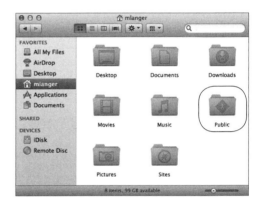

Ⓑ You can find your Public folder in your Home folder; anyone can open it and read its contents.

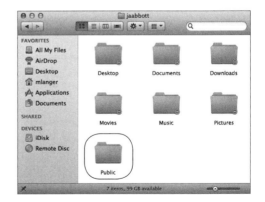

Ⓒ You can also find a Public folder in another user's Home folder; anyone can open and read its contents.

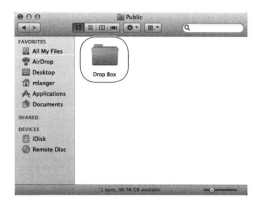

D Your Public folder includes a Drop Box folder where other users can copy files for your use; only you can open this folder and read its contents.

E Although you can copy files into another user's Drop Box folder, you can't open it and read its contents.

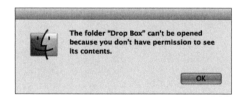

The folder "Drop Box" can't be opened because you don't have permission to see its contents.

OK

F If you try to open a folder you don't have read access to, a dialog like this appears.

To make a file accessible to all other users:

Do one of the following:

- Place the file in the Shared folder in the Users folder **A**.

- Place the file in the Public folder in your Home folder **B**.

TIP If your computer is managed by a system administrator, check to see where the administrator prefers public files to be stored.

To access a file another user has made accessible to all users:

1. Find out where the user has put the file: in the Shared folder in the Users folder **A** or in the user's Public folder **C**.

2. Open the folder and move or copy the file to a folder in your Home folder.

TIP If you don't need a copy of the file, you don't have to move or copy it. You can simply open it from the folder in which it resides.

To make a file accessible to a specific user:

1. Drag the file's icon onto the Drop Box folder icon inside the Public folder in the user's Home folder **E**.

   A warning dialog appears **G**.

2. Click OK.

   The file moves into the Public folder.

CAUTION When you drag a file into a Drop Box folder, the file is moved—*not copied*—there. You cannot open someone else's Drop Box folder to remove its contents. If you need to keep a copy of the file, hold down the Option key while dragging the file into the Drop Box folder to place a copy of the file there. You can then continue working with the original.

TIP To use the Drop Box, be sure to drag the file icon onto the Drop Box folder icon **E**—not simply into the open Public folder. If you drag a file into another user's public folder, a warning dialog appears **H**. If you have an administrator account, you can click the **Authenticate** button and enter your user name and password in the dialog that appears **I** to override the warning and move the file.

To access a file another users has made accessible only to you:

Open the Drop Box folder inside your Public folder **D**. The file should be there.

TIP Remember, you are the only one who can open your Drop Box folder.

G Mac OS warns you when you try to put a file into a folder where it can't be retrieved.

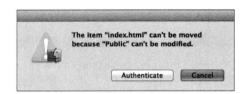

H You can't place files into another user's Public folder or any other locked folder...

I ...unless you're an administrator.

Using
Applications

In This Part

Application Basics

Applications, which are also known as apps or programs, are computer software packages you use to get work done.

For example, if you sit down at your computer to write a letter, you're likely doing it with a word processing application. If you spend some time browsing websites, you're using a web browser application. And if you import photos from your camera onto your computer and then email one of them to a friend, you might be using a photo management app and an email app.

Without applications, a computer would be pretty much useless—it simply wouldn't be able to do anything.

Mac OS X comes with some applications, most of which are discussed throughout this book. This chapter covers the basics of using applications, including multitasking, opening applications, and creating documents. Along the way, it'll show some new features in OS X Lion, including Launchpad, Auto Save, and Versions.

In This Chapter:

Applications

Applications are often classified based on what they do. There are as many kinds of applications as tasks you can perform with your computer.

Here are some examples:

- **Word processors**, such as Text-Edit, iWork's Pages, and Microsoft Office's Word, are used to create letters, reports, and other text-based documents.

- **Spreadsheets**, such as iWork's Numbers and Microsoft Office's Excel, have built-in calculation features that are useful for creating number-based documents such as worksheets and charts.

- **Databases**, such as FileMaker Pro, are used to organize information, such as the names and addresses of customers or the artists and titles in a music collection.

- **Personal information management apps**, such as Address Book and iCal, help you keep track of contacts and appointments.

- **Presentation apps**, such as iWork's Keynote and Microsoft Office's PowerPoint, are used to create presentations and animations.

- **Internet access apps**, such as the Safari and Firefox web browsers and the Mail and Microsoft Outlook email apps, let you access and share information on the Internet.

- **Photo and Graphics apps**, such as Apple Aperture, iLife's iPhoto, and Adobe Photoshop, let you organize and edit images.

- **Movie editing apps**, such as iLife's iMovie and Apple Final Cut Pro, enable you to edit videos.

- **Utility apps**, such as Disk Utility and Activity Monitor, perform tasks to manage computer files or operations or keep your computer in good working order.

- **Games**, such as Angry Birds and Portal, let you use your computer for fun and relaxation.

These are just some examples. Nowadays, there's an app for just about anything you need to do.

TIP Unless you have Windows installed on your Mac, you need to make sure that the software you buy is Mac OS-compatible.

TIP A good source of Mac OS applications is the App Store, which is covered in Chapter 13.

ⓐ A typical installation of Mac OS X installs 25 applications in the Applications folder...

ⓑ ...and another 24 in the Utilities folder within it.

Mac OS X Applications

A standard installation of Mac OS X installs about 50 applications on your computer's hard disk. These applications can be found in the Applications folder **ⓐ** and in the Utilities folder **ⓑ** within it.

Most of these applications and utilities are discussed in some level of detail throughout this book. Here's a quick summary of what you can find in the Applications folder and where you can learn more about it:

- **Address Book** (Chapter 15) manages contact information for the people and organizations you know.

- **App Store** (Chapter 13) enables you to find, buy, install, and update Mac OS applications.

- **Automator** (Chapter 24) lets you automate repetitive tasks.

- **Calculator** (Chapter 18) enables you to perform calculations and conversions.

- **Chess** (chapter 18) is a computerized version of the game of chess.

- **Dashboard** (Chapter 19) offers access to simple applications called widgets.

- **Dictionary** (Chapter 18) provides word definitions and synonyms and access to other reference materials.

- **DVD Player** (Chapter 17) enables you to play DVD-video on your Mac.

- **Facetime** (Chapter 27) lets you conduct live video conversations with others using a Mac, iPhone, or iPad.

- **Font Book** (Chapter 21) helps you manage your fonts.

- **iCal** (Chapter 16) manages your appointments and to-do lists.

continues on next page

- **iChat** (Chapter 27) enables you to conduct live text, voice, or video chats.

- **Image Capture** (Chapter 18) enables you to download image files from a digital camera or import images from a scanner and save them on disk.

- **iTunes** (Chapter 17) enables you to organize, purchase, and play audio and video content, including music, podcasts, movies, and TV shows.

- **Launchpad** (this chapter; page 150) makes it quick and easy to find and open any application installed on your computer.

- **Mail** (Chapter 27) is email client software for sending and receiving email messages.

- **Mission Control** (Chapter 20) helps you manage applications and documents as you work with them.

- **Photo Booth** (Chapter 18) enables you to use your computer's built-in camera to take photos and apply special effects to them.

- **Preview** (Chapter 18) enables you to view images, PDF files, and a variety of other file types.

- **QuickTime Player** (Chapter 17) enables you to view, record, and share Quick-Time-compatible movies and audio.

- **Safari** (Chapter 27) is web browser software, which you can use to view web pages and RSS feeds.

- **Stickies** (Chapter 18) enables you to place colorful notes on your computer screen.

- **System Preferences** (Chapters 30 through 34) enables you to customize your computer's operating system so it looks and works the way you want it to.

- **TextEdit** (Chapter 14) enables you to create, open, edit, and save text-based documents.

- **Time Machine** (Chapter 9) provides automated back up features, along with a method to restore lost or damaged files.

TIP This book does *not* include coverage of the iLife and iWork applications—iPhoto, iWeb, iMovie, iDVD, Pages, Numbers, and Keynote—because these applications are not part of a standard Mac OS X installation, although they may come preinstalled on some new Mac OS computers. For more information about these applications, I recommend checking out other titles in Peachpit's *Visual QuickStart Guide* series.

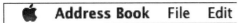

A The Application menu always displays the name of the active application.

Multitasking & the Dock

Mac OS uses a form of *multitasking*, which makes it possible for more than one application to be open at the same time. One application that is always open is Finder, which is covered in detail in Parts I and II of this book. You can open other applications as you need to use them.

Only one application can be *active*. The active application is the one whose name appears at the top of the *application menu* **A** (page 160) on the menu bar. You must make an application active to work with it—one of the easiest ways to do this is to click its icon in the Dock **B** (page 38). Other open applications continue running in the background.

Mac OS X uses *preemptive multitasking*, a type of multitasking in which the operating system can interrupt a currently running task to run another task, as needed.

Mac OS X also features *protected memory*, a memory management system in which each program is prevented from modifying or corrupting the memory partition of another program. This means that if one application freezes up, your computer won't freeze up. You can continue using the other applications that are running.

B The Dock offers a quick and easy way to switch from one open application to another. In this illustration, the open application indicator bubbles are enabled to show which applications are running.

To learn which applications are running:

1. If necessary, enable the indicator lights for open applications feature in Dock preferences (page 484).

2. Look at the Dock.

   A tiny blue bubble appears beneath each application that is running .

TIP The ability to toggle the display of the Dock's application indicator "lights" is new in OS X Lion.

To switch from one open application to another:

Use one of the following techniques:

- In the Dock **B**, click the icon for the application you want to activate.

- Click any of the open windows for the application you want to activate.

- Hold down the Command key and press Tab to display a large icon for each open application **C**. Press Tab repeatedly to cycle though the icons until the one you want to activate is selected. Then release the keys.

The windows for the application you selected come to the front and the application name appears on the Application menu **A**.

TIP You can also use Mission Control (page 295) and Exposé (page 297) to activate an application.

C Pressing Command-Tab displays a large icon onscreen for each of the active applications.

(A) The Applications folder is where you'll find most applications on your computer. This example shows the applications that come with Mac OS X, as well as those that are part of the iLife suite of programs that may have come with your Mac.

(B) A generic document icon appears on documents for which the parent application is unknown or not installed.

Reservation Form

Using Applications & Creating Documents

You use an application by opening, or *launching*, it. It loads into the computer's memory. Its menu bar replaces the Finder's menu bar and offers commands that can be used only with that application. It may also display a document window and tools specific to that program.

Most applications create *documents*—files written in a format understood by the application. When you save documents, they remain on disk so you can open, edit, print, or just view them at a later date.

For example, you may use iWork's Pages application to write a letter. When you save the letter, it becomes a Pages document file that includes all the text and formatting you put into the letter, written in a format that Pages can understand.

Your computer keeps track of applications and documents. It automatically associates documents with the applications that created them. That's how your computer is able to open a document with the correct application when you open the document from the Finder.

Mac OS stores applications in the Applications folder **(A)** on your hard disk. Additional applications can be found in the Utilities folder within the Applications folder.

TIP You can launch an application by opening a document that it created.

TIP A document created by an application that is not installed on your computer is sometimes referred to as an *orphan* document since no parent application is available. An orphan document often has a generic document icon **(B)**.

To launch an application:

Use one of the following techniques:

- Double-click the application's icon.

- Select the application's icon **C** and choose File > Open **D**, or press Command-O.

- If an icon for the application is in the sidebar or Dock, click that icon once.

The application opens **E**.

TIP If the application you opened supports the Auto Save feature and you had open documents the last time you quit it, those documents should automatically reopen so you can continue working with them. This is part of Mac OS X's Resume feature.

To open a document & launch the application that created it at the same time:

Use one of the following techniques:

- Double-click the icon for the document that you want to open.

- Select the icon for the document that you want to open **F** and choose File > Open **D**, or press Command-O.

- If an icon for the document is in the sidebar or Dock, click that icon once.

If the application that created the document is not already running, it launches. The document appears in an active window **G**.

C Select the icon for the application you want to open.

File

New Finder Window	⌘N
New Folder	⇧⌘N
New Folder with Selection	^⌘N
New Smart Folder	⌥⌘N
New Burn Folder	
Open	⌘O
Open With	▶
Print	⌘P
Close Window	⌘W
Get Info	⌘I
Compress "TextEdit"	
Duplicate	⌘D

D Choose Open from the File menu.

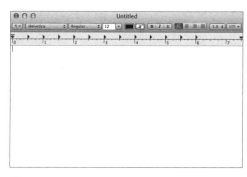

E When you launch TextEdit by opening its application icon, it usually displays an empty document window.

F Select the icon for the document you want to open.

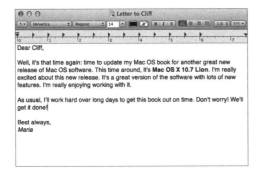

G When you launch TextEdit by opening one of its documents, it displays the document.

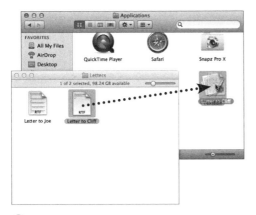

H Drag the icon for the document you want to open onto the icon for the application you want to open it with.

I The Open With submenu lists installed applications that can open a selected document. The options that appear depend on what type of document is selected and what applications are installed on your computer.

To open a document with drag & drop:

1. Drag the icon for the document that you want to open onto the icon for the application with which you want to open it.

2. When the application icon becomes selected **H**, release the button. The application launches and displays the document **G**.

TIP In step 1, the application icon can be in a Finder window (or on the desktop), in the sidebar, or on the Dock.

TIP Drag and drop is a good way to open a document with an application other than the one that created it.

TIP Not all applications can read all documents. Dragging a document icon onto the icon for an application that can't open it either won't launch the application, will open the document but display only gibberish, or will display an error message.

To open a document with the Open With command:

1. Select the icon for the document that you want to open **F**.

2. Choose File > Open With to display the Open With Submenu **I** and choose the application you want to use to open the file.

   The application you chose opens and displays the document.

TIP The Open With submenu **I** will only list applications that are installed on your computer and are capable of opening the selected document.

Launchpad

Launchpad, which is brand new in OS X Lion, offers another way to open the applications on your computer. Simply click the Launchpad icon in the Dock and watch as open windows fade away, to be replaced with a full-screen view of icons for all the applications on your Mac **A**.

You can scroll (or swipe) through multiple pages to see all installed applications. Just click an icon to launch its app. And when you decide you no longer want to use an application, you can use Launchpad to uninstall it.

TIP Launchpad can be customized to rearrange icons (page 456) or group them into folders (page 457).

To open an application with Launchpad:

1. Click the Launchpad icon in the Dock.

   The Launchpad interface appears on your desktop **A**.

2. If necessary, navigate through Launchpad's folders or screens to find the icon you want:

   ▶ To view the contents of a folder, click the folder's icon **B**.

   ▶ To return to the parent folder, click the folder's icon again.

   ▶ To view the icons on another Launchpad page, drag (or two-finger swipe on a Multi-Touch device) to the left or right.

3. Click the icon for the application you want to launch.

   The Launchpad's interface disappears and the application opens.

A Launchpad displays icons for your installed applications.

B Clicking the icon for a folder displays the contents of that folder.

C Non-Apple applications appear on a separate screen.

TIP In Launchpad, a folder looks like a box with tiny icons representing the applications it contains **A B**.

TIP The first Launchpad page includes Apple applications; if you have non-Apple applications, they appear on a separate page **C**.

D Point to and press on the icon for the application you want to uninstall.

E When you click the X icon, a dialog pops up to ask whether you're sure you want to delete it.

To close Launchpad without launching an application:

Do one of the following:

- Click anywhere on the Launchpad screen other than on an icon.

- Press the Esc key.

To uninstall an application:

1. Point to the icon for the application you want to uninstall.

2. Press the button down and hold it down.

3. When an X icon appears at the application and its icon begins to wiggle **D**, release the button.

4. Click the X icon for the application you want to delete.

   A confirmation dialog pops up **E**.

5. Click Delete.

   The application is deleted from the Applications folder and its icon disappears from Launchpad.

TIP If you purchased and installed an application with the **App Store (page 182)**, you can reinstall the application (page 183) at any time.

Full-Screen Apps

Mac OS X Lion's new full-screen apps feature helps reduce distractions while you work by clearing everything off the screen except the application you're working with . Even the menu bar slides off the screen and stays out of your way until you need it.

Once you've switched to full-screen view, you can switch from one app to another with a swipe. Press the Esc key at any time to exit full-screen view.

TIP Because this feature is so new and requires applications to be written to take advantage of it, it is not supported by all applications. Unsupported applications will appear in a normal screen view.

To enter full-screen view:

1. Open or switch to an application that supports the full-screen apps feature.

2. Click the Full-Screen button in the top-right corner of a document window 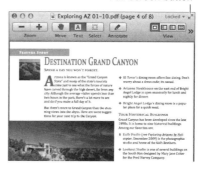.

   The application switches to full-screen view .

To display and use a menu in full-screen view:

Move the pointer to the top of the screen.

The menu bar slides back into view so you can access its menus and commands .

A In full-screen view, all you see onscreen is the application window. This is Preview, viewing a PDF file.

Full-screen button

B A small Full-Screen button appears in the upper-right corner of windows in applications that support the full-screen app feature.

C Point to where the menu bar should be and it appears, along with any toolbars that the application might display.

D In this example, I'm using Multi-Touch gestures to swipe one application (Preview) aside to see another (iPhoto).

To switch from one app to another:

Use one of the following techniques:

- With a mouse or trackpad, point to the bottom of the screen to display the Dock and click the icon for the application you want to switch to.

- With a Multi-Touch device, use three fingers to swipe to the left or right **D**. The current app's screen moves aside to display the next app's. Repeat as necessary to display the app you want.

TIP Dashboard (Chapter 19) always appears in full-screen view and is always accessible by clicking or swiping as described above.

To exit full-screen view:

Use one of the following techniques:

- Press the Esc key.

- Display the menu bar **C** and click the tiny blue icon on the far right end.

The current application returns to normal screen view.

TIP If multiple applications are displayed in full-screen view, each one is returned to regular screen view independently.

Auto Save, Versions, Revert, & Resume

Mac OS X Lion introduces Auto Save, which combines multiple new features to create an automated solution for people who sometimes forget to save their documents as they work:

- **Auto Save** automatically saves changes to a document as you work on it. Not only does Auto Save save changes to documents that have already been manually saved (page 166) once, but it also saves changes to documents that have not yet been manually saved at all.

- **Versions** creates snapshots of a document each time it is saved. This makes it possible to go back to a previous version of a document, thus undoing many changes at once. You can even go back to a version that was saved before it was last manually saved—something the Undo command normally can't do.

- **Revert** enables you to revert to the last manually saved version of a document.

- **Resume** automatically reopens all document windows that were open when you last quit an application. This makes it easy to continue (or resume) working on the same documents after a computer restart or even days later.

Auto Save places a versions menu in the title bar of a document window, just to the left of the document name:

- If the document has not been edited since it was last manually saved, no indicator appears **Ⓐ**.

- If the document has been edited since it was last manually saved, the word *Edited* appears **Ⓑ**.

- If the document has been locked for editing, the word *Locked* appears **Ⓒ**.

Point to the indicator or just to the right of the document title to display a triangle; click it to display a menu with several options **Ⓓ**, including various combinations of these:

- **Lock/Unlock** enables you to lock the document, thus preventing any changes to the document.

- **Duplicate** makes a copy of the document, leaving the original unchanged.

- **Revert to Last Opened Version** or **Revert to Last Saved Version**, which is available only if the document has been edited since the last time it was opened or saved, restores the last opened or saved version of the document, thus removing all edits.

- **Browse All Versions** uses an interface similar to that of Time Machine (page 125) to display all existing versions of the document so you can revert to a previous version.

This part of the chapter explains how you can use all of these features.

TIP Because these features are so new and require applications to be written to take advantage of them, they are not supported by all applications. An application that does not display a versions menu in the title bar and always prompts you to save changes when you quit does not support Auto Save.

TIP These features can not only work together to prevent data loss in the event of a computer problem but also help protect your work from errors you might make by allowing you to go back to an earlier version of the document.

TIP The Resume feature also works when you shut down or restart your computer (page 39) or log out of your account (page 133).

Letter to Cliff
Letter to Cliff — Edited
Letter to Cliff — Locked

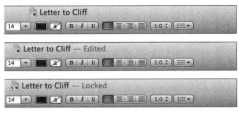

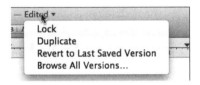

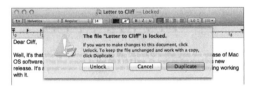

A B C If the document has not been changed since last manually saved, no menu indicator appears (top); if it has been changed since last saved, *Edited* appears (middle); and if it is locked, *Locked* appears (bottom).

— Edited
Lock
Duplicate
Revert to Last Saved Version
Browse All Versions...

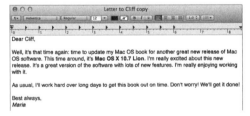

D The versions menu has four commands.

Letter to Cliff — Locked
The file "Letter to Cliff" is locked.
If you want to make changes to this document, click Unlock. To keep the file unchanged and work with a copy, click Duplicate.
Unlock
Cancel
Duplicate

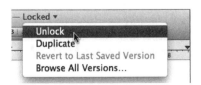

E When you try to edit a locked document, a dialog like this appears.

Letter to Cliff copy
Dear Cliff,
Well, it's that time again: time to update my Mac OS book for another great new release of Mac OS software. This time around, it's Mac OS X 10.7 Lion. I'm really excited about this new release. It's a great version of the software with lots of new features. I'm really enjoying working with it.
As usual, I'll work hard over long days to get this book out on time. Don't worry! We'll get it done!
Best always,
Maria

F Clicking the Duplicate button creates an unlocked copy of the document so you can edit it.

— Locked
Unlock
Duplicate
Revert to Last Saved Version
Browse All Versions...

G To unlock a document, choose Unlock from the versions menu.

To lock an Auto Save document for editing:

Choose Lock from the versions menu **D** in the document's title bar.

The word *Locked* appears in the versions menu indicator **C**.

To work with a locked document:

1. Try to make any change to a locked document.
2. A dialog with three options appears **E**. Click a button:
   - **Unlock** unlocks the document so you can make and save changes.
   - **Cancel** cancels the changes without unlocking the document.
   - **Duplicate** creates a duplicate copy of the document that is unlocked **F** so you can make and save changes to it. The original locked document remains open.

To unlock a document:

Choose Unlock from the versions menu **G**.

The word *Locked* disappears from the versions menu indicator.

To revert to the last saved version:

Use one of the following techniques:

- Choose File > Revert to Saved .
- Choose Revert to Last Saved Version from the versions menu in the document's title bar ❶.

TIP Not all applications include a **Revert to Saved** command on the **File** menu.

TIP The **Revert to Last Saved Version** command is not available if the document has not been edited since the last time it was manually saved.

To browse versions & restore to a previous version

1. Choose Browse All Versions from the versions menu in the document's title bar ❶.

   The version browsing interface fills the screen, displaying the current version on the left and a series of older versions on the right ❶.

2. Use one of the following techniques to browse through the versions:

   ▸ Click the timeline on the right side of the screen to go to a specific version.

   ▸ Click the title bar of the window for the version you want to see.

3. Do one of the following:

   ▸ To close the version browser without restoring to another version, click Done.

   ▸ To restore the document to the version currently displayed on the right side of the version browser, click Restore.

   The version browser closes so you can continue working on the same or restored version of the document.

H Some applications, such as TextEdit, include a Revert to Saved command on the File menu.

I You can use the version browser to scroll backward through time and view previous versions of a document.

Ⓐ You can use the Force Quit command to force an unresponsive application to quit.

Force Quitting Applications

Occasionally, an application may freeze, lock up, or otherwise become unresponsive. When this happens, you can no longer work with that application or its documents.

The Force Quit command Ⓐ enables you to force an unresponsive application to quit. Then you can either restart it or continue working with other applications.

CAUTION When you use the Force Quit command to quit an application, any unsaved changes in that application's open documents may be lost. Use the Force Quit command only as a last resort, when the Quit command (page 162) cannot be used.

TIP Mac OS X's protected memory (page 143) makes it possible for applications to continue running properly on your computer when one application locks up.

TIP If more than one application experiences problems during a work session, you might find it helpful to restart your computer. This clears out RAM and forces your computer to reload all applications and documents into memory.

To force quit an application:

1. Choose Apple > Force Quit , or press Option-Command-Esc.

2. In the Force Quit Applications window that appears **B**, select the application you want to force to quit.

3. Click Force Quit.

4. A confirmation dialog appears **C**.

   Click Force Quit.

   The application immediately quits.

TIP If you selected Finder in step 2, the button to click in step 3 is labeled Relaunch **D**. Finder must always be running in Mac OS X.

B You can choose the application you want to force to quit and then click the Force Quit button.

C Mac OS confirms that you really do want to force the application to quit.

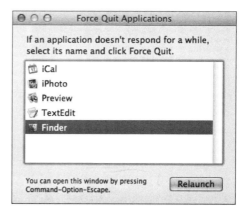

D If you select Finder in the Force Quit Applications window, the Force Quit button turns into a Relaunch button.

Standard
Application Menus

One of the great things about Mac OS is the level of standardization in basic interface elements such as menus. Apple user interface guidelines mandate that each application include a number of standard menus where specific commands can be found.

For example, every application will have a File menu and that menu will always include the application's Open, Close, New, and Print commands (if applicable). This makes it very easy to learn the basics of new software. After all, if every application's Open command is always on its File menu, you don't have to go looking for it each time you need to open a file in a different application.

This chapter covers the standard menus you'll find in just about all Mac OS applications and tells you a little about the commands you'll find there. It also provides some basic information about dialog boxes and their standard parts.

The Application Menu

The application menu takes the name of the currently active application—for example, the TextEdit application menu **A** or the iTunes application menu **B**. It includes commands for working with the entire application.

There are a number of commands that appear on most application menus:

- **About** provides information about the application.

- **Preferences** gives you access to application preference settings that you can use to customize the way the application works.

- **Services** **C** is a submenu full of commands you can use with the application or selected items within it.

- **Hide/Show** is a group of commands to hide or show applications.

- **Quit** closes the application when you're finished working with it.

Here's a closer look at what each of these commands does.

To learn about an application:

1. From the application menu, choose About *application name* **A** **B**.

2. A window with version and other information appears **D** **E**. Read the information it contains.

3. When you're finished reading about the application, click the window's close button.

A **B** The TextEdit application menu (left) and the iTunes application menu (right).

C Here's what the Services submenu looks like in TextEdit when some text is selected.

D **E** The About window for TextEdit (top) and iTunes (bottom) provide version number and copyright information.

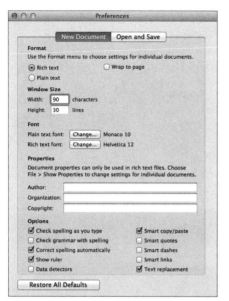

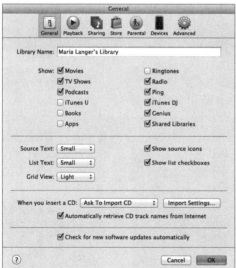

F G The Preferences window for TextEdit (top) and the Preferences dialog for iTunes. Note that each one has individual panes of information.

To set application preferences:

1. From the application menu, choose Preferences **A B**.

2. The application's Preferences window **F** or dialog **G** appears. Set options as desired.

3. Do one of the following to save your changes and dismiss the window or dialog:

   ▸ Click the window's close button **F**.

   ▸ Click the dialog's OK **G** or Save button.

TIP Preference options vary greatly from one application to another. To learn more about an application's preferences, check its documentation or onscreen help.

TIP Preference windows **F** or dialogs **G** often include multiple *panes* of settings. You can switch from one pane to another by clicking a button that's usually near the top of the window or dialog.

TIP One of the first things I do to learn about a new application is explore the options in its preferences window or dialog. The settings help me get a good idea of the features the program offers.

To use application services:

1. From the application menu, select the Services option to display its submenu **C**.

2. Choose the command you want.

TIP The options on the Services submenu vary greatly by application, as well as what's currently selected in the application.

TIP You can customize the Services submenu by setting options in the Keyboard Shortcuts pane (page 514) of Keyboard preferences (page 512).

To hide an application:

From the application menu, choose Hide *application name* Ⓐ Ⓑ, or press Command-H.

All of the application's windows, as well as its menu bar, are hidden from view.

To hide all applications except the active one:

From the application menu, choose Hide Others Ⓐ Ⓑ or press Option-Command-H.

To hide the active application and display another application:

Hold down the Option key while switching to another application.

To display a hidden application:

Click the application's icon (or any of its minimized document icons) in the Dock.

To unhide all applications:

From the application menu, choose Show All Ⓐ Ⓑ.

To quit an application:

From the application menu, choose Quit *application name* Ⓐ Ⓑ, or press Command-Q.

The application automatically saves the status of any open windows, saves preferences (if applicable), and quits.

TIP **Closing all of an application's open windows is not the same as quitting. An application normally remains running until you quit it.**

TIP **If an application is unresponsive and you cannot access its menus or commands, you can use the Force Quit command (page 157) to make it stop running.**

A B C The File menu in TextEdit (top), Safari (middle), and Address Book (bottom).

The File Menu

The File menu **A B C** includes commands for working with files or documents. Most applications will include the following commands:

- **New** creates a new document or window.
- **Open** opens an existing document.
- **Close** closes the active document window.
- **Save/Save As/Save a Version** saves the active document.
- **Page Setup** enables you to set page options for the active document.
- **Print** lets you set print options and output the document to a printer or other output method.

This section discusses the New, Open, Close, Save, and Save As commands; the Page Setup and Print commands are discussed in detail in Chapter 22.

To create a new document or window:

Do one of the following:

- Choose File > New **A**.
- Choose File > New Window **B**.
- Press Command-N **A B C**.

A new untitled document or window appears.

TIP The exact wording of the command for creating a new document or window varies depending on the application and what the command does **A B C**. This command, however, is usually the first one on the File menu.

To open a file:

1. Choose File > Open  or press Command-O to display the Open dialog **D**.

2. Use standard Finder window techniques (Chapter 2) to navigate within the window in the dialog and locate the document you want to open. Here are some tips:

    ▸ Use the pop-up menu at the top of the dialog **E** to backtrack from the current location to an enclosing folders or to a recently accessed folder.

    ▸ Click sidebar buttons to quickly view a specific folder, volume, or other location.

    ▸ Click buttons near the top of the dialog to change the window view (Chapter 4).

    ▸ Enter all or part of the file's name or contents in the Spotlight search field to display a list of files that match **F**.

3. When the file you want to open appears, open it:

    ▸ Select the file and then click Open or press Return or Enter.

    ▸ Double-click the file.

TIP The exact wording of the Open command varies depending on the application and what you want to open. For example, the Open command on Safari's File menu **B** is Open File.

TIP The Open dialog **D** has many standard elements that appear in all Open dialogs.

TIP The Open Recent command, which is available on the File menu of some applications **A**, displays a submenu of recently opened items **G**. Choose the item you want to open it again.

D TextEdit's Open dialog includes all of the elements found in a standard Open dialog.

E The pop-up menu at the top of the Open dialog lets you backtrack from the currently displayed location to the folders in which it resides or a recently accessed folder.

F The Spotlight search feature works within the open dialog, too. In this example, I've searched for the phrase *letter to* on my entire computer.

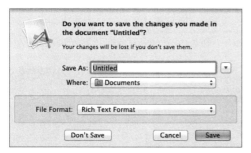

G TextEdit's Open Recent submenu makes it easy to reopen a recently opened document.

H When you close a TextEdit document that has not yet been saved, a dialog like this appears.

To close a window:

1. Use one of the following techniques:
   - ▶ Choose File > Close **A C** or File > Close Window **B**.
   - ▶ Press Command-W.
   - ▶ Click the window's close button.

2. If the window contains a document that has not yet been saved, a dialog sheet appears **H**.
   - ▶ Click Don't Save to close the window without saving the document.
   - ▶ Click Cancel or press Esc to keep the window open.
   - ▶ Click Save or press Return or Enter to save the document.

TIP The exact appearance of the dialog sheet that appears when you close a document with unsaved changes **H** varies depending on the application. All versions of the dialog should offer the same three options, although they may be worded differently.

TIP Mac OS X Lion's new AutoSave feature (page 154) automatically saves changes to existing documents periodically as you work and when you close them. If a document has been saved at least once, you will not be prompted to save changes when you close it.

To manually save a document for the first time:

1. Choose File > Save 🅐🅒, or press Command-S to display the Save dialog 🅘🅙.

2. If necessary, click the disclosure triangle beside the Save As field 🅘 to expand the dialog 🅙.

3. Use standard Finder window techniques (Chapter 2) to navigate within the window in the dialog and select a location in which to save the document. Here are some tips:

   ▸ Use the pop-up menu at the top of the dialog 🅔 to backtrack from the current location to an enclosing folders or to a recently accessed folder.

   ▸ Click sidebar buttons to quickly view a specific folder, volume, or other location.

   ▸ Click buttons near the top of the dialog to change the window view (Chapter 4).

   ▸ Enter all or part of a folder or volume name in the Spotlight search field to display a list of matches.

   ▸ Click the New Folder button to create a new folder inside the currently selected folder. You can enter a name for the new folder while it is selected 🅚.

4. When the name of the folder in which you want to save the document appears on the pop-up menu above the file list area, enter a name for the document in the Save As box and click Save.

   The document is saved in the location you specified. The name of the file appears in the document window's title bar 🅛.

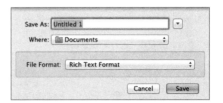

🅘 The Save As dialog might be collapsed, like this...

🅙 ...or expanded, like this.

🅚 Clicking the New Folder button creates an untitled folder in the currently displayed location.

🅛 The name of the newly saved file appears in the window's title bar.

M Microsoft Word is an example of an application with both a Save and a Save As command.

N Once a TextEdit document has been saved, the Save command turns into a Save a Version command.

TIP Not all applications enable you to save documents. iTunes, for example, does not include a Save command on its File menu.

TIP The Save dialog **I J** is also known as the Save Location dialog because it enables you to select a location in which to save a file.

TIP In step 1, you can also use the Save As command (if available **M**). The first time you save a document, the Save and Save As commands do the same thing: display the Save dialog.

TIP Some applications automatically append a period and a three-character *extension* to a file's name when you save it. Extensions are used by Mac OS X and Windows applications to identify the file type. You can toggle the display of file name extensions in Advanced Finder preferences (page 451).

To manually save changes to a document:

Use one of the following techniques:

- Choose File > Save **C M**.

- Choose File > Save a Version **N**.

- Press Command-S.

How the document is saved depends upon whether the application you are using supports the new versions feature (page 154) in OS X Lion:

- If the application supports versions (for example, TextEdit), a snapshot of the document is saved in the file as a version. It is possible to revert to an earlier version of the document, if necessary.

- If the application does not support versions (for example, Microsoft Word as of spring 2011), the document is saved in the same location with the same name, thus overwriting the existing version of the document with the updated contents.

To save a document with a new name or in a new location:

Use one of the following techniques, depending on whether the application you are using supports the versions feature (page 154).

- If the application supports versions, choose File > Duplicate  and then save the duplicate document that is created, following the instructions in the section titled "To save a document for the first time" on page 166.

- If the application does not support versions, choose File > Save As to display the Save dialog sheet . Then follow steps 2 though 4 in the section titled "To save a document for the first time" on page 166.

TIP Saving a document with a new name or in a new location creates a copy of the existing document. Applications that support the versions feature create a second document window, so there is no confusion over which document is the copy.

TIP If you use the Save dialog to save a document with the same name as a document in the selected location, a warning dialog appears . You can either click Cancel to return to the Save dialog and change the document's name or save location or click Replace to replace the document on disk with the current document.

"Letter to Mike" already exists. Do you want to replace it?

A file or folder with the same name already exists in the folder Documents. Replacing it will overwrite its current contents.

Cancel   Replace

O A dialog like this appears when you try to save a file with the same name as another file in a folder. This is what the dialog looks like in TextEdit.

Bullet in   *Faded*
close button   *document icon*

P Two indications of unsaved changes in a document created by an application that does not support versions—in this example, Microsoft Word.

Edited indicator

Q This TextEdit document has been edited since the last version was saved.

To identify unsaved documents:

How you identify a document with unsaved changes depends upon whether the document supports the new OS X Lion versions feature.

- In applications that do not support versions one or more of the following indicators may appear:
  - ▸ A bullet or X character appears in the close button on the title bar of the window **P** for a document with unsaved changes.
  - ▸ The document icon appears faded on the title bar of the window **P** for a document with unsaved changes.
  - ▸ In some applications, a bullet character appears in the Window menu beside the name of the window for a document with unsaved changes.
- In applications that do support versions, an Edited indicator may appear on the far right end of the title bar **Q**.

TIP The versions feature is brand new in OS X Lion, so not all applications support it. As support grows, you'll find more applications indicating unsaved changes in documents like TextEdit does **Q**.

The Edit Menu

The Edit menu **A** **B** includes commands for modifying the contents of a document. Here's a quick list of the commands you're likely to find, along with their standard keyboard equivalents:

- **Undo** (Command-Z) reverses the last editing action you made.

- **Redo** (Shift-Command-Z) reverses the last undo.

- **Cut** (Command-X) removes a selection from the document and puts a copy of it in the Clipboard.

- **Copy** (Command-C) puts a copy of a selection in the Clipboard.

- **Paste** (Command-V) inserts the contents of the Clipboard into the document at the insertion point or replaces selected text in the document with the contents of the Clipboard.

- **Clear** or **Delete** removes a selection from the document. This is the same as pressing D when document contents are selected.

- **Select All** (Command-A) selects all text or objects in the document.

It's important to keep in mind that Edit menu commands usually work with selected text or graphic objects in a document. Not all Edit menu commands are available in all applications at all times; it really depends on what is selected and what you're doing.

Most Edit menu commands are discussed in detail in Chapter 14, which covers TextEdit.

A B The Edit menus for TextEdit (top) and Address Book (bottom).

Edit	
Undo Typing	⌘Z
Redo	⇧⌘Z
Cut	⌘X
Copy	⌘C
Paste	⌘V
Paste and Match Style	⌥⇧⌘V
Delete	
Complete	⌥⏎
Select All	⌘A
Insert	▶
Add Link...	⌘K
Find	▶
Spelling and Grammar	▶
Substitutions	▶
Transformations	▶
Speech	▶
Special Characters...	⌥⌘T

Edit	
Undo	⌘Z
Redo	⇧⌘Z
Cut	⌘X
Copy	⌘C
Paste	⌘V
Delete	
Remove From Group	
Select All	⌘A
Find	▶
Spotlight: "Michael Chilingerian"	
Rename Group	
Edit Smart Group	
Edit Card	⌘L
Edit Distribution List...	
Special Characters...	⌥⌘T

<A /> The Window menu in TextEdit (top) and iTunes (bottom).

<B /> The Help menu in TextEdit (top), Preview (middle), and Microsoft Word (bottom).

The Window Menu

The Window menu <A /> includes commands for working with open document windows as well as a list of the open windows. The commands you'll find most often are:

- **Minimize** (Command-M; page 31) shrinks a window down to the size of an icon and slips it into the Dock.
- **Zoom** (page 31) toggles a window's size between two custom sizes you create by dragging a window border.
- **Bring All to Front** (page 29) displays all of the application's open windows on top of open windows for other applications.

These commands are discussed as they relate to the Finder in Chapter 2; the page references above will take you right to each topic. Just as application windows have the same parts and controls as Finder windows, these commands work the same way in the Finder and other applications.

The Help Menu

The Help menu <B /> includes commands for viewing onscreen help information specific to the application. Choosing the primary Help command opens the Help window with information and links.

Using onscreen help is discussed in detail in Chapter 5; refer to that chapter for more information about using standard Help features with Mac OS and its applications.

TIP The top option on the Help menu is a Spotlight search box you can use to search for help (page 79).

Dialogs

Mac OS applications use *dialog boxes* or *dialogs* **A** **B** **C** to tell you things and get information from you. Think of a dialog as the way your computer has a conversation—or dialog—with you.

Mac OS X has three main types of dialogs:

- **Modeless dialogs** **A** enable you to work with the dialog while interacting with document windows. These dialogs usually have their own window controls to close and move them.

- **Document modal dialogs** **B** appear as dialog sheets attached to a document window. You must address and dismiss these dialogs before you can continue working with the window, although you can switch to another window or application while the dialog is displayed.

- **Application modal dialogs** **C** appear as movable dialogs. These dialogs must be addressed and dismissed before you can continue working with the application, although you can switch to another application while the dialog is displayed.

Dialogs contain a variety of components to gather information and enable you to interact with them. This part of the chapter explains what these standard dialog parts are and how you can use them.

TIP You don't need to remember modeless vs. modal terminology. Just understand how dialogs differ and what the differences mean in terms of what you can do when they appear.

TIP Some standard dialogs covered in this chapter are very similar from one application to another, including Open (page 164), Save (page 166), and warning (page 168). Two more standard dialogs—Page Setup and Print—are covered in Chapter 22.

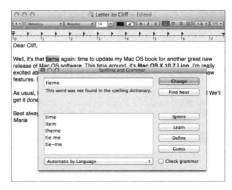

A The Spelling and Grammar dialog in TextEdit is an example of a modeless dialog—you can interact with the document while the dialog is displayed.

B This dialog sheet, which is attached to the TextEdit document window, is an example of a document modal dialog; you must address and dismiss it before you can continue working with the window it's attached to.

C An Open dialog, like this one in TextEdit, is an example of an application modal dialog; you must address and dismiss it before you can continue working with the application.

Pane   *Pane buttons*   *Preview area*

D The Screen Saver pane of Desktop & Screen Saver preferences.

Push buttons

Scrolling lists   *Combination box*

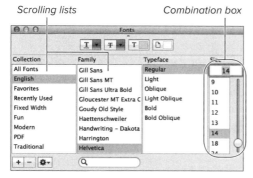

E The Fonts panel.

To use dialog parts:

- Click a *pane button* to view a *pane* full of related options **D**.

- Scroll to view the contents of *scrolling lists* **D E**. Click a list item once to select it or to enter it in a *combination box* **E**.

- Enter text or numbers into *entry fields* **F**, including those that are part of *combination boxes* **E**.

- Click a *pop-up menu* **F** to display its options; click an option to choose it.

- Click a *check box* **G** to toggle it on or off. (A check box is turned on when a check mark or X appears inside it.)

- Click a *radio button* **G** to choose its option. (A radio button is chosen when a bullet appears inside it.)

- Drag a slider control **G** to change a setting.

- Consult a preview area **D** to see the effects of your changes.

- Click a push button **D F** to activate it.

Here are a few additional things to keep in mind when using dialog parts:

- An entry field with a colored border around it is the active field **E F**. Typing automatically enters text in this field. You can advance from one entry field to the next by pressing the Tab key.

- If an entry field has a pair of arrows or triangles beside it you can click the triangles to increase or decrease a value already in the field.

- The default push button is the one that pulsates. You can always select a default button by pressing the Enter key and often by pressing the Return key.

continues on next page

- You can usually select a Cancel button ❶ by pressing the Esc key.
- You can select as many check boxes ❷ in a group as you like.
- One and only one radio button in a group can be selected ❷. If you try to select a second radio button, the first button becomes deselected.
- If you click the Cancel button in a dialog ❶, any options you set are lost.
- To select multiple items in a scrolling list, hold down the Command key while clicking each one. Be aware that not all dialogs support multiple selections in scrolling lists.

TIP There are other standard controls in Mac OS X dialogs, but these are the ones you'll encounter most often.

Pop-up menu   *Entry fields*

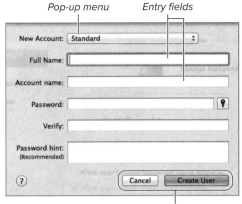

❶ This is the dialog you'd use to create a new user account.   *Push buttons*

Check boxes   *Slider control*   *Radio buttons*

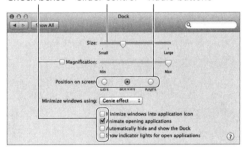

❷ The Dock preferences pane.

The
App Store

Apple's App Store combines the convenience of an online shopping service with the ease of use of a Mac OS application. The result: a system that makes it easier than ever to find, buy, install, and update Mac OS applications on your computer.

The App Store, which works with your Apple ID, automatically maintains a list of the software you've purchased, so it's easy to download and reinstall if necessary. It also notifies you of updates to software you've purchased through the App Store so you can obtain and install those updates as soon as they become available.

This chapter will introduce the features of the App Store and help you get connected so you can shop for applications online. It'll also explain how you can download, install, and update the applications you buy.

In This Chapter:

Launching & Quitting App Store

Like any other application, you must launch App Store before you can use it. This loads it into your computer's memory so your computer can work with it.

To launch App Store:

Use one of the following techniques:

- Open the App Store application icon in the Applications folder window (page 147).

- Click the App Store icon in Launchpad (page 150).

- Click the App Store icon in the Dock (page 38).

App Store launches and displays its Featured window **B**.

TIP The applications that appear in screenshots of App Store throughout this chapter will vary from what you see when you access App Store on your computer. New applications are constantly being added to the App Store, so you'll likely see much newer offerings than what's shown here.

To quit App Store:

Choose App Store > Quit App Store, or press Command-Q.

App Store quits.

A The App Store application icon.

App Store

B The App Store's Featured window displays featured applications.

(A) When you don't have an Apple ID, a screen like this prompts you through the process of creating one.

(B) You'll need to agree to the terms of service and privacy policy before you can continue.

(C) Enter basic ID information in a form like this.

Signing In & Out

To make the most of the App Store, you need to sign in with an Apple ID. Although you can browse the store to your heart's content without one, you'll need an account set up with Apple to make a purchase.

If you've every bought anything online from Apple, chances are you already have an Apple ID:

- If you've purchased anything from the iTunes Store for your iPod, iPhone, or iPad, your Apple ID is the same email address and password you use with iTunes.

- If you're a MobileMe subscriber, your Apple ID is the same email address and password you use to log into MobileMe.

If you're new to Apple products and don't have an Apple ID, you can easily create one. This part of the chapter explains how. It also tells you how you can use your Apple ID to log in to and out of the App Store.

To get an Apple ID:

1. In the App Store, choose Store > Create Account.

   The App Store window displays the Welcome to the App Store screen **(A)**.

2. Click Continue.

3. After reading (or at least skimming!) the information in the Terms and Conditions screen that appears next **(B)**, turn on the check box at the bottom of the window and click Agree.

4. Fill in the form in the Provide Apple ID Details page that appears next **(C)** and click Continue.

continues on next page

5. Enter payment information in the Provide a Payment Method screen **D** and click Create Apple ID.

   if everything has been filled in correctly, Apple sends you a verification email message.

6. Use your email client software to locate and open the verification message **E** and click the Verify Now link.

   Your default Web browser opens to a sign-in page **F**.

7. Enter your Apple ID (your email address) and your password in the appropriate boxes and click Verify Address.

   If you did everything right, your address is verified and a message in the Web browser window tells you so.

8. In the Dock, click the App Store icon to return to the App Store application.

9. Click OK in the Verify Your Apple ID screen.

10. In the Congratulations screen, click Start Shopping.

    You are returned to the Featured screen of the App Store.

D Apple asks for payment information up front to make purchasing quick and easy. It will not charge your credit card until you buy something.

E Apple sends you an email message to verify your email address.

F You'll need to enter your Apple ID and password in this Web browser form to complete the sign up process.

G Use this dialog to sign in to the App Store.

H When you're not signed in, you'll see a Sign In link in the Quick Links area.

I When you're signed in, you'll see a Welcome link in the Quick Links area.

To sign in to the App Store:

1. Use one of the following techniques to display a Sign In dialog **G**:

   ▸ Click the Sign In link in the Quick Links area **H** of any App Store screen.

   ▸ Choose Store > Sign In.

2. Enter your Apple ID and password in the appropriate boxes and click Sign In.

   The dialog disappears and you are signed into the App Store.

TIP You can tell if you're signed in by looking at the Quick Links area on any App Store screen. If a Log In link appears **H**, you're not logged in; if a Welcome link with your name appears **I**, you are logged in.

TIP Even when you're signed in, you may be required to reenter your password to access certain features. This is a security feature that prevents unauthorized access by others when you step away from your computer.

To sign out of the App Store:

Choose Store > Sign Out.

You are signed out of the App Store.

TIP Always be sure to sign out if you are accessing the App Store from a shared computer.

Browsing the App Store

The App Store is organized into five different screens, each of which is accessible from a button at the top of the window:

- **Featured** Ⓐ shows featured applications.

- **Top Charts** Ⓑ shows the top-selling applications, organized by Top Paid, Top Free, and Top Grossing.

- **Categories** organizes applications by category Ⓒ. You can click the name of a category to display a page full of applications in that category Ⓓ.

- **Purchases** shows a list of software you've purchased. This list will be empty if you haven't purchased anything yet.

- **Updates** shows a list of updates to software you've purchased. This list will be empty if there aren't any updates or you haven't purchased anything yet.

You can also search the App Store using a Spotlight search box in the upper-right corner of any window.

Ⓐ The Featured page shows featured apps. Be sure to scroll down to see them all.

Ⓑ The Top Charts screen shows the top-selling apps, divided into three different groups.

Ⓒ The Categories screen shows icons and titles for more than 20 categories.

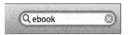

D When you click a category icon **C**, you can see the apps listed within that category.

E When you click an app icon, you can see details about the app.

F Enter a search word in the search box at the top of the window.

G Apps that match the search word or phrase appear in the window.

To browse the App Store:

1. Click one of the first three buttons at the top of the App Store window: Featured, Top Charts, or Categories.

2. In the screen that appears, use any of the following techniques to browse available applications:

   ▸ Click a See All link **A B D** to see all the apps in a group.

   ▸ Click a category icon **C** to see all the apps in a category **D**.

   ▸ Click an application icon **A B D** to see details about that app **E**.

   ▸ Click the Back or Forward button at the top of the App Store window **A B C D E** to move backward or forward through screens you've already viewed.

TIP When shopping for an app, you might want to read the customer reviews before making a purchase decision—especially if the app isn't free. Be sure to scroll down in an app description **E** to see them. I've found that the more ratings an app has, the more realistic the overall rating will be.

To search the App Store:

1. Enter a search word or phrase in the search box at the top-right corner of the App Store window **F**.

2. Press Return.

   The App Store searches for the word you entered and displays search results in its window **G**.

TIP If there are many search results, you might consider sorting them. Use the Sort By pop-up menu near the top of the window to sort by Relevance, Most Popular, Release Date, or Customer Rating.

Buying & Installing Apps

When you see an app you want to buy, all you need do is click the price (or Free) button for it Ⓐ. That begins the process of purchasing, downloading, and installing the app on your computer.

To buy an app:

1. Click the price or Free button Ⓐ for the application you want to buy.

2. If a Sign In dialog appears, enter your Apple ID and Password and click Sign In.

   Your Mac switches to Launchpad where the App is added to one of Launchpad's screens. A message beneath the icon says "Downloading" and a progress bar appears in the icon Ⓑ.

3. When the download is complete, one of two things happens:

   ► If the application does not have an installer, it simply appears in Launchpad Ⓒ where you can click it to open it and begin using it.

   ► If the application has an installer, the installer will launch and display prompts to guide you through the installation process. Follow the instructions that appear to install the software.

TIP If the app contains age-restricted material, a dialog may appear during the purchase process confirming that you are 17 or over. If you are, click OK.

TIP After installing an app, the BUY/FREE button for the app turns into an Installed button Ⓓ wherever the app appears in the App Store when you're signed in.

Ⓐ Click the BUY or FREE button to begin the purchase and installation process.

Ⓑ Ⓒ An icon for the app appears in Launchpad as it downloads (left) and when the download is complete and the app is ready to launch (right).

Ⓓ You don't have to worry about buying an app twice; the BUY/FREE button turns into an Installed button once it has been purchased and installed.

E The Purchases screen lists the apps you've purchased, including any that have not yet been installed.

F A progress bar appears in the Purchases screen while an app is being downloaded.

To review your purchases:

In the App Store window, click the Purchases button.

The Purchases screen displays a list of all your App Store purchases and indicates whether they have been installed **E**.

To reinstall a purchased app:

1. In the App Store window, click the Purchases button to display a list of purchases **E**.

2. Click the Install button beside any application that has not yet been installed.

   A download progress bar indicates that the app is being downloaded **F**. When the progress bar disappears, the Install button is replaced with an Installed button and the app is ready to use.

TIP You can download and install your app store purchases on any computer you own.

TIP You can uninstall an app with Launchpad (page 151).

Updating Apps

If an application you installed with the App Store is updated, the update will be available in the App Store's Updates screen . You'll know that an update is available because a numbered badge will appear on the Update button **B** and in the Dock, indicating the number of updates that are available.

You can install the updates from within the App Store with just a click. Here's how.

To update an app:

1. In the App Store window, click the Updates button to display a list of available updates **A**.

2. Beside each update you want to install, click the Update button.

3. If prompted for your password, enter it.

4. Wait while the software update is downloaded and installed.

   When installation is complete, the app is removed from the Updates list and the updated app is ready to use.

A Available updates appear in the Updates screen of App Store.

B A number on the Updates button indicates how many updates are available.

TextEdit

TextEdit is a text editing application that comes with Mac OS. As its name implies, TextEdit lets you create, open, edit, and print text documents.

Over the years, TextEdit's feature set has been improved and expanded to offer many of the features found in more advanced word processing applications, such as iWorks' Pages and Microsoft Word. Indeed, TextEdit can open and edit documents created with either of those applications. You might even find that it meets most of your word processing needs.

This chapter explains how to use TextEdit to create, edit, and format documents. You'll find that many of the techniques you learn here for working with text and documents will be virtually the same in most other applications.

TIP If you're new to computers, don't skip this chapter. It not only explains how to use TextEdit but provides instructions for basic text editing skills—such as text entry and the Copy, Cut, and Paste commands—that you'll use in all Mac OS applications.

In This Chapter:

Launching & Quitting TextEdit

Like any other application, you must launch TextEdit before you can use it. This loads it into your computer's memory so your computer can work with it.

To launch TextEdit:

Use one of the following techniques:

- Open the TextEdit application icon **A** in the Applications folder window (page 142).

- Click the TextEdit icon in Launchpad (page 150).

TextEdit launches. Because TextEdit supports Auto Save (page 154), you'll see one of two things:

- If this is the first time you're using Text-Edit or if you closed all document windows the last time you used TextEdit, you'll see a blank, untitled document window **B**.

- If you didn't close all document windows the last time you used TextEdit, those windows will reopen.

TIP The TextEdit document window has many of the same standard window parts found in Finder windows (page 27). They work the same way in TextEdit and other applications.

To quit TextEdit:

Choose TextEdit > Quit TextEdit, or press Command-Q.

TextEdit quits. Because TextEdit supports Auto Save, it automatically saves the current version of any open documents. Those documents will automatically reopen the next time you launch TextEdit.

A The TextEdit application icon can be found in the Applications folder.

TextEdit

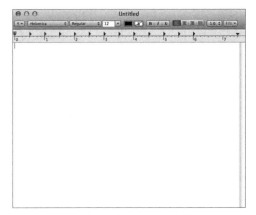

B A blank, untitled TextEdit document window.

A The text you type appears at the blinking insertion point.

B If you have an iPhone or an iPad, the autocomplete/autocorrect feature in TextEdit should look familiar.

Entering & Editing Text

You enter text into a TextEdit document by typing it in. Don't worry about making mistakes; you can fix them as you type or when you're finished. This section explains how.

TIP The text entry and editing techniques covered in this section work exactly the same in most word processors, as well as many other Mac OS applications.

To enter text:

Type the text you want to enter. It appears at the blinking insertion point **A**, which moves as you type.

Here are a few additional things to keep in mind:

- It is not necessary to press Return at the end of a line. When the text you type reaches the end of the line, it automatically begins a new line. This is called *word wrap* and is a feature of all word processors. By default, in TextEdit, word wrap is determined by the width of the document window.

- To correct an error as you type, press the Delete key. This key deletes the character to the left of the insertion point.

- The version of TextEdit that's part of OS X Lion includes an autocomplete/ autocorrect feature similar to the one on iOS devices such as the iPhone and iPad. You may see it in action as you type. To accept a suggested completion/correction **B**, keep typing. To reject it, click the X button on the tag. This feature works with TextEdit's automatic spelling check feature (page 197).

To move the insertion point:

Use one of the following techniques:

- Press one of the arrow keys to move the insertion point left, right, up, or down one character or line at a time.

- Position the pointer, which looks like an I-beam, where you want the insertion point to appear **C** and click once. The insertion point appears at the pointer **D**.

TIP Since the text you type appears at the insertion point, it's a good idea to know where the insertion point is *before* you start typing.

TIP When moving the insertion point with the mouse or trackpad, you *must click* to complete the move. If you simply point with the I-beam pointer, the insertion point will stay where it is.

To insert text:

1. Position the insertion point where you want the text to appear **E**.

2. Type the text you want to insert.

   The text appears at the insertion point **F**.

TIP Word wrap changes automatically to accommodate inserted text.

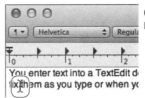

C Position the I-beam pointer...

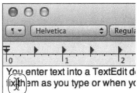

D ...and click to move the blinking insertion point.

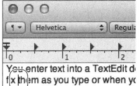

E Position the insertion point where you want to insert text...

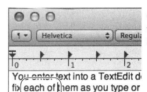

F ...and type the text you want to insert.

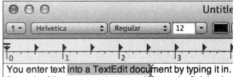

G Drag over text to select it.

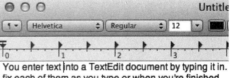

H Position the insertion point at the beginning of the text you want to select...

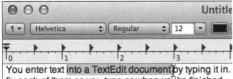

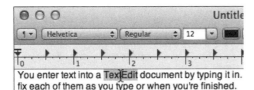

I ...and then hold down Shift while clicking at the end of the text you want to select.

You enter text into a TextEdit document by typing it in. fix each of them as you type or when you're finished.

J Double-click a word to select it.

K To select all text in a document, choose Select All from the Edit menu.

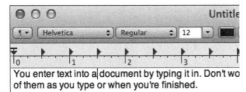

L Press Delete to remove selected text.

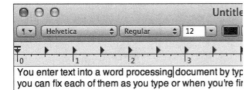

M Type new text to replace selected text.

To select text by dragging:

Drag the I-beam pointer over the text you want to select **G**.

To select text with Shift-click:

1. Position the insertion point at the beginning of the text you want to select **H**.

2. Hold down the Shift key and click at the end of the text you want to select.

   All text between the insertion point and where you clicked becomes selected **I**.

TIP The Shift-click technique is a good way to select large blocks of text. After positioning the insertion point as instructed in step 1, scroll to the end of the text you want to select. Then Shift-click as instructed in step 2 to make the selection.

To select a single word:

Double-click the word **J**.

To select all document contents:

Choose Edit > Select All **K**, or press Command-A.

To delete text:

1. Select the text that you want to delete **J**.

2. Press the Delete key.

   The selected text disappears **L**.

To replace text:

1. Select the text that you want to replace **J**.

2. Type the new text.

   The selected text is replaced by what you type **M**.

Basic Text Formatting

TextEdit also offers formatting features that you can use to change the appearance of document text.

- **Font formatting** enables you to change the appearance of individual text characters. This includes the font typeface and family, character style, character size, and character color.

- **Text formatting** enables you to change the appearance of entire paragraphs of text. This includes alignment, line spacing, and ruler settings such as tabs and indentation.

This chapter introduces the most commonly used formatting options in TextEdit.

TIP TextEdit offers other formatting options that you can explore on your own. You'll find them all on the Format menu and its submenus.

TIP Some text formatting options are on the ruler. If the ruler is not showing, you can display it by choosing Format > Text > **Show Ruler** or by pressing Command-R.

A Select the text you want to format.

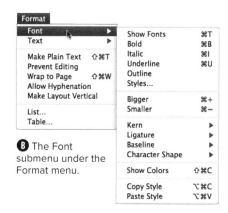

B The Font submenu under the Format menu.

C The Fonts window.

D You can see your changes immediately, as you make them.

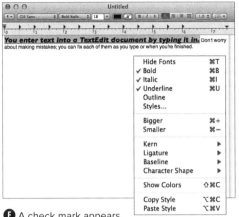

E A check mark appears on the Font submenu beside the name of each style applied to selected text.

Font formatting buttons and menus

G You can use buttons and menus on the toolbar to apply font formatting to selected text.

TABLE 14.1 Shortcut Keys for TextEdit Font Formatting

Keystroke	Formatting Applied
Command-B	Bold
Command-I	Italic
Command-U	Underline
Command-+	Bigger (increase font size)
Command-–	Smaller (decrease font size)
Shift-Command-T	Make Plain Text (remove formatting)

To apply font formatting:

1. Select the text characters you want to apply font formatting to **A**.

2. Use any combination of the following techniques to apply font formatting:

   ▸ Choose Format > Font > Show Fonts **B**, or press Command-T, to display the Fonts window **C**, where you can set options as desired. You'll immediately see the results of your changes in the document window **D**; make changes if you don't like what you see. You can also select different text and format it without closing the Fonts window.

   ▸ Choose options from the Format menu's Font submenu **B** to apply formatting. You can choose any combination of options. A check mark appears beside the type of formatting applied to selected text **E**.

   ▸ Use TextEdit window toolbar buttons and menus **F** to set the font family, typeface, font size, text color, and style. You can point to a button or menu to see a Help Tag (page 74) that describes what it does.

   ▸ Press the shortcut key (**Table 14.1**) for the type of formatting you want to apply.

TIP To remove an applied style, choose it from the Font submenu or select its toolbar button or menu again.

TIP Fonts are covered in greater detail in Chapter 21.

To apply text formatting:

1. Select the paragraph(s) you want to format.

2. Use any combination of the following techniques to apply text formatting:

- ‣ Choose an option from the Format menu's Text submenu **G** to apply formatting.

- ‣ Use TextEdit window toolbar buttons and menus **H** to set the alignment, line spacing, paragraph spacing, and bullet or number formatting. You can point to a button or menu to see a Help Tag (page 74) that describes what it does.

- ‣ Press the shortcut key (**Table 14.2**) for the type of formatting you want to apply.

To set tab stops:

Add, remove, and modify tab stops on the ruler as follows:

- ■ To remove a tab stop, drag it from the ruler into the document window **I**. When you release the button, the tab is removed.

- ■ To add a tab stop, click the ruler where you want to place it.

- ■ To move a tab stop, drag it to a new position on the ruler **J**.

- ■ To change a tab type, right-click it to display a menu of options **K** and choose the one you want.

TIP A tab stop is the position the insertion point moves to when you press the Tab key.

TIP Tab settings affect entire paragraphs. When you press Return to begin a new paragraph, the tab stops you set for the current paragraph are carried forward.

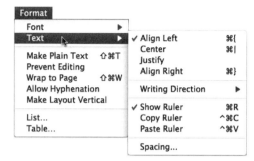

G Choose an option from the Text submenu under the Format menu.

Text formatting buttons and menus

H You can use these buttons and menus to apply text formatting to selected paragraphs.

TABLE 14.2 Shortcut Keys for TextEdit Text Formatting

Keystroke	Formatting Applied
Command-{	Align Left
Command-I	Center
Command-}	Align Right

I Drag the tab off the ruler. (The pointer disappears, so it's tough to illustrate.)

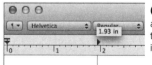

J Drag the tab to a new position on the ruler. (Again, invisible pointer!)

K Right-click to display a menu of tab types and choose the one you want.

L If desired, type text at the beginning of the line.

M Press Tab and enter text at the first tab stop.

N The first line of a table created with tabs.

O A complete table using left and decimal tabs.

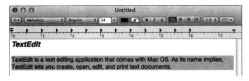

P Select the text you want to set indentation for.

First line indent
    Left indent   *Right indent*

Q TextEdit
Indent markers.

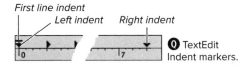

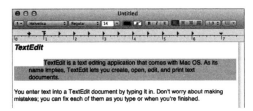

R In this example, all three indent markers were shifted to set indentation for this paragraph.

To use tab stops:

1. Add and remove tab stops as instructed in the section titled "To set tab stops" on page 192.

2. Position the insertion point at the beginning of the paragraph that tab stops are set for.

3. If desired, enter text at the beginning of the line **L**.

4. Press the Tab key.

5. Enter text at the tab stop **M**.

6. Repeat steps 4 and 5 until you have entered text as desired at all tab stops **N**.

7. Press the Return key to start a new paragraph.

8. Repeat steps 2 through 7 for each paragraph in which you want to use the tab stops **O**.

To set indentation:

1. Select the paragraph(s) for which you want to set indentation **P**.

2. Drag one of the icons on the end of the ruler **Q** to the left or right:

   ▸ To set the first line indentation for a paragraph, drag the horizontal rectangle icon.

   ▸ To set the left indent, drag the triangle on the left end of the ruler.

   ▸ To set the right indent, drag the triangle on the right end of the ruler.

   As you drag, a yellow box indicates the position of the indent. When you release a marker, the text shifts **R**.

Undoing & Redoing Actions

The Undo command **A** enables you to reverse your last action, thus offering an easy way to fix errors immediately after you make them. The Redo command **A**, which is available only when your last action was to use the Undo command, reverses the undo action.

TextEdit supports multiple levels of undo (and redo). That means you can undo (or redo) several actions, in the reverse order that they were performed (or undone).

TIP The Undo and Redo commands are available in most applications and can be found at the top of the Edit menu (page 170).

TIP The exact wording of the Undo (and Redo) command depends on what was last done (or undone). For example, if the last thing you did was to apply font formatting to selected text, the Undo command will be Undo Set Font **A**.

To undo the last action:

Choose Edit > Undo **A**, or press Command-Z.

The last thing you did is undone.

TIP To undo multiple actions, choose Edit > Undo repeatedly.

To redo an action:

After using the Undo command, choose Edit > Redo **A**, or press Shift-Command-Z.

The last thing you undid is redone.

TIP To redo multiple actions, choose Edit > Redo repeatedly.

Edit	
Undo Set Font	⌘Z
Redo Center	⇧⌘Z
Cut	⌘X
Copy	⌘C
Paste	⌘V
Paste and Match Style	⌥⇧⌘V
Delete	
Complete	⌥⎋
Select All	⌘A
Insert	▶
Add Link...	⌘K
Find	▶
Spelling and Grammar	▶
Substitutions	▶
Transformations	▶
Speech	▶
Special Characters...	⌥⌘T

A The Edit menu with Undo and Redo commands displayed. If one of these commands were not available, it would be gray.

Edit	
Undo Typing	⌘Z
Redo	⇧⌘Z
Cut	⌘X
Copy	⌘C
Paste	⌘V
Paste and Match Style	⌥⇧⌘V
Delete	
Complete	⌥⎋
Select All	⌘A
Insert	▶
Add Link...	⌘K
Find	▶
Spelling and Grammar	▶
Substitutions	▶
Transformations	▶
Speech	▶
Special Characters...	⌥⌘T

Ⓐ You can find the Cut, Copy, and Paste commands on the Edit menu.

Copy, Cut, & Paste

The Copy, Cut, and Paste commands Ⓐ enable you to duplicate or move document contents. Here's what each of these commands do:

- **Copy** copies selected content to the Clipboard. The selected text remains in the document.

- **Cut** copies selected content to the Clipboard and removes it from the document.

- **Paste** copies the contents of the Clipboard into the document at the insertion point.

Because the Clipboard is shared by all Mac OS applications, the Copy, Cut, and Paste commands work between applications. So, for example, you can copy text from a TextEdit document and then paste it into a Microsoft Word document.

TIP Almost all Mac OS-compatible applications include the Copy, Cut, and Paste commands on the Edit menu (page 170). These commands work very much the same in all applications.

TIP The Copy, Cut, and Paste commands also work with images and other content.

TIP TextEdit and many other Mac OS applications also support drag-and-drop text editing. Simply select the text you want to move and drag it to a new position in the document. Holding down the Option key while dragging copies the selection to the new location. Try it for yourself and see!

Quick Quiz: The Clipboard

Right *after* using the Paste command, what's in the Clipboard?

Answer: The same thing that was in it right *before* using the Paste command.

Using the paste command pastes a *copy* of what's on the Clipboard. That content remains on the Clipboard to use again and again—until you use the Copy or Cut command to replace it with new content.

To copy text:

1. Select the text that you want to copy **B**.

2. Choose Edit > Copy **A**, or press Command-C.

   The text is copied to the Clipboard so it can be pasted elsewhere. The original text remains in the document.

To cut text:

1. Select the text that you want to cut **B**.

2. Choose Edit > Cut **A**, or press Command-X.

   The text is copied to the Clipboard so it can be pasted elsewhere. The original is removed from the document.

To paste Clipboard contents:

1. Position the insertion point where you want the Clipboard contents to appear **C**.

2. Choose Edit > Paste **A**, or press Command-V.

   The Clipboard's contents are pasted into the document **D**.

TIP The Clipboard contains only the last item that was copied or cut. Using the Paste command, therefore, pastes in the most recently cut or copied selection.

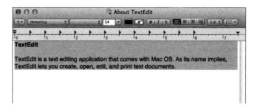

B Select the text you want to copy or cut.

C Position the insertion point where you want to paste the contents of the Clipboard.

D When you use the Paste command, the contents of the Clipboard are pasted at the insertion point.

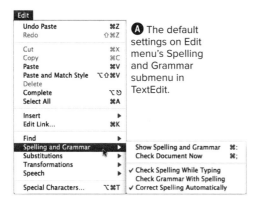

A The default settings on Edit menu's Spelling and Grammar submenu in TextEdit.

Checking Spelling & Grammar

TextEdit includes a spelling checker and a grammar checker. These two features can be used either automatically, to check a document as you create it, or manually, to check a document that is fully or partially completed. Together, they can help you identify problems in your documents so you can correct them before sharing them with others.

TextEdit also has an automatic spelling correction feature similar to that on iOS devices such as the iPhone and iPad. This feature can automatically correct misspelled words as you type.

This part of the chapter takes a look at how you can set up and use TextEdit's spelling and grammar checking and correction features.

To check and correct spelling as you type:

1. Display the Spelling and Grammar submenu under the Edit menu **A** and choose the following options to place a check mark beside the ones you want:
   - ▸ **Check Spelling While Typing** enables the automatic spelling check feature.
   - ▸ **Check Grammar With Spelling** enables grammar checking.
   - ▸ **Correct Spelling Automatically** enables the automatic spelling correction feature.

2. As you enter text in the document, TextEdit checks its spelling (and grammar, if enabled) and does one the following when it encounters a potential error:

continues on next page

Word of Advice: Don't Rely on Spelling and Grammar Checkers!

Don't depend solely on the spelling and grammar checkers in TextEdit (or any other application, for that matter) to make your documents perfect. Spelling checkers will not identify misspelled words that correctly spell other words—for example, *then* and *them*. Grammar checkers cannot identify all grammatical errors—and sometimes they inaccurately identify errors that aren't errors at all. These tools are no substitute for a good, old-fashioned proofreading!

- If automatic spelling correction is enabled and a possible correction is available, TextEdit may display an autocorrect tag 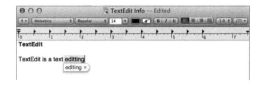. To accept the correction, just keep typing; the incorrect spelling is automatically replaced. To reject the correction, click the X on the tag.

- If automatic spelling checking is enabled, TextEdit places a dashed red underline under each word that isn't in its dictionary ⓒ. You can either manually correct the error using standard text editing techniques (page 187) or right-click the error to display a menu of options ⓓ and choose the option you want.

- If automatic grammar checking is enabled, TextEdit places a green dashed underline under each word or phrase that could be a grammar error ⓒ. You can either manually correct the error using standard text editing techniques (page 187) or right-click the error to display a menu of options ⓔ and choose the option you want.

TIP Sometimes TextEdit's autocorrection feature will automatically correct a word's spelling without displaying a tag.

ⓑ TextEdit might display an autocorrect tag to offer to make a correction.

ⓒ TextEdit identifies potential errors with dashed underlines.

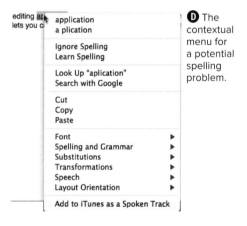

ⓓ The contextual menu for a potential spelling problem.

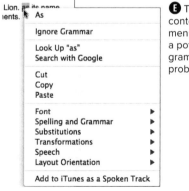

ⓔ The contextual menu for a potential grammar problem.

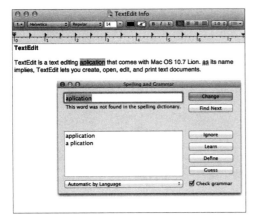

F Use the Spelling and Grammar window to resolve possible spelling and grammar errors.

To manually check spelling & grammar:

1. Choose Edit > Spelling and Grammar > Show Spelling and Grammar **A**, or press Command-: (colon), to display the Spelling and Grammar window.

    TextEdit selects and underlines the first possible misspelled word it finds. The word appears in a field in the Spelling and Grammar window and any suggested corrections appear in a list **F**.

2. You have several options:
    - ▸ To replace the word with a listed word, select the replacement word and click Change.
    - ▸ To enter a new spelling for the word, enter it in the box where the incorrect spelling appears and click Change.
    - ▸ To ignore the word, click Ignore.
    - ▸ To skip the word and continue checking, click Find Next.
    - ▸ To add the word to Mac OS X's dictionary, click Learn. TextEdit will never stop at that word again in any document.

3. Repeat step 2 for each word that TextEdit identifies as a possible misspelling or grammar error.

4. When you're finished checking spelling, click the Spelling and Grammar window's close button to dismiss it.

TIP To ensure that TextEdit uses the correct spelling dictionary, you can choose the language your document is written in from the pop-up menu at the bottom of the Spelling and Grammar window **F**.

TIP If you want to check grammar with spelling, make sure the Check Grammar check box is turned on in the Spelling and Grammar window **F**.

Saving Documents

When you're finished working with a TextEdit document, you may want to save it. You can then open it another time to review, edit, or print it or send it to someone else who might want to work with it.

TextEdit supports Mac OS X's new Auto Save feature (page 154), so it automatically saves all documents you create. It isn't until you close a document's window that Text-Edit asks if you want to save it . If you don't save an unsaved document when closing it, TextEdit discards any information it may have automatically saved for it.

If you quit TextEdit, the next time you launch it, it automatically reopens all the document windows that were open when you quit—even if those documents were never saved. This is Mac OS X's new Resume feature in action.

Once you save a TextEdit document, it can be closed, reopened, or shared with someone else—just like any other document file. The Auto Save feature will also automatically save versions (page 154) of the file as you continue working on it. But you can manually save a version (page 167) any time you like. This makes it possible to restore a document to a previously saved version (page 156).

You use the Save command (page 163) and Save dialog to save a document for the first time (page 166) and to save subsequent changes to it (page 167).

Ⓐ It isn't until you close a document window that TextEdit asks if you want to save it.

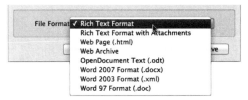

B You can use the File Format pop-up menu to save a TextEdit file in a specific format.

C To save a document as a plain text file, you must convert it to plain text first.

TextEdit supports the following file formats, which can be specified when you save the file for the first time, by choosing an option from the File Format pop-up menu in the Save dialog **B**:

- **Rich Text Format** (**RTF**) is supported by most word processing applications and enables you to include text formatting in the document file. This is TextEdit's default file format.

- **Rich Text Format with Attachments** is the same as Rich Text Format, but it enables you to include file attachments such as images in the file.

- **Web Page (.html)** and **Web Archive** are an HTML format files that can be read by a Web browser such as Safari.

- **OpenDocument Text (.odt)** is a format that can be read by Open Office compatible word processing applications, such as Google Docs.

- **Word 2007 Format (.docx)**, **Word 2003 Format (.xml)**, and **Word 97 Format (.doc)** are three different Microsoft Word compatible formats.

TIP Remember that until you manually save a document, thus giving it a name and placing a copy of it on disk, that document is accessible through TextEdit only. Don't rely on the Auto Save feature—be sure to save all your important documents.

TIP You can also save a document as a plain text document if you convert it to plain text *before* saving it. To do this, choose Format > Make Plain Text **C**. This strips out all formatting in the document and displays different options in the File Format pop-up menu when you save the file.

Opening Documents

You can open any compatible text or word processing document with TextEdit. This includes documents in plain text, RTF, Word, and OpenDocument format (page 200).

You open a TextEdit document like any other document:

- Double click its icon in the Finder (page 148).

- Drag its icon onto the TextEdit document icon (page 149).

- Select the icon and use the Open With command (page 149).

- Choose File > Open from within TextEdit and use the Open dialog that appears to locate, select, and open the file (page 164).

Because TextEdit supports Mac OS X's new Resume feature, when you open TextEdit, any document windows that were open the last time you quit it are automatically reopened.

Address Book

Address Book is a contact management application that enables you to keep track of the names, addresses, phone numbers, e-mail addresses, Web URLs, and similar information for people and businesses that you know. Data you enter into Address Book can be grouped, sorted, searched, and printed. When you search your Mac using the Spotlight search menu on the menu bar (page 100), search results can include Address Book contact records.

The information you store in Address Book can be used by Mail (page 418) to send email messages, iChat (page 427) to send instant messages, FaceTime (page 434) to initiate video calls, and iCal (Chapter 16) to invite people to events.

Address Book records can be shared with others through the use of compatible servers, such as CardDAV and Exchange. They can also be synchronized with online services such as Google and mobile devices such as iPad and iPhone.

This chapter, provides enough information to get you started using Address Book for your contact management needs.

In This Chapter:

Launching & Quitting Address Book

Like any other application, you must launch Address Book before you can use it. This loads it into your computer's memory so your computer can work with it.

To launch Address Book:

Use one of the following techniques:

- Open the Address Book application icon in the Applications folder window (page 147).

- Click the Address Book icon in Launchpad (page 150).

- Click the Address Book icon in the Dock (page 38).

Address Book launches **B**.

TIP If the Address Book window displays just a single contact card **C**, you can click the book button in its lower-left corner to expand the view and display it as a book with a list of records on the left and details about the selected record on the right **B**.

TIP You can resize the Address Book window by dragging any of its edges (page 30). You can move the Address Book window to a new location on screen by dragging it from any location except an edge, button, or data.

A Address Book's application icon.

Address Book

B When you first open Address Book, it only has two records: one for Apple and one for you.

C The Address Book window can also be displayed as a single contact card.

D Here's what the List and Card view of Address Book might look like with a bunch of contacts entered.

E Group view lists the groups on the left and the contacts within a selected group on the right.

F Here's List and Card view for a specific group.

G Use View menu commands or their keyboard shortcuts to quickly switch view.

To navigate Address Book's Interface:

Address Book's interface has been significantly changed for OS X Lion. Instead of a multicolumn display that includes groups, contacts, and contact details, it now appears as a book with a list on the left and details for a selected list item on the right **D E F**. Here are some tips for navigating this new interface; you'll use this information throughout this chapter and whenever you work with Address Book:

- To view the items in a list, scroll through the list using standard scrolling techniques (page 16).

- To switch from one Address Book view to another, use commands under the View menu **G** or their corresponding keyboard shortcuts.

- To view all the contacts in a group, in Group view, click the name of the group **E**.

- To view all the contacts in a group in List and Card view **F**, in Group view, double-click the name of the group.

- To view all contacts in List and Card view **D**, in Group view, double-click the All Contacts group **E**.

- To view contact details, in List and Card view, select the contact name. Details appear on the right side of the window **D F**.

To quit Address Book:

Choose Address Book > Quit Address Book, or press Command-Q.

Address Book quits. Any changes you made to contact records are automatically saved.

Working with Contact Cards

As you work with Address Book, you'll be adding, removing, and editing *contact cards*. A contact card is a collection of information about a specific person or business. Information is entered into pre-defined fields to keep data entry consistent throughout the Address Book database.

To add a new card:

1. Use one of the following techniques:

   ▸ Click the Create a new card button (+) at the bottom of the Address Book window.

   ▸ Choose File > New Card **A**, or press Command-N.

   A few things happen **B**:

   ▸ A *No Name* record is created in the list of contacts on the left.

   ▸ A blank address card appears on the right, with the First field selected.

   ▸ Address Book switches to edit mode.

2. Enter information about the contact into appropriate fields:

   ▸ When a field is active, text appears within it to prompt you for information **B**. Type to replace selected text.

   ▸ Press Tab or click a field to move from field to field.

   ▸ Additional fields appear automatically when you enter data into all available fields of a specific type. For example, if you enter information into both phone number fields, another phone number field appears **C**.

A Choose New Card from the File menu.

B Address Book creates a new blank contact card and selects the first field for data entry.

C Address Book automatically adds fields when you use up all fields of an available type.

D You can use a pop-up menu to change a field's label.

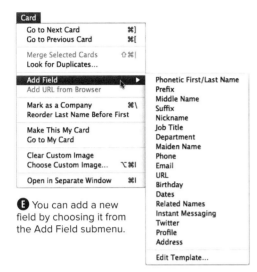

E You can add a new field by choosing it from the Add Field submenu.

F A completed contact card shows only the fields that contain data.

G To list a record by company name, turn on the Company check box.

3. To change the label that appears beside a field, click label to display a menu **D**, and then choose the label you prefer.

4. To add another field, choose the field you want from the Add Field submenu under the Card menu **E**.

5. To remove a field, click the red minus button beside it. The field is removed. (Empty fields that do not have a red minus button **C** will not appear on completed contact record.)

6. When you are finished entering contact information, click the Done button to view the completed card **F**.

TIP You can enter information into any combination of fields; if you do not have information for a specific field, skip it and it will not appear in the completed card.

TIP To list an entry by company name rather than the person's name **F**, turn on the Company check box beneath the Company field **G**. A contact that does not include a person's name is automatically listed by the company name.

To delete a contact record:

1. On the left side of the Address Book window, select the contact you want to delete.

2. Press the Delete key.

3. In the confirmation dialog that appears, click Delete or press Return.

   The contact disappears.

To edit a contact card:

1. On the left side of the Address Book window, select the contact you want to edit **F**.

2. Click the Edit button at the bottom of the window to switch to edit mode **H**.

3. Make changes as desired in the record's address card.

4. Click Done to save your changes and view the modified card.

To add an image to a contact card:

1. On the left side of the Address Book window, select the contact that you want to add a picture or logo to.

2. If necessary, click the Edit button to switch to edit mode **H**.

3. Drag the icon for the file containing the photo or logo you want to add from a Finder window to the image well in the address card window **I**.

4. When you release the button, the image appears in a pop-up window **J**.

5. Drag the slider at the bottom of the dialog to resize the image. You can then drag the image around in the frame to determine the resized image's edges.

6. Click Set. The image appears in the contact card **K**.

TIP Another way to add an image to a card is to choose Card > Choose Custom Image to display the image pop-up window **J**. Then either drag the image into that window or click the Choose button to use another dialog to locate and select the image you want to use.

TIP To remove a photo or logo from a contact record, select the contact and choose Card > Clear Custom Image or simply click the image while the record is in edit mode and press Delete.

H When you click the Edit button, you can make changes to the currently displayed contact card.

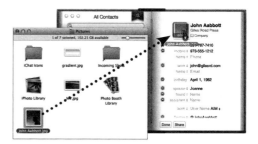

I Drag the image file's icon to the image area in the contact card.

J The image appears in a pop-up window.

K An Image in a contact card.

A A vCard file icon, as it appears in Mac OS. Note the custom image; this card file includes the contact's photo.

Chuck Joiner.vcf

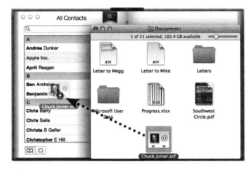

B One way to add a vCard's information to Address Book is to drag the icon into Address Book's list of contacts.

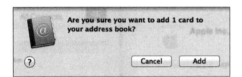

C A dialog confirms that you want to add the card to Address Book.

D The card appears in Address Book with all of the information it contains.

Importing & Creating vCards

vCard, or *virtual address card*, files are commonly used to share contact information electronically. A vCard file, which normally has a .vcf filename extension **A**, can contain all of the contact information for an individual or organization. Because the file uses a standard format, it is readable by most contact management software.

If you receive a vCard file from a contact, you can import it into Address Book to quickly add that contact's record to your Address Book file. Similarly, you can create a vCard file for anyone in Address Book and share it with someone else so they can add it to their contact management application.

To import a vCard:

1. Use one of the following techniques:

   ▸ Double-click a vCard file icon **A**.

   ▸ Drag a vCard file icon from a Finder window to the left side of the Address Book window **B**.

   A dialog appears, asking if you're sure you want to add the card **C**.

2. Click Add.

   An Address Book contact card is created based on the vCard contents **D**.

To save contact information as a vCard:

Drag the name of a contact from the right side of the Address Book window to the Desktop or a Finder window **E**.

The vCard file's icon appears where you dragged it **F**.

TIP You can save multiple vCards at once. Simply hold down the Command key while clicking contact names to select multiple contacts. Then drag any of them to a Finder window as discussed above.

To share a contact's card with someone else:

1. In the left side of the Address Book window, select the card you want to share **D**.

2. In the bottom of the Address Book windows, click the Share button **D**.

   Address Book opens your default email application. A new email message is created with a vCard file for the contact you selected attached **G**.

3. Complete and send the email message (page 422).

TIP You can send your vCard via email to anyone you like. This makes it easy for people to add your contact information to their contact database.

E Drag the name of a contact from Address Book to a Finder window.

F The icon for the contact's vCard file appears where you dragged the name.

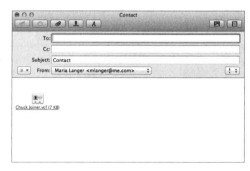

G The Share button in the Address Book window creates a vCard file and attaches it to an email message.

A Address Book's General preferences window offers options for changing the display and sort order of contacts.

B Address Book offers two options for sorting its contacts list.

C You can sort contacts by last name.

Organizing Contact Cards

Once Address Book has more than just a few contact cards, it's important to be able to locate the ones you want quickly, when you want them. Address Book includes a number of features you might find helpful for keeping contacts organized:

- Sort cards based on first or last name.
- Search for cards based on any field of information.
- Organize cards into groups.
- Create smart groups to keep cards organized automatically based on criteria you specify.

This part of the chapter takes a look at all of these features.

TIP The Last Import group is automatically created (or modified) by Address Book when you import one or more contacts.

To sort contact cards:

1. Choose Address Book > Preferences, or press Command-, (comma) to open the Address Book Preferences window.

2. If necessary, click the General button at the top of the window to display General preferences **A**.

3. Choose an option from the Sort By pop-up menu **B**.

   The contacts are immediately sorted by the option you chose **C**.

4. Click the General preferences window's close button to dismiss it.

TIP By default, contact cards are sorted by first name.

To search for a contact card:

1. Begin entering a search word or phrase in the Search box at the top of the Address Book window.

   Address Book immediately displays all records that match what you've typed **D**.

2. Continue typing to narrow down the list of contacts that match the search word or phrase.

   Each character you type reduces the list of matches **E**.

TIP You can search by any text that might appear in a contact's record. For example, if you're trying to find a person who works at a certain company but can't remember the person's name, you can enter the company name to display a list of all contacts at that company.

TIP If you have set up multiple groups (as dis-cussed next), make sure you select either the All Contacts group or the group you expect to find the contact before beginning your search. If the contact you're looking for is not in the group you're searching, you won't find him.

D In this example, searching for the characters *jo* instantly displays a bunch of matches.

E Adding another character narrows down the search results.

F Address Book's File menu.

G An untitled group appears in the group list.

H When you type in a new name and press Return the untitled group is named.

I Drag a name from the contact list to the group.

J Select a group name to see the contact cards within it.

To organize contact cards into groups:

1. Use one of the following techniques:

   ▸ Switch to Group view and then click the Create New Group button at the bottom of the Address Book window.

   ▸ Choose File > New Group **F**, or press Shift-Command-N.

   A new entry appears in Group view with its name, *untitled group*, selected **G**.

2. Enter a name for the group and press Return to save it **H**.

3. In the list of groups, select All Contacts.

4. In the contact list on the right side of the window, locate a contact you want to add to the new group.

5. Drag the contact's name from the list of contacts onto the name of the group you want to add him to **I**.

   When you release the button, the contact is added to the list.

6. Repeat steps 4 and 5 to add as many contacts as you like to the group.

TIP To see which contact cards are in a group, click the name of the group on the left side of the window. The names of the contacts in the group appear on the right **J**.

TIP You can create as many groups as you need to organize your contacts.

TIP A contact can be included in more than one group.

To remove a contact from a group:

1. In Group view, select the group you want to remove the contact from ❶.

2. In the list of contacts on the right side of the window, select the contact you want to remove.

3. Press the Delete key.

4. Click the appropriate button in the confirmation dialog that appears ❻:

   ▸ **Cancel** does not delete the contact.

   ▸ **Delete** deletes the contact from the Address Book database and any other groups it might be part of.

   ▸ **Remove from Group** removes the contact from the group. The contact remains in the Address Book database and any other groups it might be part of.

TIP Deleting a contact from the All Contacts group completely removes it from Address Book.

To delete a group:

1. In Group view, select the group you want to remove ❶.

2. Press the Delete key.

3. In the confirmation dialog that appears ❶, click Delete.

   The group is removed but all contacts that were in it remain in Address Book.

TIP You cannot remove the All Contacts group.

❻ A dialog like this appears when you try to delete a contact from a specific group.

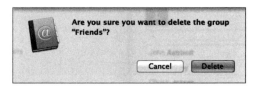

❶ Use this dialog to confirm that you want to delete the selected group.

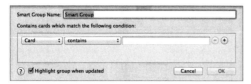

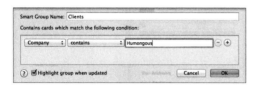

M A dialog like this appears when you use the New Smart Group command.

N Set criteria by choosing options and entering match text.

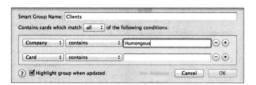

O You can add lines for additional criteria if necessary.

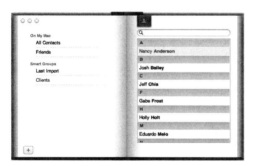

P In this example, I used a smart group to automatically group contacts who work at specific companies.

To create a smart group:

1. Choose File > New Smart Group **F**, or press Option-Command-N.

   A smart group settings dialog appears **M**.

2. Enter a name for the group in the Smart Group Name box.

3. Use options in the middle of the dialog to set criteria for matching contacts **N**.

4. To add more matching criteria, click the + button at the far right end of the line of criteria you already set. The dialog expands to offer an additional line and a pop-up menu for matching options **O**. Set options as desired.

5. Repeat step 4 as necessary to add more matching criteria.

6. If you have set more than one line of criteria, choose a matching option from the pop-up menu beneath the smart group name field.

7. Click OK.

   The smart group is created and populated with contacts that match the criteria you specified **P**.

TIP To create a smart group from search results, perform a search and then choose File > **New Smart Group from Current Search.**

TIP You can delete a smart group the same way you delete a regular group (page 214).

TIP You cannot manually remove a contact from a smart group. The only way a contact can be removed from a smart group is if it no longer matches the criteria you specified when you set up the smart group.

TIP To edit a smart group's criteria, select the group and choose Edit > **Edit Smart Group.** Then use the dialog that appears to modify settings and click OK.

Printing Contact Cards

Address Book makes it possible to print individual contact cards, selected contact cards, or groups of contact cards in a number of formats. Start by selecting the cards you want to print and then using the Print dialog to set printing options and send the print job to your printer.

Although printing in Mac OS X is discussed in detail in Chapter 22, here's a quick overview of how you can print your contacts.

TIP Before you can print, you must have a printer set up to use with your computer. You can learn more about printing in Chapter 22.

To print contact cards:

1. Select the card(s) you want to print:

   ▸ To print just one card, in Group or List and Card view, select the card.

   ▸ To print multiple cards, in Group or List and Card view, select the cards. (You can hold down the Command key to select multiple cards at once.)

   ▸ To print all the cards in a group, in Group view, select the group.

2. Choose File > Print **A**, or press Command-P.

   The Print dialog appears **B** **C** **D** **E**.

3. Choose the name of the printer you want to use from the Printer pop-up menu.

4. Choose an option from the Style pop-up menu:

   ▸ **Mailing Labels** **B** prints mailing labels on a variety of widely available label sheets.

   ▸ **Envelopes** **C** prints envelopes on common envelope sizes.

A You can find the Print command on the File menu.

B Some of the mailing labels options in the Print dialog.

C Some of the Envelopes options in the Print dialog.

D List options in the Print dialog.

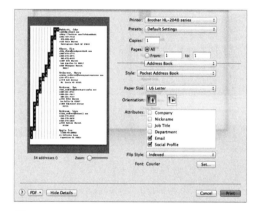

E Pocket Address Book options in the Print dialog.

- **Lists D** prints contact lists that include the database fields you specify.
- **Pocket Address Book E** prints pocket-sized address books.

5. Set options as desired in the dialog:

- For mailing labels **B**, click the Layout button and set label layout options. Then click the Label button and set options for label content, sort order, color, and font.

- For envelopes **C**, click the Layout button and set envelope layout options. Then click the Label button and set options for envelope content, print order, color, and font. Finally, click the Orientation button and select an envelope print orientation.

- For lists **D**, set Paper Size, Orientation, and Font Size options. Then turn on check boxes in the Attributes area to specify what information you want to print for each record.

- For pocket address books **E**, set Orientation, Flip Style, and Font options. Then turn on check boxes in the Attributes area to specify what information you want to print for each record.

Note the changes in the dialog's preview area as you change settings.

6. Click Print.

Address Book sends the information to your printer, and it prints.

TIP After step 3, if the Print dialog that appears is small and does not offer many options, click the Show Details button at the bottom of the dialog to expand it.

16

iCal

iCal is a personal calendar application that enables you to keep track of appointments and other events. With iCal, you can:

- Create multiple color-coded calendars for different categories of events—for example, home, business, or school.

- View calendars individually or together.

- View calendars by day, week, or month.

- Send email invitations for events to people in your Mac OS X Address Book.

- Get notification of upcoming events on screen or by email.

- Create and manage a priorities-based reminders list.

- Share calendars on the Web with family, friends, and business associates.

This chapter provides basic instructions for setting up and using iCal.

In This Chapter:

Launching & Quitting iCal

Like any other application, you must launch iCal before you can use it. This loads it into your computer's memory so your computer can work with it.

To launch iCal:

Use one of the following techniques:

- Open the iCal application icon in the Applications folder window (page 147).

- Click the iCal icon in Launchpad (page 150).

- Click the iCal icon in the Dock (page 38).

iCal launches and displays its main calendar window **B**.

TIP The appearance of the iCal window varies depending on which calendar view is displayed.

TIP iCal supports OS X Lion's new full-screen apps feature (page 152).

To quit iCal:

Choose iCal > Quit iCal, or press Command-Q.

iCal quits. Any changes you made to events or Reminders are automatically saved.

A The iCal application icon.

iCal

B The main calendar window for iCal, shown in Week view.

View	
By Day	⌘1
By Week	⌘2
✓ By Month	⌘3
By Year	⌘4
Next	⌘→
Previous	⌘←
Go to Today	⌘T
Go to Date...	⇧⌘T
Make Text Bigger	⌘+
Make Text Smaller	⌘−
Show Calendar List	
Show Notifications	
Show Search Results	
Show Reminders	⌥⌘T
✓ Show All-Day Events	
Show Declined Events	
Enter Full Screen	

🅐 Use the View menu to show or hide iCal window elements a number of ways.

Working with the Calendar Window

iCal's main calendar window can be displayed in a number of different views. Once you've chosen a view you like, you can view any date in the year.

Here's a quick rundown of how you can change the calendar view and see specific dates.

To change the calendar view:

Choose an option from the top of the View menu 🅐, press one of the corresponding keyboard shortcuts, or click one of the view buttons at the top of the calendar window 🅑🅒🅓🅔.

- **By Day** shows a day at a glance, along with an agenda of upcoming events 🅑.
- **By Week** shows a week at a glance 🅒.
- **By Month** shows a month at a glance 🅓.
- **By Year** shows a year at a glance, with colored squares indicating dates with events scheduled 🅔.

🅑 The iCal window with events viewed By Day.

🅒 The iCal window with events viewed By Week.

🅓 The iCal window with events viewed By Month.

To scroll through calendar dates:

1. Switch to the calendar view you prefer (page 221).

2. Click the Back or Forward buttons near the top right corner of the window 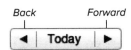 to scroll backward or forward through calendar views. For example, in Week view, the calendar will scroll a week at a time; in month view, it will scroll a month at a time.

TIP You can use standard window scrolling techniques (page 16) to scroll the contents of the iCal window whenever necessary.

To view a specific day, week, or month:

1. Choose View > Go to Date **A**, or press Shift-Command-T.

2. Enter the date you want to go to in the tiny dialog sheet that appears **G**.

3. Click Show.

   The calendar page changes (if necessary) to display that date.

To view today's date:

Use one of the following techniques:

- Click the Today button near the top-right corner of the window **F**.

- Choose View > Go to Today **A**.

- Press Command-T.

The Calendar page changes (if necessary) to display the current date.

E The iCal window with events viewed By Year.

F Use these buttons to scroll backward or forward through calendar pages.

G Use this dialog to enter the date you want to view.

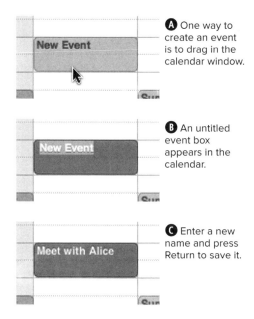

A One way to create an event is to drag in the calendar window.

B An untitled event box appears in the calendar.

C Enter a new name and press Return to save it.

Working with Events

An event is a date-based activity that you might include on your calendar. Meetings and appointments are examples of events. Events can be one-time or recurring. They can also be scheduled for a specific time of day or last all day.

This part of the chapter explains how to create events, add and modify event details, and delete events.

TIP iCal also supports to-do items or reminders, which are activities that are not necessarily associated with a specific date—although they could be. You can learn more about reminders on page 229.

To add an event by clicking or dragging in the calendar window:

1. Display the date you want to add the event to.

2. Use one of the following techniques:

   ▶ In Day or Week view, drag from the event's start time to end time **A**.

   ▶ in Month or Year view, double-click inside the event's date box.

   A box for the event appears in the calendar window with its default name (*New Event*) selected **B**.

3. Enter a new name for the event, and press Return **C**.

4. Continue following instructions in the section titled "To set event details" on page 224.

TIP Double-clicking a calendar date number switches to Day view for that date.

TIP When you create a new event by double-clicking in the date box, iCal uses the next hour after the current time as the event time.

To add an event with the Quick Event feature:

1. Use one of the following techniques:

   ▸ Click the + button near the top-left of the iCal window.

   ▸ Choose File > New Event .

   ▸ Press Command-N.

   A Create Quick Event pop-up window with sample event text appears beneath the + button **E**.

2. Type some descriptive text for the event that includes the date and time **F** and press Return.

   iCal switches to the day of the event, creates a box at the specified time, and opens the inspector so you can enter more event details **G**.

3. Continue following instructions in the section titled "To set event details" on page 225.

TIP Whether iCal properly schedules the event depends on how you enter its descriptive text. Practice with this feature to see how you can get the best results.

D Choose New Event from the File menu.

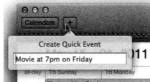

E The Quick Event pop-up window appears with sample event text.

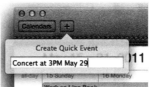

F Type some descriptive text for your event.

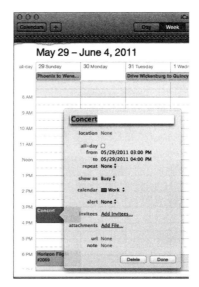

G When you press Return, iCal creates the event and opens its detail window in edit mode.

H Double-clicking an event box displays its details.

I But you must click the Edit button to enter edit mode and make changes.

J Turning on the All Day check box, hides the time fields.

K Use this pop-up menu to choose a repeating option.

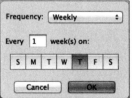

L This pop-up dialog enables you to set custom repeating options for an event.

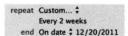

M A repeating event with an end date.

To set event details:

1. If necessary, in the calendar window, double-click the event you want to set details for to open the event's detail window **H**.

2. If necessary, click the Edit button to switch to edit mode **G** **I**.

3. To modify the event name, click the existing name to display an edit box and edit the contents of the box **G** **I**.

4. To specify a location for the event, click to the right of the location label and type what you want to appear.

5. To set the beginning and ending dates for the event, click numbers in the date fields and type new values.

6. Set the event times as follows:
   ▸ To indicate that the event lasts all day (or multiple days), turn on the all-day check box. The time fields disappear **J**.
   ▸ To specify starting and ending times for the event, make sure the all-day check box is turned off and then enter the starting and ending times in the two time areas.

7. To set the event to repeat on a regular basis, choose an option from the repeat pop-up menu **K**. If none of the standard options apply, you can choose Custom and use the dialog that appears **L** to set a custom repeating schedule. Then, if necessary, set an ending option in the end field that appears **M**.

8. To specify how the event time should appear on a shared calendar, choose an option from the Show as pop-up menu. Your options are Free or Busy.

continues on next page

9. To specify the calendar to add the event to, choose a calendar from the calendar pop-up menu. The menu lists all calendars you have created.

10. To be reminded about the event, choose an option from the alarm pop-up menu . Then set other alarm options as necessary 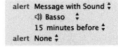. You can repeat this process to set multiple alarms.

11. To invite others to the event, click the Add Invitees link. Then enter contact names or email addresses in the box that appears. As you type, iCal attempts to match names to those in Address Book with an email address recorded ; select the name you want to add. You can repeat this step to invite multiple people.

12. To attach a file to the event, click the Add File link. Then use the standard Open dialog that appears to locate, select, and open the file you want to attach. When you click Open, the file is added to the event details . You can repeat this step to attach multiple files.

13. To associate a webpage with the event, click to the right of the url label and type a URL in the box that appears.

14. To add notes about the event, click to the right of the note label and type what you want to appear 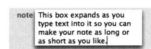.

15. When you're finished entering event details **S**, click Done. The details are saved with the event; some details appear in the main calendar window **T**.

N If you choose an option from the alarm pop-up menu...

O ...you can set options for one or more event reminders.

P As you enter a name in the invitees field, iCal attempts to match it to an Address Book contact with an email address.

Q An event can include one or more file attachments.

R You can enter a note about the event in the note field.

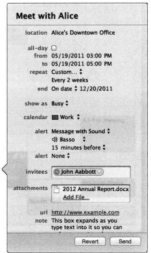
S Here's an example of a completed event's details before saving them.

T Some of the event's details appear in the iCal window.

U Clicking an invitee name displays a menu of options like this one.

V If you change a repeating event, a dialog like this one asks if you want to change all of the events or just one.

TIP You can follow these steps to add details for a new event or make changes to an existing event.

TIP The all-day event check box is handy for entering information about vacations and other events that span multiple days.

TIP In steps 5 and 6, the ending time or date must be *after* the starting time or date. It may be necessary to change AM to PM before entering the second time.

TIP A quick way to change an event's time is to drag its top or bottom border in Day or Week view of the main calendar window. This automatically changes the time information in the event details dialog.

TIP A quick way to change an event's date is to drag its event box from one date to another in the main calendar window. This automatically changes the date information in the event details dialog.

TIP You can click an invitee's name to access a menu of options for that invitee and the invitee field **U**.

TIP If an event has invitees who have not yet been invited to the event, the Done button appears as a Send button at the bottom of the event details dialog **S**. Clicking Send sends email invitations to invitees.

TIP You can enter multiple invitees for an event by separating each name with a comma.

TIP If you set an event to repeat, any time you change that event's details, a dialog appears **V**. Click the appropriate button for the change.

To view event details:

In any view of the main calendar window, double-click the event.

Details appear in a pop-up window **S**.

To delete an event:

1. In the calendar window, select the event you want to delete.

2. Press the Delete key.

   What happens next depends on the settings for the event.

   ► If the event has no special settings, it simply disappears.

   ► If the event has an attachment, a dialog appears to warn you 🚫. You must click Continue to delete the event.

   ► If the event is a recurring event, a dialog appears with three options 🚫: **Cancel** does not delete the event, *Delete All Future Events* deletes just the events in the future, and **Delete Only This Event** deletes only the event for the date and time that you've selected.

   ► If the event has invitees, a dialog appears with three options 🅨: **Cancel** does not delete the event, **Delete and Don't Notify** deletes the event but does not notify invitees that it has been canceled, and **Delete and Notify** deletes the event and notifies the attendees that it has been canceled.

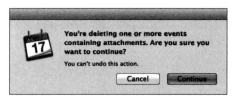

🚫 A dialog like this appears to warn you that deleting an event with an attachment can't be undone.

🚫 Use this dialog to determine which repeating event(s) should be deleted.

🅨 Use this dialog to determine whether invitees should be notified when an event is cancelled.

View	
By Day	⌘1
✓ By Week	⌘2
By Month	⌘3
By Year	⌘4
Next	⌘→
Previous	⌘←
Go to Today	⌘T
Go to Date...	⇧⌘T
Make Text Bigger	⌘+
Make Text Smaller	⌘–
Show Calendar List	
Show Notifications	
Show Search Results	
Show Reminders	⌥⌘T
✓ Show All-Day Events	
Show Declined Events	
Enter Full Screen	

Ⓐ To show or hide the Reminders list, use a command on the View menu.

Ⓑ The Reminders list appears on the right side of iCal's main window.

Working with Reminders

Reminders are iCal items that may or may not be associated with a specific date or time. Perhaps the best way to differentiate between them and calendar events is that reminders don't usually have a timespan. They're things you need to do that don't need to be scheduled on your calendar.

Like events, reminders can be associated with a specific calendar. If a reminder does have a due date associated with it, it can be set up with an alert. A reminder can also include a URL and note. But unlike calendar events, reminders can be assigned one of three priorities, which can be used for sorting them in the reminders list.

In this part of the chapter, you'll learn how to display, create, set options for, remove, and sort reminders in iCal.

TIP Previous versions of Mac OS referred to reminders as to-do items.

To show the Reminders list:

Choose View > Show Reminders Ⓐ, or press Option-Command-T.

The Reminders list appears on the right side of the iCal window Ⓑ.

To add a reminder:

1. Choose File > New Reminder **C**, or press Command-K.

   If the Reminders list was not already showing, it appears. An untitled reminder appears in the list with its default name (*New Reminder*) selected **D**.

2. Enter a name for the reminder, and press Return **E**.

To set reminder details:

1. If necessary, display the Reminders list.

2. In the Reminders list, double-click the item you want to modify.

   Details about the item appear in a pop-up window **F**.

3. To modify the item name, click the existing name to display an edit box **F** and edit the contents.

4. To mark the item as completed, turn on the completed check box.

5. To set a priority for the item, choose an option from the priority pop-up menu **G**.

6. To set a due date for the item, turn on the due date check box and enter a date in the field beside it **H**.

7. To set an alert for the reminder, choose an option from the alert pop-up menu and set associated options **H**.

8. To specify a calendar to add the item to, choose one from the calendar pop-up menu. The menu lists all calendars you have created.

9. To associate a Web page with the item, click to the right of the url label and type a URL in the box that appears.

C Choose New Reminder from the File menu.

D A new, untitled reminder is added to the Reminders list.

E Type a new name for the reminder and press Return to save it.

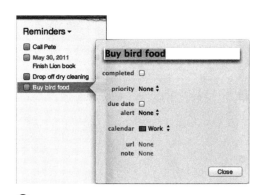

F Double-clicking a reminder displays its details in a pop-up window.

G You can use a pop-up menu to set a priority for the reminder.

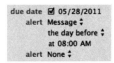

H In this example, a reminder item has a due date and alert set.

note Sale at Tropic Zone ends May 30; get there before they run out of the Organic food Alex likes.

Ⓘ A reminder can also include a note.

Ⓙ Here's an example of a reminder with plenty of details.

10. To add notes about the item, click to the right of the note label and type what you want to appear **Ⓘ**.

11. When you're finished entering information **Ⓙ**, click Close.

TIP The stack of lines to the left of a reminder in the Reminders list **ⒹⒺ** indicates its priority: the more lines, the more important the item is. You can click this button to change the priority **Ⓚ**.

To sort the Reminders list:

1. Click the Reminders heading to display a menu of sort and display options **Ⓛ**.

2. Choose the sort order you want.

   The list is immediately resorted.

To mark a reminder as complete:

Click the check box beside the reminder in the Reminders list **Ⓜ**.

A check mark appears in the box, indicating that the item is complete.

TIP If the Reminders list is configured to hide completed items, when you turn on the check box for a reminder, it is removed from the Reminders list.

To delete a reminder:

1. If necessary, display the Reminders list.

2. In the Reminders list, select the item you want to delete.

3. Press the Delete key.

   The item disappears.

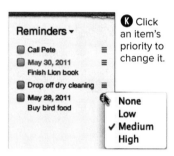

Ⓚ Click an item's priority to change it.

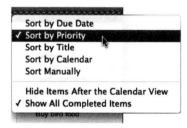

Ⓛ Click the Reminders list heading to display a menu with sort and display options.

Ⓜ Clicking an item's check box marks it as complete.

Creating & Deleting Calendars

iCal comes preconfigured with two calendars: Home and Work. But you can create additional calendars if necessary to better organize your calendar items. You can also display any combination of calendars at once, making it possible to focus on one aspect of your schedule or see the whole thing.

This part of the chapter explains how to create, display, and delete calendars.

To display the Calendar list:

Use one of the following techniques:

- Choose View > Show Calendar list 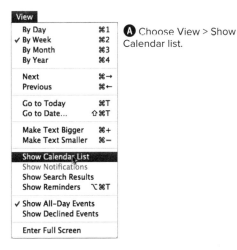.

- Click the Calendars button in the upper-left corner of the iCal window.

The Calendar list appears as a pop-up menu beneath the Calendars button ⓑ.

To add a calendar:

1. Choose File > New Calendar ⓒ, or press Option-Command-N.

   An untitled calendar appears on the Calendar list with its default name (*Untitled*) selected ⓓ.

2. Enter a name for the calendar, and press Return to save it ⓔ.

TIP You can use the New Calendar Group command on the File menu ⓒ to add calendar groups. You can then organize your calendars by dragging them into groups on the Calendar list.

ⓐ Choose View > Show Calendar list.

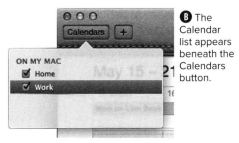

ⓑ The Calendar list appears beneath the Calendars button.

ⓒ Choose New Calendar from the File menu.

ⓓ A new untitled calendar appears in the calendar list.

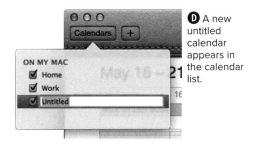

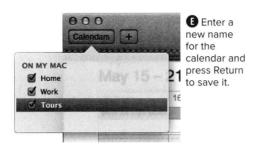

E Enter a new name for the calendar and press Return to save it.

F Choose Delete from the Edit menu to delete a selected calendar.

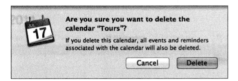

G You'll need to click Delete in this dialog to delete a calendar with events.

To rename a calendar:

1. If necessary, display the Calendar list **B**.

2. Click the name of the calendar you want to rename.

   A selection box appears around it and its name becomes selected.

3. Enter a new name for the calendar and press Return to save it.

To display events from only certain calendars:

1. If necessary, display the Calendar list **B**.

2. Click to toggle the check boxes beside the calendars you want to show or hide.

   The calendars with check marks beside them will appear in the iCal window.

To delete a calendar:

1. If necessary, display the Calendar list **B**.

2. Select the calendar you want to delete.

3. Choose Edit > Delete **F**, or press Command-Delete.

4. If a confirmation dialog appears **G**, click Delete.

   The calendar and all of its events are removed.

Sharing Calendars

You can use iCal to share your calendars with others by publishing it on MobileMe or a compatible WebDAV server. You can then give others the URL they need to access your calendar on the Web or subscribe to it with their calendar software.

Likewise, you can subscribe to a calendar published by someone else. All you need is the calendar's URL to add it to iCal.

This part of the chapter explains how you can publish your calendars and subscribe to someone else's.

TIP iCal also supports calendars shared via CalDAV, Exchange, Google, Yahoo!, and other popular formats. A discussion of these advanced features is beyond the scope of this book; consult iCal help for more information.

TIP You must have a connection to the Internet to publish or subscribe to a calendar.

To publish a calendar:

1. If necessary, display the Calendar list.

2. Select the calendar you want to publish **A**.

3. Choose Calendar > Publish **B**.

   The publish calendar dialog appears **C**.

4. Set options as desired:

   ▸ **Publish calendar as** is the name of the calendar as it will be published.

   ▸ **Publish on** enables you to specify whether the calendar should be published on your MobileMe account or on a private server. If you choose a private server, the dialog expands to offer more options **D**.

A Select the calendar you want to publish.

B The Calendar menu includes commands to Subscribe to and Publish a calendar.

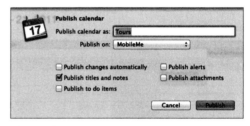

C These are the options for publishing to MobileMe...

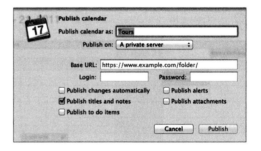

D ...and these are the options for publishing to a private server.

E This dialog appears when your calendar has been published.

F iCal can generate an email message with information about accessing the calendar online.

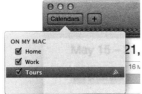

G A broadcast icon appears beside the name of a calendar that has been published.

TIP Your Mac must be configured for a MobileMe account (page 536) to publish a calendar on MobileMe.

TIP In the Calendar list, a broadcast icon appears beside the name of a calendar that has been published **G**.

TIP In step 3, if you choose not to automatically update the calendar, you can do so manually. Select the calendar in the Calendar list and choose Calendar > Refresh or press Command-R.

▸ **Base URL** is the Web address for accessing your calendar. This option only appears if you are publishing to a private server.

▸ **Login and Password** is your login information for the server you are publishing on. These options only appears if you are publishing to a private server.

▸ **Publish changes automatically** updates the calendar online whenever you make changes to it in iCal.

▸ **Publish titles and notes** includes event or item names and notes in the published calendar.

▸ **Publish to do items** includes reminders in the published calendar.

▸ **Publish alerts** includes event or item alarms in the published calendar.

▸ **Publish attachments** includes file attachments as clickable links in the published calendar.

5. Click Publish.

6. Wait while your computer connects to the server and uploads the calendar. When the upload is complete, the Calendar Published dialog appears **E**. You have three options:

   ▸ **Visit Page** launches your Web browser, connects to the Internet, and displays the calendar page.

   ▸ **Send Mail** launches your default email application and creates a message with the calendar's access information. You can address the message and send it to people you want to inform about the calendar **F**.

   ▸ **OK** simply dismisses the dialog.

To unpublish a calendar:

1. In the Calendar list, select the calendar you want to remove from the Web.

2. Choose Calendar > Unpublish .

3. In the confirmation dialog that appears ❶, click Unpublish.

To subscribe to a calendar:

1. Choose Calendar > Subscribe ❶, or press Option-Command-S.

2. In the dialog that appears ❶, enter the URL for the calendar you want to subscribe to and click Subscribe.

3. iCal displays a dialog you can use to set subscription options ❶:

   ▸ **Name** is the name of the calendar as it should appear in your Calendar list.

   ▸ **Subscribed to** is the URL of the calendar on the Web.

   ▸ **Location** is where the calendar data is stored.

   ▸ **Remove** enables you to toggle check boxes to remove or disable alerts, attachments, and To Do items for the calendar.

   ▸ **Last updated**, which cannot be changed, indicates the date and time the calendar was last refreshed.

   ▸ **Auto-refresh** lets you set a frequency for iCal to automatically update the calendar. Choose an option based on how often you expect the calendar to change. Choosing No disables automatic refreshing.

4. Click OK.

   The calendar's events appear in the iCal window and the calendar name appears under Subscriptions in the Calendar list ❶.

❶ The Calendar menu looks like this when you select a published calendar in the Calendar list.

❶ iCal confirms that you want to unpublish a calendar.

❶ Enter the URL for the calendar you want to subscribe to in a dialog like this.

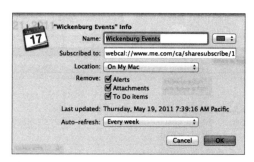

❶ iCal lets you set options for the calendars you subscribe to.

❶ The Calendars you subscribe to also appear on the Calendar list.

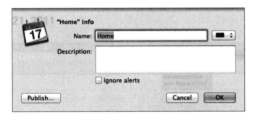

N Here are the calendar settings for an unpublished calendar.

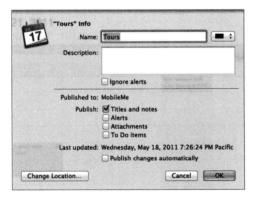

O These are the settings for a published calendar.

M With a calendar selected, choose Get Info from the Edit menu.

TIP You cannot add, modify, or delete events on a calendar that you subscribe to.

TIP To manually update the contents of a calendar you have subscribed to, select the name of the calendar in the Calendar list and choose **Calendar > Refresh H** or press Command-R.

TIP To unsubscribe from a calendar, delete it from the Subscriptions list (page 233).

TIP To find more calendars you can subscribe to, choose **Calendar > Find Subscriptions H**. This launches your Web browser and takes you to Apple's website, where you can find everything from Apple Store events to professional sports game dates.

To modify calendar settings:

1. In the Calendar list, select the calendar you want to modify settings for.

2. Choose Edit > Get Info **M**, or press Command-I.

   A dialog appears. The options it offers varies depending on whether the calendar is unpublished **N**, published **O**, or subscribed to **K**.

3. Set options as desired:

   ▸ **Name K N O** is the name of the calendar as it appears in iCal.

   ▸ **Description N O** is a description of the calendar.

   ▸ **Ignore alerts N** tells iCal to ignore any alerts associated with the calendar.

   ▸ **Published to O** is the location the calendar is published to.

   ▸ **Publish O** enables you to toggle check boxes to publish titles and notes, alerts, attachments, and to do items with the calendar.

continues on next page

- **Last updated (K)(O)**, which cannot be changed, indicates the last time the calendar was refreshed.

- **Publish changes automatically (O)** refreshes the calendar each time you make a changes to it.

- **Subscribed to (K)** is the URL of the calendar on the Web.

- **Location (K)** is where the calendar data is stored.

- **Remove (K)** enables you to toggle check boxes to remove or disable alerts, attachments, and to do items for the calendar.

- **Auto-refresh (K)** enables you to set a frequency for iCal to refresh the calendar automatically. Choose an option based on how often you expect the calendar to change. Choosing No disables automatic refreshing.

4. Click OK to save your changes.

TIP To publish an unpublished calendar, you can click the Publish button in its info window **(N)**. Consult the section titled "To publish a calendar" on page 234 for more information.

TIP To change the location of a published calendar, click the Change Location button in its info window **(O)**. Consult the section titled "To publish a calendar" on page 234 for more information.

Music & Video Applications

Mac OS X comes with three applications that enable you to enjoy music and video on your Mac:

- **iTunes** lets you play audio and video files, as well as purchase or rent content to listen to or watch on your Mac.

- **QuickTime Player** enables you to view, record, edit, and share QuickTime-compatible media files.

- **DVD Player** allows you to play movies and other video stored on DVD media on your Mac.

This chapter introduces these three applications and explains how you can get started using them to play and share music and video on your Mac.

In This Chapter

iTunes

iTunes is a digital media application that enables you to do several things:

- Play digital audio files saved in a variety of common audio file formats.
- Encode music from audio CDs on your Macintosh in a variety of audio file formats.
- Organize music into playlists.
- Buy music, audio books, television shows, movies, and iOS apps from the iTunes Store.
- Subscribe to and listen to podcasts.
- Download free educational content from iTunes U.
- Save digital audio files in AAC and MP3 format.
- Create custom CDs of your favorite music.
- Listen to Internet-based radio stations.
- Share your iTunes library with other users on your local network.
- Play video content via AppleTV.
- Sync content and apps with your iPod, iPhone, or iPad.

This part of the chapter explains how you can get started using iTunes to manage, buy, and play music and other media files.

TIP iTunes supports the following audio file formats: AAC, AIFF, Apple Lossless, MP3, MPEG-4, AAC (.m4a), and WAV.

TIP You can learn a lot more about all of iTunes' features at www.apple.com/itunes/features/.

A The iTunes application icon.

iTunes

B The iTunes window before you have stored any media files.

C iTunes includes access to a number of video tutorials that can help you learn more about it.

To launch iTunes:

1. Use one of the following techniques:

▸ Open the iTunes application icon **A** in the Applications folder window (page 147).

▸ Click the iTunes icon in Launchpad (page 150).

▸ Click the iTunes icon in the Dock (page 38).

2. If you are opening iTunes for the first time, a license agreement window appears. You must click Accept to use iTunes.

3. If you are opening iTunes for the first time, two iTunes windows appear:

▸ The main iTunes window **B** displays some general information about iTunes. Once you have begun storing media files in iTunes, this window will display that media.

▸ The iTunes Tutorials window **C** offers access to video tutorials to help you learn how to use iTunes. You can always display this window by choosing Help > iTunes Tutorials.

To quit iTunes:

Choose iTunes > Quit iTunes, or press Command-Q.

iTunes quits. Any changes you made to playlists or other settings are automatically saved.

To add songs from an audio CD to the iTunes Library:

1. Insert an audio CD in your CD drive.

   A few things may happen:

   - If your computer has access to the Internet, it goes online to get CD song information.

   - The CD's name appears in the source list and a list of its tracks appears in the song list **D**.

   - A dialog offers to import the songs **E**.

2. Do one of the following:

   - If the import dialog appeared **E**, click Yes to start the import.

   - If the import dialog did not appear, in the song list, turn on the check box beside each song you want to add and click the Import CD button at the bottom of the window.

   iTunes begins importing the songs on the CD. The status area provides progress information **F**. The songs may play while they are imported. When iTunes is finished importing songs, it plays a sound.

3. Click the eject button beside the CD name in the source list **D** to eject the disc.

TIP Please observe copyright law and only import music you own into iTunes.

TIP You can specify an import format by setting iTunes preferences. Choose iTunes > Preferences, click the General button, and then click the Import Settings button to get started.

D iTunes displays the CD in the Devices list and a list of the songs it contains in the song list.

E iTunes displays a dialog asking if you want to import the CD.

F The status area at the top of the iTunes window reports import progress.

G Drag the icon for a music file from a Finder window into the iTunes window.

H The song you dragged is imported into iTunes.

I Here's an iTunes music library displayed in grid view with album artwork downloaded by iTunes.

To import music files on disk to the Library:

Drag the icon for the music file from the desktop or a Finder window to the iTunes window's Library list **G**.

After a moment, the song appears in the Library window **H**.

TIP You can use this technique to add several music files or folders full of music files at once. Simply select their icons and drag any one of them into the window.

TIP You can also import music with the Add to Library command on the iTunes File menu. Personally, I think the drag-and-drop technique is quicker and easier.

To get album art:

1. Choose Advanced > Get Album Artwork.

2. If a dialog prompts you to sign into your iTunes Store account, click OK, choose Store > Sign In, and use the dialog that appears to sign in to the iTunes store. Then repeat step 1.

3. If a dialog ask if you're sure you want to get album artwork, click Get Album Artwork.

   iTunes goes online to search for and download missing album artwork for your iTunes library. When it's finished, it displays the artwork it's found with the album information in the song list **I**.

TIP You can use this feature to ensure you have artwork to take advantage of iTunes Cover Flow view.

To browse the source list:

Click one of the items in the source list on the left side of the iTunes window to display the contents of that source:

- **Library** is a list of all the content you have stored in your iTunes library. Categories within this area can include Music ⓙ, Movies, TV Shows, Podcasts, iTunes U, Books, Apps, Ringtones, and Radio.

- **Store** displays iTunes Store related items, including the iTunes Store ⓚ, Ping, and Downloads. You must have an Apple ID to use iTunes Store features.

- **Devices** displays iTunes-compatible devices connected to your computer, including inserted CDs ⓑ and iOS devices.

- **Shared** displays content available via network from a shared library.

- **Genius** displays playlists created for you by the Genius feature ⓛ, which creates playlists and mixes from your iTunes music library and suggests music you might like. You must have an Apple ID and turn on the Genius feature to use it; click Genius and follow the instructions that appear.

- **Playlists** displays the iTunes DJ feature, which automatically chooses songs to play from your iTunes music library, as well as any smart or regular playlists you may have created.

TIP Some features, such as the iTunes Store and Radio, require access to the internet to use.

ⓙ Your Music library includes all the music stored in iTunes. Here's what it looks like in Album list view.

ⓚ The iTunes Store is a great source of content for iTunes.

ⓛ The Genius feature can create playlists of similar songs. Here's what a Genius mix looks like in Cover Flow view.

Song list, Album list, Grid, Cover Flow

M The view buttons.

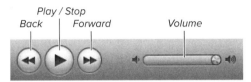

Back, Play / Stop, Forward, Volume

N Buttons at the top of the iTunes window let you control play and volume.

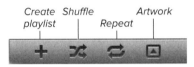

Create playlist, Shuffle, Repeat, Artwork

O Use buttons beneath the source list to add playlists, control play order and repeating, and display artwork or the movie viewer.

P You'll need to authorize your computer to play protected songs purchased from the iTunes store. (Yes, I did buy "Valley Girl" by Frank Zappa. Gonna make somethin' of it?)

To change the window view:

Click one of the view icons at the top of the iTunes window to change the view of items you are browsing:

- Song list view displays a list of songs.
- Album list view **J** displays a list of albums and, within each album group, the album's songs.
- Grid view **I** displays music by album cover.
- Cover Flow view **L** displays content in a split pane view, with artwork in the top pane and a list in the bottom pane.

To play content:

1. In the source list, select the source of the content you want to play.

    Individual items appear in the main part of the window **I J K L**.

2. Double-click the item you want to play.

    iTunes begins playing what you double-clicked.

TIP When you play music, iTunes automatically plays all music in the list that was displayed when you started playing.

TIP You can use buttons at the top of the iTunes window **M** to control play and volume.

TIP You can use buttons at the bottom of the source list **O** to work with the list and change the way music is played.

TIP To listen to protected songs purchased from the iTunes Store or accessible via shared library, you may have to authorize your computer. If so, a dialog will appear **P**; enter the account name and password for the owner of the music and click Authorize. You only need to do this once on your computer to listen to protected music. You can authorize up to five computers to play the protected songs you purchase.

To create a playlist:

1. Use one of following techniques:

   ▸ Click the New Playlist button beneath the source list .

   ▸ Choose File > New Playlist.

   ▸ Press Command-N.

   A new untitled playlist appears in the Playlist area of the source list **Q**.

2. Type a name for the playlist, and press Return to save it.

Q A new playlist appears at the bottom of the Playlists area in the source list.

To add songs to a playlist:

1. If necessary, select the source of the music you want to add to the playlist.

2. Drag a song from the song list to the playlist name in the source list **R**.

3. Repeat step 2 for each song you want to add to the playlist.

4. When you're finished adding songs, click the playlist name.

   The songs appear in the list.

R Drag a song from the song list to the playlist.

> **TIP** In step 2, you can hold down the Command key while selecting songs to select more than one and then drag them to the playlist.

To remove a song from a playlist:

1. In the source list, select the playlist you want to modify.

2. In the song list, select the song you want to remove.

3. Press Delete.

4. If a confirmation dialog appears, click Remove.

   The song is removed from the playlist.

> **TIP** Removing a song from a playlist does not remove it from the iTunes Library.

S The Smart Playlist dialog starts off like this.

T Here's an example of smart playlist settings with two criteria.

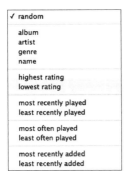

U Use this pop-up menu to specify how iTunes should select songs when you limit the selection.

V Here's the smart playlist showing the results of my criteria **T**.

To create a smart playlist:

1. Choose File > New Smart Playlist or press Option-Command-N to display the Smart Playlist dialog **S**.

2. Choose an option from the first pop-up menu, which includes all data fields that iTunes tracks for each item. Then set criteria using options on that line.

3. To add additional matching criteria, click the + button. The dialog expands to offer an additional line for criteria. Set criteria as desired in this line **T**. You can repeat this step to set all criteria.

4. If you set up multiple criteria in step 3, choose an option from the Match pop-up menu: **All** matches all criteria you set and **Any** matches any criteria.

5. To limit the size of the playlist, turn on the Limit to check box, choose an option from the pop-up menu: minutes, hours, MB, GN, or items. Then enter a value in the box beside it. You can also use the selected by pop-up menu **U** to specify how songs should be chosen.

6. To include only songs that are checked in the song list, turn on the Match only checked items check box.

7. To automatically update the playlist each time songs are added or removed from the Library, turn on the Live updating check box.

8. Click OK.

   A new smart playlist appears in the source list with a suggested name based on what you entered. When the list is selected, you can see the songs iTunes selected **V**.

To delete a playlist:

1. In the source window, select the playlist you want to delete.

2. Press the Delete key.

3. If a confirmation dialog appears, click Delete.

   The playlist is removed.

TIP Deleting a playlist does not delete the songs on the playlist from your music library.

To create a Genius playlist:

1. If the Genius feature has not already been enabled, choose Store > Turn on Genius. Then follow the instructions that appear onscreen to turn it on.

2. Select or play any song in your library.

3. Click the Start Genius button in the lower-right corner of the iTunes window.

   iTunes displays the Genius playlist, with a list of 25 songs it thinks are a good match for the one you selected ⑥.

4. Play the playlist like any other playlist.

To save iTunes songs as audio files:

Drag the name of the song you want to export from the iTunes Library window to the desktop or a Finder window **W**.

After a moment, an audio file icon for the exported song appears in the Finder **X**.

TIP You can use this technique to export a bunch of audio files at once. Simply hold down the Command key while clicking each song you want to select. Then drag any one of them to the Finder window.

TIP Audio export format is determined by Import Settings in iTunes preferences. Choose iTunes > Preferences, click the General button, and then click Import Settings to get started.

W Drag the song file from the iTunes window into a Finder window.

X The song is exported as an audio file.

Y The Burn Settings dialog offers options for burning a CD from within iTunes.

To burn iTunes content to disc:

1. Create a playlist that contains the content you want to include on the disc.

2. Select the playlist.

3. Choose File > Burn Playlist to Disc.

4. In the Burn Settings dialog that appears **Y**, set options as desired:

   ▸ **Preferred Speed** is the burn speed. Options vary depending on your CD/DVD writer.

   ▸ **Disc Format** enables you to choose from three formats: Audio CD, which will play in any CD player; MP3 CD which will play in any CD player that supports MP3 CDs, including your computer; and Data CD or DVD, which stores the files as data. If you select Audio CD, you can set additional options.

5. Click Burn.

6. When prompted, insert a blank disc.

7. Wait while iTunes prepares and burns the disc.

   A progress indicator appears at the top of the iTunes window as it works. When iTunes is finished, it makes a sound and the disc icon appears on your desktop.

TIP Your computer must have a compatible CD-R drive or SuperDrive to burn audio CDs or data to CD or DVD. You can learn more about burning CDs and DVDs on page 118.

TIP If you are creating an audio CD and the playlist you have selected won't fit on a single disc, iTunes offers to split the songs over multiple CDs.

TIP You cannot burn an audio or MP3 CD containing protected audio files.

To share content with other network users:

1. Choose iTunes > Preferences.

2. Click the Sharing button to display Sharing preferences 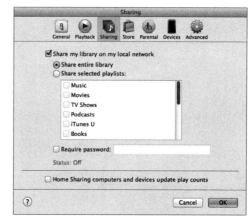.

3. To share your iTunes content with other network users, turn on the Share my library on my local network check box. Then select one of the radio buttons:

   ▸ **Share entire library** shares all of your music.

   ▸ **Share selected playlists** enables you to toggle check boxes for individual playlists you want to share.

4. To require other network users to enter a password to listen to your music, turn on the Require password check box and enter a password in the box.

5. To allow devices sharing your music to update song play counts, turn on the Home Sharing computer and devices update play counts check box.

6. Click OK.

7. A dialog reminding you that sharing music is for personal use only may appear. Click OK.

TIP Once sharing is enabled, the Status area in the Sharing preferences dialog reports whether your music is being accessed by other users on the network **Z**.

TIP You can learn more about networking and sharing files with Mac OS in Part V of this book.

Z Use the Sharing preferences window within iTunes to set music sharing options.

The QuickTime
Player icon.

QuickTime Player

QuickTime Player

QuickTime is a video and audio technology developed by Apple Inc. It is widely used for digital movies as well as for streaming audio and video available via the Internet.

QuickTime Player is an application you can use to:

- View QuickTime movies and streaming Internet content.

- Create your own audio, video, and screencast recordings.

- Share your QuickTime files on a variety of Internet services.

TIP To share content on MobileMe, YouTube, Vimeo, Flickr, or Facebook, you must have an account on the service you want to use.

TIP You can learn more about QuickTime technology on Apple's QuickTime Web site, www.apple.com/quicktime/.

To launch QuickTime Player:

Use one of the following techniques:

- Open the QuickTime Player application icon **A** in the Applications folder window (page 147).

- Click the QuickTime Player icon in Launchpad (page 150).

- Open a QuickTime-compatible audio or video file.

Because QuickTime Player supports OS X Lion's new Auto Save feature, the movie files that were open when you last quit QuickTime are automatically reopened. In addition, if you launched QuickTime Player by opening a QuickTime-compatible file, that file opens.

TIP QuickTime Player supports the new full-screen apps feature of OS X Lion.

To quit QuickTime Player:

Choose QuickTime Player > Quit Quick-Time Player, or press Command-Q.

QuickTime Player quits. Any changes to open files are automatically saved. The files that were open when you Quit are automatically reopened the next time you launch QuickTime Player.

To open a QuickTime movie file:

Use one of the following techniques:

- Double-click a QuickTime movie file icon **B**.

- Drag the icon for a QuickTime movie onto the QuickTime Player icon in the Applications folder window.

If QuickTime Player is not already running, it launches. The movie's first frame appears in a window **C**.

TIP You can also open a QuickTime movie by using the Open File command on QuickTime Player's File menu. You can learn more about opening documents from within applications on page 164.

TIP If you point to a QuickTime movie's document icon, a play button appears **D**. Clicking that button plays the movie in its icon using enhanced icon view (page 26). This technique also works in the Finder's column view (page 65) and in the Info window (page 94) for a QuickTime movie.

B A QuickTime-compatible movie file's icon normally displays a preview frame from its movie.

Phoenix to Lake
   Powell.m4v

C QuickTime's no-nonsense window hides all controls until you need them.

D Pointing to a QuickTime-compatible movie file's icon displays a play button you can click to play the movie right in its icon.

Phoenix to Lake
   Powell.m4v

E When you point to a movie window, a title bar and movie controls appear.

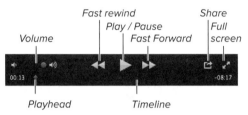

F QuickTime's movie controls.

G Use the Share pop-up menu to share a movie with friends.

View

Enter Full Screen	⌘F
Float on Top	
✓ Actual Size	⌘1
Fit to Screen	⌘3
Fill Screen	⌘4
Panoramic	⌘5
Increase Size	⌘+
Decrease Size	⌘−
Show Closed Captioning	⌥⌘T
Languages	▶
Subtitles	▶
Show Chapters	⌘R
Next Chapter	⇧⌘→
Previous Chapter	⇧⌘←
Show Clips	⌘E
Show Audio Track	⌘U
Loop	⌥⌘L

H The View menu offers options for changing the size of the movie window.

To control movie play:

When you point to a QuickTime Player window, a group of buttons and controls appears **E F**. Use them to control movie play:

- **Volume** changes movie volume; drag the slider left or right or click the volume icon to mute/unmute.

- **Fast rewind** plays the movie backward quickly, with sound.

- **Play** starts playing the movie. When the movie is playing, the Play button turns to a **Pause** button, which pauses movie play.

- **Fast Forward** plays the movie forward quickly, with sound.

- **Share** displays a menu you can use to copy the movie to iTunes or share it online with others **G**.

- **Full screen** toggles between normal and full screen view.

- **Timeline** tracks movie progress. By dragging the **Playhead**, you can quickly move or "scrub" to a specific scene in the movie.

TIP Each time you click the fast rewind or fast forward button, the speed is increased up to 8x normal speed. To play at normal speed, click the Play button.

TIP You can drag the play controls to another location within the QuickTime Player window.

To specify movie size:

Select a size option from the View menu **H**. The size of the movie's window changes accordingly.

To record a movie with QuickTime Player:

1. Choose File > New Movie Recording or press Option-Command-N.

   QuickTime Player displays a Movie Recording window , using the video input from your computer's built-in FaceTime camera or another compatible camera connected to your computer.

2. Click the red Record button to begin recording your movie.

   A timer appears on the bottom-left corner of the control area and the volume level bar shows how well QuickTime Player can "hear" you **J**.

3. To stop recording, click the Stop button. (If the Stop button isn't showing, move the pointer to the window to display it.)

   QuickTime Player saves the movie in your Movies folder. The movie remains open so you can play it.

TIP Clicking the Options button in the Movie Recording window displays a menu with options for fine-tuning movie settings **K**.

TIP You can use similar techniques to record audio or to make a movie of what appears on your computer screen as you work. Just start with commands under the File menu: **New Audio Recording** or **New Screen Recording.** The controls that appears are very similar to those that appear when you record a movie.

I A Movie Recording window shows anything in front of the camera. (I knew I should have tried makeup this morning.)

J These are the controls in the Movie Recording window while a movie is being recorded. Note the movie length timer, sound level, and movie file size information that is displayed along the bottom of the controls.

K You can use this pop-up menu to set options for your movie.

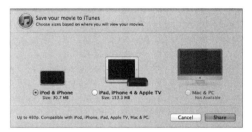

L The Share menu offers several ways to share your movies with friends (and strangers).

M For some types of sharing, such as sharing to iTunes, QuickTime Player will ask what size you prefer.

N For some types of sharing, such as sharing on YouTube, QuickTime Player will prompt you for sign in information.

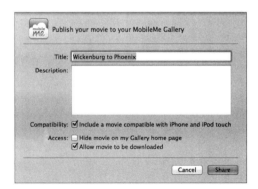

O For some types of sharing, such as sharing via a MobileMe Gallery, QuickTime Player will prompt you for descriptive information.

To share movies:

1. If necessary, open the movie you want to share.

2. Choose an option from the Share menu on the menu bar **L** or in the QuickTime Player window **G**:

   ▸ **iTunes** adds the movie to your iTunes library. Once there, you can watch it in iTunes or an Apple TV or copy it to an iPad, iPod, or iPhone.

   ▸ **MobileMe Gallery** saves the movie to your MobileMe account.

   ▸ **YouTube**, **Vimeo**, **Flickr**, or **Facebook** saves the movie to your account on one of these services.

   ▸ **Mail** saves the movie and attaches it to an email message you can send to others.

3. What happens next depends on which option you chose. QuickTime Player may prompt you to do any combination of the following things:

   ▸ **Specify a file size M**. Normally, when sending a file out on the Internet, smaller is better. But sometimes you might want a larger size to preserve quality.

   ▸ **Sign In to your account N**. If you're sharing your movie on an online service, you'll need to sign in so Quick-Time Player can upload it.

   ▸ **Provide descriptive information O**. Some services will include a video name, description, category, and/or key words with your movie.

   Follow the prompts that appear onscreen to set options and provide information.

continues on next page

4. When you're finished entering all required information, click the Share button in the last dialog.

QuickTime Player exports the movie in a compatible format. This could take some time, depending on the speed of your computer and the size of the movie.

What happens next depends on the share option you chose:

▸ For movies shared via iTunes, the exported movie is automatically copied into iTunes.

▸ For movies shared via one of the online services, the movie is automatically uploaded to that service.

▸ For movies shared via mail, Quick-Time Player launches your default email application, creates a new message, and attaches the exported file to it. All you need to do is address and send the message.

TIP Some online services have limits on length or size of movies they will accept. QuickTime Player will warn you if your movie is longer or bigger than what they service you selected accepts.

TIP Please respect all copyrights and terms of service when sharing movies with friends and online.

DVD Player

DVD Player is a simple application that enables you to play DVD-video discs on your Mac. All you need is an optical drive capable of reading DVD media, and DVD Player does the rest.

To launch DVD Player:

Insert a DVD-Video disc into your Mac.

DVD Player should launch and do one of two things:

- Display a black Viewer window with a floating Controller palette **A**.
- Immediately begin DVD play **B**.

If DVD Player does not launch at all, then use one of the following techniques to open it:

- Open the DVD Player application icon **C** in the Applications folder window (page 147).
- Click the DVD Player icon in Launchpad (page 150).

A If DVD Player hasn't loaded a movie, it'll display a black player window with is floating controller palette.

B What's more likely is that DVD Player will simply begin playing the movie. (Now *this* is a classic.)

C The DVD Player application icon.

DVD Player

TIP If a Drive Region Code dialog appears the first time you play a DVD-Video, click the Set Drive Region button to set DVD Player's region to match that of the disc you inserted. Then click OK to dismiss the confirmation dialog that appears.

To quit DVD Player:

Choose DVD Player > Quit DVD Player (the menu appears, if necessary, when you point to it), or press Command-Q.

DVD Player quits.

To display the Controller:

Use one of the following techniques:

- Move the mouse or drag your finger across the trackpad while the DVD is playing.

- Choose Window > Show Controller (the menu appears, if necessary, when you point to it), or press Control-Command-C.

The Controller appears **D** **E**.

To show or hide additional DVD controls on the Controller **E**, double-click the pair of tiny lines on the right end of the Controller.

To control DVD play:

Use one of the following techniques:

- Click buttons on the Controller **D** **E**.

- Choose a command from the Controls menu **F**.

TIP The Pause command on the Controls menu **F** changes into a Play command when a DVD is not playing.

To resize the Viewer window:

Choose an option from the View menu **G** or press the corresponding shortcut key.

DVD menu controls | Title/Chapter indicator | Go to DVD Menu | Go to Title Menu | Eject Disc

Rewind | Stop | Volume
Play/Pause | Fast Forward

D DVD Player's Controller.

E The Controller, expanded to show additional control buttons. Point to a button to learn its name.

Controls	
Pause	Space bar
Stop	⌘.
Slow Motion	⌥⇧→
Scan Forward	⇧⌘→
Scan Backwards	⇧⌘←
Scan Rate	▶
Slow Motion Rate	▶
Volume Up	⌘↑
Volume Down	⌘↓
Mute	⌥⌘↓
Timer	▶
New Bookmark...	⌘=
Use Current Frame as Jacket Picture	
Close Control Drawer	⌘]
Eject DVD	⌘E

F You can use the Controls menu to control DVD play.

View	
Half Size	⌘0
Actual Size	⌘1
Double Size	⌘2
Fit to Screen	⌘3
Enter Full Screen	⌘F
Deinterlace	▶
Viewer Above Other Apps	

G The View menu offers options for changing the size of the viewer window.

Other Mac OS X Applications

In addition to the applications discussed in detail in various places throughout this book, Mac OS X includes a variety of more basic applications that you can use to perform tasks on your computer.

This chapter provides instructions for getting started with applications you can find in the Applications folder on your hard disk. Among these, you'll find applications for performing calculations, working with images and PDF files, looking up words, taking notes, and even challenging your computer to a nice game of chess.

You can find a complete list of the applications that are part of a standard OS X Lion installation—along with chapter references where you can learn more about each one—on page 143.

In This Chapter:

Calculator

Calculator displays a simple calculator that can perform addition, subtraction, multiplication, and division, as well as complex mathematical calculations and conversions.

TIP If you use the Calculator application often, you might be interested in the Calculator widget (page 288), which is part of the Mac OS X Dashboard (Chapter 19).

To launch Calculator:

Use one of the following techniques:

- Open the Calculator icon **A** in the Applications folder window (page 147).
- Click the Calculator icon in Launchpad (page 150).

The Calculator window appears **B**.

To quit Calculator:

When you're finished using Calculator, use one of the following techniques to quit:

- Choose Calculator > Quit Calculator, or press Command-Q.
- Click the Calculator window's close button.

To perform basic calculations:

Use any combination of the following techniques:

- Use your mouse or trackpad to click buttons for numbers and operators.
- Press keyboard keys corresponding to numbers and operators.

The numbers you enter and the results of your calculations appear at the top of the Calculator window **B**.

A Calculator's application icon.

Calculator

B Calculator looks and works like the calculator on your cell phone.

C Calculator's Window menu.

D The Paper Tape window makes it easy to keep track of your entries.

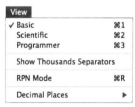
E Calculator's View menu enables you to choose a different type of calculator.

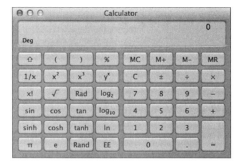

F The Scientific calculator.

G The Programmer calculator.

H The Basic calculator with Reverse Polish Notation turned on.

To keep track of your entries:

Choose Window > Show Paper Tape **C**, or press Command-T.

The Paper Tape window appears. It displays your entries as you make them **D**.

TIP To hide the Paper Tape window, choose Window > Hide Paper Tape, press Command-T. or click the Paper Tape window's close button.

TIP To start with a fresh tape, click the Clear button.

TIP You can use commands under the File menu to save or print the paper tape.

To use other kinds of calculators:

Choose a command from the View menu **E** to choose the type of calculator you want to work with:

- **Basic** (Command-1) is the basic calculator **B**.

- **Scientific** (Command-2) is a calculator with scientific functions **F**.

- **Programmer** (Command-3) is a calculator with functions and features of interest to programmers **G**.

- **RPN Mode** (Command-R) enables Reverse Polish Notation for the currently displayed calculator. Note that the letters RPN appear on the calculator when this feature is enabled **H**.

TIP Reverse Polish Notation, or RPN, is an alternative format for entering calculations. It is commonly used on Hewlett-Packard brand calculators. (If you don't know what RPN is, you probably don't want to use it.)

To perform conversions:

1. Enter the value you want to convert.

2. Choose the conversion you want from the Convert menu **I**.

3. In the dialog that appears **J**, set options for the conversion you want to perform.

4. Click Convert.

   The original value you entered is converted and appears at the top of the Calculator window.

TIP The Convert menu's Recent Conversions submenu makes it easy to repeat conversions you have done recently.

I Use the Convert menu to choose a type of conversion.

J In the dialog that appears, enter specifics about the units you want to convert from and to.

A The Chess application icon.

Chess

B The Chess window displays a colorful, three-dimensional chess board.

Chess

Chess is a computerized version of the classic strategy game of chess. You can play against the computer or a friend. If you play against the computer, your pieces are white and you go first; the computer's pieces are black.

TIP Chess is one of the Mac OS X applications that supports the full screen apps (page 152) and Auto Save (page 154) features.

To launch Chess:

Use one of the following techniques:

- Open the Chess icon **A** in the Applications folder window (page 147).

- Click the Chess icon in Launchpad (page 150).

The Chess window appears **B**.

To quit Chess:

Choose Chess > Quit Chess, or press Command-Q.

To move a chess piece:

Drag the piece onto any valid square on the playing board.

TIP The computer moves automatically after each of your moves.

TIP If you attempt to make an invalid move, an alert sounds and the piece returns to where it was.

TIP If Speakable Items is enabled (page 572), you can use spoken commands to move chess pieces.

To start a new game:

1. Choose Game > New , or press Command-N.

   The Start a New Game dialog appears **D**.

2. Choose an option from the Players pop-up menu **E**.

3. If desired, choose an option from the Variant pop-up menu **F**.

4. Click Start.

C The Game menu for Chess.

D Set options in this dialog to begin a new game.

E F The Players (top) and Variant (bottom) pop-up menus enable you to customize a new game.

Ⓐ The Dictionary application icon.

Dictionary

Ⓑ The DIctionary application window, right after launching Dictionary.

Ⓒ Dictionary begins displaying search results immediately.

Dictionary

Dictionary is like a reference library with all the features of a dictionary, thesaurus, and encyclopedia—but without all that paper. You can use it to get word definitions, pronunciations, and synonyms, as well as information from Wikipedia.

TIP If you use the Dictionary application often, you might be interested in the Dictionary widget (page 288), which is part of the Mac OS X Dashboard (Chapter 19).

To launch Dictionary:

Use one of the following techniques:

- Open the Dictionary icon **Ⓐ** in the Applications folder window (page 147).
- Click the Dictionary icon in Launchpad (page 150).

The Dictionary window appears **Ⓑ**.

To quit Dictionary:

Use one of the following techniques:

- Choose Dictionary > Quit Dictionary, or press Command-Q.
- Click the Dictionary window's close button.

To look up a word or phrase:

1. Near the top of the Dictionary window **Ⓑ**, click the button for the reference you want to search:
   - ▸ **All** searches all references.
   - ▸ **Dictionary** searches the *New Oxford American Dictionary*. Use this option to look up pronunciations and definitions.

continues on next page

- ▸ **Thesaurus** searches the *Oxford American Writer's Thesaurus*. Use this option to look up synonyms.
- ▸ **Apple** searches the *Apple Dictionary*. Use this option to look up Apple-related terms.
- ▸ **Wikipedia** searches the Wikipedia online encyclopedia. Use this option to look up more detailed information than what you'd find in a dictionary.

2. Enter the word or phrase you want to look up in the search box at the top of the Dictionary window.

   As you type, Dictionary begins displaying a list of matches **C**.

3. Double-click the word or phrase that interests you.

   The window displays information for that entry from the reference you selected in step 1 **D E F**.

TIP To change the size of font characters in the Dictionary window, click one of the font size buttons in the window's toolbar.

TIP To print an entry, choose File > Print. You can learn more about printing in Chapter 22.

TIP You can click a word in an entry to look up that word, too.

D The definition of a selected word appears in Dictionary's window.

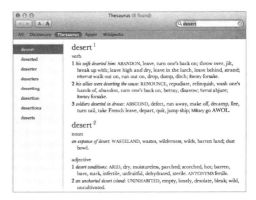

E Here are the synonym entries for the same word in Dictionary's Thesaurus.

F And here's the Wikipedia entry for the same word.

A Image
Capture's icon.

Image Capture

B The Image Capture window with two devices connected but neither selected.

Image Capture

Image Capture is an application that performs three functions:

- Import image files from a digital camera to your computer's hard disk.
- Operate your scanner to scan and save images.
- Share images from a camera on a website or in a slide show.

In this part of the chapter, I explain how to import images from a digital camera and scan a document with Image Capture.

TIP Some devices require that driver software be installed on Mac OS X before the camera or scanner can be used. Consult the documentation that came with your scanner or camera or check the device manufacturer's website for Mac OS X compatibility and driver information.

TIP Not all devices are compatible with Image Capture. Generally speaking, if Image Capture does not "see" your camera or scanner when it is connected and turned on, the camera or scanner is probably not compatible.

TIP If you have Apple's iLife suite of products, you can also import images from a digital camera using iPhoto, which offers additional features for managing photos saved to disk.

To launch Image Capture:

Use one of the following techniques:

- Open the Image Capture icon **A** in the Applications folder window (page 147).
- Click the Image Capture icon in Launchpad (page 150).

The Image Capture window appears **B**.

TIP Image Capture may also open automatically when you connect a scanner or camera or insert a media card in your computer or connected card reader.

To quit Image Capture:

Use one of the following techniques:

- Choose Image Capture > Quit Image Capture, or press Command-Q.

- Click the Image Capture window's close button.

To download images from a digital camera or media card:

1. Do one of the following:

  ▶ Attach your digital camera to your computer's USB or FireWire port, using the applicable cable. Then turn the camera on and, if necessary, set it to review mode.

  ▶ Insert your camera's media card into a USB card reader and plug the reader into one of your computer's USB ports.

  ▶ Insert your camera's SD card in your computer's SD card slot.

2. If necessary, select your camera or media card in the Devices list.

  Thumbnail images of the photos on the camera or card appear in the window **C**.

3. Use the Import To pop-up menu at the bottom of the window to select the location you want to import images to. There are four groups of options **D**:

  ▶ Folders that are commonly used for storing downloaded items or images.

  ▶ Applications that can open images.

  ▶ Tasks you can use to automate the creation of a webpage or PDF file of the imported images.

  ▶ Other enables you to choose a disk location or application for saving or opening the images.

C Image Capture displays thumbnail images of the photos it finds on the device. In this example, I've attached an SD card reader from my camera to my Mac via USB.

D Use this pop-up menu to specify where you want to import images to.

E A progress indicator appears as images are copied to your computer.

For this example, I chose the default option, which is the Pictures folder in the Home folder.

4. Do one of the following:

   ▶ To import all images, click the Import All button.

   ▶ To import some of the images on the camera, select the images you want to import and click the Import button. (You can hold down the Command key while clicking each image you want to add it to the selection.)

   A progress indicator appears while the photos are imported **E**. When it disappears, the import is complete; check marks appear beside each imported photo.

5. If necessary, click the Eject icon beside the camera or media card name in the Devices list before disconnecting or removing it.

TIP If iPhoto is installed on your computer, it may launch instead of Image Capture when you connect a digital camera. If so, you can quit iPhoto and launch Image Capture to use it.

TIP You can also use the thumbnail window **C** to delete images on the device. Select the images you want to delete, click the Delete button at the bottom of the window, and click Delete in the confirmation dialog that appears.

TIP You can set default actions for the selected device with options in the bottom-left corner of the Image Capture window **C**.

To scan a document:

1. Make sure your scanner is properly installed, connected, and turned on.

2. Place the document you want to scan on the scan bed.

3. Open Image Capture.

4. If necessary, select your scanner in the Devices list **F**.

5. Choose an option from the Scan Size pop-up menu **G**:

   ▸ **Detect Separate Items** is for a document with individual images on it.

   ▸ **Detect Enclosing Box** is for a document with one item that does not occupy the entire scanner bed.

   ▸ **A4** and **US** Letter are two common paper size.

6. Choose the location you want to scan the document to from the Scan To pop-up menu **H**. There are three groups of options:

   ▸ Folders that are commonly used for storing scanned documents.

   ▸ Applications that can open scanned documents.

   ▸ Other enables you to choose a disk location or application for saving or opening the scanned document.

7. Click Scan.

8. Wait while the scanner scans the document. This could take a few moments and multiple scanner passes, depending on your scanner model. You may see an Overview image as it works.

   When it's finished, an image of the document you scanned appears in the Image Capture window and the document is saved to the location you selected in step 6 **I**.

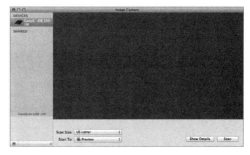

F Select the scanner in the Devices list.

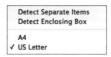

G Choose a Scan Size option.

H Use this pop-up menu to determine where images should be scanned to.

I In this example, I've scanned a photo to Preview. By double-clicking the name of the Scan in Image Capture's Scan Results window, I've opened it in Preview.

TIP Clicking the Show Details button at the bottom of the Image Capture window **F** may offer additional options for scanning a document, including resolution, type of document, and size. The options vary depending on your scanner model and installed driver software.

A The Photo Booth application icon.

Photo Booth

B Photo Booth's main window displays whatever your camera sees. (The deadline is *when*?)

Photo Booth

Photo Booth is an application that enables you to take snapshots with a FaceTime camera or digital video camera. You can take still photos or short movies and can include special effects with the photos you take. Once you've made an image, you can email it to a friend or use it as a personal icon for your Mac OS account or iChat.

To launch Photo Booth:

Use one of the following techniques:

- Open the Photo Booth icon **A** in the Applications folder window (page 147).

- Click the Photo Booth icon in Launch-pad (page 150).

- Click the Photo Booth icon in the Dock.

The Photo Booth window appears **B**.

To quit Photo Booth:

Use one of the following techniques:

- Choose Photo Booth > Quit Photo Booth, or press Command-Q.

- Click the Photo Booth window's close button.

To create a snapshot or movie:

1. Click one of the three buttons on the left side beneath the video preview:

   ▸ **Take a still picture** takes a single still photo.

   ▸ **Take four quick pictures** takes four still photos a second or so apart.

   ▸ **Take a movie clip** records a movie.

2. Click the Camera button.

   A countdown timer appears beneath the video preview **C**. When it reaches the end, one of three things happens:

   ▸ For still photos, the photo is snapped and appears as a thumbnail in the bottom of the window **D**.

   ▸ For four quick photos, four photos are snapped, one after the other. They appear in a single frame at the bottom of the window **D**.

   ▸ For a movie clip, the camera begins recording. Click the stop button to stop recording movie frames. A thumbnail of the movie appears at the bottom of the window **D**.

C Photo Booth counts down before snapping photos. (Just *once* I'd like to look presentable while writing about Photo Booth.)

D In this example, there are two single photos, one 4-shot photo, and one video. With an image selected, the buttons above the thumbnails offer options to work with the selected image.

E F The first two screens of effects apply visual effects to the image.

G Photo Booth comes with some fun backdrops, including ones suitable for video.

To include special effects or a background image in a photo:

1. Click the Effects button.

2. Click the arrow buttons on either side of the Effects button to scroll through the four screens of effects **E F G H** until you find one you like.

3. Do one of the following:

   ▸ To apply a visual effect **E F**, click to select it.

   ▸ To apply a backdrop **G H**, click to select the backdrop you want. Then move out of the frame, as instructed until the background is detected.

4. Follow the steps on the previous page to create a snapshot or movie.

TIP The fourth screen of effects **H** is for your own backdrop images. Drag the image you want to use to one of the blank spaces to add it to those available for use.

TIP To turn off an effect, choose Normal in any of the effects screens.

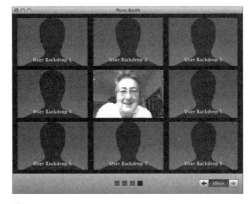

H You can use this last effects screen to add your own backdrops to Photo Booth.

To work with Photo Booth images:

1. At the bottom of the Photo Booth window, select the thumbnail for the image you want to use **D**.

2. Do one of the following:

   ▸ To use the photo as your account Picture, click the Account Picture button. Photo Booth opens the Users & Groups preferences pane (page 579) for your account and pastes in the image **I**.

   ▸ To use the photo as your iChat buddy picture, click the Buddy Picture button. Photo Booth opens iChat (page 427) and displays its Buddy Picture window. You can use the zoom slider at the bottom of the window to change the magnification of the image **J**. Click Set to save it.

   ▸ To email an image, click the Email button. Photo Booth launches your default email application and creates a new message with the image attached. Complete the form and click Send.

3. When you're finished using the application you worked with (System Preferences, iChat, or your email application), press Command-Q to quit it.

To export an photo or movie:

Drag the thumbnail image for the photo or movie into a Finder window **K**.

When you release the thumbnail, an icon for the exported item appears where you dragged it. You can then work with it like any other image or movie file.

TIP You can also choose File > Export and use the dialog that appears to choose a disk location for the exported file.

I You can use a Photo Booth image as an account picture, ...

J ...or an iChat buddy picture.

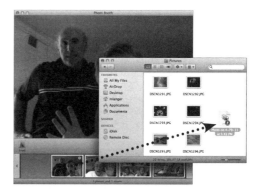

K Exporting an item is as easy as dragging its thumbnail into a Finder window.

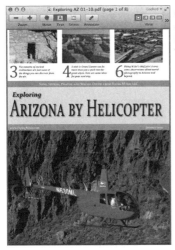

Ⓐ Preview can open PDF files like this one...

Preview

Preview is a program that enables you to open and view a variety of file types:

- **Image files Ⓐ**, including JPG, GIF, HDR, TIFF, PSD, PICT, PNG, BMP, RAW, and SGI.

- **PDF**, or **Portable Document Format**, files **Ⓑ** created with Mac OS X's Print command, Adobe Acrobat software, or other software capable of creating PDFs.

- **Microsoft Office files**, including those created with Word **Ⓐ** and Excel.

Preview also includes tools you can use to edit images and annotate images and PDFs.

TIP Preview supports the new full-screen apps (page 152) and Auto Save (page 154) features of OS X Lion.

TIP When you open PostScript (PS) or EPS format files, Preview automatically converts them to PDF files for viewing.

TIP Although you can open and view Microsoft Office files in Preview, you cannot edit them. You can, however, open and edit most Microsoft Word files in TextEdit (Chapter 14).

TIP You can also open PDF files with Adobe Reader software. You can learn more about Adobe Reader—and download a free copy of the software—on the Adobe Systems website, get.adobe.com/reader.

Ⓑ ...image files like this one, ...

Ⓒ ... and even Microsoft Word files like this one.

To launch Preview:

Use one of the following techniques:

- Open the Preview icon  in the Applications folder window (page 147).

- Click the Preview icon in Launchpad (page 150).

- Click the Preview icon in the Dock (page 38).

Any documents that were open in Preview when you last used it automatically reopen.

To quit Preview:

When you're finished using Preview, choose Preview > Quit Preview, or press Command-Q.

To open a file with Preview:

Use one of the following techniques:

- Drag the document file's icon onto the Preview icon in the Applications folder **E**.

- Right-click the file's icon and choose Preview from the Open With submenu on the contextual menu that appears **F**.

- Double-click the file icon for a Preview-compatible document. (This technique, however, might open the document in another compatible application installed on your computer.)

Preview launches and displays the file in its window **A B C**.

TIP You can also use Preview's Open command (page 164) to open any compatible file.

D The Preview application icon.

Preview

E Drag the document onto the Preview application icon.

F Choose Preview from the Open With submenu on a contextual menu (or the File menu).

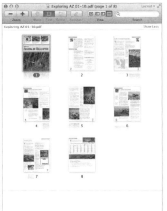

G If you open more than one image at a time in Preview, you can use thumbnails to move from one to another in the same window.

H Contact Sheet view displays thumbnail images of all pages in the document.

I You can search a PDF file for a specific word or phrase.

To change the view of a document:

Click buttons in Preview's toolbar to change the view of the document:

- **Zoom** buttons reduce and increase the size of the image in the window.

- **View** button change the window's view:

  - **Content Only** **A** shows only the document's pages.

  - **Thumbnail** **C** **G** displays clickable thumbnail images of pages.

  - **Table of Contents** displays clickable headings in a structured document.

  - **Contact Sheet** **H** displays a printable view of thumbnail images of all pages in the document.

To search for text in a PDF file:

1. Open the PDF file you want to search.

2. In the search box at the top-right corner of the window, enter a search word or phrase.

   As you type, Preview searches the document for the text you entered. It displays thumbnail images and excerpts of pages containing that text on the left side of the window. It also highlights the occurrences of the search text in the page that is displayed **I**.

3. To display a specific occurrence of the search text, click its page thumbnail. The search text is highlighted in yellow wherever it appears on that page **I**.

To select text in a PDF file:

1. On Preview's toolbar, click the Text tool button.

2. Position the pointer over text in the document window.

    The pointer turns into an I-beam pointer.

3. Press the button down and drag to select text .

TIP Once text is selected, you can use the Copy command (page 195) to copy it to the Clipboard and use it in another document.

TIP If a document is protected for copying or editing, you may not be able to select text.

To select part of a picture:

1. On Preview's toolbar, click the Select tool button.

2. Position the pointer in the upper-left corner of the area you want to select.

3. Drag down and to the right.

    A selection box appears over the image, along with an indicator that shows the size of the selection in pixels .

4. Release the button to complete the selection .

TIP Once you have selected part of a picture, you can use the Copy command (page 195) to copy it to the Clipboard for use in another document.

To crop an image:

1. Select the part of the image you want to keep .

2. Choose Tools > Crop, or press Command-K.

    The image is trimmed to the selection.

J Drag over text to select it.

K Drag a box around the part of the image you want to select.

L Release the button to complete the selection.

M The Crop command trims the image to your selection.

A The Stickies application icon.

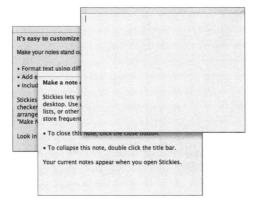
B When you first open Stickies, it displays three sticky notes, one of which is blank and all ready to use.

Stickies

Stickies is an application that displays computerized "sticky notes" that you can use to place reminders on your screen.

TIP If you use the Stickies application often, you might be interested in the Stickies widget (page 288), which is part of the Mac OS X Dashboard (Chapter 19).

To launch Stickies:

Use one of the following techniques:

- Open the Stickies icon **A** in the Applications folder window (page 147).
- Click the Stickies icon in Launchpad (page 150).

Any sticky notes that were open when you last used Stickies automatically reopen **B**.

TIP Read the text in the default Stickies windows **B** to learn more about Stickies.

To quit Stickies:

When you're finished using Stickies, choose Stickies > Quit Stickies, or press Command-Q.

TIP When you quit Stickies, all notes are automatically saved to disk and will reappear the next time you launch Stickies.

To create a new sticky note:

1. Choose File > New Note **C**, or press Command-N to display a blank new note **D**.

2. Type the text that you want to include in the note **E**.

TIP You can use options under the Color and Font menus to change the appearance of notes or note text.

To print a sticky note:

1. Click the note to activate it.

2. Choose File > Print **C** or press Command-P.

3. Use the Print dialog that appears (page 325) to set options for printing and click the Print button.

To close a sticky note:

1. Do one of the following:

   ▸ Click the sticky note's close box.

   ▸ Activate the sticky note and choose File > Close, or press Command-W.

2. In the confirmation dialog that appears **F**, click a button:

   ▸ **Don't Save** closes the note without saving its contents.

   ▸ **Cancel** leaves the note open.

   ▸ **Save** displays the Export dialog **G**, which you can use to save the note as plain or formatted text in a file on disk. Enter a name, select a disk location, choose a file format, and then click Save.

TIP Once a sticky note has been saved, it can be opened and edited with TextEdit or any other text editing application.

C The File menu in Stickies.

D Start with a blank new note.

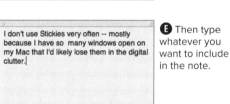

E Then type whatever you want to include in the note.

F A dialog like this appears when you close a note.

G Use the Export dialog to save the note's contents as plain or formatted text.

(19)

Dashboard

Dashboard is a feature of Mac OS X that gives you instant access to simple applications called *widgets*. Widgets work with other applications such as iTunes, iCal, and Address Book to provide you with quick access to the most commonly used features. They also work with the Internet to get up-to-date information such as stock quotes, weather, and business listings.

Mac OS X comes with a bunch of widgets, all accessible from the widget bar that you can display at the bottom of your screen. Click a widget to display and use it.

In this chapter, I explain how to use Dashboard to display the widget bar and widgets. I also tell you how to use the widget manager to add, remove, and disable widgets. Finally, I provide a brief summary of the widgets that come with Mac OS X.

In This Chapter:

Opening & Closing Dashboard

The main purpose of Dashboard is to make widgets easily accessible without interfering with your work. Apple achieves this by making Dashboard quick and easy to open and close.

To open Dashboard:

Use one of the following techniques:

- Open the Dashboard icon in the Applications folder (page 147).

- Click the Dashboard icon in the Dock (page 38).

- Click the Dashboard icon in Launchpad (page 150).

- Press F12 or, on a laptop, press fn-F12.

- On a Multi-Touch device, use three fingers to swipe to the right until Dashboard appears.

Dashboard sweeps into view from the left, displaying the last widgets you used **B**.

TIP The keyboard shortcuts provided here assume your Mac has default settings in the Mission Control preferences pane (page 494).

TIP If you have an Apple Mouse, you can use the Mouse preferences pane (page 516) to configure one of its buttons to activate Dashboard.

To close Dashboard:

Use one of the following techniques:

- In the lower-right corner of the Dashboard screen, click the Return arrow.

- Press Esc, F12, or, on a laptop, fn-F12.

- On a Multi-Touch device, use three fingers to swipe to the left.

Dashboard sweeps away to the left.

A The Dashboard application icon.

Dashboard

B By default, these four widgets are open when you first launch Dashboard.

(A) The widget bar appears at the bottom of the Dashboard screen.

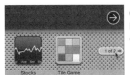

(B) Click the button at the end of the widget bar...

(C) ...to display more widgets.

Working with the Widget Bar

The widget bar gives you access to all installed widgets.

To display the widget bar:

With Dashboard open, click the + button in the lower-left corner of your screen.

A few things happen **(A)**:

- The widget bar slides up into view from the bottom of the screen.
- Close buttons appear for each widget that is open.
- The Manage Widgets button appears.

To see other installed widgets:

Click the arrow button on the left or right end of the widget bar **(B)**.

The widget bar scrolls to show more installed widgets **(C)**.

To hide the widget bar:

Click the x button near the lower-left corner of your screen.

The widget bar slides back down out of sight, leaving Dashboard ope.

Using Widgets

To use a widget, you must open it. If you want a widget to appear automatically every time you open Dashboard, you can leave it open when you close Dashboard. Otherwise, you can close the widget.

Once a widget is open, you can work with the controls and options on its face to get the information you want. Widgets tend to be simple, so in most cases, you won't need help using them.

What isn't always obvious, however, is that most widgets offer the ability to set options on their reverse side. These can control the way the widget works.

This part of the chapter explains how to open, move, and close a widget, as well as how you can flip a widget over to access options normally hidden from view.

To open a widget:

1. Open Dashboard.

   If the widget you want to open is already displayed, you can skip the remaining steps; the widget is already open and ready to use.

2. If the widget you want to open is not already displayed or you want to open a second copy of it, open the widget bar **Ⓐ**.

3. Do one of the following:

   ▸ Click the icon for the widget you want to open.

   ▸ Drag the icon for the widget you want to open from the widget bar to the location you want it to appear onscreen **Ⓑ**.

   The widget appears onscreen and is ready to use **Ⓒ**.

Ⓐ To open a widget, start by displaying Dashboard and the widget bar.

Ⓑ Drag the icon for the widget you want to open from the widget bar into the Dashboard window.

Ⓒ The widget appears in Dashboard, all ready to use.

TIP Why would you want to open more than one copy of a widget? Well, suppose you want to view the weather for Phoenix, AZ, and Wenatchee, WA. You simply open the Weather widget twice and configure one for each of the cities.

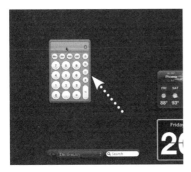

D To move a widget, just drag it.

E Pointing to the Weather widget displays its settings button in the lower-right corner.

F Here are the settings for the Weather widget.

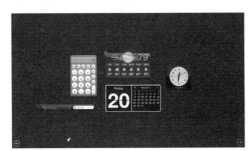

G You can hold down the Option key while pointing to a widget to display its close button.

To move a widget:

Once a widget is displayed, you can drag it to move it to a new position onscreen **D**.

TIP Arrange the widgets you keep open so you know exactly where to look onscreen when you open Dashboard to access their features.

To set widget options:

1. Point to the widget.

   If settings are available, you should see a tiny *i* button, which normally—but not always—appears in the lower-right corner of the widget **E**.

2. Click the i button.

   The widget turns over so you can access settings on its reverse side **F**.

3. Set options as desired.

4. Click Done to save your settings and flip the widget back over.

To close a widget:

1. If necessary, display the close button:

   ▸ If the widget bar is displayed, an X button should appear at the upper-left corner of the widget **A**.

   ▸ If the widget bar is not displayed, hold down the Option key and point to the widget you want to close. An X button appears at its upper-left corner **G**.

2. Click the X button. The widget closes.

TIP Keep in mind that many widgets lose their settings when you close them. If you plan to use a widget with custom settings often, you may want to keep it open so you don't have to reset it each time you use it.

Installing Widgets

You can customize Dashboard by adding or removing widgets.

Additional widgets are available on Apple's Dashboard Widgets Web page, **www.apple.com/downloads/dashboard/**. You can also find widgets on shareware distribution websites and on websites for third-party vendors.

To install a widget:

1. Download or copy the widget file you want to install to your computer.

2. Double-click the widget file's icon **A**.

   A widget installer window appears **B**.

3. Click Install.

   Dashboard opens. The widget appears within a "test drive" window **C**.

4. Test the widget to make sure it works as expected.

5. Do one of the following:

   ▸ To complete the installation, click Keep. The test drive window disappears, but the widget remains open **D**.

   ▸ To remove the widget without installing it, click Delete. The installation and widget disappear, but Dashboard remains open.

> **TIP** If you download a widget with Safari, the Widget Installer window **B** may open automatically when the download is complete. Follow steps 3 through 5 to complete the installation.

> **TIP** Installing a widget moves its file to the Widgets folder inside the invisible Library folder in your Home folder.

A Although many widgets have custom icons, this is what the default widget icon looks like.

B When you open a widget icon, an installer dialog like this appears.

C Dashboard opens the widget in a "test drive" window.

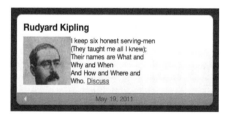

D When installation is complete, the widget remains open in Dashboard.

A You can open the Widget Manager by clicking the Manage Widgets button or by opening the Widgets widget.

B The Widget Manager lists all installed widgets and enables you to sort, disable, or delete them.

C The Widget Manager confirms that you really do want to delete a widget before removing it.

Managing Widgets

You can use Dashboard's Widget Manager to open, disable, enable, or delete widgets on your Mac.

To open the Widget Manager:

1. Open Dashboard and display the widget bar.

2. Click the Widgets icon (in the first row of widgets in the widget bar) or the Manage Widgets button **A**.

   The Widget Manager opens among your other widgets **B**.

To manage widgets:

In the Widget Manager window **B**:

- To open a widget, double-click its name.

- To sort the widgets in the Widget Manager window, choose an option from the pop-up menu: Sort by Name or Sort by Date.

- Toggle the check box beside a widget name to disable or enable it. Disabled widgets do not appear on the widget bar.

- To delete a widget, click the red – (minus) button beside the widget. Then click OK in the confirmation screen that appears **C**.

TIP You cannot use the Widget Manager to delete widgets that are installed with Mac OS X. Instead, consider disabling them. If you really must remove one of the Mac OS X widgets, you can delete its widget file from the Widgets folder in the Library folder of your hard disk.

Mac OS X Widgets Overview

Mac OS X Lion comes with 17 widgets that you might find useful as you work with your computer. Here's a quick summary of what each of them can do for you.

- **Widget Manager** (page 287) enables you to manage your Dashboard widgets.

- **Address Book** Ⓐ works with the Address Book application (Chapter 15) to give you quick access to your contacts.

- **Calculator** Ⓑ, which is a lot like the Calculator application (page 260), puts simple calculations at your fingertips.

- **Dictionary** Ⓒ, which is a lot like the Dictionary application (page 265), offers a quick way to look up the definitions, pronunciations, and synonyms for a word. The Dictionary widget also includes Apple Inc. terminology.

- **ESPN** Ⓓ puts sports news links and scores on your Dashboard. You can configure it to show the sport that interests you most.

- **Flight Tracker** Ⓔ can provide you with information about airline flights all over the world, including arrival and departure times, en route progress, and delays.

Ⓐ The Address Book widget offers a quick way to look up information stored in the Address Book application.

Ⓑ Calculator puts a simple calculator at your fingertips.

Ⓒ The Dictionary widget, which is one of my personal favorites, can help ensure that you always use the right words.

Ⓓ ESPN offers up-to-date news and scores for current sports.

Ⓔ Use Flight Tracker to see the status of a specific flight.

F The iCal widget displays events from iCal. (Yes, today is my husband's birthday.)

G The Movies widget helps you find out what's playing near you.

H Ski Report provides current conditions at the ski resort of your choice. (It ain't easy to find a ski resort with snow in late May.)

I The Stickies widget puts virtual sticky notes in Dashboard.

J The Stocks widget helps you keep track of stock prices. (Looks like the tech world is having a bad day.)

- **iCal** **F** gives you access to the events you manage with the iCal application (Chapter 16).

- **Movies** **G** can help you learn what's playing at nearby movie theaters.

- **Ski Report** **H** provides information of interest to skiers about ski resorts all over the world, including new snow, base depth, and trails open.

- **Stickies** **I**, which is a lot like the Stickies application (page 279), enables you to create reminder notes that look a lot like the sticky notes you might already have all over your workspace.

- **Stocks** **J** enables you to keep track of your favorite securities throughout the day.

- **Tile Game** **K** tests your puzzle-solving skills with a familiar—at least to old-timers like me—interface from your childhood.

- **Translation** **L** can translate text on the fly from one language to another.

continues on next page

K Tile Game is a great digital version of the analog classic.

L Who needs a translator when there's one built into your Mac?

- **Unit Converter** ⓜ enables you to convert from one unit of measurement to another.

- **Weather** ⓝ provides basic weather information for cities throughout the world.

- **Web Clip** ⓞ is a do-it-yourself widget that works with the Safari Web browser (page 438) to capture information from the Web and display it in your Dashboard. As the source information changes, so does the information in the Web Clip widget.

- **World Clock** ⓟ enables you to check the time in any major city in the world.

ⓜ Use Unit Converter to convert from one unit's measure to another's.

ⓝ The Weather widget puts a 7-day forecast in Dashboard.

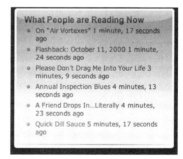

ⓞ Use Web Clip to create custom widgets of content from the Web. This is a list of recently read posts on my blog that will be updated each time I open Dashboard.

ⓟ The World Clock widget lets you see the time of day anywhere in the world.

Desktop Management

Mac OS X includes a number of desktop management tools that you might find helpful to work more efficiently and productively:

- **Stacks** puts expandable folders in the Dock. Clicking a folder displays its contents, making it quick and easy to open files you use often.

- **Mission Control** combines two existing Mac OS X features with a brand new interface for accessing them:

  - ▸ **Exposé** helps you cope with screen clutter by arranging open windows so you can see their contents or your desktop with a press of a button.

  - ▸ **Spaces** enables you to organize windows into groups, thus helping you to manage projects or tasks.

In this chapter, I explain how to take advantage of these features to keep your workspace organized and clutter-free while you work.

In This Chapter:

Stacks

Mac OS X's Stacks displays the contents of any folder in the Dock as a fan **A**, grid **B**, or list **C**. Click the folder icon to display the stack. Then click the item in the stack to open it. This makes it easy to organize Dock items and access the applications, folders, and files you use most.

By default, OS X Lion is preconfigured with two stacks folders **D**:

- **Documents** is your Documents folder—the default location for saved documents.

- **Downloads** is your Downloads folder—the default location for files you download from the Internet.

You can add your own stacks to the Dock by simply adding folders.

TIP Whether a stack appears as a fan, grid, or list depends, in part, on settings for the stacks folder (page 455) or the number of items in the folder.

TIP If you upgraded to OS X Lion from a previous version of Mac OS, you may also have a stacks folder for Applications, which is the contents of your Applications folder.

TIP A stack's Dock icon can appear as a pile (or stack) of icons with the most recently added item on top **D**. This helps give you an idea of the folder's contents.

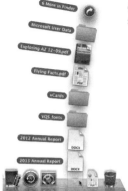

A You can display stacks as a fan, ...

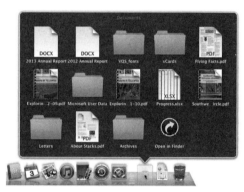

B ...a grid, ...

C ...or a list.

D The Documents and Downloads stacks folder appear beside the Trash on the Dock.

To display a stack:

In the Dock, click the icon for the stack folder you want to display.

The contents of the folder appear in a fan Ⓐ, grid Ⓑ, or list Ⓒ.

To hide a stack:

Use one of the following techniques:

- Click anywhere other than a stack item.
- Click the stack folder again.

The stack collapses back into the stack icon in the Dock.

To open an item in a stack:

1. Display the stack containing the item you want to open ⒶⒷⒸ.
2. Click the item you want to open.

   The item opens.

To open a stack folder:

1. In the Dock, click the folder to open to display its stack ⒶⒷⒸ.
2. Click the appropriate button:

   - For a fan Ⓐ, click the Show in Finder or More in Finder button at the top of the fan. The wording of this command varies depending on whether all items are showing.

   - For a grid Ⓑ, click the Open in Finder button at the bottom of the grid. (You may have to scroll down in the grid to display this button.)

   - For a list Ⓒ, click the Open in Finder command at the bottom of the list.

   The stacks folder opens in its own Finder window.

To navigate folders within a stack grid:

1. Display the stack grid you want to navigate Ⓑ and, if necessary, scroll to display the folder you want to open.

2. Use any combination of the following techniques:

   ▸ To open a folder in the grid, click it. The grid displays the contents of the folder you clicked Ⓔ. You can repeat this step as necessary to dig deeper into the folder hierarchy Ⓕ.

   ▸ To back out of a folder, click the Back arrow in the upper left corner of the grid ⒺⒻ.

To navigate folders within a stack list:

1. Display the stack list you want to navigate Ⓒ.

2. To open a folder in the list, point to it.

   The list turns into a hierarchical menu with the folder's contents displayed in a submenu Ⓖ.

3. Repeat step 2 as necessary to open multiple submenus for deeply nested folders Ⓗ.

TIP This is a great way to organize the files and folders you need to access using the stacks feature.

Ⓔ Click a folder to display a grid of items within it.

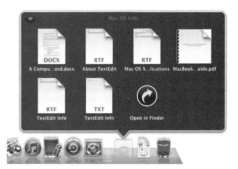

Ⓕ You can continue clicking folders to dig deeper into the folder hierarchy.

Ⓖ Point to a folder in the list to display a submenu of items within that folder.

Ⓗ You can display multiple levels of subfolders.

Mission Control

Mission Control **Ⓐ**, which is brand new in OS X Lion, combines the functionality of two existing Mac OS features—Exposé (page 297) and Spaces (page 299)—into one interface. These features work together to make it easier to stay organized and focused when working with multiple applications and documents on your Mac.

This part of the chapter introduces Mission Control's interface and explains how you can access it. The rest of this chapter goes into detail on using the features of Exposé and Spaces within the Mission Control environment.

TIP The gestures and keystrokes discussed in this section are based on default Mac OS settings; if you changed them, the corresponding techniques may not work.

Dashboard   *User-defined Spaces*   *Full-screen app*   *Add Space button*

Ⓐ Mission Control in action.   *Dock (always visible)*   *Individual apps in currently displayed space (Desktop 1)*

To open Mission Control:

Use one of the following techniques:

- Open the Mission Control icon in the Applications folder .

- Click the Mission Control icon in Launchpad.

- On a Multi-Touch device, swipe up with three fingers.

- Press the Mission Control key (normally F3, if present on your keyboard) or Control-Up Arrow.

Mission Control opens Ⓐ.

TIP The Control-Up Arrow keystroke replaces the F9 keystroke associated with Exposé (page 297) in previous versions of Mac OS.

To switch to a specific space with Mission Control:

1. Open Mission Control Ⓐ.

2. Along the top of the top of the screen, click the space you want to switch to.

   Mission Control closes and the screen displays just those applications and windows in the space you clicked Ⓒ.

To close Mission Control:

Use one of the following techniques:

- Press the Esc key.

- On a Multi-Touch device, swipe down with three fingers.

- Press the Mission Control key (normally F3, if present on your keyboard) or Control-Up Arrow.

TIP The gesture and keystroke here are based on default Mac OS settings; if you changed either, the corresponding technique may not work.

Ⓑ You can find the Mission Control icon in the Applications folder.

Mission Control

Ⓒ Clicking the Desktop 2 icon in Ⓐ displays the application windows open in that Space.

 Pressing Control-Down Arrow opens the Application Windows view of Exposé.

 Pressing F11 (or FN-F11 on a laptop) opens the Show Desktop view of Exposé, which can be handy if you keep a lot of icons on your desktop. (You know who you are.)

TABLE 20.1 Exposé Keyboard Shortcuts

Key	Description
Control-Down Arrow	Displays all open windows for the current application.
F11 or FN-F11 on a laptop	Displays the desktop for the current Space.

Exposé

If you're like most Mac OS X users, you probably have multiple applications and windows open at the same time while you work. The result can be a cluttered screen, with many layers of windows hiding other windows and the desktop.

Exposé helps solve the problem of screen clutter by making it easy to see all open windows in a single application **A** or the entire desktop **B** at once. Simply press one of Exposé's keyboard shortcuts (**Table 20.1**) to see what you need to see.

In OS X Lion, Exposé's features have been worked into Mission Control (page 295) and combined with Spaces (page 299), to create a unified interface for accessing spaces, applications, and application windows.

TIP The keyboard shortcut for displaying all of an applications windows has been changed for OS X Lion. You can customize Exposé's keyboard shortcuts or add additional Exposé triggers in the Mission Control preferences pane (page 494).

To see all open windows in the active application:

Press Control-Down Arrow.

All open windows in the active application resize and arrange themselves into a grid while other windows simply disappear **A**.

To switch to a specific application window:

1. Press Control-Down Arrow.

   Exposé displays all of the open windows for one application **A**.

2. Press the Tab key.

   Exposé displays all open windows for the next application **C**.

3. Repeat step 2 until the application you want to work with is displayed.

4. Use one of the following techniques to activate a specific window in the displayed application:

   ▸ Press the Right Arrow or Left Arrow key to move a blue border from one window to the next **D**. Press Return when the blue border is around the window you want to activate.

   ▸ Click the window you want to activate.

   Three things happen **E**:

   ▸ Exposé closes.

   ▸ If your Mac is set up with multiple spaces, it switches to the space the window you clicked is part of.

   ▸ The window you clicked becomes active.

To see the desktop:

Press F11, or, on a laptop, press FN-F11.

All open windows shift to the edges of the screen so you can see the desktop **B**.

To close Exposé:

Press the Esc key.

C Pressing the Tab key while Exposé is activate switches to the next application.

D When you point to a window, a blue border appears around it.

E Clicking a window in Exposé activates it in its Space.

A Spaces appear at the top of the Mission Control screen.

B Point to the corner of the screen to display and click an Add Space button.

C An empty space is added to the top of the Mission Control screen.

Spaces

Mac OS X's Spaces feature enables you to organize groups of windows into multiple spaces. Then, when you work in a space, only the windows that are part of that space appear onscreen.

For example, while working on a chapter of this book, I might have a space that includes my InDesign chapter document, Photoshop (which I use to edit screen-shots), and the three Finder windows that I use for the chapter's documents. I might also have another space set up with Mail, iChat, and Safari. I can then quickly switch from my work space to my communica-tion space when I need to check email or track down someone for a chat. When I want to return to work without distractions from those other applications, I can quickly switch back to my work space.

In OS X Lion, Apple changed the way you set up and switch spaces, making it part of the new Mission Control feature (page 295). This part of the chapter explains how to set up and remove spaces, assign applications to specific spaces, and switch from one space to another.

TIP By default, Mac OS creates separate spaces for Dashboard (Chapter 19) and for each full-screen app (page 152).

To add a space:

1. Press Control-Up Arrow to open Mis-sion Control **A**.

2. Move the pointer to the top-right corner of the screen and click the Add Space button that appears **B**.

   An icon for a new empty space appears at the top of the screen **C**.

To remove a space:

1. Open Mission Control **C**.

2. Point to the space you want to remove.

3. Click the black delete button that appears **D**.

   The space is removed. All of its windows appear in the previous space.

To switch from one space to another:

Use one of the following techniques:

- Open Mission Control **C** and click the icon at the top of the screen for the space you want to switch to.

- On a Multi-Touch device, use three fingers to swipe to the left or right until the space you want to switch to appears.

   If Mission Control was open, it closes. Your Mac switches to the space you clicked **E**.

To add windows to a space:

1. Activate the window you want to move to another space.

2. Drag the window to the edge of the screen and pause **F**.

   After a moment, the current space slides away to the side, displaying the next space.

3. Repeat this process as necessary until the space you want to move the window to is displayed.

4. Release the window **G**.

   The window moves to the currently displayed space.

TIP In case you're wondering, it is possible to display different windows for the same application in different spaces.

D When you point to a space and pause, a delete button appears.

E A new, empty space.

F Drag the window you want to move to the edge of the screen and pause.

G Release the window in the space you want to place it.

H The contextual menu in the Dock for an application that is running.

I The Options submenu includes commands for assigning the application to a specific space.

To assign a specific application to a specific space:

1. Switch to the space you want to assign the application to.

2. In the Dock, right-click the icon for the application you want to assign to that space.

   A contextual menu appears for that application **H**.

3. Point to the Options menu to display a submenu **I**.

4. Choose This Desktop.

   The application's windows move to the current space. From that point forward, every time you open that application, it will open in the same space.

To open an application in all spaces:

1. In the Dock, right-click the icon for the application you want to open in all spaces.

   A contextual menu appears **H**.

2. Point to the Options menu **I**.

3. Choose All Desktops.

   From that point forward, every time you open that application, it will open in all spaces.

To remove an application's space assignment:

1. In the Dock, right-click the icon for the application you want to open in all spaces.

   A contextual menu appears **H**.

2. Point to the Options menu **I**.

3. Choose None.

   From that point forward, the application will open in whatever space is active.

Mac OS
Utilities

In This Part

Fonts

Fonts are typefaces that appear onscreen and in printed documents. When they're properly installed, they appear on all Font menus and in font lists.

Mac OS, which has long been a favorite operating system among design professionals who work extensively with fonts, has several tools for managing fonts and using them in documents:

- **Font Book** is an application that enables you to install, preview, search, activate, and deactivate fonts with an easy-to-use interface.

- The **Fonts panel** enables you to apply and manage fonts within documents.

- The **Characters Palette** makes it easy to insert special characters in your documents.

This chapter tells you more about fonts and explains how to use all of these Mac OS font features.

Font Formats

Mac OS X supports several types of fonts in both Mac OS and Windows specific formats:

- **PostScript Type 1 fonts** are used primarily for printing. These fonts must be accompanied by corresponding screen font files. PostScript font technology was developed by Adobe Systems, Inc.

- **TrueType font** (.ttf) and **TrueType font collections** (.ttc), can display high-quality output onscreen and in print.

- **Multiple Master** is a special PostScript format that enables you to create custom styles, called instances, by setting font weight, width, and other variables. Mac OS X supports Multiple Master instances.

- **System or Data fork suitcase format** (.dfont) stores all information in the data fork of the file, including resources used by Mac OS drawing routines.

- **OpenType font format** (.otf), which can contain 65,000 different glyphs or characters, are popular for non-Roman languages. OpenType format fonts come in two versions: PostScript-based fonts from Adobe and TrueType-based fonts from Microsoft.

Do you need to know all this to install and use fonts with your Mac? Not really. Just make sure the fonts you buy are Mac OS X compatible and you shouldn't have any trouble with them.

Font Book

A Font Book is an application that makes it easy to manage your fonts.

Font Book **A** is a Mac OS X application that enables you to install, uninstall, organize, preview, search, activate, and deactivate fonts.

Font Book organizes all of your fonts into collections and libraries:

- Installation-based collections, which appear at the top of the Collection list, are groups of fonts organized by where they are installed (Table 21.1).

- User Libraries, which appear in the middle of the Collection list, are user-defined groups of fonts stored anywhere on your computer—not just in a Fonts folder.

- Other collections, which appear in the bottom of the list, are predefined groups of fonts organized by purpose or user-defined font collections.

Within each library or collection is one or more *font families*, each of which may contain one or more *typefaces*. Each typeface is a slightly different version of the font—for example, bold, italic, or condensed.

Font Book makes it possible to turn fonts on or off. This helps keep your applications' font menus and lists neat by letting you display only those fonts that you want to display.

TABLE 21.1 Font Collections

Collection Name	Installation Location	Purpose
All Fonts	Various	All fonts available for use.
Computer	Hard Disk/Library/Fonts	Fonts available to all user accounts on your computer. This collection only appears on the list if one of the next two collections appears.
User	~/Library/Fonts	Fonts available only for your user account.
Network	Network Hard Disk/Network/Library/Fonts	Fonts available only when connected to the network computer on which the fonts are installed.

To launch Font Book:

Use one of the following techniques:

- Double-click the Font Book icon in the Applications folder .

- Double-click a font file **C**. This also displays the font's characters in a preview window **D**.

- Choose Manage Fonts from the action pop-up menu in the Fonts Panel **E**.

Font Book's main window opens **A**.

TIP The Fonts Panel can be displayed in a variety of applications, including TextEdit (Chapter 14) and Mail (Chapter 27).

To quit Font Book:

When you are finished using Font Book, choose Font Book > Quit Font Book.

To install a font from the Finder:

1. Double-click the font file **C**.

   The font opens in Font Book's preview window **D**.

2. Click Install Font.

   The font is added to the default install location.

TIP The default installation location for adding fonts is the User collection. You can change this option in Font Book Preferences. Choose Font Book > Preferences to get started.

B You can find the Font Book application icon in the Applications folder.

Font Book

C Here's an example of a font file icon.

ITC Zapf Dingbats

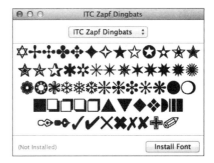

D Double-clicking the file icon for a font that has not yet been installed opens a preview window like this in Font Book.

E Another way to open Font Book is to choose Manage Fonts from the action pop-up menu in the Fonts panel.

F Font Book's File menu.

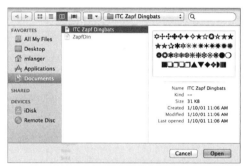

G Use an Open dialog to locate, select, and open the font you want to install.

To install a font from within Font Book:

1. In the Collection list, select the collection or library you want to add the font to.

2. Choose File > Add Fonts **F**, or press Command-O.

3. Use the Open dialog that appears **G** to locate and select the font you want to install.

4. Click Open.

   One of two things happens:

   ▸ If you selected a collection in the Collection list, the font's files are installed by copying them to the collection's location on disk.

   ▸ If you selected a library in the Collection list, the font's files are *not* copied. Instead, Font Book installs them by creating a reference to them within Font Book.

   Either way, the font's files are installed and ready to use.

TIP You can also install a font by dragging the font's file icon(s) onto a library or collection name in the main Font Book window.

To uninstall a font:

1. Select the name of the font in the Font list of the main Font Book window **A**.

2. Press the Delete key.

3. In the confirmation dialog that appears **H I**, click Remove.

   One of two things happens:

   ▸ If you selected a font installed in a collection **H**, the font's files are moved to the Trash. Emptying the Trash permanently removes them from your computer.

   ▸ If you selected a font installed in a library **I**, Font Book removes its reference to the font's files.

   Either way, the font's files are uninstalled and no longer available to use.

TIP You may find it more convenient to disable a font than to delete it. You can learn how on page 314.

TIP Font Book won't let you uninstall a font needed by the System for operation **J**.

To view fonts by library or collection:

In the Collection list of the main Font Book window, select the name of the library or collection you want to view.

The fonts in that library appear in the Font list **A**.

TIP A font can be in more than one library or collection.

TIP You can copy a font from one collection to another by dragging it from the Font list to the name of another collection.

H A dialog like this appears when you remove a font from a collection.

I This dialog appears when you remove a font from a library.

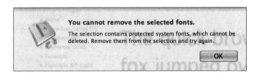

J You can't remove a system font.

K To view a typeface within a font family, select its name.

L You can change the size of the sample text.

M Choose an option from the Preview menu.

N You can display a repertoire of all characters in a selected font or typeface.

O You can also display sample text. (Having a home office is not always what its cracked up to be.)

To preview font or typeface characters:

1. In the Collection list of the main Font Book window, select All Fonts or the name of a library or collection that the font is part of **A**.

2. In the Font list, select the name of the font family you want to preview.

   The characters for the regular typeface of the font appear on the right side of the window **A**.

3. To see a specific typeface in the font family, click the disclosure triangle to the left of the font name to display all typefaces **A**. Then click the name of the typeface you want to see.

   The typeface characters appear on the right side of the window **K**.

TIP To change the size of characters in the preview part of the window, enter a value in the Size box, choose a value from the Size drop-down list, or drag the slider on the far right side of the window. The size changes accordingly **L**.

To change the preview text:

Choose one of the first three options on the Preview menu **M**:

- **Sample** (Command-1) displays the characters shown throughout this chapter.

- **Repertoire** (Command-2) displays all characters in ASCII order **N**.

- **Custom** (Command-3) enables you to specify your own sample text **O**.

The text changes accordingly.

To add a collection or library

1. Do one of the following:

   ‣ To add a collection, choose File > New Collection ⓕ, or press Command-N.

   ‣ To add a library, choose File > New Library ⓕ, or press Option-Command-N.

   An unnamed collection or library appears in the appropriate section of the Collection list with its name selected ⓟ.

2. Enter a new name for the collection or library and press Return to save it ⓠ.

3. To add fonts to the library or collection, follow the instructions in the section titled "To install a font from within Font Book" on page 309 and make sure the collection or library is selected in step 1.

TIP You can also add fonts to a collection by dragging them from another collection. Dragging a font from one collection to another does not duplicate the font's files on your computer. It just adds a reference to the font to the collection.

ⓟ In this example, I've created a new collection, which appears in the bottom area of the Collection column.

ⓠ When you enter a name and press Return, the collection (or library) is sorted alphabetically in the appropriate section of the Collection column.

R Click Remove in this dialog to remove the selected collection or library.

To remove a collection or library:

1. In the Collection list, select the library or collection you want to remove.

2. Use one of the following techniques:

    ▸ Press the Delete key.

    ▸ Choose File > Delete "*Collection Name.*"

    ▸ Choose File > Delete "*Library Name.*"

3. Click Remove in the confirmation dialog that appears **R**.

    The collection or library is removed.

TIP Removing a library or a collection does not delete font files from disk.

TIP When you remove a library, its fonts are no longer available for use in applications. When you remove a collection, the collection name no longer appears in the Fonts panel, but the fonts it contains are still available for use in applications.

TIP You may find it more convenient to disable a library or collection than to delete it. Learn how on page 314.

TIP You cannot remove the collections that appear at the top of the Collection list.

To disable a collection, library, or font:

1. In Font Book, select the name of the collection, library, font family, or typeface you want to disable.

2. Do one of the following:

   ▸ Choose Edit > Disable "*Collection Name*" 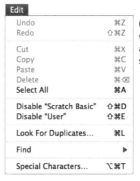, choose Edit > Disable "*Library Name*," or press Shift-Command-E.

   ▸ Choose Edit > Disable "*Font Name*" Family , choose Edit > Disable "*Typeface Name*" 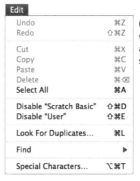, press Shift-Command-D, or click the check box at the bottom of the Font list.

3. If a confirmation dialog appears, click Disable.

   What happens depends on what you disabled :

   ▸ If you disabled a collection or library, its name appears in gray in the Collection list.

   ▸ If you disabled a font family or typeface, its name appears in gray with the word *Off* in the Font list.

TIP When you disable a library, you disable all of its fonts.

TIP A disabled library or collection will not appear in the Fonts panel.

TIP If a font appears in only one collection and that collection is disabled, the font is also disabled.

TIP When you disable a font in a collection, that font will not appear in the Font panel when the collection is selected. When you disable a font in a library, that font is not available for use in any application.

TIP Font Book does not allow you to disable a font that is used by the System.

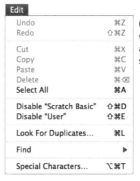 The Edit menu when a typeface and collection are selected.

 The Edit menu when a font family and collection are selected.

 In this example, I've disabled several collections, font families, and typefaces.

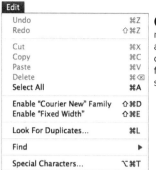

V The Edit menu with a disabled collection and font family selected.

W A yellow warning icon appears beside any fonts families or typefaces with problems.

X Font Book resolves the conflict by simply disabling one of the typefaces.

Y Font Book can resolve all font conflicts at once.

To enable a library, collection, font, or font family:

1. In Font Book, select the name of the disabled collection, library, font family, or typeface that you want to enable.

2. Do one of the following:

   ▸ Choose Edit > Enable "*Collection Name*" **V**, choose Edit > Enable "*Library Name*," or press Shift-Command-E.

   ▸ Choose Edit > Enable "*Font Name*" Family **V**, choose Edit > Enable "*Typeface Name*," press Shift-Command-D, or click the check box at the bottom of the Font list.

   The selected collection, library, font family, or typeface is enabled.

To resolve font conflicts:

1. In the Font list, locate and select a font family with a yellow warning icon to the right of its name **W**.

2. If necessary, click the triangle to the left of the font name to display its typefaces. At least one of them should have a yellow warning icon beside its name.

3. Click the Resolve Automatically button at the bottom of the preview area **W**.

   Font Book disables one of the conflicting typefaces **X**.

TIP Font conflicts like the one in **W** are often caused when multiple copies of a font family or typeface are installed in the same computer but in different places. Disabling one of the copies stops the conflict.

TIP You can resolve all conflicts on your computer at once. Choose Edit > Look for Duplicates **S T V**, or press Command-L. In the dialog that appears **Y**, click Resolve Automatically.

To validate a font:

1. In the Font list, select the Font or Font family you want to validate.

2. Choose File > Validate Font 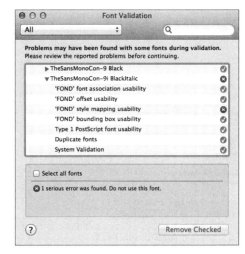.

   Font Book checks the font and display results in the Font Validation window **Z**.

3. Consult the results summary at the bottom of the Font Validation window.

4. To get detail about a minor or serious problem, click the disclosure triangle beside a problem to see details **Z**.

5. To remove problem fonts, turn on the Select all fonts check box and click Remove Checked. Then click Remove in the Confirmation dialog that appears.

TIP It's a good idea to uninstall any fonts with font errors.

TIP In step 1, you can select multiple fonts by holding down the Command key and clicking each font you want to select.

TIP By default, Font Book automatically validates each font you install with it.

TIP The Font menu's Validate File command **F** displays an Open dialog you can use to validate a font file that is not installed on your computer.

Z The Font Validation window displays font error details and enables you to remove the bad fonts.

The Fonts Panel

The Fonts panel Ⓐ offers a standard interface for formatting font characters in a document. This Mac OS X feature is fully integrated with Font Book, so the time you spend organizing your fonts there will help you be more productive when working with the Fonts panel.

The Fonts panel is *not* a dialog box (page 172). That means you can leave it open and switch back and forth between your documents and the Fonts panel's formatting options. Changes are applied immediately; there's no need to click an Apply or OK button. You can even leave the Fonts panel open all the time when you work with an application.

In this part of the chapter, I explain how to use the Fonts panel to format text.

Ⓐ The Fonts panel closely resembles the layout of Font Book.

Ⓑ Choose Show Fonts from the Font submenu under TextEdit's Format menu.

Ⓒ You can access other features with the action pop-up menu.

Ⓓ The Preview pane can help you see what your font settings look like applied to text.

> **TIP** This chapter looks at the Fonts panel as it appears in TextEdit, the text editor that comes with Mac OS X. You can learn more about using TextEdit in Chapter 14.

To open TextEdit's Fonts panel:

In TextEdit, choose Format > Font > Show Fonts Ⓑ, or press Command-T.

> **TIP** The command to open the Fonts panel in other applications that support it is similar.

> **TIP** You can open Font Book from within the Fonts panel by choosing Manage Fonts from the action pop-up menu Ⓒ.

> **TIP** To display a preview of font formatting in the Fonts panel, choose Show Preview from the shortcut menu Ⓒ. A pane appears at the top of the Fonts panel with a preview of the selected font settings Ⓓ.

To apply basic font formatting:

1. Select the text you want to apply font formatting to or position the insertion point where you want the formatting change to begin.

2. If necessary, open the Fonts panel 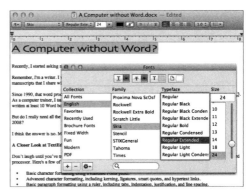.

3. Select a collection from the Collection list.

4. Select a font family from the Family list.

5. Select a style from the Typeface list.

6. Set the font size by entering a value in the Size box, selecting a size from the Size list, or dragging the Size slider up or down Ⓕ.

   The changes you make are applied to the selected text or text typed at the insertion point.

TIP The styles that appear in the Typeface list vary depending on the font selected in the Family list. Some font families offer more styles than others.

TIP Oblique is similar to italic. Light, regular, medium, bold, and black refer to font weights or boldness.

Ⓔ In this example, I've used the Fonts panel to change the formatting of some selected text.

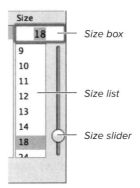

Ⓕ The Fonts panel offers three different ways to set the font size.

Size box — Size box

Size list — Size list

Size slider — Size slider

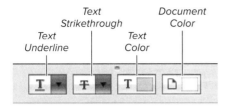

Text Underline — Text Strikethrough — Text Color — Document Color

G Use these menus and buttons to apply additional font formatting options.

H Use the Colors panel to choose a color to apply.

To apply font effects:

Use the effects controls at the top of the Fonts panel window **G** to apply other font formatting options to selected text or start formatting at the insertion point:

- **Text Underline** offers four underline options: None, Single, Double, and Color. If you choose Color, you can use the Colors panel **H** to set the underline color.

- **Text Strikethrough** offers four strike-through options: None, Single, Double, and Color. If you choose Color, you can use the Colors panel **H** to set the strikethrough color.

- **Text Color** enables you to set the color of text. When you click this button, the Colors panel appears **H** so you can choose a color for text.

- **Document Color** enables you to set the color of the document background. When you click this button, the Colors panel appears **H** so you can choose a color for the entire document's background.

TIP The Colors panel is covered in more detail on page 489.

The Characters Palette

The Characters Palette 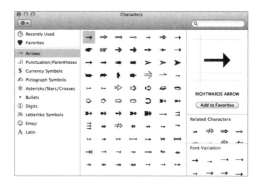 enables you to insert any character in any installed font in a document. It is especially useful for typing special characters, like mathematical symbols, arrows, and dingbats characters.

TIP The Characters Palette is available within some Mac OS X applications, including TextEdit.

To display the Character Palette:

Use one of the following techniques:

- In TextEdit, choose Edit > Special Characters **B**, or press Option-Command-T.

- In the Fonts panel, choose Characters from the action pop-up menu **C**.

TIP You can also display the Character Palette by choosing Show Character Palette from the Input menu (page 493).

To insert a character with the Character Palette:

1. In a document window, position the insertion point where you want the character to appear.

2. Display the Character Palette **A**.

3. Select a character group in the left column.

4. Select one of the characters or groups in the middle part of the window.

5. In the middle or Font Variation pane of the window, double-click the character you want to insert.

   The character appears at the insertion point in your document.

A The Characters Palette offers a visual way to insert special characters.

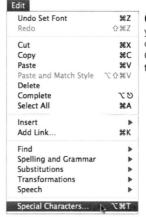

B In TextEdit, you can choose Special Characters from the Edit menu.

C Choose Characters from the action pop-up menu.

Printing

In a Mac OS, printing is handled by the operating system rather than individual applications. You choose the Print command in the application that created the document you want to print. Mac OS steps in, displaying the Print dialog and telling the application how to send information to the printer.

There are two main benefits to this:

- If you can print documents created with one application, you can probably print documents created with any application.

- The Page Setup and Print dialogs look very much the same in most applications.

This chapter covers most aspects of printing documents on a computer running Mac OS X. It also explains how you can use the Print dialog to create and email PDF files and fax documents right from your computer.

Printing: An Overview

To print on your Mac, you need to complete three basic steps, two of which you may only have to do once. Here's a quick overview of the process.

1. If necessary, add your printer to the Printers list in the Print & Scan preferences pane. You only need to do this once for each printer you use. You can find complete instructions starting on page 523.

2. If necessary, in the document you want to print, open the Page Setup dialog, set options, and save them. In most cases, the default or last-used options will be fine for your document, so you won't need to change them. You can learn more about the Page Setup dialog in this chapter, on page 324.

3. Open the Print dialog, set options, and click Print. This is the one step you'll need to do with most of the documents you print. You can learn about using the Print dialog in this chapter, starting on page 325.

There are a few additional things you might want to keep in mind about printing. I'll discuss them briefly here.

Printer Drivers

A *printer driver* is software that Mac OS uses to communicate with a specific kind of printer. It contains information about the printer and instructions for using it. You can't open and read a printer driver, but your computer can.

A standard installation of OS X Lion installs printer drivers for the printers it detects during installation. If you have an Internet connection, Mac OS checks to make sure you have the most up-to-date version of

Do You Really Need to Print It?

Let's face it: these days, most documents don't need to be printed at all.

Before you click that Print button, take a moment and think about it. Do you really need hard copy? What will you do with it? Is it just a quick printout for proofreading? Will it wind up in the wastepaper basket or shredder when you're done? Can't you just work with it onscreen?

If you need to share a document with someone else, consider creating a PDF file of the document instead. It's quick and easy to e-mail it, right from within the Print dialog. Or you could put it on a network server or file sharing service such as Dropbox or your iDisk. Not only is this a much quicker and cost-effective way to share a document, but it prevents the waste of paper, ink, or toner.

And look at it this way: The less you print, the longer your printer will last. My primary document printer is nearly 15 years old—can you say the same about yours?

So think about it—and don't print when you don't have to.

the installed printer drivers. It can also install printer drivers on the fly when you set up a new printer.

When you buy a printer, it should come with a CD or access to a website that includes Mac-compatible printer driver software; if your computer does not recognize your printer, you'll need to install this software to use it.

Sharing Printers

If your Mac is connected to a network, you may be able to access printers that are shared or otherwise available on the network. This means you can print without having a printer directly connected to your Mac.

You can also share a printer that is directly connected to your Mac with other users on your network. As long as your computer is turned on and connected to the network, other network users can use it to print.

If you have access to multiple printers, you can create a *printer pool*, or group of shared printers. When you or another user prints to a printer pool, the document prints on the first available printer in the pool. This is especially helpful on a busy network when many users have access to just a handful of printers.

You can set up printer sharing features using various System Preferences panes:

- Use the Sharing preferences pane (page 546) to enable printer sharing for your printers.

- Use the Print & Scan preferences pane (page 522) to add network printers to your computer and create a printer pool.

The Page Setup Dialog

The Page Setup dialog 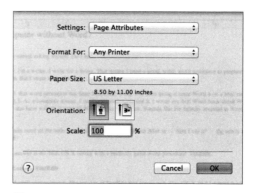 lets you set page options prior to printing, including the printer the document should be formatted for, paper size, orientation, and scale.

TIP Not all applications offer access to the Page Setup dialog. If Page Setup does not appear on the File menu for the application you're printing from, this dialog is not available in that application.

To set Page Attributes:

1. In the application you plan to print from, choose File > Page Setup  to display the Page Setup dialog.

2. If necessary, choose Page Attributes from the Settings pop-up menu to display Page Attributes options .

3. Set options as desired:

   ▸ To format the document for a specific printer, choose the printer's name from the Format For pop-up menu . This menu includes all of the printers listed in the Print & Scan preferences pane (page 522).

   ▸ To change the paper size, choose an option from the Paper Size pop-up menu . This menu lists common paper sizes or, if you chose a specific printer, all the paper sizes supported by that printer.

   ▸ To change the page orientation, click the Orientation option you want.

   ▸ To change the print scale, enter a scaling percentage in the Scale box.

4. Click OK to save your settings and dismiss the Page Setup dialog.

TIP Default printer and paper size are set in the Print & Scan preferences pane (page 525).

A The Page Setup dialog, as it appears for a TextEdit document.

B Choose Page Setup from the File menu. Here's what it looks like in TextEdit.

C To format for a specific printer, choose the printer from this menu.

D Choose a paper size from the Paper Size pop-up menu.

A The Print dialog can appear with few options...

Setting Options in the Print Dialog

The Print dialog **A** **B** enables you to set printing options and output the document to a printer, fax modem, or PDF file.

Like the Page Setup dialog, the Print dialog is a standard dialog, but two things can cause its appearance and options to vary:

- Print options vary depending on the selected printer.

- Additional options may be offered by specific applications.

The Print dialog offers two modes: a simple view with few options **A** and a detailed view with all options **B**. Simply click a Show Details or Hide Details button to toggle from one view to the other.

This section explains how to set Print options available for most printers and applications.

TIP If your Print dialog includes options that are not covered here, consult the documentation that came with your printer.

TIP For information about using Print options specific to an application, consult the documentation that came with the application.

B ...or expanded to show many options.

C Choose Print from the File menu. Here's what it looks like in TextEdit.

To open the Print dialog:

1. Choose File > Print **C**, or press Command-P.

   The Print dialog appears **A** **B**.

2. If necessary, click the Show Details button at the bottom of the dialog to expand it and show all of its options **B**.

To set basic printing options:

On the top-right corner of the Print dialog **B**, set options as desired:

D The Printer menu includes all printers in the Print & Scan preferences pane.

- **Printer D** is the printer you want to print to. This menu includes all of the printers listed in the Print & Scan preferences pane (page 522).

- **Presets E** is a set of predefined options. I explain how to use this feature later in this section.

E The Presets menu enables you to save or select predefined options

- **Copies** is the number of copies to print.

- **Pages** enables you to enter a range of pages to print:

    - **All** prints all pages in the document.

    - **From** enables you to enter values in the From and to boxes to set a range of pages to print.

F Use this pop-up menu to select the paper size you want to print to.

- **Paper Size F** is the size of paper you want to print to. This menu includes all the paper sizes supported by the selected printer.

- **Orientation** is the paper orientation for printing: portrait or landscape.

G Use this pop-up menu to select the type of option you want to edit. This menu varies depending on the printer you're printing to.

TIP Choosing Add Printer from the Printer pop-up menu **D** opens the Add Print dialog, which you can use to add a printer to the Print & Scan preferences pane (page 524).

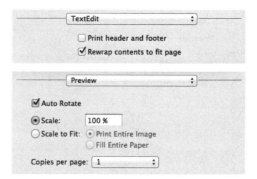

H I Application-specific settings vary from one application to another. These are the settings for TextEdit (top) and Preview (bottom).

To save settings as a preset:

1. Follow the instructions on the previous two pages to set options as desired in the Print dialog **B**.

2. Choose Save Current Settings as Preset from the Presets pop-up menu **E**.

   The Save Preset As dialog appears **U**.

3. Enter a name for the settings in the Preset Name box.

4. Choose a Preset Available For option to specify whether it should be available for just the current printer or all printers.

5. Click OK.

   The name you entered is added to the Presets menu and chosen **V**.

TIP It's a good idea to save settings if you often have to change the Print dialog's settings. This can save time when you need to print.

TIP To save changes to a preset, follow these steps and save the preset with the same name.

To use preset settings:

In the Print dialog **B**, choose the name of the preset settings you want to use from the Presets pop-up menu **V**.

All Print dialog settings are set according to the saved settings.

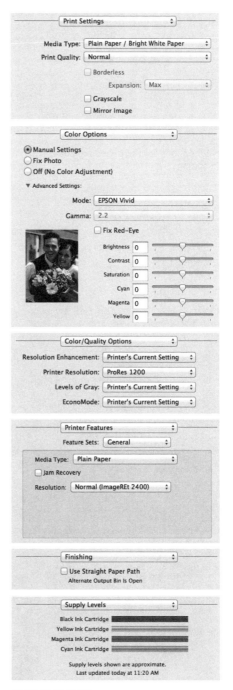

O P Q R S T Examples of printer-specific settings in the Print dialog for various printers.

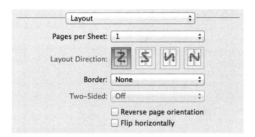

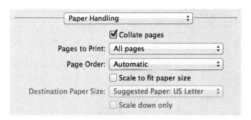

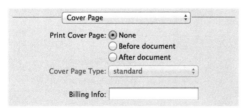

J Layout options control pages per sheet and related settings.

K Color Matching options enable you to select a color matching method.

L Paper Handling options control collation, page selection and order, and print scaling.

M Paper Feed options control how paper is fed into the printer.

N Cover page options enable you to print a cover page for the print job.

To set other options:

1. In the lower-right corner of the Print dialog, choose an option from the pop-up menu at the divider line **G**. Here are some of the possible options:

   ▸ *Application name* **H** **I** displays application-specific options.

   ▸ **Layout J** enables you to set the number of pages per sheet, layout direction, border, two-sided printing, and reverse page orientation, which prints the pages in reverse order.

   ▸ **Color Matching K** enables you to set color-matching options.

   ▸ **Paper Handling L** enables you to specify which pages to print (all, even, or odd), set scaling options, and set the page order (normal or reverse).

   ▸ **Paper Feed M** enables you to specify whether paper will be fed automatically or manually.

   ▸ **Cover Page N** enables you to set options for a cover page that can be printed before or after the document.

   ▸ Print Settings **O**, Color Options **P**, Color/Quality Options **Q**, Printer Features **R**, Finishing **S**, and Supply Levels **T**, all of which are illustrated on the next page, are examples of printer-specific options you might see for your printers.

2. Set options as desired in the bottom half of the Print dialog.

3. Repeat steps 1 and 2 for each group of options you want to set.

TIP Many of the options that appear in the lower half of the print dialog customized for specific printers, so what you see may vary from what is shown in this book.

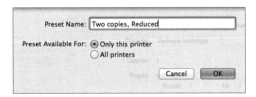

Use this dialog to name and save a preset.

The preset you created appears on the Presets menu.

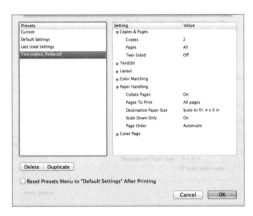

You can view, duplicate, or delete settings for each preset in a dialog like this.

To view preset settings:

1. In the Print dialog ⓑ, choose Show Presets from the Presets menu ⓥ.

2. In the Presets dialog that appears, select the preset you want to view ⓦ.

3. If necessary, click disclosure triangles on the right side of the dialog to display setting information.

4. Repeat steps 2 and 3 for each preset you want to view.

5. When you are finished viewing presets, click OK to dismiss the dialog.

TIP You can click the Duplicate button in the Presets dialog ⓦ to make a copy of a selected preset. You can then make changes to the original or copy to create a different preset.

To delete a preset setting:

1. In the Print dialog ⓑ, choose Show Presets from the Presets menu ⓥ.

2. In the Presets dialog that appears, select the preset you want to delete ⓦ.

3. Click the Delete button.

   The preset setting is deleted.

Previewing Documents

The Print dialog includes a preview area **Ⓐ** that you can use to get a large thumbnail preview of each page of the document. This is a good way to see how a document will print before actually printing it.

TIP You can also use the Print dialog's Open PDF in Preview command, which I discuss on page 331, to create a PDF of the document and open it in Preview (page 275). This gives you a full-sized version of the document to examine before printing.

To preview a document in the Print dialog:

1. Follow the instructions on pages 326 and 328 to set options as desired in the Print dialog's panes.

2. Look at the Preview area on the left side of the Print dialog to see what the first page looks like **Ⓐ**.

3. If the document has multiple pages, use the controls beneath the preview to scroll through the document.

TIP Some applications include a Print Preview command. This displays a preview of the document from within the application and does not open the Print dialog.

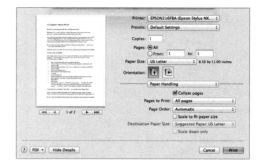

Ⓐ The left side of the Print dialog shows a preview of the document as it will print.

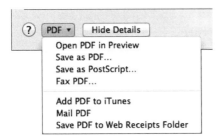

A Use options on this menu to create and distribute PDF files.

B Opening a document as a PDF in Preview is a good way to see what the document will look like before printing. You can then print right from Preview.

TIP The commands below the split line on the PDF menu are PDF workflows created with AppleScript or Automator. I tell you about Mac OS X's automation tools on page 373.

Saving Documents as PDF Files

PDF, which stands for *Portable Document Format*, is a standard file format that can be opened and read by Preview, Adobe Reader, and some other applications. PDF is a good format for distributing a formatted document when you're not sure what software the document's recipient has. Most computer users have some kind of PDF reader software; if they don't, they can download Adobe Reader for free.

The PDF menu in the Print dialog offers several options for saving a document as a PDF file **A**:

- **Open PDF in Preview** opens the document as a PDF file in Preview. This is useful for seeing a full-sized preview of a document you plan to print.

- **Save as PDF** saves the document as a PDF file in the location you specify.

- **Save as PostScript** saves the document as a PostScript format file, which can then be sent to a PostScript output device.

- **Fax PDF** uses a fax modem to fax the document as a PDF.

- **Add PDF** to iTunes adds the file to iTunes as a PDF. Once there, it can be copied to an iPad or iPhone.

- **Mail PDF** creates a PDF file of the document and attaches it to an email message form.

- **Save PDF to Web Receipts Folder** saves the document as a PDF file in the Web Receipts folder in your Documents folder.

To save a document as a PDF file:

1. Follow the instructions on pages 326 and 328 to set options as desired in the Print dialog's panes.

2. Choose Save as PDF from the PDF menu **A**.

3. A Save dialog (page 166) appears. If necessary, click the disclosure triangle beside the Save As field to expand it to show all options **C**.

4. Enter a name and select a disk location for the PDF file.

5. If desired, provide additional information about the file in the Title, Author, Subject, and Keywords boxes in the bottom part of the dialog.

6. To secure the document against unauthorized access or use, click the Security Options button. Then set options in the PDF Security Options dialog that appears **D** and click OK.

7. Click Save.

   The file is saved as a PDF file in the location you specified.

TIP You can use the PDF Security Options dialog **D** to require separate passwords to Open the document or copy and print its content.

C Use this Save dialog to name and choose a destination for the PDF file.

D Use the PDF Security Options dialog to secure your PDF from unauthorized access or to restrict copying or printing.

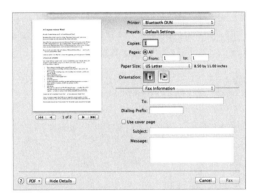

E You can choose your fax modem from the Printer pop-up menu.

F Use the form in the bottom-right of the window to fill in fax recipient and cover sheet information.

G If you choose Fax Modem from the pop-up menu near the bottom of the dialog, you can set options for your fax modem.

To fax a document:

1. Set options as desired in the Print dialog's panes.

2. Do one of the following:

   ▸ Choose Fax PDF from the PDF menu **A**.

   ▸ Choose a fax modem from the Printer pop-up menu **E**.

   The bottom half of the Print dialog changes to offer options for faxing the document **F**.

3. Enter the fax phone number you are faxing the document to in the To box.

4. If you need to dial a number to get a dial tone (like in an office or hotel) or a 1 for long distance, enter these numbers in the Dialing Prefix box.

5. To include a fax cover page, turn on the Use cover page check box, type a subject in the Subject box, and type a message in the Message box.

6. Click Fax.

   A Print status dialog appears briefly as the document is spooled to the fax modem's queue. A moment later, the computer dials and sends the fax.

TIP You must add a fax modem to the Print & Scan preferences pane before you can fax a document. Learn how on page 523.

TIP The header on each page of the faxes you send includes the date, time, and page number.

TIP You can set options for a fax modem from within the Print dialog. While a fax modem is chosen from the Printer menu, choose Fax Modem from the pop-up menu on the divider line in the bottom half of the Print dialog **G**. Then set options for dialing, sound, and dial tone.

Printing Documents

As you've probably figured out, the Print dialog also enables you to send a document to a printer to be printed.

To print a document:

1. Follow the instructions on pages 326 and 328 to set options as desired in the Print dialog's panes.

2. Click Print.

   The print job is sent to the print queue, where it waits for its turn to be printed.

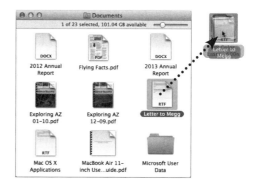

Ⓐ A quick way to print a document is to drag its icon on top of a desktop printer.

Desktop Printers

Mac OS X's desktop printers feature lets you create an icon for a printer you use frequently. Then, when you want to print a document on that printer, simply drag the document icon onto the printer icon.

TIP You can learn how to set up a desktop printer on page 527.

To print with a desktop printer:

1. Drag the icon for the document you want to print onto the printer icon **Ⓐ**.

2. When you release the button, the document is sent to the printer's print queue and prints.

   The Print dialog does not appear.

TIP You can drag any number of document icons onto the printer icon. They will all be spooled to the printer.

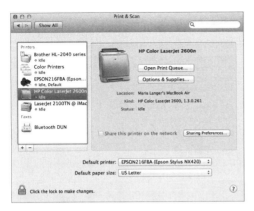

A One way to open a print queue is to select the printer in the Print & Scan preferences pane and then click Open Print Queue.

B You can also open a print queue by double-clicking the printer's icon if it appears in the Dock.

C If you've created a desktop printer icon for a printer, you can double-click it to open its print queue.

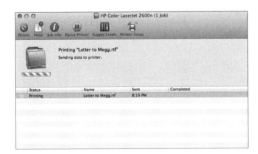

D A typical print queue with one job queued and printing.

Print Queues

A print queue is a list of documents or print jobs waiting to be printed. When you click the Print button to send a document to a printer, you're really sending it to the printer's queue, where it waits its turn to be printed.

You can open a printer's queue window to check the progress of print jobs that are printing; to stop printing; and to hold, resume, or cancel a specific print job.

TIP Although this section discusses printer queues, a fax modem also has a queue that works exactly the same way.

To open a printer's queue window:

Use one of the following techniques:

- Open the Print & Scan preferences pane **A** (page 522), select the name of the printer you want to open the print queue for, and click Open Print Queue.

- If the printer has at least one print job spooled, click the printer's icon in the Dock **B**.

- Double-click the desktop printer icon for a printer **C**.

The printer's queue window opens **D**.

TIP Clicking the tiny button to the left of a document's status in the print queue displays a preview of the document.

To control printing:

In the print queue window **D**, use any of the following techniques:

- To pause all printing, click the Pause Printer button. Any printing stops and the words *Printer Paused* appear in the print queue window.

- To restart print jobs, click the Resume button in the print queue window. The next print job starts printing.

- To hold a specific print job, select the print job you want to hold and click the Hold button. *On Hold* appears in the Status column beside the job name in the print queue window. If the job was printing, it stops and another queued job prints.

- To resume a specific print job, select the print job you want to resume and click the Resume button. *On Hold* disappears from the Status column beside the job name in the print queue window. If no other jobs are printing, the job begins to print.

- To cancel a specific print job, select the print job you want to cancel and click the Delete button. The job is removed from the print queue. If it was printing, printing stops.

TIP You can use commands under the Printer **E** and Jobs **F** menus to access other print queue options. The commands that are available vary depending on the printer and how your computer is connected to it.

E Use this menu to access other options for your printer.

F This menu offers options for working with a selected print job.

A You can use the Finder's print command to send selected documents to the default printer.

The Finder's Print Command

The Finder's File menu also includes a Print command **A**. This is a quick-and-dirty command for sending a selected document to the default printer, without even displaying the Print dialog.

TIP The Finder's Print command works very much like the Print One command available in some applications.

To use the Finder's Print command:

1. In a Finder window, select the document(s) you want to print.

2. Choose File > Print **A**, or press Command-P.

   If necessary, the application that created the document opens. The document is sent to the default printer and prints. The application that opened it remains open.

23

Disk Utility

Disk Utility is a utility application for working with disks and volumes. As discussed in Chapter 8, a *disk* is a storage device and a *volume* is a part of a disk formatted for storing files.

Disk utility can:

- Provide general information about a disk or volume.
- Verify and repair a disk or volume.
- Erase a selected disk or volume.
- Divide a disk into several volumes or partitions.
- Create disk images.
- Mount a disk image as a disk.
- Burn a disk image to CD or DVD.
- Set up a RAID disk.
- Restore a disk from a backup image.

This chapter explains how to use Disk Utility's most commonly used features.

In This Chapter:

Launching & Quitting Disk Utility

Like any other Mac OS application, you need to launch Disk Utility to use it. You can find Disk Utility's application icon  in the Utilities folder inside the Applications folder on your hard disk.

TIP Certain features of disk utility cannot be used on the startup disk. If you need to repair or format your startup disk, you must start your Mac with another startup disk or DVD or your computer's recovery partition (page 130).

To open Disk Utility:

Use one of the following techniques:

- Open the Disk Utility icon in the Utilities folder in your Applications folder **A**.

- Click the Disk Utility icon in the Utilities folder in Launchpad (page 150).

Disk Utility's main window appears **B**. It lists mounted disks with their volumes, as well as recently opened or created disk images files on the left side of the window.

To quit Disk Utility:

Use one of the following techniques:

- Choose Disk Utility > Quit Disk Utility, or press Command-Q.

- Close Disk Utility's window **B**.

A Disk Utility's application icon.

Disk Utility

B The main Disk Utility window with the First Aid button selected.

A Some information about a selected disk appears at the bottom of the Disk Utility window.

B Information about a selected disk...

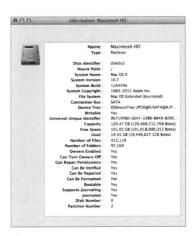

C ...and for a selected volume.

Learning More about a Disk or Volume

Disk Utility can provide additional information about a mounted disk or volume that can't be found in the Info window (page 94). You might find this information useful for troubleshooting problems.

To get information about a disk or volume:

1. On the left side of the Disk Utility window, select the disk or volume you want information about.

   Some information about the item appears at the bottom of the window **A**.

2. Use one of the following techniques:

   ▶ Click the Info button on the toolbar.

   ▶ Choose File > Get Info, or press Command-I.

   A window with additional information appears **B** **C**.

3. When you are finished reviewing the information in the window, click its close button to dismiss it.

Verifying & Repairing Disks

One of the main components of Disk Utility is Disk First Aid, which can be used to verify and repair permissions and disks that can get damaged during regular use, unexpected power outages, or by disconnecting an external disk before it has been properly unmounted.

Mac OS X automatically checks the startup disk when you start your Mac and can repair any minor directory problems it finds. You may, however, want to run Disk First Aid to verify or repair disk permissions and disks occasionally as a general maintenance routine.

TIP Permissions (page 398) determine how users can access files. If permissions are incorrectly set for a file, it may not be accessible by the users who should be able to use it. If permissions are really messed up, your computer might not work correctly.

TIP Disk Utility's First Aid feature cannot repair all disk problems. For severely damaged disks, you may need to acquire third-party utilities.

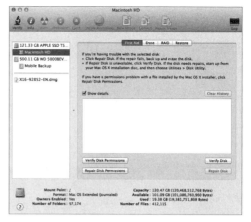

A In this example, I've selected the startup volume. I can verify or repair disk permissions or verify the disk, but I can't repair the disk.

B As shown here, Disk Utility found and repaired quite a few permissions problems on my startup volume.

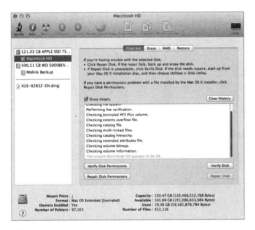

C While verifying my startup volume, Disk Utility did not find any problems.

To verify or repair a disk or volume or its permissions:

1. In the Disk Utility window, click the First Aid button.

2. In the left side of the window, select the disk or volume you want to verify or repair **A**.

3. Click the button for the action you want to perform:

   ▸ **Verify Disk Permissions** verifies file permissions on a Mac OS X startup volume.

   ▸ **Repair Disk Permissions** repairs file permissions on a Mac OS X startup volume.

   ▸ **Verify Disk** verifies the directory structure and file integrity of a disk or volume.

   ▸ **Repair Disk** repairs damage to the directory structure of any disk or volume other than the startup disk, as long as it is not write-protected.

4. If you are verifying the startup volume, a dialog may appear to warn you that your computer may be slow or unresponsive while the startup disk is being verified. Click Verify Disk to continue.

5. Wait while your computer checks and/ or repairs the selected disk or volume and its permissions.

   When it's done, it reports its results on the right side of the window **B C**.

TIP To repair your startup volume, start your computer from its recovery partition (page 130). After specifying a language, click the Disk Utility option in the Mac OS Utilities window that appears. Then follow these steps.

TIP To select more than one disk or volume in step 2, hold down the Command key while clicking each item.

Erasing & Partitioning Disks

You can use Disk Utility to erase and partition disks.

When you *erase* a disk, you remove all files and directories on that disk. This prepares the disk to accept new data.

An erased disk has a single *volume* or *partition*, which is what appears in the Finder. You store files on the volume. If you want to, you can split a disk into multiple partitions so that multiple volumes appear in the Finder. Each partition is treated by Mac OS as a separate disk.

To erase a disk or volume:

1. In the Disk Utility window, click the Erase button.

2. In the column on the left side of the window, select the disk or volume you want to erase **A**.

3. Set options for the volume:

   ▸ **Format B** is the format applied to the volume.

   ▸ **Name** is the name of the volume.

4. To specify how disk space occupied by deleted files should be erased, click the Erase Free Space button. (This option is only available if you have selected a volume to erase.) Then select an option in the Erase Free Space Options dialog **C** and click OK.

5. To increase security and prevent the disk from being unerased, click the Security Options button. Then select an option in the Secure Erase Options dialog **D** and click OK.

6. Click Erase.

   A confirmation dialog appears **E**.

A In this example, I've selected a USB storage device and set options to erase and rename it.

B There are several Format options, depending on the type of media you are erasing.

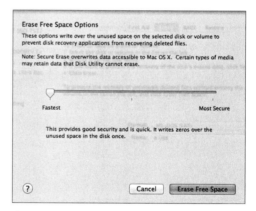

C You can use the slider in this dialog to determine how quickly or securely you want to erase free space on a volume.

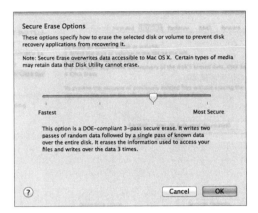

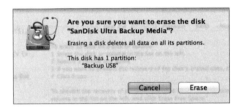

D Use the slider in this dialog to determine how quickly or securely a disk is erased.

E Disk Utility asks one more time if you're sure you want to erase the disk.

F The newly erased disk appears in the Finder.

CAUTION Erasing a disk or volume permanently removes all data. Do not erase a disk if you think you will need any of the data it contains.

7. If you're sure you want to continue, click Erase.

8. Wait while your computer erases the disk or volume. A progress dialog appears as it works.

   When it's finished, an icon for the erased disk or volume reappears in Disk Utility and in the Finder **F**.

TIP You cannot erase the startup disk. (And that's a good thing.) If you want to erase your computer's startup disk, you must start your computer with another disk.

TIP When you erase a disk, you replace all volumes on the disk with one blank volume. When you erase a volume, you replace that volume with a blank volume.

TIP If you're not sure which volume format to choose in step 3, choose Mac OS Extended (Journaled). If you wanted one of the other formats, you'd know it.

TIP In steps 4 and 5, dragging the slider to different settings displays the corresponding explanation for that setting. This should be enough information to help you decide which option is right for you.

TIP Using the security options in steps 4 and 5 can considerably lengthen the amount of time it takes to erase the disk, especially for high capacity disks.

TIP After erasing a disk or volume, a dialog may appear, asking if you want to use that volume to back up with Time Machine (page 125). Click the appropriate button for your situation.

TIP If you're concerned about unauthorized persons recovering data from files you erase, be sure to check out the Secure Empty Trash feature (page 56).

To partition a disk:

1. Select the disk you want to partition.

2. In the Disk Utility window, click the Partition tab **G**.

3. Choose an option from the Partition Layout pop-up menu **H**.

   The area beneath the pop-up menu changes accordingly **I**.

4. In the Partition Layout area, select a volume. Then set options in the Partition Information area as desired **J**:

   ▸ **Name** is the name of the volume.

   ▸ **Format K** is the format applied to the volume.

   ▸ **Size** is the amount of disk space allocated to that partition.

5. Repeat step 4 for each partition.

6. Click Apply.

   A confirmation dialog appears **L**.

CAUTION Partitioning a disk permanently removes all data. Do not partition a disk if you think you will need any of the data on an existing partition.

7. If you're sure you want to continue, click Partition.

8. Wait while your computer creates the new partitions.

   When it's finished, icons for each partition appear in Disk Utility beneath the disk name **M** as well as in the Finder **N**.

TIP You can also change the partition size in step 4 by dragging the divider between partitions in the Partition Layout area **O**.

TIP If you select Free Space as the format for any partition in step 4, that partition cannot be used to store files.

G Choose the disk you want to partition and then click the Partition button.

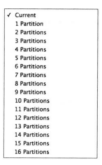

H Use the Partition Layout pop-up menu to choose how many partitions you want.

I In this example, I chose 2 partitions.

J Partition Format options.

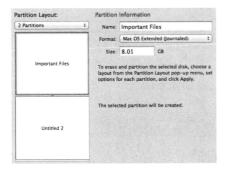

K Select a partition and set options for it.

TIP If you're not sure what volume format to choose in step 5, choose Mac OS Extended (Journaled). If you wanted one of the other formats, you'd know it.

TIP If you are partitioning removable media that may be used as a startup disk for a Macintosh or a Windows PC, before step 6, click the Options button in the Partition pane. Select the appropriate option in the dialog that appears **P** and click OK.

L Disk Utility confirms that you really do want to repartition the disk.

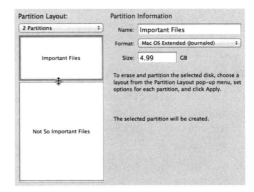

O You can drag the border between two partitions to resize them.

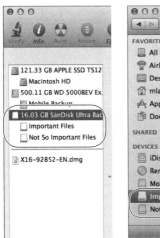

M The partitions appear under the disk in Disk Utility.

N The partitions also appear as individual volumes in the Finder.

P If necessary, set options in a dialog like this to create a bootable disk partition.

Working with Disk Image Files

A *disk image* is a single file that contains everything on a disk. You can mount a disk image on your desktop just like any other disk **B**.

Disk images are often used to distribute software on the Internet. They usually have a .dmg filename extension.

Disk Utility enables you to create disk image files, store data on them, mount them as disks, and burn them to CD or DVD.

To create a blank disk image file:

1. On the left side of the Disk Utility window, click beneath the list of disks and volumes so that none of them are selected.

2. Click the New Image button in Disk Utility's toolbar.

3. At the top of the dialog that appears **C**, enter a file name and specify a disk location to save the disk image file. (You can click the disclosure triangle beside the Save As field to display additional location options if necessary.)

4. Set options in the bottom part of the dialog:

   ▸ **Name** is the name of the volume within the Disk Image file. This is the name that will appear on the disk's icon in the Finder when the disk image is mounted.

   ▸ **Size** is the size of the volume. Choose an option from the pop-up menu **D**. If you choose Custom, use a dialog sheet to set the size.

A The icon for a disk image file looks like this.

Example Disk.dmg

B When you open a disk image file, a mounted disk appears in the Finder. You can use this like any other disk.

C Set options for a new disk image file in this dialog.

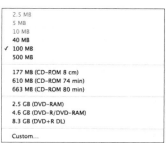

D The size of the disk determines the size of the disk image file.

```
✓  Mac OS Extended (Journaled)
   Mac OS Extended
   Mac OS Extended (Case-sensitive, Journaled)
   Mac OS Extended (Case-sensitive)
   MS-DOS (FAT)
   ExFAT
```

E Disk images can be formatted the same as any other disk.

```
✓  none

   128-bit AES encryption (recommended)
   256-bit AES encryption (more secure, but slower)
```

F You can encrypt a disk image file.

```
   Hard disk
   CD/DVD
✓  No partition map
   Single partition – Apple Partition Map
   Single partition – Master Boot Record Partition Map
   Single partition – GUID Partition Map
   Single partition – CD/DVD
   Single partition – CD/DVD with ISO data
```

G You can also set custom partition options for a disk image.

```
   sparse bundle disk image

   sparse disk image

✓  read/write disk image
   DVD/CD master
```

H In most cases, you'll want to create a read/write disk image.

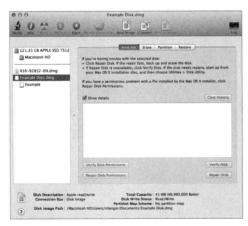

I Once you've created a disk image, it's mounted on your computer and appears in Disk Utility's window.

- ▸ **Format E** enables you to select the format of the volume.

- ▸ **Encryption F** offers file encryption options for the disk image file.

- ▸ **Partitions G** enables you to set a partition map for the disk image file.

- ▸ **Image Format H** refers to the type of disk image. In most cases, you'll want to select read/write disk image.

5. Click Create.

   Disk Utility creates a disk image file to your specifications, adds it to the list in Disk Utility **I**, and mounts it on the desktop **B**.

TIP The size of a disk image file is determined by the size specified in step **4**.

TIP If you're not sure what to choose for options in step **4**, leave them set to the default values.

TIP Once you have created and mounted a blank disk image, you can copy items to it as if it were a regular disk (page **51**). The items you copy to the disk are automatically copied into the disk image file.

To create a disk image file from a folder or disk:

1. In Disk Utility, do one of the following:

   ▸ To create a disk image file from a folder, choose File > New > Disk Image from Folder **J**, or press Shift-Command-N.

   ▸ To create a disk image file from a disk, select the disk on the left side of Disk Utility's window and then choose File > New > Disk Image from "*Disk Name*" **J**.

2. If you are creating a disk image from a folder, use the Select Folder to Image dialog **K** to locate and select the folder you want to create a disk image of and then click Image.

3. In the top part of the dialog that appears **L**, enter a name and choose a disk location for the image file.

4. In the bottom part of the dialog, set options as desired:

   ▸ **Image Format M N** refers to the type of disk image.

   ▸ **Encryption F** offers file encryption options for the disk image file.

5. Click Save.

   Disk Utility creates a disk image file containing the contents of the folder or disk, adds it to the list in Disk Utility's window, and saves it in the location you specified.

TIP The size of a disk image file is determined by the amount of data in the folder or disk and the Image Format option you chose in step 4.

TIP If you choose read/write from the Image Format pop-up menu in step 4, you can add files to the mounted disk image disk. Otherwise, you cannot.

J Use the New menu to create a disk image from a folder or a disk.

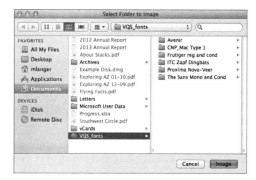

K If you're creating a disk image from a folder, you need to tell Disk Utility which folder.

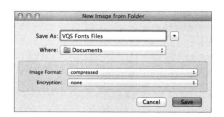

L Set options for the new disk image file in a dialog like this.

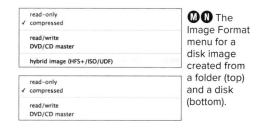

M N The Image Format menu for a disk image created from a folder (top) and a disk (bottom).

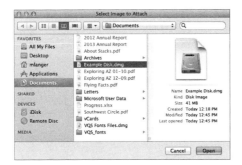

O Use this dialog to locate, select, and open a disk image file.

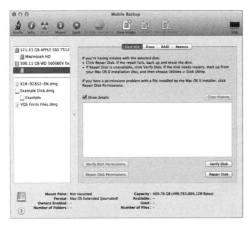

P In this example, the selected volume is not mounted. I can click the Mount button to mount it.

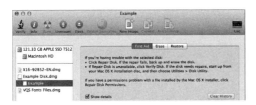

Q Select the volume you want to unmount and click the Unmount button.

To mount a disk image:

Use one of the following techniques:

- Double-click the disk image file's icon in the Finder **A**.

- On the left side of the Disk Utility window, select the name of the disk image you want to mount **I** and click the Open button in the toolbar.

- In Disk Utility, choose File > Open Disk Image, or press Option-Command-O. Then use the Select Image to Attach dialog that appears **O** to locate, select, and open the disk image file.

The disk image file's disk icon appears in the Finder and, if Disk Utility is open, in the list of disks and volumes.

TIP To mount an unmounted disk or partition, select it in the list on the left side of Disk Utility's main window **P** and click the Mount button in the toolbar.

To unmount a disk image:

Use one of the following techniques:

- In the Finder, drag the icon for the mounted disk to the Trash.

- In a Finder window's sidebar, click the Eject button beside the name of the mounted disk.

- In the Disk Utility main window, select the disk image volume you want to unmount **Q** and click the Unmount button in the toolbar.

Although the icon disappears from the desktop, all of its contents remain in the disk image file.

To burn a disc from a disk image:

1. In the Disk Utility window, select the disk image you want to burn to CD or DVD 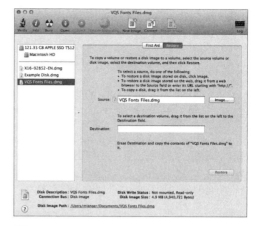.

2. Click the Burn button in the toolbar.

   A burn disc dialog appears **S**.

3. Insert a writable CD or DVD disc in your drive.

4. Click Burn.

5. Wait while Disk Utility writes to the disc. A progress dialog appears as it works.

   When the disc finished, Disk Utility ejects the disc and displays a dialog **T**.

6. Click OK.

   The disc appears mounted in Disk Utility as well as in the Finder.

TIP You must have a Combo Drive, Super-Drive, or compatible disc writer to burn CD or DVD discs.

TIP If a disk image file you want to burn to disc does not appear in the Disk Utility window, mount it as instructed in the section titled "To mount a disk image" on page 351 and then follow these instructions.

TIP If you click the disclosure triangle in the burn disc dialog **S**, the dialog expands to offer additional options **U**.

TIP Burning content to CD or DVD disc in the Finder is covered in detail starting on page 118.

R Select the disk image you want to burn to disc.

S When you click the Burn button on the toolbar, a dialog like this prompts you to insert a disc.

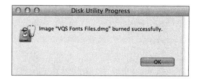

T This dialog confirms a successful disc burn.

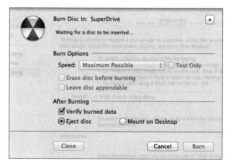

U Clicking the disclosure triangle in the burn disc dialog **S** displays more options.

Mac OS Utility Applications

Mac OS X includes utility applications that you can use to work with your computer and its files.

This chapter provides instructions for getting started with a number of utilities, most of which you find in the Utilities folder inside the Applications on your hard disk. Among these, you'll find applications for monitoring system activity, installing Windows on your Mac, entering Unix commands using a command-line interface, creating screen shots, and automating repetitive tasks.

This chapter does not cover utilities that are discussed elsewhere in this book: AirPort Utility (page 380), Bluetooth File Exchange (page 390), Disk Utility (Chapter 23), or Network Utility (page 407). A discussion of Audio MIDI Setup, Java Preferences, Podcast Capture, Podcast Publisher, RAID Utility, and X11 is beyond the scope of this book.

In This Chapter:

Activity Monitor

Activity Monitor enables you to get information about the various processes running on your computer. It also displays, in graphical format, CPU activity, memory usage, and disk and network statistics. You may find this information helpful if you are a programmer or network administrator or you are trying to troubleshoot a computer problem.

TIP A *process* is a running program that performs a task.

To monitor computer activity:

1. Open the Activity Monitor icon in the Utilities folder **A**.

   The Activity Monitor window appears **B**.

2. To view only specific types of processes, choose an option from the pop-up menu at the top of the window **C**.

   The list of processes in the top half of the window changes accordingly.

3. Click a button at the bottom of the window to view other information:

   ▸ **CPU B** displays CPU activity.

   ▸ **System Memory D** displays RAM usage.

   ▸ **Disk Activity E** displays disk access activity.

   ▸ **Disk Usage F** displays free and utilized disk space. Use the pop-up menu to choose other available disks.

   ▸ **Network G** displays network activity.

TIP To sort processes in the Activity Monitor window, click the column you want to sort by. You can reverse the sort order by clicking the same column again.

A Activity Monitor can be found in the Utilities folder.

Activity Monitor

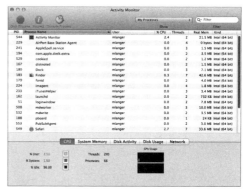

B The main Activity Monitor window lists active processes.

C Use this menu to specify which processes you want to show.

D E F G The bottom part of the Activity Monitor window can show System Memory, Disk Activity, Disk Usage, or Network information.

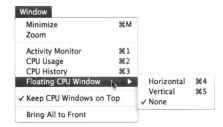

 H Use options under the Window menu and its Floating CPU Window submenu to display various Activity Monitor windows.

I The CPU Usage window displays activity for your computer's CPU(s).

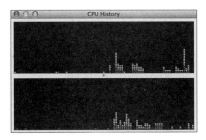

J The CPU History window displays CPU usage over time for your computer's CPU(s).

K The tiny Floating CPU window displays CPU activity anywhere you like onscreen.

L The Activity Monitor Dock icon offers menu commands for displaying various windows.

To display other monitor windows:

Choose an option from the Window menu or its Floating CPU Window submenu **H**:

- **Activity Monitor** displays the Activity Monitor window **B**.

- **CPU Usage I** displays a graphical representation of current CPU usage.

- **CPU History J** displays a window with a chart of CPU usage over time.

- **Floating CPU Window** submenu commands display a horizontal **K** or vertical bar with a graphical representation of current CPU usage.

TIP You can also use the contextual menu that appears when you right-click the Activity Monitor's Dock icon **L** to show various windows.

TIP You can use the Update Frequency submenu under the Monitor menu to change how often monitor windows are updated.

TIP If your computer has multiple processors, it will display a separate graph for each one **I J**.

Boot Camp Assistant

Boot Camp is an Apple technology that makes it possible to run Microsoft Windows on your Intel-based Macintosh computer. Once installed and configured, you can boot, or start, your Macintosh in either Mac OS X or Windows and use the software you have installed for the system you've booted.

Boot Camp Assistant is a utility application that installs the software you need to use Boot Camp. You run it once, install Boot Camp and Windows, and shouldn't have to run it again.

Boot Camp has some very specific requirements:

- Mac OS X 10.7 Lion or later.

- A USB keyboard and mouse or a built-in keyboard and trackpad.

- A built-in or compatible external optical disc drive.

- Windows 7 Home Premium, Professional, or Ultimate. Boot Camp does not include Windows; it must be purchased separately.

Although this chapter doesn't provide step-by-step instructions for installing and using Boot Camp, it does explain how you can get illustrated instructions prepared by Apple.

TIP A discussion of Windows is beyond the scope of this book. I highly recommend Peachpit Press's *Windows 7: Visual QuickStart Guide*.

A Book Camp Assistant helps you install Windows on your Mac.

Boot Camp Assistant

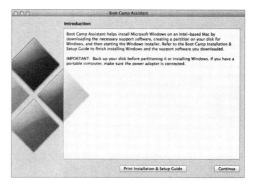

B The Introduction window tells you a little about the installation process and offers a button you can click to print complete instructions.

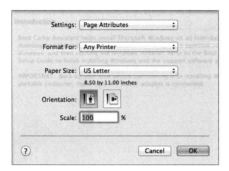

C Set options for your printer in the Page Setup dialog.

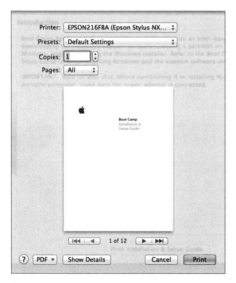

D Use the Print dialog to print or create a PDF of the instructions.

To print a Boot Camp installation & setup guide:

1. Open the Boot Camp Assistant icon in the Utilities folder **A**.

   The Boot Camp Assistant's window and Introduction screen appears **B**.

2. Click the Print Installation & Setup Guide button.

3. In the Page Setup dialog that appears **C**, set options for your printer and click OK.

4. In the Print dialog that appears **D**, set options for your printer and click Print.

   A 12-page illustrated document is printed. It includes complete instructions for installing and using Boot Camp.

TIP To print, you must have a printer set up for use with your Mac. You can learn more about printing in Chapter 22.

TIP If you'd rather save paper, you can save the document as a PDF. In step 4, choose Save as PDF from the PDF menu, set options for the PDF in the dialog that appears, and click Save. You can learn more about saving documents as PDFs on page 331.

ColorSync Utility

ColorSync is an industry-standard technology that helps designers match the colors they see onscreen to those in devices such as scanners, printers, and imagesetters. For the average user, color matching may not be very important, but for a designer who works with color, correct reproduction makes it possible to complete complex projects on time and within budget.

In this section, I explain how to use the ColorSync utility to check ColorSync profiles and view profiles and devices.

TIP A complete discussion of ColorSync is far beyond the scope of this book. To learn more about ColorSync features and settings, visit www.apple.com/colorsync.

To verify or repair ColorSync profiles:

1. Open the ColorSync Utility icon in the Utilities folder **A**.

2. In the window that appears, click the Profile First Aid icon **B**.

3. Click one of the buttons at the bottom of the window:

   ▸ **Verify** checks all installed profiles for errors.

   ▸ **Repair** repair any errors in installed profiles.

   ColorSync Utility checks or repairs installed profiles. When it's finished, it displays results in its window **C**.

TIP You can use this feature to check or fix ColorSync Profiles if you notice a difference between what you see on your monitor and what you see on printed documents.

A The ColorSync Utility icon.

ColorSync Utility

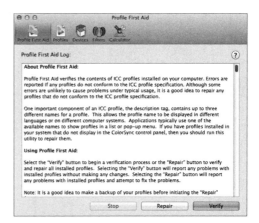
B The main Profile First Aid window provides information about what this feature does.

C The results of verifying (or repairing) profiles appears in the Profile First Aid window.

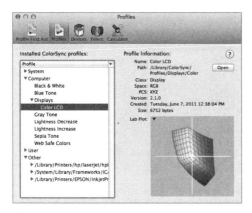

D The Profiles pane displays a list of all installed profiles. Click a profile to learn more about it.

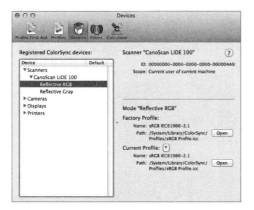

E The Devices pane displays a list of registered devices. Click a device to learn more about it.

F The Filters pane lists all available filters.

To view lists of installed profiles, registered devices, & available filters:

1. Open the ColorSync Utility icon in the Utilities folder **A**.

2. In the ColorSync Utility window, click an icon in the toolbar:

   ▸ **Profiles D** displays a list of installed ColorSync profiles.

   ▸ **Devices E** displays a list of registered ColorSync devices.

   ▸ **Filters F** displays a list of available ColorSync filters.

3. If necessary, click triangles beside a folder pathname to view a list of the items in the folder **D E** or settings for the item **F**.

TIP A *registered device* is one that is recognized by the system software and has a ColorSync profile assigned to it.

TIP Clicking the name of a profile or device displays information about it in the right side of the window **D E**.

TIP You can change a device's profile by choosing an option from the Current Profile pop-up menu when the item is displayed **E**.

TIP The filters that are installed with Mac OS X are locked and cannot be changed.

To convert color values:

1. Open the ColorSync Utility icon in the Utilities folder **A**.

2. In the ColorSync Utility window, click the Calculator icon **G**.

3. On the left side of the window, use the pop-up menus to set the color space or profile you are converting from.

4. Use the sliders on the left side of the window to enter color values.

5. On the right side of the window, use the pop-up menus to set the color space or profile you are converting to.

   The converted color values appear on the right side of the window **G**.

TIP To find the color value for a pixel on your screen, click the magnifying glass icon to change the mouse pointer into a magnified cross-hairs pointer **H**. Click the pixel you want to get the color values for to insert the values on the left side of the screen. This feature is similar in functionality to DigitalColor Meter, which I discuss a little later in this chapter.

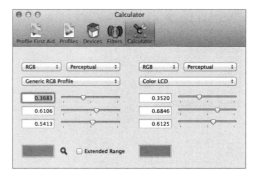

G This example shows a conversion from a Generic RGB profile to the profile for my MacBook Air's LCD display.

H Clicking the magnifying glass icon enables you to use a magnified cursor to select a single pixel onscreen.

 **Ⓐ** The Console application icon.

Console

Ⓑ In this example, Console is displaying all messages recorded by the system.

Console

The Console application enables you to read messages from Mac OS X system software and applications. You might find this useful if you handle text support or are troubleshooting a problem. (If not, you'll probably think it looks like a bunch of gibberish.)

To view system messages:

1. Open the Console icon in the Utilities folder **Ⓐ** to display Console's main window.

2. On the left side of the window, select the log or report you want to read. You can click a disclosure triangle to view lists of individual reports.

3. Read the messages in the right side of the window **Ⓑ**.

TIP You can click the Clear Display button in the Console window **Ⓑ** to erase the contents of the window and start a fresh log.

To save a copy of the log:

1. Choose File > Save a Copy As, or press Shift-Command-S.

2. Use the standard Save As window that appears to save the contents of the currently displayed window as a plain text file.

TIP Following these steps makes it possible to send a copy of a log file to someone helping you to troubleshoot a problem on your Mac.

DigitalColor Meter

DigitalColor Meter enables you to measure colors that appear on your display as a variety of standard values. This makes it possible to precisely record or duplicate colors that appear onscreen.

TIP A discussion of color technology is far beyond the scope of this book. To learn more about how your Mac can work with colors, visit the ColorSync page on Apple's Website, www. apple.com/colorsync/.

To measure color values:

1. Open the DigitalColor Meter icon in the Utilities folder to display the DigitalColor Meter window **B**.

2. Point to the color onscreen that you want to measure.

   Its values appear in the right side of the DigitalColor Meter window **B**.

3. If desired, choose a different option from the pop-up menu above the measurements **C**.

   The value display changes to convert values to that measuring system **D**.

TIP You can use commands under the Image menu **E** to work with the color sample image.

TIP You can change the amount of color that is sampled by dragging the Aperture Size slider to the right or left. A large aperture size will average the colors within it **F**.

A The DigitalColor Meter icon.

DigitalColor Meter

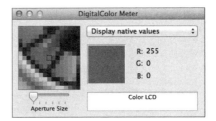

B Point to a color onscreen, and Digital-Color Meter displays measurements for it.

C Use a pop-up menu to choose a different measuring system.

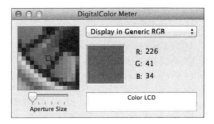

D If you change the measuring system, the values change accordingly.

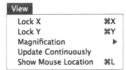

E Use the View menu to work with the sample image.

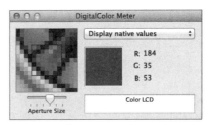

F Changing the Aperture Size averages the colors within the selection area.

A The Grab application icon.

Grab

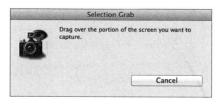

B Use the Capture menu to specify what you want to capture.

Drag over the portion of the screen you want to capture.

Cancel

C The Selection Grab dialog provides instructions for capturing a portion of the screen.

D Drag a selection box around the portion of the screen you want to capture.

Grab

Grab is an application that can capture screen shots of Mac OS X and its applications. You tell Grab to capture what appears on your screen, and it creates a TIFF file. You can then view the TIFF file with Preview or any application capable of opening TIFFs.

TIP You might find screen shots useful for documenting software—or for writing books like this one.

TIP Although Grab is a handy screen shot utility, it isn't the best available for Mac OS X. Snapz Pro X, a shareware program from Ambrosia Software, is far better. If you take a lot of screen shots, be sure to check it out at www.ambrosiasw.com.

To create a screen shot:

1. Set up the screen so it shows what you want to capture.

2. Do one of the following:
   ▸ If Grab is not already running, open the Grab icon in the Utilities folder **A**.
   ▸ If Grab is already running, click its icon on the Dock to make it active.

3. Choose an option from the Capture menu **B** or press its corresponding shortcut key:
   ▸ **Selection** (Shift-Command-A) enables you to capture a portion of the screen. When you choose this option, the Selection Grab dialog **C** appears. Use the mouse pointer to drag a box around the portion of the screen you want to capture **D**. Release the mouse button to capture the screen.

continues on next page

▸ **Window** (Shift-Command-W) enables you to capture a window. When you choose this option, the Window Grab dialog  appears. Click the Choose Window button, then click the window you want to capture.

E The Window Grab dialog.

▸ **Screen** (Command-Z) enables you to capture the entire screen. When you choose this option, the Screen Grab dialog **F** appears. Click outside the dialog to capture the screen.

F The Screen Grab dialog assures you that it won't be included in your screen shot.

▸ **Timed Screen** (Shift-Command-Z) enables you to capture the entire screen after a ten-second delay. When you choose this option, the Timed Screen Grab dialog **G** appears. Click the Start Timer button, then activate the program you want to capture and arrange onscreen elements as desired. In ten seconds, the screen is captured.

G You can start a timer in the Timed Screen Grab dialog.

4. Grab makes a camera shutter sound as it captures the screen. The image appears in an untitled document window **H**.

5. Do one of the following:

▸ If you are satisfied with the screen shot, choose File > Save or press Command-S and use the Save As dialog that appears to save it as a file on disk.

▸ If you are not satisfied with the screen shot, choose File > Close or press Command-W to close the window. In the Close dialog, click Don't Save.

H The screen shot appears in a Grab window.

A The Grapher icon.

Grapher

B Set basic options in the New Graph dialog.

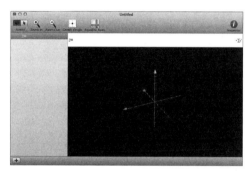

C A graph begins with a frame like this.

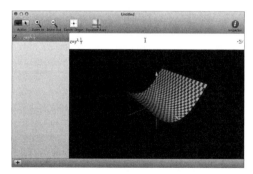

D Here's an example of a 3D graph for a simple formula.

Grapher

Grapher is a charting tool that can create static and dynamic 2-D and 3-D graphs based on formulas.

To graph a formula:

1. Open the Grapher icon in the Utilities folder **A**.

2. If necessary, choose File > New or press Command-N to display the New Graph dialog **B**.

3. Click a button near the top of the dialog to list either 2D or 3D document types.

4. In the list on the left side of the dialog, select the type of graph you want.

   A preview appears in the right side of the dialog **B**.

5. Click Choose.

   An untitled window with an empty graph appears **C**.

6. Type the formula you want to chart in the box at the top of the window.

7. Press Return.

   The formula's graph appears in the window and the formula is added to the Definitions list **D**.

8. If desired, click the + button at the bottom of the formula list and repeat steps 6 and 7 to add other formulas to the graph.

TIP Grapher's Equation Palette makes it a bit easier to enter complex formulas. To display it, choose Window > Show Equation Palette or press Shift-Command-E.

TIP Once you've created a graph, you can save or print it using commands under the File menu.

Keychain Access

Mac OS X's keychain feature offers users a way to store passwords for accessing password-protected applications, servers, and Internet locations.

Mac OS X automatically creates a keychain for each user. This is the default, or *login*, keychain. Each user's keychain is automatically unlocked when he logs in, so the passwords it contains are available when needed to access secured files and sites.

Keychain Access gives you direct access to the keychain items stored for your account. You can use it to manually add, modify, or remove keychain items.

TIP The keychain feature only works with applications that are keychain-aware.

TIP Your keychain is automatically maintained by Mac OS as you access various websites, servers, and applications. You might never need to open Keychain Access.

To add a keychain item when accessing a secure application, server, or Internet location:

1. Follow your normal procedure for accessing the secure item.

2. Enter your password when prompted.

3. Use a check box or other control to indicate that your Mac should remember the site or your password. The way this appears varies based on what you're accessing; **B** and **C** show two examples.

4. Finish accessing the secure item.

   Later, if you open Keychain Access **D**, you'll see that a keychain items has been created for accessing that item.

A Keychain Access is an application for working with keychain items.

Keychain Access

B C Two examples of login dialogs you may encounter. The top one is an example of a Wi-Fi network login dialog; the bottom one is an example of a server login dialog. In both examples, you use a check box to remember the network or password.

D Here are the two keychain items created based on the examples in **B** and **C**.

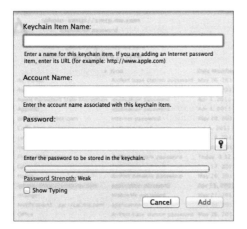

E You can make changes to a keychain item in a dialog like this.

F It's possible to manually add a keychain item using a dialog like this one.

G Keychain Access asks if you're sure you want to delete the keychain item.

To view or modify your keychain:

1. Open the Keychain Access icon in the Utilities folder **A**.

   A list of items in your keychain appears **D**.

2. Do one of the following:

   ▸ To view a keychain item's information, select it and consult the information at the top of the window **D**.

   ▸ To modify a keychain item, select it and choose File > Get Info or press Command-I. Then make changes in the dialog that appears **E** and click Save Changes.

   ▸ To manually add a keychain item, click the + button at the bottom of the window. In the dialog that appears **F**, enter details about the keychain item and click Add.

   ▸ To delete a keychain item, select it and press the Delete key. In the confirmation dialog that appears **G**, click Delete.

3. When you are finished making changes, choose Keychain Access > Quit Keychain Access, or press Command-Q to quit. Your changes are saved automatically.

TIP As you work with Keychain items, you may be prompted to authenticate by entering an administrator user name and password. If you cannot do so, you will not be able to proceed.

TIP Removing a keychain item does not prevent you from accessing an item. It just prevents you from accessing it without entering a password.

Migration Assistant

Migration Assistant enables you to copy user accounts, applications, computer settings, and files between Macs or from a PC to a Mac. This makes it possible to transfer your information from an old Mac to a new one, restore user information with Time Machine, or add user accounts from or to another Mac.

When you first start Migration Assistant , it offers two options:

- From another Mac, PC, Time Machine backup, or other disk enables you to transfer user information from another computer or backup to the computer you're working on **B**. If you choose this option, you'll be able to specify whether you want to transfer from another computer or from a backup **C**.

- To another Mac enables you to transfer user information from the Mac you're working on to another Mac.

The Migration Assistant is very easy to use. It provides clear instructions for completing every step and walks you through the process of copying user information. Simply double-click its icon to get started and follow the prompts.

> **TIP** The Mac OS X Setup Assistant (page 9) may automatically perform the same tasks as the Migration Assistant, depending on your answers to questions during setup.

> **TIP** The Migration Assistant requires that you provide an Administrator user name and password to use it. This prevents unauthorized users from adding accounts to the computer.

> **TIP** Most users will never need to use the Migration Assistant after completing the setup process for a Mac.

A The Migration Assistant icon.

Migration Assistant

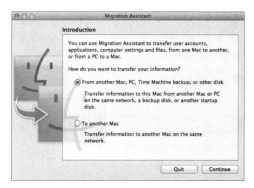

B The first screen of Migration Assistant asks whether you want to transfer data from or to another computer.

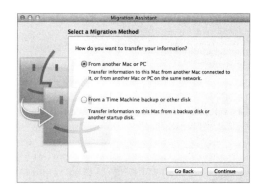

C If you indicate that you want to transfer data from another computer or backup, Migration Assistant prompts you for more information.

A The System Information icon.

System Information

B Maria Langer's MacBook Air ▶ Hardware

C Maria Langer's MacBook Air ▶ Network ▶ AirPort

D Maria Langer's MacBook Air ▶ Software ▶ Applications ▶ 5DonPaletteServer

B C D Three examples of the kind of information you can get from the System Information application: general hardware information, general network information, and a complete list of applications.

System Information

The System Information application, which was known as System Profiler in previous versions of Mac OS, provides information about your computer's hardware, software, network, and logs. This information can come in handy when you are troubleshooting problems or just need to know more about the hardware and software installed on your computer.

TIP Clicking the More Info button in the About This Mac window launches System Information.

To view system information:

1. Open the System Information icon in the Utilities folder **A** to display the System Information window for your computer.

2. In the list on the left side of the window, click the type of information you want to view **B C D**.

3. The information appears in the window **B C D**.

TIP Clicking an item in the top-right portion of a System Information window displays details about that item **C D**.

TIP You can use the File menu's Save and Print commands to save or print the information that appears in System Information. You might find this handy if you need to document your system's current configuration for troubleshooting or backup purposes.

Terminal

Terminal is an application that enables you to enter command line instructions into your Mac. These instructions are interpreted by Unix, the operating system beneath Mac OS X. This makes it possible to modify your Mac's internal settings with Unix and run Unix applications.

CAUTION **Don't know anything about Unix? Then you'd probably want to steer clear of Terminal. Typing an incorrect command into Terminal can render your Mac useless.**

TIP **A discussion of Unix is beyond the scope of this book.**

To use Terminal:

1. Double-click the Terminal icon in the Utilities folder **A**.

   A Terminal window with a shell prompt appears **B**.

2. Use your keyboard to enter commands into Terminal. Be sure to press Return to send each command to Unix.

   The results of your commands appear in the Terminal window **C**.

A The Terminal icon.

Terminal

B When you open Terminal, it displays the current date and a shell prompt.

C In this example, I used the ls command to get a list of the items in my home folder. (Aren't you glad you don't have to deal with this on a regular basis?)

About the Shell Prompt

The shell prompt shown in **B** and **C** (maria-langers-MacBook-Air: ~mlanger$) includes the following components:

- *Computer name* is the name of the computer you're logged in to.

- *Directory* is the current directory.

- ~ (the tilde character) is Unix shorthand for your home directory.

- *User name* is your user name, which, in this example, is mlanger.

- $ is the end of the prompt.

A The VoiceOver Utility icon.

VoiceOver Utility

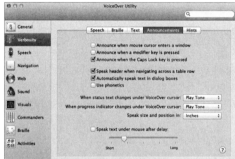

B C D Examples of settings screens in Voice-Over Utility: General, Verbosity Announcements, and Speech Pronunciation.

VoiceOver Utility

VoiceOver is a built-in screen reader that helps visually impaired people use their computers. Once configured, VoiceOver enables you to hear descriptions of everything onscreen, move around the screen, select items, and read and manipulate text.

A complete discussion of VoiceOver is beyond the scope of this book. This section, however, provides enough information to get started with the VoiceOver Utility, the application you use to configure VoiceOver.

TIP VoiceOver can be enabled or disabled in the Universal Access preferences pane, which is discussed on page 504.

TIP To learn more about configuring and using VoiceOver, open VoiceOver Utility and choose Help > VoiceOver Help. Then follow the links to get the information you need.

To configure VoiceOver:

1. Open the VoiceOver Utility icon in the Utilities folder **A**.

2. The VoiceOver Utility window appears. Click buttons to set options in each of nine categories:

   ▸ **General B** lets you set the greeting and how portable preferences are used.

   ▸ **Verbosity C** includes four panes of settings that control how much speaking VoiceOver does.

   ▸ **Speech D** enables you to select the default voice and voices for various types of spoken text.

continues on next page

- ▶ **Navigation ❺** controls how VoiceOver moves and tracks the cursor and text selections.
- ▶ **Web ❻** controls how Voice-Over works with your Web browser.
- ▶ **Sound** enables you to set sound-related preferences.
- ▶ **Visuals ❼** enables you to set the size of the VoiceOver cursor and menu magnification, as well as configure the Caption Panel.
- ▶ **Commanders ❽** enables you to map commands to the trackpad, numeric keypad, or keyboard.
- ▶ **Braille ❶** lets you set the way Braille display works.
- ▶ **Activities** lets you create custom settings groups that you can use with the applications you specify.

3. Choose VoiceOver Utility > Quit Voice-Over Utility, or press Command-Q, to save your settings.

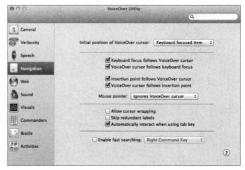

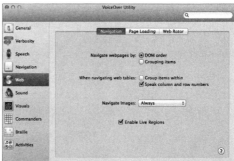

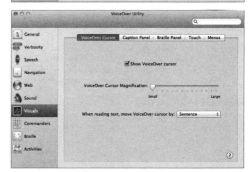

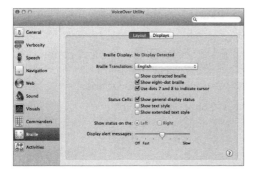

❶ Braille Layout settings in VoiceOver Utility.

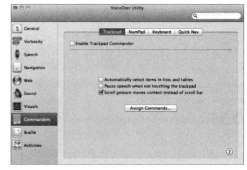

❺❻❼❽ Examples of settings in VoiceOver Utility: Navigation, Web Navigation, Visuals VoiceOver Cursor, and Commanders Trackpad.

A You can find the Automator application icon in the Applications folder.

Automator

B This example Automator workflow retrieves movie trailers from Apple's Web site and displays them in Safari.

C AppleScript Editor can be found inside the Utilities folder.

AppleScript Editor

D This sample AppleScript duplicates an image and saves it as a TIFF file.

Automation Tools

Computers are supposed to make our lives easier, right? They can—if we "teach" them to perform repetitive tasks automatically.

For example, when I begin work in the morning, I start my computer and launch the applications I use every day: Mail, iCal, iTunes, InDesign, and Photoshop. I check my email, delete junk mail, and start playing one of my iTunes playlists. Then I open book chapter files and folders. When I'm done with a chapter, I save it as a PDF file, create an archive of the chapter's folder, and upload it all to my publisher's FTP site. There are many repetitive tasks here—tasks my computer has been trained to do automatically at my request. This saves time; my Mac can do things a lot faster than I can.

Mac OS X includes two tools for automating repetitive tasks:

- Automator **A** enables you to build workflows **B** that automate tasks in multiple applications—all without knowing a single line of programming code. You can find Automator in the Applications folder on your hard disk.

- AppleScript is a scripting language that enables you to automate tasks and extend the functionality of Mac OS. You use AppleScript Editor **C** to create and edit scripts **D** and save them in a variety of formats—including formats that work with Automator. You can find AppleScript Editor in the Utilities folder on your hard disk.

A discussion of these two automation tools is beyond the scope of this book. But once you've mastered the basics of Mac OS, why not give them a try?

Network & Internet Connectivity

In This Part

25

Networking

Networking uses wired or wireless connections and network protocols to link your computer to others on a *network*. Once connected, you can share files, access email, and run special network applications on server computers.

This chapter looks at peer-to-peer networking, which uses the built-in features of Mac OS X to connect to other computers for sharing. It explains how to configure an AirPort base station for use as a networking tool. It also covers some of the advanced network configuration applications available as Mac OS X utilities.

This chapter touches only briefly on using networks to connect to the Internet. Connecting to the Internet is discussed in detail in Chapter 26. A discussion of Mac OS X Server, which is designed to meet the demands of large workgroups and corporate intranets, is beyond the scope of this book.

In This Chapter:

Network Interfaces

Mac OS computers support the following types of network interfaces:

- **Wi-Fi** is a wireless networking technology. Through the use of *AirPort* (page 380), Apple's Wi-Fi connectivity device, your Mac can join wireless networks using the 802.11a, b, g, or n specifications.

- **Bluetooth** (page 390) is a wireless technology designed for short-range (less than 30 feet) connections between devices. Although Bluetooth is commonly used to connect to input devices such as a keyboard or mouse, it's also a viable connection method between computers or handheld computing devices such as smart phones.

- **Ethernet** (page 390) is a network connection method that uses Ethernet cables to connect computers, network printers, routers, and hubs. Ethernet was a common method of networking until a few years ago, when the benefits of wireless networking—no wires!—started providing a real alternative.

- **FireWire** (page 396), which is also known as *IEEE 1394*, is an Apple technology for extremely fast data connections. Although it's commonly used for data transfer between computers and hard disks or video devices, it can also be used to attach two computers for networking using IP over FireWire.

- **Modem** can establish a connection between two computers over a phone line. This older technology is used primarily for Internet connections when faster alternatives are not available.

You can check the status of a network interface or add additional interfaces in the Network preferences pane **A**.

A You can check network status for any connection to your computer in the Network preferences pane.

TIP Other network technologies supported by OS X Lion include VPN, PPPoE, and 6 to 4. A discussion of these technologies is beyond the scope of this book.

TIP Network hardware configuration details involving hubs and routers are far beyond the scope of this book. If you need help setting up a complex network, refer to a detailed networking reference or contact a network consultant.

TIP Not all Macs support all network interfaces. For example, my MacBook Air does not have Ethernet or FireWire ports, so without special adapters, it would not support either of these network interfaces.

To check network status:

1. Use one of the following techniques to open System Preferences:

   ▶ Choose Apple > System Preferences.

   ▶ Click the System Preferences icon in the Dock.

   The System Preferences window opens.

2. Choose View > Network to display Network preferences **A**.

3. To get details about the status and settings for a specific connection, select it in the list on the left side of the window.

   Details appear in the right side of the window **A**.

TIP You can set advanced options for a selected interface by clicking the Advanced button near the bottom of the Network preferences window. You can learn more about the Network preferences pane starting on page 540.

AirPort

AirPort is Apple's version of the Wi-Fi local area network technology. It enables your computer to connect to a network or the Internet via radio waves instead of wires. All new Macintosh computers come with AirPort functionality pre-installed.

In addition to a Mac's AirPort capabilities, Apple offers three different AirPort devices:

- **AirPort Extreme Base Station** is an external device that works as a router to share an incoming Internet connection, printer, and external hard disk with other computers.

- **Time Capsule** is an AirPort Extreme Base Station with a built-in hard disk. It's designed for use with the Time Machine feature for automated backup, but it can be used for a centralized storage space for network users.

- **AirPort Express Base Station** is an external device that can connect to a network via Ethernet or can extend an existing AirPort network. It also supports AirPlay, which makes it possible to receive data from iTunes to play music on compatible stereo speakers.

Mac OS X includes AirPort Utility, which enables you to configure an AirPort device for networking. This part of the chapter explains how to configure two kinds of AirPort base stations: a Time Capsule and an AirPort Express. It explains how to get started with AirPort base station manual settings. And finally, it tells you how to connect to an AirPort network with a Mac.

TIP An AirPort network can include multiple base stations and computers.

TIP You can learn more about AirPort devices and networking on Apple's Website at www.apple.com/wifi/.

TIP It's not possible to show every single combination of configuration option. Instead, I've done my best to show the configuration options you're most likely to use for your setup.

TIP If you're not sure how to set an option in an AirPort Utility configuration screen, consult your ISP.

TIP If a firmware update for your base station is available, a dialog or notification in the AirPort Utility window may appear to tell you. Follow onscreen instructions to install any updates that are available.

TIP The base station and network passwords you're prompted for when setting up a base station are for different things. The base station password controls access to the device's configuration. The network password controls access to the network by wireless users.

TIP If you are the only user of your AirPort network, it's OK to have the same password for the network as the base station. But if multiple users will be using the network, you should assign a different password to the base station to prevent other users from changing base station settings.

A The AirPort Utility application icon can be found in the Utilities folder.

AirPort Utility

B In this example, AirPort utility found three devices: an AirPort Express, an old AirPort Extreme, and a Time Capsule (selected). (Yes, I admit that I never throw any computer equipment away.)

C Set Time Capsule name and security options.

To launch AirPort Utility:

Use one of the following techniques:

- Open the AirPort Utility icon **A** in the Utilities folder inside the Applications folder.

- In LaunchPad (page 150), click Utilities and then click AirPort Utility.

AirPort opens, scans for AirPort base stations within range, and displays what it finds **B**.

To create a Time Capsule network:

1. In AirPort Utility's main window, select the Time Capsule you want to configure **B** and click Continue.

2. If a dialog asking if you want to switch networks appears, click Switch.

3. AirPort Utility scans the Time Capsule for current settings and displays its first screen **C**. Set options.

   ▸ **Time Capsule Name** is the name you want to assign to the Time Capsule.

   ▸ **Time Capsule Password** and **Verify Password** is the same password for the Time Capsule, entered twice. You'll need this password to make changes to the Time Capsule configuration in the future.

   ▸ **Remember this password in my keychain** automatically creates a keychain item for the Time Capsule password.

   ▸ **Use a different password** to secure disks enables you to specify a different password to protect the data on disks inside and connected to the Time Capsule.

4. Click Continue.

continues on next page

5. The next screen 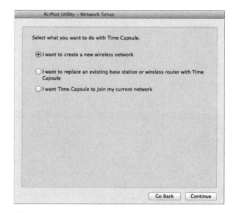 asks what you want to do:

   ▶ **I want to create a new wireless network** uses the Time Capsule to create a wireless network. Choose this option to continue following instructions here.

   ▶ **I want to replace an existing base station or wireless router with Time Capsule** enables you to swap out another wireless router with the Time Capsule.

   ▶ **I want Time Capsule to join my current network** adds the Time Capsule to an existing network, thus extending the network's reach and adding the devices connected to Time Capsule to the network.

6. Click Continue.

7. The next screen  enables you to set network name and security options:

   ▶ **Wireless Network Name** is the name of the network. If you have multiple networks, you may want to give it a name related to its location or use.

   ▶ You have two security options: WPA2 Personal password-protects your network so no one can join it without a password. If you choose this option, enter a password of 8 to 63 characters in both boxes. **No security** leaves your network open so anyone can join it without a password.

8. Click Continue.

9. A screen offering to create a guest network appears next . This allows other people to use your Internet connection without being able to access the computers on the network. To enable this feature, turn on the check box, enter a name for the guest network, choose a

D Choose an option to proceed.

E Set network name and security options.

F You can set up a guest network.

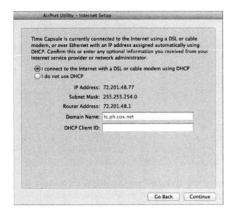

G Indicate whether you use DHCP.

H If you want to set up Time Machine, say so.

I At the end of the process, AirPort Utility displays a summary of settings.

security option, and if necessary, enter the same password in each Password box.

10. Click Continue.

11. In the next screen **G**, indicate whether you use DHCP.

- ▸ **I connect to the Internet with a DSL or cable modem using DHCP** uses the DHCP information you receive from your Internet connection to set IP addresses for the computers on your network.

- ▸ **I do not use DHCP** disables IP address sharing on your network.

12. Click Continue.

13. Next, you're asked if you want to set up Time Machine (page 125) to back up your computer **H**. If you choose yes, you'll be prompted as part of the setup to configure Time Machine (page 577).

14. Click Continue.

15. A summary of your settings appears **I**. Click Update.

16. A dialog warns you that the network will be temporarily unavailable. Click Continue.

The Time Capsule restarts. It may take a while. When it's finished, it appears in AirPort Utility's list of base stations with a green bullet beside it and the name you specified.

17. Click Quit.

To create an AirPort Express network:

1. In AirPort Utility's main window, select the AirPort Express you want to configure **J** and click Continue.

2. If a dialog asking if you want to switch networks appears, click Switch.

3. AirPort Utility scans the AirPort Express for current settings and displays its first settings screen **K**. Set options.

   ▸ **AirPort Express Name** is the name you want to assign to the AirPort Express.

   ▸ **AirPort Express Password** and **Verify Password** is the same password for the AirPort Express, entered twice. You'll need this password to make future changes to the configuration.

   ▸ **Remember this password in my keychain** automatically creates a keychain item (page 366) for the AirPort Express password.

4. Click Continue:

5. Next, select an option to proceed **L**:

   ▸ **I want to create a new wireless network** uses the AirPort Express to create a wireless network. Choose this option to continue following instructions here.

   ▸ **I want to replace an existing base station or wireless router with AirPort Express** enables you to swap out another wireless router with the AirPort Express.

   ▸ **I want AirPort Express to join my current network** adds the AirPort Express to an existing network, thus extending the network's reach and adding the devices connected to AirPort Express to the network.

J Select the AirPort Express you want to configure. In this example, the selected base station has never been configured.

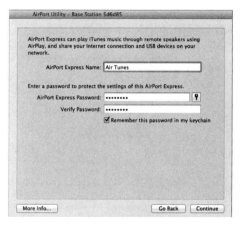

K Use this screen to name your AirPort Express.

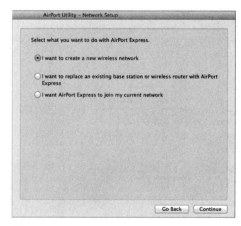

L Choose an option for setup.

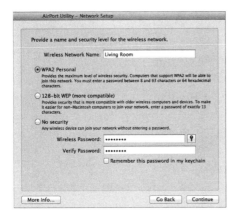

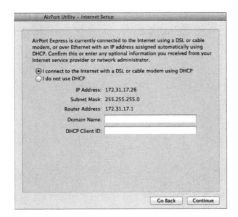

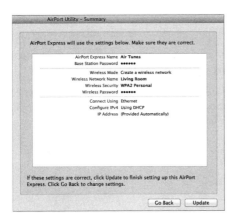

M Enter a network name and set security options.

N Indicate DHCP use.

O AirPort Utility summarizes settings.

6. Click Continue.

7. Next, enter a name and set security options for the network **M**. There are three security options:

   ▸ **WPA2 Personal** is a security method that works with computers that support WPA2. Enter a password of 8 to 63 characters in both Password boxes.

   ▸ **128-bit WEP** is an older and less secure but more compatible security method. Enter a password of exactly 13 characters in both Password boxes.

   ▸ **No security** does not secure the network at all. Anyone within range can connect.

8. Click Continue.

9. In the next screen **N**, indicate how you use DHCP.

   ▸ **I connect to the Internet with a DSL or cable modem using DHCP** uses the DHCP information you receive from your Internet connection to set IP addresses for the computers on your network.

   ▸ I do not use DHCP disables IP address sharing on your network.

10. Click Continue.

11. A summary of your settings appears **O**. Click Update.

12. A dialog warns you that the network will be temporarily unavailable. Click Continue.

    The base station restarts. This might take a while. When it's finished, it appears in AirPort Utility's list of base stations with a green bullet beside it and the name you specified.

13. Click Quit.

To manually set AirPort base station options:

1. In AirPort Utility's main window, select the AirPort base station you want to configure  and click Manual Setup.

2. If necessary, enter the base station password when prompted.

3. The manual configurations window appears. It offers several categories of options, depending on the Base Station model you selected in Step 1 and the peripherals attached to it. Click a button in the toolbar at the top of the window to display and set options in a variety of panels:

   ▸ **AirPort** includes basic AirPort options, which include Summary ❶, Time Capsule, Wireless, Guest Network, and Access Control.

   ▸ **Internet** displays Internet configuration options, which include Internet Connection ❷, TCP/IP, DHCP, and NAT.

   ▸ **Music** (not shown) displays options for enabling and configuring AirPlay.

   ▸ **Printers** ❸ shows printers connected to the base station.

   ▸ **Disks** shows disks connected to the base station ❹ and enables you to set file sharing options for AirPort Disks.

   ▸ **Advanced** includes a number of advanced networking options, such as Logging & Statistics ❺, Port Mapping, MobileMe, and IPv6.

4. Repeat step 3 for each screen of options you want to change.

5. Click update to save your changes to the base station and restart it.

❶ In this example, I've selected a Time Capsule.

❶ The Summary pane of AirPort settings.

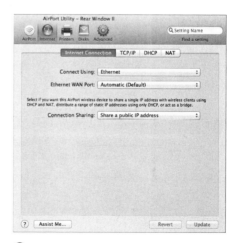

❷ The Internet Connections pane of Internet settings.

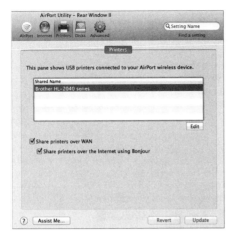

S The Printers settings.

TIP The manual configuration options offered by AirPort Utility are advanced and powerful. Do not make changes to these options unless you know what you're doing, or you may inadvertently disable your network.

TIP Want more advanced information about setting up an AirPort network? Consult the Apple documentation that can be downloaded from support.apple.com/manuals/airport/.

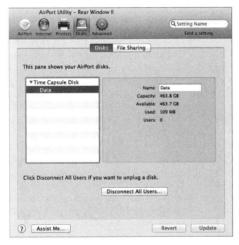

T The Disks pane of Disks settings.

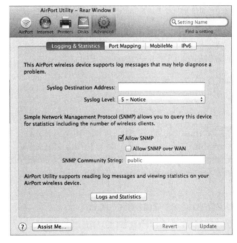

U The Logging & Statistics pane of Advanced settings.

Using the Wi-Fi Status Menu

The Wi-Fi Status menu  can be displayed at the right end of the menu bar. it indicates the status of your Wi-Fi connection:

- If the icon has one or more black arcs, you are connected to a network .
- If the icon has gray arcs, Wi-Fi is turned on but you are not connected to a network.
- If the icon looks like an empty fan 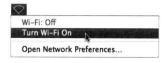, Wi-Fi is turned off.

The menu also has options for enabling or disabling your computer's AirPort connectivity, connecting to Wi-Fi networks, creating your own Wi-Fi network, and accessing networking preferences options.

This part of the chapter explores the options you'll likely use most.

TIP To use the Wi-Fi Status menu **A**, it must be enabled. You can enable it in the Network preferences pane (page 540) when your AirPort interface is selected (page 379).

To enable or disable your computer's AirPort connectivity:

Do one of the following:

- To enable AirPort, choose Turn Wi-Fi On from the Wi-Fi Status menu **B**.
- To disable AirPort, choose Turn Wi-Fi Off from the Wi-Fi Status menu **A**.

TIP When your computer's AirPort connectivity is enabled, the command reads *Turn Wi-Fi Off* **A**. When it is turned off, the command reads *Turn Wi-Fi On* **B**.

A You can use the Wi-Fi Status menu to connect to a wireless network or perform other tasks.

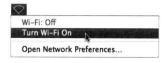

B If Wi-Fi is disabled, you can use the Turn Wi-Fi On command to enable it.

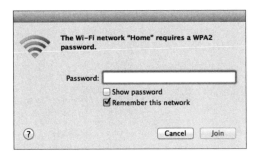

C Use this dialog to enter a password, if one is necessary to join the network.

D You can use a dialog like this one to connect to an unlisted network, provided you know its name and security settings.

To connect to a Wi-Fi network:

1. Choose the name of the network you want to connect to from the Wi-Fi Status menu **A**.

2. If the network requires a password, a dialog appears **C**. Enter the password and set other options as desired:

   ▸ **Password** is the network password. You must enter the correct password for the Join button to work.

   ▸ **Show password** displays the password as plain text characters instead of bullets so you can see what you're typing.

   ▸ **Remember this network** adds the network to the Network preferences pane so your computer can automatically connect to it in the future. It also adds the password to your keychain so you don't have to type it in every time you connect.

3. Click Join.

   The Wi-Fi menu's indicator displays black arcs to indicate you are connected to a network.

TIP An available network's signal strength and password requirement are indicated in the menu with black arcs to indicate signal strength and a padlock icon to indicate password is required **A**.

TIP If the network you want to join is not listed on the Wi-Fi Status menu, you can use the Join Other Network command to connect. Just enter the network name and security information in the dialog that appears when you choose this command **D** and click Join.

TIP If the base station has a dial-up connection to the Internet, a Connect command will also appear on this menu. Use this command to connect to the Internet.

Bluetooth

Bluetooth is a very short-range—30 feet or less—wireless networking technology. It enables you to connect Bluetooth-enabled computers, smart phones, and other mobile devices to each other. It also lets you connect Bluetooth-enabled input devices, such as a mouse or keyboard, to your Mac.

Mac OS X includes two tools for working with Bluetooth:

- **Bluetooth preferences pane** (page 543) allows you to configure Bluetooth and pair Bluetooth devices with your computer.

- **Bluetooth File Exchange** enables you to send files from one Bluetooth device to another or browse files on another Bluetooth-enabled computer.

This part of the chapter explains how to configure and use Bluetooth to exchange files between two computers.

TIP You can learn more about Bluetooth technology at www.bluetooth.com.

TIP Don't confuse Bluetooth with AirPort (page 380). AirPort makes it possible for an AirPort-enabled computer to connect to and exchange information on an AirPort network. Bluetooth enables your computer to exchange information with a single Bluetooth-enabled device.

TIP Before you can use a Bluetooth connection to another device, your computer and the other device must be paired. You can learn how to pair devices on page 545.

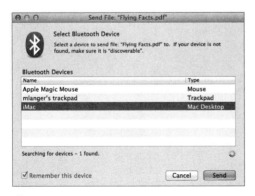

A Bluetooth File exchange makes it possible to send files from one computer to another via Bluetooth.

Bluetooth File Exchange

B The Bluetooth Status menu offers options for working with Bluetooth devices.

C Use this dialog to locate and select the file you want to send.

D Choose the receiving device from the list in this dialog.

To transfer a file from one computer to another via Bluetooth:

1. If necessary, do all the following:
   - Enable Bluetooth (page 543).
   - Enable Bluetooth sharing on the receiving computer (page 552).
   - Set up Bluetooth pairing between your computer and the receiving computer (page 545).

2. Use one of the following techniques to open Bluetooth File Exchange:
   - Double-click the Bluetooth File Exchange icon **A** in the Utilities folder inside the Applications folder.
   - In LaunchPad (page 150), click Utilities and then click AirPort Utility.
   - Choose Send File from the Bluetooth Status menu **B**.

3. Use the Select File to Send dialog that appears **C** to locate and select the file you want to send.

4. Click Send.

5. In the Bluetooth Devices list of the Send File dialog that appears **D**, select the computer you want to send the file to.

continues on next page

6. Click Send.

A dialog appears while your computer waits for the receiving computer to accept the file **E**.

7. On the receiving computer, click Accept in the Incoming File Transfer dialog **F**.

8. Wait while the file is transferred.

You'll see a progress dialog on the sending Mac **G**; one will also appear on the receiving computer.

When the file has been transferred, the receiving computer displays a dialog with information about it **H**.

TIP In step 3, you can select multiple files by holding down the Command key while clicking each one.

TIP In step 7, you can turn on the Accept all check box **F** to receive all files without giving you an opportunity to accept or decline.

TIP You can click the magnifying glass button in the Incoming File Transfer window **H** to open the folder where the file has been saved.

E Your Mac waits for the receiving device to accept the file.

F On the receiving device, click Accept.

G A progress bar appears to indicate transfer progress.

H On the receiving device, a dialog indicates that the file has been received.

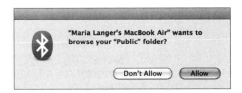

I Click Allow in this dialog to allow another computer to browse via Bluetooth.

J The contents of the device's public folder appear in a window.

To browse another device via Bluetooth:

1. If necessary, do all the following:
   - ‣ Enable Bluetooth (page 543).
   - ‣ Enable Bluetooth sharing on the receiving computer (page 552).
   - ‣ Set up Bluetooth pairing between your computer and the computer you want to browse (page 545).

2. Do one of the following:
   - ‣ In Bluetooth File Exchange, choose File > Browse Device or press Shift-Command-O.
   - ‣ Choose Browse Device from the Bluetooth Status menu **B**.

3. In the Browse Device dialog (which looks a lot like the Send File dialog **D**), select the computer you want to browse.

4. Click Browse.

   On your computer, an empty window named for the device appears.

5. On the computer you want to browse, a dialog asks if your computer can browse its Public folder **I**. Click Allow.

   On your computer, the device window fills with the contents of the other computer's Public folder **J**.

6. Use standard Finder techniques to navigate and copy files between your computer and the other computer.

7. When you are finished working with the device window, click its close button to dismiss it and stop browsing.

To use the Bluetooth status menu:

Choose commands on the Bluetooth status menu **B** to perform the following tasks:

- **Turn Bluetooth Off** disables Bluetooth on your computer.

- **Send File** launches Bluetooth File Exchange so you can send a file to a Bluetooth device, as explained on page 391.

- **Browse Device** launches Bluetooth File Exchange so you can add another Bluetooth device, as discussed on page 393.

- *Device Name* displays a submenu for the device with options that are appropriate for the device **K**.

- **Set up Bluetooth Device** launches the Bluetooth Setup Assistant, so you can set up a Bluetooth device (page 545).

- **Open Bluetooth Preferences** opens the Bluetooth preferences pane (page 543).

TIP The Bluetooth Status menu can be displayed from within the Bluetooth preferences pane (page 543).

K The Bluetooth Status menu offers options for each Bluetooth device paired with your Mac.

Ethernet

Despite the rush to connect without wires, Ethernet is still a familiar and widely used networking option, especially in business environments and in places where network administrators see Wi-Fi as a security challenge.

A simple Ethernet connection involves stringing an Ethernet cable between the Ethernet port—which looks like a big fat telephone port—on two computers . A more complex setup involves hubs and routers.

Once a Mac is connected to an Ethernet network, it knows it and takes advantage of all that network has to offer, including Internet sharing (page 551) and printer sharing (page 550), if available. So, for example, if you have access to the Internet via Wi-Fi on one computer but not the other, you can connect the two computers with an Ethernet cable and share the Internet connection over that cable.

Ⓐ In this example, the Ethernet connection consists of a cable connected from one Mac to another.

TIP Not all Macs have an Ethernet port. If your computer doesn't have an Ethernet port and you need one, you can buy an Apple USB Ethernet Adapter from the Apple Store.

TIP Apple's AirPort Extreme and Time Capsule base stations, which are discussed on page 380, offer three Ethernet ports for connecting computers and other devices that do not have wireless capabilities.

TIP A discussion of Ethernet hubs and routers is far beyond the scope of this book.

FireWire

Although FireWire can be used to connect two computers for networking, it isn't often used that way. Instead, it's more often used to exchange information between two Macs when transferring configuration information as part of a Mac OS X installation (as mentioned in Chapter 1) or to use one computer's hard disk in target disk mode. And, of course, it's most often used to connect peripheral devices, including hard disks and digital video cameras.

There's not much to say about connecting two computers for networking via FireWire. It's pretty straightforward. Just connect a FireWire cable to each computer's FireWire port. Your Mac will use the FireWire cable to make a connection **A**.

TIP Not all Macs have FireWire ports.

TIP If you want to share an Internet connection over FireWire, be sure to set up Internet sharing (page 551).

TIP Using a FireWire connection to transfer configuration information or to set up a disk in target disk mode is beyond the scope of this book. If you need to use either of these features, you can learn more on Apple's website.

A In this example, I've connected two computers with a FireWire cable.

Users, Groups, & Privileges

Network file sharing access is determined by the users and groups set up for the computer, as well as the privileges settings for each file or its enclosing folder.

Before you start setting up file sharing on your computer, it's a good idea to know a little bit about how this works.

TIP The concept of users, groups, and privileges is also referred to as *permissions*.

Users & Groups

Each person who connects to a computer (other than with Guest access) is considered a *user*. Each user has his own user name or ID and a password.

User names are set up by the computer's system administrator, using the Users & Groups preferences pane (page 579). The password is also assigned by the system administrator, but in most cases, it can be changed by the user in the Users & Groups preferences pane when logged in to his account. This enhances security.

Each user can belong to one or more *groups*. A group is one or more users who have the same privileges. Some groups are set up automatically by Mac OS X when you install it. A system administrator can also add groups with the Users & Groups preferences pane.

Privileges

Each file or folder can be assigned a set of privileges. Privileges determine who has access to a file and how it can be accessed.

There are four possible privileges settings:

- **Read & Write** privileges allow the user to open and save files.

- **Read only** privileges allow the user to open files but not save files.

- **Write only** (Drop Box) privileges allow the user to save files but not open them.

- **No Access** means the user can neither open nor save files.

Privileges can be set for three categories of users:

- **Owner** is the user or group who can access and set access privileges for the item. In Mac OS X, the owner can be you (if it's your computer and you set it up), system, or admin.

- **Group** is a group that has access to the item.

- **Everyone** is everyone else on the network, including users logged in as Guest.

TIP You can check or set an item's privileges in the Sharing & Permissions area of the Info window for the item **A B C**.

A B C Privileges settings in the Info window for the Applications folder (top), Public folder (middle), and a document (bottom).

D You may have to enter an administrator's name and password in a dialog like this to make changes to an item's permissions.

E Use this dialog to add a specific user or group to the Permissions list.

F Choose an option from the pop-up menu beside the user or group.

G You can use the action pop-up menu to apply your changes to all items within a folder.

To set an item's permissions:

1. Select the icon for the item you want to change permissions for.

2. Choose File > Get Info or press Command-I to display the Info window.

3. If necessary, click the triangle beside Sharing & Permissions to display permissions information **A** **B** **C**.

4. If the padlock icon at the bottom of the window indicates that settings are locked, click it. Then enter an administrator name and password in the dialog that appears **D** and click OK.

5. To add specific user or group privileges, click the + button under the Name column. Then use the dialog that appears **E** to select an existing account from Users & Groups or your Address Book. Or click the New Person button to add a new user account on the fly. When you click Select, the additional user is added to the Name list.

6. To set permissions for a user or group, choose an option from the pop-up menu that appears beside its name **F**.

7. If the item is a folder, you can choose Apply to enclosed items from the Action pop-up menu at the bottom of the window **G** to apply the settings to all folders within it.

8. Close the window to save your changes.

TIP You cannot change privileges for an item if you are not the owner **A** unless you have an administrator password.

TIP The Write only (Drop Box) privilege is only available for folders and disks.

Connecting for File Sharing

Once your computer is connected to a network, as discussed earlier in this chapter, and set up for file sharing, as discussed on page 548, you can connect to another computer and access its files. Mac OS X offers two ways to do this:

- The Go menu's Connect to Server command **A** prompts you to enter the address of the server you want to connect to. You enter a user name and password to connect, choose the volume you want to access, and display its contents in Finder windows.

- The network browser enables you to browse the computers on the network—from the Finder **B** and from within Open and Save dialogs. You open an alias for another computer and you're prompted for a user name and password. Enter login information, choose a volume, and work with the files just as if they were on your computer.

The main difference between these two methods is that the Connect to Server command makes it possible to connect to servers that are not listed in the network browser.

The next few pages provide instructions for connecting to other computers using both methods, along with some tips for speeding up the process in the future.

TIP Mac OS X's networking features refer to network-accessible computers as *servers*.

TIP To mount a server volume, you must have access as a user or guest (page 397).

A The Go menu.

B In this example, the Network Browser "sees" a Windows PC, an iMac, a MacBook Pro, and a remote Time Capsule.

Click to log in with a user account

C When you connect to a server as a guest, you have limited access to files.

D You can connect to the server as a registered user by providing a user name and password.

E Once you connect as a registered user, you have access to whatever files and folders that user account can access.

To use the network browser:

1. Choose Go > Network **A**, or press Shift-Command-K.

   The Network window opens, displaying the servers you have access to **B**.

2. Do one of the following:

   ▸ To connect to a server as a guest, double-click its icon or click its name in the sidebar. Folders that guests have access to appear in the server's window **C**. Use these folders as you would any other Finder item. Skip the remaining steps.

   ▸ To connect to a server with a registered user account, select the server's name in the sidebar. Then click Connect As in the connection bar near the top of the window **C**.

3. In the Login dialog that appears **D**, select Registered User, enter a user name and password that is recognized by the server, and click Connect.

4. Folder icons for the available volumes appear in the window **E**. Use these folders as you would any other Finder item.

TIP If guest access is disabled, you will not be able to connect as a guest, or, if you can connect, you will not have access to any items.

TIP When you are connected to a server using a registered user account and have accessed a volume, an eject button appears beside the server name in the sidebar **F**. Click the button to disconnect from the server.

TIP In step 3, turning on the Remember this password in my keychain check box enables you to connect in the future without entering your password.

To use the Connect to Server command:

1. In the Finder, choose Go > Connect to Server **A**, or press Command-K.

2. In the Connect to Server dialog that appears **F**, enter the network address of the server you want to connect to and click Connect.

3. In the Login dialog that appears **D**, select Registered User, enter a user name and password that is recognized by the server, and click Connect.

4. In the dialog that appears **G**, select the volume(s) you want to mount and click OK.

   The name of the server appears in the Shared area of the sidebar with an eject button beside it. You can open the volume you selected like any other disk to work with its contents.

TIP You can specify a server address by IP or server name. This information appears in the Sharing preferences pane (page 546) when File Sharing is enabled and selected.

TIP After step 2, you can click the + button to add the server address to the Favorite Servers list in the Connect to Server dialog **F**. You can then access a favorite server by double-clicking its address in the list.

TIP In step 2, to open a recently opened server, choose its address from the Recent Servers pop-up menu **H**.

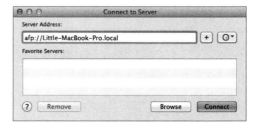

F Enter the server address in this dialog and click Connect.

G Choose the volume you want to open.

H Your Mac remembers recently opened servers.

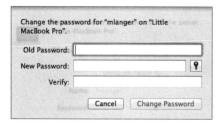

I Use this dialog to change your password on the server.

To change your password on the server:

1. Follow the steps on page 401 or 402 to display a login window **D**.

2. Select the Registered User option and enter your user name in the Name box.

3. Click the Change Password button.

4. In the password dialog that appears **I**, enter your current password in the Old Password box and your new password in the New Password and Verify boxes.

5. Click Change Password.

   Your password is changed and you are connected to the server.

TIP It's a good idea to change all of your passwords occasionally, just to enhance security.

AirDrop

AirDrop is a brand new feature of Mac OS that makes it easy to share files with other OS X Lion users. There's no complex configurations, no pairing devices or logging into servers. Just start AirDrop, identify the icon of the computer you want to share with, and drag the file you want to share onto it. When the recipient accepts the file, it's transferred.

TIP **AirDrop works within Wi-Fi range—that is, the range your computer can pick up a Wi-Fi connection.**

TIP **As this book went to press, AirDrop required Mac OS X 10.7 Lion or later running on a Mac with a recent version of AirPort. I was able to run it successfully on my early-2011 MacBook Air and mid-2009 MacBook Pro. Older computers may not support it. iOS devices may support it in the future.**

To open AirDrop:

In the Finder, use one of the following techniques:

- In the sidebar, click AirDrop **A**.
- Choose Go > AirDrop **B**, or press Shift-Command-R.

Three things happen:

- The AirDrop icon in the sidebar changes from a parachute to a sweeping radar scope **A** to indicate that it's working.
- Your computer begins broadcasting that it is available to share files via AirDrop.
- Your computer looks for other computers with AirDrop open and displays their icons in the AirDrop window **C**.

TIP **If AirDrop does not appear in the sidebar, you can add it. I explain how on page 451.**

AirDrop icon

A Starting AirDrop is as easy as opening its Finder window.

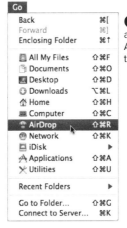

B You could also choose AirDrop from the Go menu.

C AirDrop displays icons for the AirDrop computers it finds.

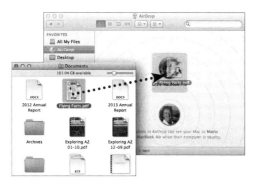

D Drag a file from a Finder window onto the icon for the computer you want to send it to.

E A pop-up dialog confirms that you really do want to send the file.

F On the recipient's computer a pop-up dialog asks whether the file should be received.

To share a file with AirDrop:

1. With AirDrop open **C**, identify the icon of the computer you want to share a file with.

2. Drag a file from a Finder window onto the icon of the computer you want to share with **D**.

3. A pop-up dialog asks if you're sure you want to send the file **E**. Click Send.

4. On the recipient's computer a pop-up dialog announces that your computer wants to send a file **F**. Click one of three buttons:

   ▸ **Save and Open** accepts the file and immediately opens it.

   ▸ **Decline** refuses to accept the file.

   ▸ **Save** accepts the file and saves it to the Downloads folder without opening it.

5. If the recipient accepts the file, it is transferred from your computer to his.

TIP This shouldn't need saying, but just in case: don't accept files from people you don't know.

TIP I think one of my favorite fun features of Lion is AirDrop's animation of a file being saved to the Downloads folder.

To close AirDrop:

Do one of the following:

■ Close the AirDrop window.

■ Select any other item in the sidebar.

AirDrop stops broadcasting and makes your computer invisible to other AirDrop users.

Using a Remote Disc

If your Mac doesn't have an optical drive—for example, a MacBook Air—you can use DVD or CD Sharing (page 546) to utilize the optical drive on another computer on your network.

To access an optical disc on another computer:

1. In the Finder, use one of the following techniques:

   ▸ Select Remote Disc in the sidebar **A**.

   ▸ Choose Go > Computer, or press Shift-Command-C. In the computer window that appears **B**, double-click Remote Disc.

   Computers configured to share their optical drives appear in the window.

2. Double-click the icon for the computer with the optical drive you want to access.

3. If the other computer is set up to require permission before access, click the Ask to use button in the network browser window **C**. A dialog on the other computer appears, asking for permission **D**. Click Accept.

4. If a disc is inserted in the other computer's optical drive, it appears in the window **E**. Access it as if it were attached directly to your computer.

TIP DVD or CD Sharing must be enabled and configured in the Sharing preferences pane (page 546) of the computer with the optical drive for this to work.

A The Remote Disc window displays computers set up to share their optical drive.

B You can open the Remote Disc window from the Computer window.

C You may have to ask permission to access another computer's optical drive.

D This dialog appears on the other computer.

E The Inserted CD or DVD appears in the window.

A You can find Network
Utility in the Utilities
folder inside your
Applications folder.

Network Utility

B Use the Info pane to get information about a
network interface.

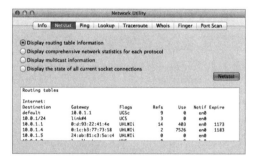

C Use the Netstat pane to get network
performance statistics.

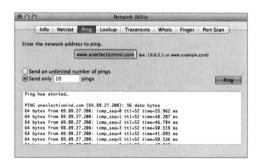

D Use the Ping pane to "ping" another computer
on the network or Internet.

Network Utility

Network Utility **A**, which can be found
in the Utilities folder in your Applications
folder, is an information-gathering tool to
help you learn more about and troubleshoot a network. Its features are made
available in eight tabs:

- **Info B** provides general information
  about the network interfaces.

- **Netstat C** enables you to review network performance statistics.

- **Ping D** enables you to test your computer's access to specific domains or IP
  addresses.

- **Lookup E** uses a domain name server
  to convert between IP addresses and
  domain names.

continues on next page

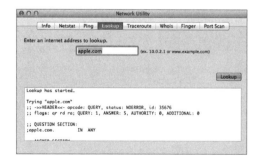

E Use the Lookup pane to get the IP address for
a specific domain name.

- **Traceroute 🄕** traces the route from your computer to another IP address or domain.

- **Whois 🄖** uses a whois server to get information about the owner and IP address of a specific domain name.

- **Finger 🄗** gets information about a person based on his email address.

- **Port Scan 🄘** scans a specific IP address for active ports.

TIP The tools within Network Utility are used primarily for troubleshooting network problems and getting information about specific users or systems.

TIP Many of these utilities are designed to work with the Internet and require Internet access.

TIP In this day and age of increased privacy and security, you'll find that Finger 🄗 and Port Scan 🄘 are seldom successful in getting information about a person or server.

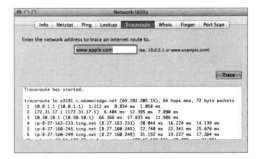

🄕 Use the Traceroute pane to trace the routing between your computer and another IP address.

🄖 Use the Whois pane to look up information about a domain name.

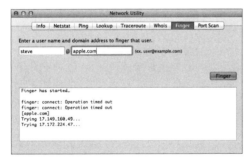

🄗 You can try to use Finger to look up information about a person based on his email address.

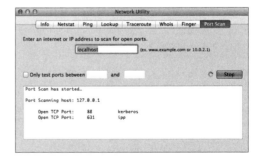

🄘 Use the Port Scan pane to check for active ports on an IP address or domain.

To use Network Utility:

1. Use one of the following techniques to open Network Utility:

   ▸ Open the Network Utility icon **A** in the Utilities folder inside the Applications folder.

   ▸ In LaunchPad (page 150), click Utilities and then click Network Utility.

2. Click the button for the utility you want to use **B C D E F G H I**.

3. Enter the domain name, IP address, or email address you want to check.

4. Click the button to start the scan process. (The name of the button varies from one utility to another.)

   The results appear at the bottom of the Network Utility window.

26

Connecting to the Internet

The Internet is a vast, worldwide network of computers that offers information, communication, online shopping, and entertainment for the whole family.

Although accessing the Internet was once just a small part of what your computer could do, these days it's pretty much assumed that your computer has access to the Internet. Indeed, when you use the Mac OS Setup Assistant (page 9) after installing OS X Lion or buying a new computer, one of the first things you're prompted for is your Internet connection method. Not only does OS X Lion use your connection to check for software updates (page 566), but it also uses the Internet to provide expanded help information (page 75), update your system clock (page 554), and enable you to shop for applications (Chapter 13).

This chapter provides some basic information about the Internet and explains how you can use the Network Setup Assistant and Network Diagnostic tools to set up and troubleshoot a connection.

In This Chapter:

Internet Connection Methods

Internet connections are provided by *Internet Service Providers* or *ISPs* for a fee. It works much like the phone company—in fact, your ISP might even be the local phone company.

Your computer uses *TCP/IP* to connect to the Internet. TCP/IP is a standard Internet protocol, or set of rules, for exchanging information.

There are two main ways to connect. Each method uses one of your computer's network interfaces (page 378). Each has its own pros and cons.

Direct, or Network, Connection

In a *direct*, or *network*, connection, your computer has a live, high-speed broadband connection to the Internet all the time. This is common for workplace computers on companywide networks. At home, cable modems and DSL offer direct connections.

The connection is made possible by physical cables that connect your home or office to the ISP's servers. In some cases, an Ethernet cable directly connects your computer to the ISP's equipment. In other cases, there's a router between the ISP's equipment and your computer. That router could connect multiple computers at your location via Ethernet cables or Wi-Fi network.

These days direct connections are most popular, primarily because they're fast, convenient, and affordable.

Modem, or Dial-up, Connection

In a *modem* (page 378) or *dial-up* connection, your computer uses a modem to dial in to a server, which gives it access to the Internet. This functionality is also available to some cell phone users utilizing *tethering* or *dial-up networking* (*DUN*). Mobile Wi-Fi *hotspots* created with a smartphone connection to an ISP make it seem, to the computer, as if it's accessing any other Wi-Fi network.

Although once the *only* way for an average user to connect to the Internet, modem connections are rare these days. That's a good thing because they're generally slow, require a phone line, and are not very convenient. Modems, which were standard equipment in many Macintosh models for years, are increasingly difficult to find.

Mobile hotspots, however, are gaining popularity among laptop users who need to be assured of an Internet connection when they're on the go. This service is available for many smartphone models—including iPhones—as well as stand-alone mobile hotspot devices such as a Novatel MiFi. To your computer, a mobile hotspot connection looks like any other Wi-Fi hotspot.

No matter how your dial-up connection to the Internet works, access speed will generally be slower than direct connections. These connections must be established or enabled to be used.

TIP You can check or change settings for your Internet connection in the Network preferences pane (page 540).

TIP DUN and mobile Wi-Fi hotspot service and setup vary based on cell phone carrier and service offered. A complete discussion of DUN and mobile hotspots is beyond the scope of this book.

Network Setup & Diagnostics

Mac OS includes two tools to help you set up network connections and diagnose problems with existing connections:

- The **Network Setup Assistant** steps you through the process of setting up an Internet connection using an Wi-Fi network, telephone modem, DSL modem, cable modem, or local area network with Ethernet connection. It automatically sets options in the Network preferences pane (page 540) for your connection.

- **Network Diagnostics** checks each part of your Internet connection to determine where a problem might be. It then provides you with tips for resolving the problem.

This part of the chapter introduces the Network Setup Assistant and Network Diagnostics so you can use them to set up or troubleshoot your Internet connection.

TIP If you set up your Internet connection when you configured your computer or OS X Lion (page 9), your computer should be ready to connect to the Internet and you can skip this part of the chapter. But if you didn't set up your connection or if your Internet connection information has changed since setup, the Network Setup Assistant is a good way to configure your computer to connect to the Internet.

TIP The Network Setup Assistant groups all settings for a connection as a location (page 542). If your computer has more than one way to connect to the Internet, you can create a location for each method.

To use the Network Setup Assistant:

1. Choose Apple > System Preferences or click the System Preferences icon in the Dock.

2. In the System Preferences window that appears, click the Network icon.

   Network preferences appears, displaying network status and connection information for one of your network interfaces **A**.

3. Click the Assist me button at the bottom of the window.

4. In the dialog that appears **B**, click the Assistant button.

   The Introduction screen of the Network Setup Assistant appears **C**.

5. Enter a name for the connection in the Location Name box and click Continue.

6. In the How Do You Connect to the Internet? screen that appears next **D**, select the method you use and click Continue.

7. Follow the remaining prompts to enter information about your connection.

8. At the last screen, click Done.

> **TIP** Before you use the Network Setup Assistant to configure your computer for an Internet connection, make sure you have all the information you need to properly configure the options. You can get all of the information you need from your ISP or network administrator.

> **TIP** In step 6, only the connections that are available for your computer can be selected. The others will be gray.

> **TIP** Switching from one location to another is covered on page 542.

A The Network preferences pane.

B Click Assistant in this dialog.

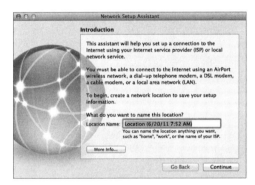

C Start by entering a name for the configuration.

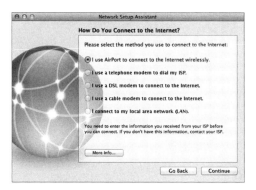

D Select the way you connect.

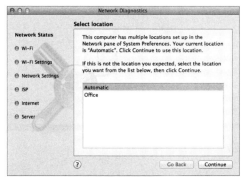

E F In these two examples, the top image shows a perfectly functioning Internet connection while the bottom one shows a connection with some problems.

To use Network Diagnostics:

1. Choose Apple > System Preferences or click the System Preferences icon in the Dock.

2. In the System Preferences window that appears, click the Network icon.

   Network preferences appears, displaying network status and connection information for one of your network interfaces **A**.

3. Click the Assist me button at the bottom of the window.

4. In the dialog that appears **B**, click the Diagnostics button.

   The Network Diagnostics window appears. Your Mac checks the selected configuration and reports its status in the left side of the window **E F**.

5. If you have more than one configuration set up, select the name of the location in the list.

6. Click Continue.

7. Follow the instructions that appear in the window to troubleshoot and repair any problems found.

TIP In many cases, you can fix an Internet connection problem by restarting your computer or shutting down and then powering up your router. In fact, that's one of the suggestions Network Diagnostics often makes.

Using Wi-Fi Hotspots

When you're on the go with your laptop, you'll likely rely on Wi-Fi hotspots available in hotels, airports, and coffee shops to connect to the Internet. You connect to these hotspots by choosing the one you want from the Wi-Fi menu on the menu bar , as discussed on page 389.

Here are a few things to keep in mind when connecting to public Wi-Fi networks.

- Networks with padlock icons beside their names are password protected. You'll need a password to connect.

- It's possible to connect to a network and still be required to provide a password or agree to some terms of service. In most cases, a window will appear to prompt you for information .

- The fan icon beside each network name indicates signal strength. Whenever possible, try to connect to a network with at least two black curved bars.

- Some public networks require that you pay a fee to access them. Before entering any credit card information into a form on a public network, make sure the form is legitimate and secure.

For safety's sake, remember the following:

- Many public networks are not secure. When you connect to an unsecured network, you run the risk of your data being accessed by others.

- It's important to disable or limit guest network access for file sharing before joining a public network.

- Networks listed under Devices are not regular Wi-Fi networks. Instead, they might connect you directly to someone else's computer, possibly for reasons not in your best interest.

A Choose a network from the Wi-Fi menu.

B Some networks allow you to connect but then prompt you for login information or credit card information to pay for access.

Internet Applications

OS X Lion includes four applications for interacting with the Internet:

- **Mail** enables you to exchange email messages, create to-do lists, and subscribe to RSS feeds.

- **iChat** enables you to exchange instant messages and conduct audio or video conferences with MobileMe, AIM, Google Talk, Jabber, and Yahoo! users.

- **FaceTime** enables you to conduct video phone calls with other OS X Lion users, as well as some iPhone and iPad users.

- **Safari** enables you to browse websites, download files from FTP sites, subscribe to RSS feeds, and save Web pages to read later.

In addition to these, if you are a MobileMe subscriber, you can take advantage of several MobileMe features integrated into OS X Lion.

This chapter provides brief instructions for using these tools—just enough to get you started. You can explore the other features on your own.

Mail

Mail is an email client application. It enables you to send and receive email messages using your Internet email account.

Here's how it works. Imagine having a mailbox at the post office. As mail comes in, the postmaster sorts it into the boxes—including yours. To get your mail, you need to go to the post office to pick it up. While you're there, you're likely to drop off any letters you need to send.

Email works the same way. Your email is delivered to your email server—like the post office where your mailbox is. The server software (like the postmaster) sorts the mail into mailboxes. When your email client software (Mail, in this case) connects to the server via the Internet, it picks up your incoming mail and sends any outgoing messages it has to send.

If you provided a MobileMe account information when you set up Mac OS or used the Mail, Contacts & Calendars preferences pane (page 534) to set up other email accounts, that information is automatically stored in Mail so it's ready to use. Just open Mail and it automatically makes that virtual trip to the post office to get and send messages.

Mail has been updated for OS X Lion to include threaded messaging and a full-height list of messages. It's interface is remarkably similar to the Mail app in iOS devices such as iPad and iPhone. It also supports Lion's Full-Screen apps feature (page 152).

In this part of the chapter, I explain how to set up an email account with Mail. I also explain how to compose, send, read, and retrieve email messages.

A Mail's application icon.

Mail

B The Welcome to Mail window appears if you do not have any email accounts set up.

 Mail's Message Viewer window lists messages on the left and the contents of a selected message on the right. (Yes, I bought a new Mac. I can't wait to get it.)

 The first screen of the Add Account window looks a lot like the Welcome to Mail window .

 Enter incoming mail server settings in this window.

To open Mail:

Use one of the following techniques:

- Open the Mail application icon  in the Applications folder.

- Click the Mail icon in the Dock.

- Click the Mail icon in Launchpad.

One of two things happens:

- If Mail has not yet been set up with at least one email account, the Welcome window appears .

- If Mail has already been set up with at least one email account, the Message Viewer window opens  and Mail checks for new mail (if your computer is connected to the Internet).

To set up an email account:

1. If necessary, choose File > Add Account to display the first screen of the Add Account window .

2. Enter basic information for the account:

   ▸ **Full Name** is your full name.

   ▸ **Email Address** is your email address.

   ▸ **Password** is your email account password.

3. Click Create (for a MobileMe account) or Continue.

   If you created a MobileMe account, you're done. You can skip the remaining steps.

4. In the Incoming Mail Server dialog , enter information for your incoming mail server and click Continue.

   ▸ **Account Type** is the type of account. Your options are POP, IMAP, Exchange, and Exchange IMAP.

continues on next page

- ▸ **Description** is an optional description for the account.

- ▸ **Incoming Mail** Server is the domain name or IP address of your incoming mail server.

- ▸ **User Name** is your user ID on the mail server.

- ▸ **Password** is your password on the mail server.

- ▸ **Also set up** (not shown) offers check boxes to set up Contacts and Calendars. This option is only available for Exchange accounts.

- ▸ **Outlook Web Access Server** (not shown) is the domain name or IP address of the Outlook server for Web access to email. This option is only available for Exchange IMAP accounts.

5. In the Outgoing Mail Server dialog **F**, enter information for your outgoing mail server and click Continue.

- ▸ **Description** is an optional description for the server.

- ▸ **Outgoing Mail Server** is the domain name or IP address of your outgoing mail server. You can choose a server from the drop-down list or enter information for a different server. If you turn on the Use only this server check box, the server you enter or select is the only one that can be used with the account.

- ▸ **Use Authentication** tells Mail to send your user name and password when sending mail. This is required by most mail servers. If you turn on this check box, be sure to enter your account user name and password in the boxes below it.

F Enter information about your outgoing server in this window.

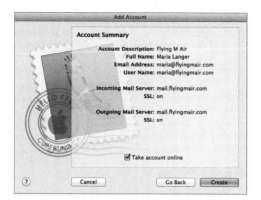

G Mail summarizes the information you entered.

H When the account is created, Mail checks for messages in that account and displays them. In this example, a junk mail message is displayed.

I If Mail can't verify your server, it displays a dialog like this.

6. When Mail has verified all information you entered, it displays the results in an Account Summary window **G**. Make sure the Take account online check box is turned on. Then click Create.

A few things happen **H**:

▸ The new account is added to Mail's Accounts list.

▸ Mail switches to that account's inbox.

▸ Mail checks for and displays mail for that account.

TIP You can also set up an email account by adding an account to the Mail, Contacts & Calendars preferences pane (page 534).

TIP You only have to set up an email account once. Mail will remember all of your settings.

TIP Your ISP or network administrator can provide all of the important information you need to set up an email account, including the account name, password, and mail servers.

TIP If Mail can't verify the identity of a mail server, it may display a dialog **I**. You have several choices to proceed: Show Certificate displays the certificate and additional information for the server. Cancel aborts the attempt to connect with the server. Connect connects with the server despite the problem.

TIP You cannot use the outgoing mail server for a MobileMe account to send email messages for an account with another ISP. The MobileMe outgoing mail server only works with MobileMe accounts. Outgoing or SMTP server information should be provided by your ISP.

To create & send a message:

1. Use one of the following techniques to open a New Message window **J**:

   ▸ Click the Compose New Message button at the top of the Message Viewer window **C**.

   ▸ Choose File > New Message, or press Command-N.

2. Use one of the following techniques to enter the recipient's address in the To box:

   ▸ Type the recipient's email address.

   ▸ If the recipient is someone in your Address Book file (Chapter 15) or someone you have received an email message from in the past, enter the person's name. As you type, Mail attempts to match the name **K**. Click the correct entry.

3. Repeat step 2 to add additional names. When you are finished, press the Tab key twice.

4. Enter a subject for the message in the Subject field, and press Tab.

5. If you have more than one email address, choose the address you want to use to send the message from the From pop-up menu. For some types of accounts, you may also have to select an outgoing mail server from a menu that appears beside it.

6. Type your message in the large box at the bottom of the window **L**.

7. Use one of the following techniques to close the window and send the message:

   ▸ Click the Send Message button in the top-left corner of the window.

   ▸ Choose Message > Send, or press Shift-Command-D.

J A New Message window.

K When you start typing the name of someone in Address Book, Mail guesses which one you want.

L A very simple message might look like this.

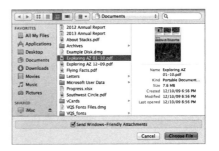

M Use this dialog to locate and select a document to attach to the email message.

N A multiple-page PDF attached to a message.

O The Format bar has buttons you can use to format selected text in a message.

P If you have iPhoto installed, you can use the Photo Browser to attach images to a message.

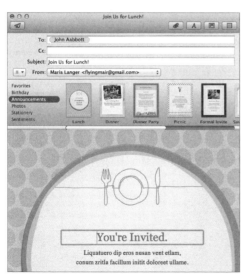

Q The Stationery Pane in action.

To enhance an outgoing message:

1. Follow steps 1 through 5 on the previous page to prepare a new mail message.

2. Click the toolbar button **J** for the task you want to perform:

   ▸ **Attach a Document to This Message** displays a standard Open dialog **M**. Locate and select a file you want to attach and then click Choose File. The file is attached **N**.

   ▸ **Show Format Bar** displays an additional row of buttons **O** that you can use to format selected text in the body of the message.

   ▸ **Show or Hide the Photo Browser** toggles the display of the Photo Browser window **P**, which you can use to select and attach iPhoto images to the message.

   ▸ **Show or Hide the Stationery Pane** toggles the display of stationery templates above the message form. Select a category in the left column and then click to select the stationery you want to use. The stationery's formatting fills the message body area **Q**. Replace sample text and/or images with your own content to complete the message.

> **TIP** Attached images and one-page PDFs appear as images in mail messages. Other types of files appear as icons **N**.

> **TIP** You can also attach a file by simply dragging its icon into the message window.

To retrieve email messages:

Click the Get New Messages in All Accounts button at the top of the Message Viewer window  🅒.

Mail accesses the Internet, connects to your email server, and downloads messages that are waiting for you. Incoming messages appear in the first column of the window with any Inbox selected 🅒🅗.

🆃🅸🅿 A blue bullet character appears beside each unread email message 🅗.

🆃🅸🅿 Messages that Mail thinks are junk mail are colored brown 🅗. To set junk mail preferences, choose Mail > Preferences and click the Junk Mail button.

🆃🅸🅿 Mail automatically creates a separate in-box for each email account. You can view a specific inbox by choosing its name from the Inbox menu in the Message Viewer window's toolbar 🆁.

To read a message:

1. On the left side of the Message Viewer window, click the message that you want to read.

    The message contents appear in the right side of the window 🅒.

2. Read the message.

🆃🅸🅿 You can double-click a message to display it in its own message window 🆂.

🆃🅸🅿 Mail's new conversations feature displays multiple messages on the right side of the window when you select a conversation 🆃. To read an entire message, click the See More link at the bottom of the message.

🆃🅸🅿 To save attachments, click the Details link at the top-right of the message to display additional information 🆄, including a Save menu for attachments. Choose a command from the menu 🆅 to save one or all attachments.

🆁 You can use this menu to view a specific inbox or click the Inbox button to view them all together.

🆂 Double-clicking a message displays it in its own window.

🆃 Mail's new conversation feature displays all the messages with the same subject line.

U Click the Details link to display additional message header information and buttons for saving attachments and using Quick Look.

V You can use the Save menu to save all or just one of a message's attached files.

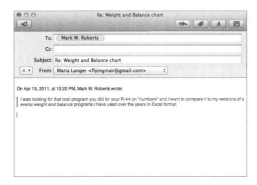

W In this example, I created a reply with just some of the original text quoted.

X In this example, I'm forwarding an entire message.

To reply to a message:

1. To quote only part of the message's original text in the reply, select the text you want to quote.

2. Click one of the Reply buttons at the top of the window:

   ‣ **Reply to Sender of Selected Message** addresses the reply to the person who sent you the message.

   ‣ **Reply to All Recipients of the Selected Message** addresses the reply to the person who sent you the message as well as everyone else who received it.

   A pre-addressed message window opens **W**. It includes the selected text or the entire message as a quote.

3. Type the text of your reply in the message body.

4. Click the Send Message button.

TIP Don't reply to all recipients of a message unless you really believe they all want or need to see your reply.

To forward a message:

1. To forward only part of the message's original text, select the text you want to forward.

2. Click the Forward Selected Messages button at the top of the window.

   A copy of the selected text or the entire message appears in a new message form **X**.

3. Enter the email address of the person you want to forward the message to in the To box.

4. If desired, enter a message at the top of the message body.

5. Click the Send Message button.

To add a message's sender to Address Book:

1. Select **C** or open **S** a message sent by the sender you want to add.

2. Click the From name at the top of the message window to display a menu of options **Y**.

3. Choose Add to Address Book.

   Mail adds the person's name and email address to the contacts in Address Book.

4. If desired, open Address Book (Chapter 15) and add additional information for the record.

TIP As shown in **Y**, the menu offers other options you might find useful while working with email.

To create a calendar event from an email message:

1. Display the email message with date or time information for the event you want to create.

2. Point to the date or time. A pop-up menu outline appears around the information **Z**.

3. Click the triangle to display the event as a calendar item **AA**.

4. Click Add to iCal to add the event to iCal.

5. If necessary, open iCal (Chapter 16) and modify the information to include the correct name, duration, calendar, and other settings.

TIP Creating an event like this automatically links it to the email message where you created it. You can click the Show in Mail link in the event's details in iCal to quickly open the linked email message.

Y Clicking a sender's email address displays a handy menu.

Z Point to a date or time (or date and time as shown here) to display the outline of a menu.

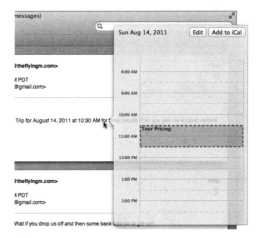

AA Click the menu button to see the event that Mail can create.

iChat

iChat enables you to conduct live chats or audio or video conferences with me.com, Mac.com, AIM, Yahoo!, Google Talk, and Jabber accounts.

Here's how it works. The first time you open iChat, you configure it with your chat account information, as well as the information for your buddies who use compatible chat networks. Then, while you're connected to the Internet with iChat running, iChat does two things:

- It tells the network that you're available to receive instant messages and participate in chats.

- It tells you when your buddies are online and available to receive instant messages and participate in chats.

When a buddy is available, sending him an instant message is as easy as clicking a button and typing what you want to say. If more than one buddy is available, you can open a chat window and invite them to participate together.

iChat also includes audio and video conferencing features. If you have a microphone or a compatible video camera (including a FaceTime camera), you can have live audio or video chats with your buddies.

In this part of the chapter, I explain how to configure iChat for your account, set up an iChat buddy list, invite a buddy to a chat, and participate in text or video chats.

TIP To use iChat, you must have a MobileMe, AIM, Yahoo!, Google Talk, or Jabber account. To use the AV features, you must have a microphone (for audio only) or compatible video camera (for audio and video) and a fast Internet connection.

To open iChat:

Use one of the following techniques:

- Open the iChat application icon **A** in the Applications folder.
- Click the iChat icon in Launchpad.

One of two things happens:

- If iChat has not yet been set up, the Welcome window appears **B**.
- If iChat has already been set up, the iChat window opens **C** and iChat checks to see which of your buddies is online.

To set up iChat:

1. Open iChat.

2. Read the information in the Welcome to iChat window that appears **B** and click Continue.

3. In the Account Setup window **D**, choose an Account Type from the pop-up menu and then enter your account information. The information you need to provide varies depending on your account type. Then click Continue.

4. Read the information in the Conclusion window **E** and click Done.

   A Buddy List window with a "Connecting" message appears next. After a moment, the window expands to list your buddies and their online status **C**.

TIP In step 3, if you don't have a chat account, click the Get an iChat Account button. This launches your Web browser and displays a site where you can sign up for a free Apple ID that you can use with iChat.

A The iChat application icon.

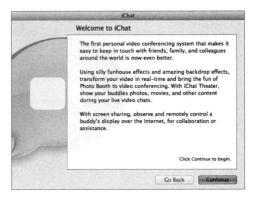

B If iChat has not yet been set up, the Welcome to iChat window appears when you open it.

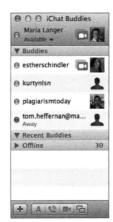

C Once iChat has been set up, opening it displays your buddy list.

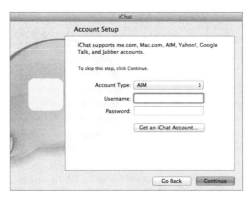

D Enter your account information in this window.

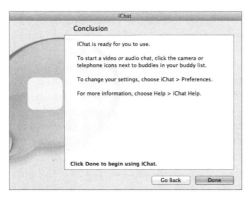

E The last screen of the setup process tells you iChat is ready to use.

F Choose Add Buddy from this pop-up menu.

G Enter your buddy's account information.

H Your buddy's account is added to the Buddy List.

To add a buddy:

1. Use one of the following techniques:
   - Choose Add Buddy from the + button menu at the bottom of the Buddy List window **F**.
   - Choose Buddies > Add Buddy.
   - Press Shift-Command-A.

2. In the New Buddy dialog **G**, fill in the form with information about your buddy's account.

3. Click Add.

   The buddy is added to the Buddy List window **H**.

TIP The Buddy List automatically includes contacts for which you have provided AIM information in Address Book, as well as buddies you may have added while using any previous version of iChat.

TIP Google Talk and Jabber buddies must authorize you as a buddy before their status appears in iChat **H**.

TIP A buddy's online status and audio or video capabilities is indicated in the buddy list with a color-coded bullet and phone or camera icons **C**.

To remove a buddy:

1. Select the name of the buddy you want to remove.

2. Press the Delete key.

3. Click Remove in the confirmation dialog that appears.

To conduct a text chat:

1. In the Buddy List **C**, select the name of a buddy who is available for chatting.

2. Click the Start a Text Chat button at the bottom of the Buddy List window **C**.

   A chat window appears **I**.

3. Enter your message in the box at the bottom of the window.

   As you type, a "cloud" appears beside your icon to indicate that you're writing something **J**.

4. Press Return.

   The comment appears in the top half of the window beside your icon **K**.

5. Wait for your buddy to answer.

   Her comments appear in the top half of the window beside his icon **L**.

6. Repeat steps 3 through 5 to continue your instant message conversation in the window **MN**.

> **TIP** To include an emoticon (smiley) in your comment **N**, click the menu on the far right end of the text entry box and select the emoticon you want. It is inserted in your comment.

I Begin by opening a chat window.

J Type your comment in the box at the bottom of the window.

K When you press Return, the comment is sent.

L When your buddy responds, her comments appear in the window.

MN Continue the conversation. Your comments and your buddy's comments appear in the window.

O While waiting for your buddy to answer your call, the video chat window shows a preview of what your buddy will see.

P When the chat begins, you can see your buddy in the window with your image inset in a smaller box. (Coffee is king!)

To conduct a video chat:

1. In the Buddy List, select the name of a buddy who is available for video chatting **C**.

2. Click the Start a Video Chat button at the bottom of the Buddy List window.

   A video chat window appears **O**.

3. Wait until your buddy responds.

   When he accepts the chat, the window changes to show his live image, with yours in a small box **P**.

4. Talk!

TIP Audio chats work a lot like video chats—but without the picture.

TIP To conduct a video chat, both you and your buddy must have video capabilities. Look for a camera icon beside a buddy's name **C**.

TIP Video chats require sufficient bandwidth to work. If your connection—or your buddy's—to the Internet is too slow, an error message will appear.

TIP If the inset picture is blocking your view, you can move it to another position in the window. Just drag it.

TIP You can use the Effects button at the bottom of the window to apply a special effect like those in Photo Booth (page 273) to your image.

To end a chat:

Click the close button in the Chat window. Be sure to say "Bye" first!

To respond to a text chat invitation:

1. When another iChat user invites you to a text chat, his message appears in a window on your desktop **Q**. Click the window to display a Chat window **R**.

2. Do one of the following:

   ▸ To accept the invitation, enter a message in the box at the bottom of the window **S** and click Accept or press Return. The message appears in the Chat window, which expands to display the chat **T**.

   ▸ To decline the invitation, click the Decline button or click the window's close button. The Chat window disappears.

   ▸ To prevent the person from ever bothering you again with an invitation, click the Block button. Then click Block in the confirmation dialog that appears. The Chat window disappears.

TIP You cannot block a Google Talk or Jabber buddy you've authorized for chat.

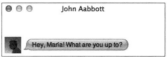

Q A chat request looks like this.

R When you click the message, a text entry field appears.

S Type your response in the text box.

T When you press Return, the chat begins.

U A video chat invitation looks like this.

V When you click it, the window expands to show a preview of what your buddy will see when you answer.

W Clicking Accept begins the video chat.

X Clicking Text Reply turns a video chat into a text chat.

To respond to a video chat invitation:

1. When another iChat user invites you to a video chat, an invitation window appears **U** and iChat makes a phone ringing sound. Click the window to display a Video Chat window **V**.

2. Do one of the following:

   ▸ To accept the invitation, click Accept or press Return. iChat establishes a connection with the caller and the window changes to show his live image, with yours in a small box **W**. Start talking!

   ▸ To decline the invitation, click the Decline button or click the window's close button. The Video Chat window disappears.

   ▸ To respond with a text message, click Text Reply. Then use the text chat window that appears **X** to conduct a text chat with your buddy.

FaceTime

FaceTime is a video communications application that makes it possible to make video calls to OS X Lion, iPad 2, iPhone 4, and some iPod touch users.

What's cool about FaceTime is that it makes it possible to see, in real time, the person you're contacting. But this goes beyond simple video conversations. You can share whatever is within sight of your FaceTime camera and the person you're connecting to can do the same. So, for example, if you're having a FaceTime conversation with a friend who wants to show you his new car or a coworker who wants to show you a problem with a job out in the field, you can see and discuss it live.

To use FaceTime, you need the following:

- **Apple ID.** This is the same ID you might already use for MobileMe or iCloud, the App Store, or the iTunes Store. If you don't have an Apple ID, you can create one from within FaceTime.

- **Internet connection.** For best results, it should be fast.

- **Camera.** This can include a FaceTime camera built into your Mac, a video camera connected via FireWire, or a UVC-compliant video camera connected by USB.

- **Microphone.** This can include the microphone built into your computer, an external microphone connected to the audio input port, or a Bluetooth or USB headset.

- **Address Book contacts.** FaceTime uses Address Book as its contact list.

This part of the chapter explains how to set up FaceTime, make a FaceTime call, and answer a FaceTime call.

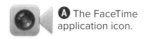

A The FaceTime application icon.

FaceTime

B When you start FaceTime for the first time, it may ask you to enter your Apple ID and password.

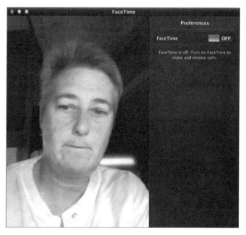

C The FaceTime window with FaceTime turned off.

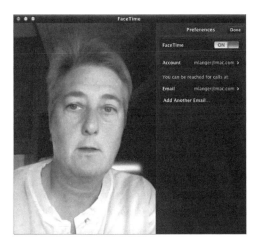

D In this example, FaceTime is turned on and the Preferences pane is displayed.

E Here's the FaceTime window showing my Address Book contacts.

F If necessary, enter your preferred email address.

To open FaceTime:

Use one of the following techniques:

- Open the FaceTime application icon **A** in the Applications folder.
- Click the FaceTime icon in the Dock.
- Click the FaceTime icon in Launchpad.

FaceTime opens and displays its main screen. What appears on the right side of the screen depends on whether you are logged into FaceTime and it is turned on:

- If you are not logged into FaceTime, the Enter Apple ID pane appears **B**.
- If you are logged into FaceTime but it has not been enabled, the Preferences pane appears with the slider set to Off **C**.
- If FaceTime has been enabled, either the Preferences pane appears with the slider set to On **D** or the Contacts pane appears **E**.

To log in and enable FaceTime:

1. If FaceTime's main window displays the login screen **B**, enter your Apple ID and password and click Sign In.
2. You may be asked which email address you want to use for people to call you **F**. If necessary, enter your preferred email address in the Address field and click Next.
3. FaceTime verifies your account, turns on, and displays the Contacts pane **E**.

TIP If FaceTime's Main window displays the Preferences pane with the slider set to Off **C**, click the slider to turn it on and then click Done.

TIP If FaceTime's Main window displays the Preferences Pane with the slider set to On **D**, just click Done.

To make a FaceTime call:

1. If necessary, click the Contacts button at the bottom of the FaceTime window to displays your contacts **D**.

2. Click the name of the contact you want to call to display his record details **G**.

3. Click the contact number or email address you want to call.

   FaceTime initiate call. The window shrinks to show just a preview of what the contact will see, along with a status message at the top of the window **H**. When the contact answers the call, his face appears in the window and yours appears in an inset at the bottom of the window **I**.

4. Talk.

G Clicking a contact name displays his record details so you can choose the contact number or email address you want to use to place your FaceTime call.

H Wait while the call connects. (I don't look too uncertain here, do I?)

I When it connects, start talking!

J An incoming FaceTime call looks like this.

K When you answer, the conversation can begin.

To answer a FaceTime call:

1. When another FaceTime user calls you, an invitation window appears **J** and FaceTime makes a phone ringing sound. Click the window to activate it.

2. Do one of the following:

   ▸ To accept the invitation, click Accept. FaceTime establishes a connection with the caller and the window changes to show his live image, with yours in a small box **K**. Start talking!

   ▸ To decline the invitation, click the Decline button or click the window's close button. The FaceTime window disappears.

To turn off FaceTime:

If you don't want to be bothered by incoming FaceTime calls, choose FaceTime > Turn FaceTime Off, or press Command-K.

FaceTime is disabled and the Preferences pane appears with the slider set to Off **C**.

Safari

Safari is a Web browser application. It enables you to view, or browse, pages on the World Wide Web.

A Web page is a window full of formatted text and graphics . You move from page to page by clicking text or graphic links or by opening *URLs* (*uniform resource locators*) for specific Web pages. These two methods of navigating the World Wide Web can open a whole universe of useful or interesting information.

Safari has been updated for OS X Lion. Not only does it support the Full-Screen Apps feature but its new Reading List feature makes it convenient to save a Web page for reading later.

TIP Safari also supports RSS (Really Simple Syndication) feeds, which make it possible to keep up to date with new content on blogs and many Web sites.

To open Safari:

Use one of the following techniques:

- Open the Safari application icon in the Applications folder.

- Click the Safari icon in the Dock.

- Click the Safari icon in Launchpad.

- Click a Web link in any email message, chat window, or document.

Safari opens. If you opened it by clicking a link, it displays the Web page for that link. Otherwise, it displays the default Home page  or the page that was open when you last quit Safari.

TIP You can change the default home page by specifying a different page's URL in Safari's preferences. Choose **Safari > Preferences** and click the **General** button to get started.

A The default home page is Apple's Start page.

B Clicking a link displays the page it links to.

C The Safari application icon.

Safari

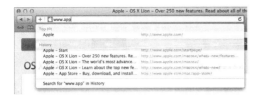

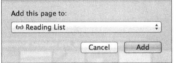

D As you type a URL, Safari tries to match it with a page you've visited in the past.

Add bookmark for the current page

E To bookmark a URL, click the Add bookmark for the current page button.

F Use this dialog to add a bookmark.

G Choose an option from the pop-up menu.

H Enter or edit a name for the bookmark.

I The bookmark appears in the location you added it—in this case, on the bookmarks bar.

To follow a link:

1. Position the mouse pointer on a text or graphic link. The mouse pointer turns into a pointing finger **B**.

2. Click.

    Safari loads and displays the location for the link you clicked **C**.

To view a specific URL:

1. Type the URL into the address box.

    As you type, Safari tries to match the URL with pages you have visited in the past. It displays results in a menu **D**.

2. Do one of the following:

    ▸ If the page you want to view appears on the menu beneath the address box, click it.

    ▸ If the page you want to view is not listed, keep typing to finish entering the URL and then press Return.

    Safari loads and displays the page.

To bookmark a page:

1. Display the Web page that you want to create a bookmark for.

2. Click the Add bookmark for the current page button **E**, choose Bookmarks > Add Bookmark, or press Command-D.

3. In the dialog that appears **F**, choose one of the options beneath the divider line on the pop-up menu **G**.

    A text box with the name of the page appears in the dialog **H**.

4. Make changes as desired to the page name and click Add.

    The bookmark is added to the location you specified **I**.

To view a bookmarked page:

Do one of the following:

- If the bookmark is on the bookmarks bar ①, click it.

- If the bookmark is in one of the book-marks bar folders, click the folder name on the bookmark bar to display a menu of bookmarks ① and click the book-mark you want to open.

- If the bookmark is on the Bookmarks menu, click the menu to display it ⓀK and then click the bookmark you want to open.

To display a grid of your top sites:

Choose History > Show Top Sites or press Option-Command-1.

A page with thumbnail images of your most frequently visited Web pages appears ①. Click a thumbnail to go to that page.

TIP You can manually add a site to the Top Sites grid. Follow the instructions in the sec-tion titled "To bookmark a page" on page 439 but choose Top Sites in step 3.

TIP Clicking the History button at the top of the Top Sites grid ① displays thumbnail images of recently visited pages.

J Folders on the bookmark bar appear as menus.

K When you add bookmarks to the Bookmarks menu they appear near the bottom of the menu.

L The Top Sites grid displays the pages you visit most.

M The Reading List feature makes it easy to save pages to read later.

N If you prefer a distraction-free version of the page, click the Reader button in the address bar.

O To remove a page from your Reading List, click the X button.

To save a page to read later:

With the page you want to read later displayed, choose Bookmarks > Add to Reading List, or press Shift-Command-D.

An animation shows the page moving into the eyeglasses icon on the bookmarks bar.

To read pages on your Reading List:

1. Click the eyeglasses button on the bookmarks bar.

   A sidebar displays large buttons for your reading list items.

2. Click the button for the page you want to read.

   The page you clicked appears in the main part of the window **M**.

TIP To list only unread items, click the Unread button at the top of the Reading List pane **M**.

TIP To remove distractions from the page such as images and advertisements, click the Reader button in the Address bar **N**. This feature may not be available for all pages.

TIP To hide the Reading List, click the eyeglasses icon in the bookmarks bar again.

To remove an item from your Reading List:

1. Point to the item you want to remove.

2. Click the X button that appears in the item's upper-right corner **O**.

   The item is removed from the list.

TIP You can remove all items from your reading list by clicking the Clear All button at the top of the Reading List pane **M**.

Using MobileMe with Mac OS

Apple's MobileMe service includes three features that are fully integrated with Mac OS:

- **Sync** enables you to synchronize information on your Mac with MobileMe and any other Mac or iOS device that has access to the Internet. This makes it easy, for example, to synchronize iCal calendars, Address Book contacts, and Safari bookmarks between a desktop Mac and a laptop or an iPad.

- **iDisk** gives you 20 GB of hard disk space on Apple's servers. You can use this space—which is accessible from the Web and the OS X Finder—to save or share files, host websites and photo galleries, and store backups.

- **Back to My Mac** makes it possible to access your computer for file and screen sharing from other Macs with Back to My Mac enabled. This can come in handy the next time you realize that you forgot to copy an important file to your laptop before hitting the road.

You can learn how to configure your Mac for use with MobileMe on page 536. That's also where you can learn how to set up the Sync feature and begin syncing data.

This part of the chapter explains how to access your iDisk space and a computer configured for use with Back to My Mac.

TIP As this book went to press, Apple had announced its new iCloud service, which would replace MobileMe by the summer of 2012. It is unclear how these features will work in iCloud. As details become available, I'll cover them in articles on my book support website, www.MariasGuides.com.

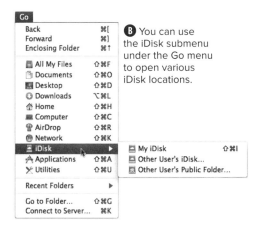

A An iDisk folder is preconfigured with a bunch of folders for storing information.

B You can use the iDisk submenu under the Go menu to open various iDisk locations.

C Use this dialog to open someone else's iDisk.

D Enter a member name and click Connect.

To open your iDisk storage space from the Finder:

Use one of the following techniques:

- Click the iDisk icon in the Sidebar **A**.
- Choose Go > iDisk > My iDisk **B**, or press Shift-Command-I.

A Finder window with your iDisk contents appears **A**.

TIP The status bar (page 37) of the Finder window **B** tells you how much space is left in your iDisk storage space.

To open another user's iDisk:

1. Choose Go > iDisk > Other User's iDisk **B**.

2. In the Connect to iDisk dialog that appears **C**, enter the user's MobileMe member name and password to open the iDisk. Then click Connect.

   A window displaying the contents of the user's iDisk appears.

To open a user's Public folder:

1. Choose Go > iDisk > Other User's Public Folder **B**.

2. In the Connect to iDisk Public Folder dialog that appears **D**, enter the MobileMe member name and click Connect.

3. If the Public folder is password-protected, a dialog appears. Enter the password to access the folder, and click Connect.

   A window displaying the contents of the user's Public folder appears.

To access a computer with Back to My Mac:

1. Make sure Back to My Mac is enabled in the Back to My Mac screen of the Mobile Me preferences pane **E** (page 539) for the computer you want to access and the computer you want to access it from.

2. Make sure File Sharing (page 548) or Screen Sharing (or both) is enabled in the Sharing preferences pane **F** for the computer you want to access and the computer you want to access it from.

3. In the Finder, choose Go > Network to display a Network browser window **G**.

4. Open the icon for the computer you want to access.

5. If a password window appears, enter your user name and password and click Connect.

   The computer's contents appear in the Network browser **H**. Open the folder you want to access.

TIP Using the Network browser to connect to network computers for File sharing is discussed in detail on page 401.

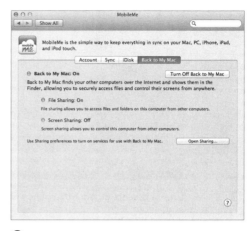

E Make sure Back to My Mac is enabled.

F Make sure File Sharing or Screen Sharing (or both) is enabled.

G The computer you are sharing with Back to My Mac appears in the Network browser.

H Connect to the computer like any other network computer.

Customizing
Your Mac

In This Part

Customizing the Finder

One of the great things about Mac OS is its user interface flexibility. Although the Mac OS X Finder looks the same on every computer when first installed, it is highly customizable, making it possible for every Mac user to set up his or her computer so it looks and works just right.

This chapter covers the following ways to customize the Finder:

- Finder preferences enable you to set general Finder options, as well as text for labels, sidebar contents, and advanced options.

- Dock icons can be added, removed, and rearranged to include the items you want in the order you want them to appear.

- Launchpad icons can be rearranged and grouped into folders.

- Menu bar icons can be added, rearranged, and removed to better suit your needs.

Setting Finder Preferences

Finder preferences enables you to customize several aspects of the desktop and Finder to change the way they look and work.

The Finder's preferences window is organized into four different panes of options:

- **General** lets you set basic options for the desktop and Finder windows.
- **Labels** enables you to set label names for the Finder's label feature.
- **Sidebar** lets you set options for the sidebar.
- **Advanced** enables you to set options for the display of file extensions and the Trash warning.

To set Finder preferences, open the preferences pane you need to change, make changes, and close the window. Your changes are automatically saved.

To open Finder Preferences:

Choose Finder > Preferences  or press Command-, (comma).

The Finder Preferences window opens, displaying the last pane of options you accessed.

Ⓐ Choose Preferences from the Finder menu.

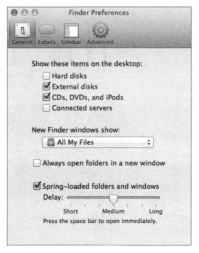

Ⓑ The default Finder General preferences settings.

C Use this pop-up menu to choose what you want to appear in new Finder windows.

D E F The top-level hard disk (top), home folder (middle), and Documents folder (bottom) are three of the options for a new Finder window.

To set General Finder Preferences:

1. In the Finder Preferences window, click the General button to display General options **B**.

2. To specify what items should appear on the desktop (page 12), toggle check boxes under Show these items on the desktop:

   ▸ **Hard disks** displays icons for internal hard disks.

   ▸ **External disks** displays icons for external hard disks and thumb drives.

   ▸ **CDs, DVDs, and iPods** displays icons for removable media, including CDs and DVDs, as well as iPods.

   ▸ **Connected servers** displays icons for mounted server volumes.

3. To specify what should appear in a new Finder window (page 28), choose an option from the New Finder windows show pop-up menu **C**:

   ▸ *Computer name* displays the icons for the computer and all mounted volumes.

   ▸ *Hard Disk name* displays the root level of your hard disk **D**.

   ▸ **iDisk** displays the top level of your iDisk. (This option only appears if you are a MobileMe subscriber.)

   ▸ *Your account name* displays the contents of your Home folder **E**.

   ▸ **Desktop** displays the contents of your Desktop folder.

   ▸ **Documents** displays the contents of your Documents folder **F**.

   ▸ **All My Files** displays the All My Files smart folder (page 106).

continues on next page

- **Other** displays a dialog that you can use to select a different folder to display **G**.

4. To set other options, toggle check boxes in the bottom half of the window:
   - **Always open folders in a new window** opens a new window to display the contents of the folder you open.
   - **Spring-loaded folders and windows** enables the spring-loaded folders feature (page 84). You can use the slider to set the delay time for this feature.

To customize labels:

1. In the Finder Preferences window, click the Labels button to display Labels options **H**.
2. To change the name of a label, select the text for the label you want to change and enter new text **I**.
3. Repeat step 2 for each label you want to change.

TIP Assigning labels to icons is covered on page 87.

TIP The names of labels appear the File menu and contextual menus when you point to a label and in a list view window when the Label column is displayed **J**, as discussed on page 466.

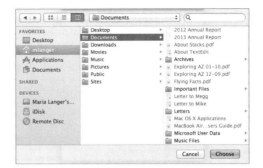

G Use a dialog like this to choose a different folder to open in a new Finder window.

H Labels preferences let you change the text assigned to colored labels.

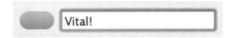

I Changing label text is easy: just type in the new text.

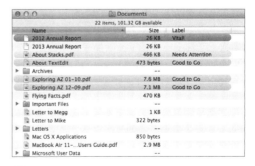

J Labels can appear in list view windows.

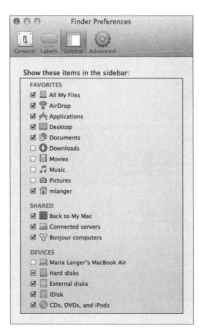

K Toggle check boxes to specify which items should appear in the sidebar.

L Default settings for Advanced Finder preferences.

M You can use Advanced Finder preferences to display file name extensions for all files.

To set Sidebar preferences:

1. In the Finder Preferences window, click the Sidebar button to display Sidebar options **K**.

2. Toggle check boxes to specify what items should appear in each area of the sidebar (page 35). The options are self-explanatory.

TIP Customizing the sidebar to add, remove, and rearrange items is covered on page 471.

To set Advanced preferences:

1. In the Finder Preferences window, click the Advanced button to display Advanced options **L**.

2. Toggle check boxes to set options:

   ▸ **Show all file extensions** tells the Finder to display file extensions in Finder windows **M**. This option, in effect, turns off the Hide extension check box in the Name & Extension area of the Info window (page 94) for all files on a go-forward basis.

   ▸ **Show warning before changing an extension** displays a warning dialog when you change a file name extension **N** (page 48).

continues on next page

N This dialog warns you of the consequences of changing a file name extension.

- ▸ **Show warning before emptying the Trash** displays a confirmation dialog  when you choose Finder > Empty Trash (page 56) or Finder > Secure Empty Trash (page 56). Turning off this check box prevents the dialog from appearing.

- ▸ **Empty Trash securely** enables the secure empty Trash feature (page 56) for each time you empty the Trash.

3. Choose an option from the When performing a search pop-up menu  to set how Mac OS X's search feature (Chapter 7) should work.

TIP As Mac OS warns ⓝ, changing a file's extension may cause the file to open in another application. If that application can't read the file, it may not open at all.

ⓞ You can use Advanced Finder preferences to prevent this dialog from appearing when you empty the Trash.

ⓟ Choose a default search location from this pop-up menu.

A Drag an icon from a Finder window to the Dock.

B The icon appears on the Dock, right where you dropped it.

Customizing the Dock

The contents of the Dock (page 38) can be customized a number of ways:

- Include icons for items that you use often. This makes them quick and easy to open any time you need them.

- Remove icons for items you seldom use. This reduces Dock clutter.

- Rearrange Dock icons to better suit your needs. This can make you more productive.

- Customize the appearance and functionality of stacks folders so they work the way you want them to.

This part of the chapter covers all of these customization options.

TIP You can also set Dock preferences to control how the Dock looks and works; learn more on page 484.

To add an item to the Dock:

1. Open the window containing the item you want to add to the Dock.

2. Drag the item from the window to the Dock.

   Items on the Dock shift to make room for the new item **A**.

3. Release the button.

   The icon appears where you released it **B**.

TIP Dragging an item to the Dock does not remove it from its original location.

TIP Add applications to the left of the Dock's divider and documents, folders, websites, and servers to the right of the divider.

To remove an item from the Dock:

1. Drag the item from the Dock to the desktop.

   As you drag away from the Dock, the space occupied by the item closes up **C**.

2. Release the button.

   The item disappears **D** in a puff of digital smoke.

TIP You cannot remove the Finder or Trash from the Dock.

TIP Removing an item from the Dock does not delete it from disk.

TIP If you remove an icon for an application that is running, the icon will not disappear from the Dock until you quit.

To rearrange Dock items:

1. Drag the item you want to move from its current place on the Dock to a new place.

   As you drag, icons shift to close up empty space and open up new space **E**.

2. Release the button.

   The item moves to its new position **F**.

C Drag an item off the Dock.

D The item is removed from the Dock.

E Drag an icon from one position to another on the Dock.

F When you release it, it moves.

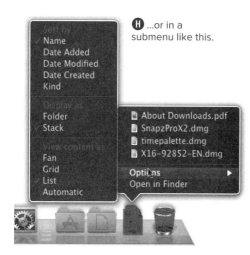

G You can view stacks options in a contextual menu like this...

H ...or in a submenu like this.

I Stacks can be displayed as folders (left and center) or stacks of icons (right).

To customize the display of a stacks folder:

1. In the Dock, point to the folder you want to set options for.

2. Use one of the following techniques to display a menu of options **G**:

   ▸ Hold down the Control key and click.

   ▸ Right-click or, on a Multi-Touch device, click with two fingers.

   ▸ If the stack is set to display as a list, click to display the list and then choose Options to display the Options submenu **H**.

3. To change the sort order of items in the stack, choose a Sort by option.

4. To set the appearance for the stack's icon on the Dock **I**, choose a Display as option:

   ▸ **Folder** displays the stack's icon using the same icon as its source folder.

   ▸ **Stack** displays the stack's icon as a stack of icons.

5. To set the appearance for the folder's open stack, choose a View content as option:

   ▸ Fan always displays the stack as a fan.

   ▸ Grid always displays the stack as a grid.

   ▸ List always displays the stack as a list.

   ▸ Automatic displays the stack as a fan unless there are too many items in the folder to fit—then it displays them as a grid.

TIP You can see examples of stack appearance in Chapter 20, where using the stacks feature is discussed.

Organizing Launchpad

Launchpad is similar to stacks in that it displays icons in a way that makes them easy to find and click. But Launchpad automatically identifies and displays only applications, making it a useful tool for opening an application quickly.

But what happens when you have many applications installed on your Mac? Launchpad can get messy and extend into multiple windows, making applications a little less easy to find. Fortunately, there are two ways you can customize Launchpad to make the applications you use most easily accessible:

- Rearrange Launchpad icons to put them in a more convenient order.

- Organize applications into Launchpad folders to group them logically.

This part of the chapter covers both of these techniques.

TIP Some applications may already be stored in folders—for example, a standard Mac OS installation gathers a bunch of applications in the Utilities folder.

TIP Do you have an iOS device such as an iPhone or an iPad? If so, Launchpad should look familiar—it's a lot like the home screen in iOS.

To rearrange Launchpad icons:

1. In Launchpad, drag the icon you want to move from its current position to a new position in Launchpad's grid.

   As you drag, icons shift to close up empty space and open up new space **A**.

2. Release the button.

   The icon moves **B**.

A To move an icon, just drag it to a new position in the grid.

B The icon appears in its new position.

C In this example, I'm dragging the Preview icon on top of the Photo Booth icon.

To organize Launchpad icons by folder:

1. In Launchpad, drag the icon for one item you want to group into a folder onto the icon for another item you want to group in the same folder **C**.

   The destination icon turns into a dark colored square and then a folder menu containing the destination icon opens beneath it **D**.

2. Release the button to drop the icon into the folder **E**.

3. Click the folder icon to go back to Launchpad's main screen.

   A square icon representing the new folder is in the grid position formerly occupied by the destination icon **F**.

4. Drag another icon onto the new folder icon and release it.

5. Repeat step 4 for every application you want to include in that folder.

D Launchpad displays a menu for a folder that it automatically created and named *Entertainment*.

TIP Each item you add to a Launchpad folder is represented by a tiny icon on the folder icon **G**.

E When I release the button, the icon I'm dragging drops into the new Launchpad folder.

F The new folder icon appears where the destination icon was in the main Launchpad screen.

G I can tell by looking at this icon that it contains four items.

To rename a Launchpad folder:

1. In Launchpad, click the folder you want to rename to display a menu of its contents **H**.

2. Click the name of the folder in the upper-left corner of the menu.

   The name becomes selected **I**.

3. Type a new name for the folder and press Return to save it.

   The folder is renamed **J**.

To remove an item from a Launchpad folder:

1. In Launchpad, click the name of the folder you want to remove the item from to display a menu of its contents **H**.

2. Drag the item you want to remove from the folder up and out of the menu **K**.

   The menu closes to reveal the main Launchpad screen **L**.

3. Drag the item into the grid position where you want it to appear.

4. Release the button.

   The item moves into its new position **M**.

H Click a folder to display a menu of its contents.

I Click the folder name to select it.

J Type a new name and press Return to save it.

K Drag the icon out of the menu.

L The menu closes to reveal the main Launchpad screen.

M When you release the button, the icon is moved into the location you dropped it.

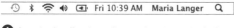

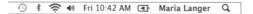

A A typical collection of menu bar icons includes Time Machine, Bluetooth, Wi-Fi, Sound, Battery Level, Date & Time, User Name, and Spotlight.

B Hold down the Command key while dragging the icon you want to move.

C When you release the button, the icon moves into its new position.

Rearranging Menu Bar Icons

The right end of the Mac OS menu bar at the top of the screen may display any combination of icons **A**. In many instances, these icons are menus that offer access to System or application features.

In addition to showing or hiding these icons with various System Preferences options (as discussed in Chapters 31 through 34), you can also rearrange many of these icons to suit your needs.

TIP Note that you cannot move the Spotlight search menu or move any icon to its right.

To move a menu bar icon:

1. Hold down the Command key and drag an icon to a new position on the end of the menu bar.

   As you drag, icons shift to close up empty space and open up new space **B**.

2. Release the button.

   The icon moves into its new position **C**.

TIP Dragging a menu bar icon off the menu is a quick way to remove it without opening System Preferences or the application that put it there.

Customizing
Finder Windows

Mac OS X makes it possible to customize the appearance and functionality of windows and the desktop a number of different ways:

- Set view options to control icon size, grid spacing, sort order, text size, background, and other options for individual windows and, on a limited basis, the desktop.

- Customize the toolbar to add, remove, and reorganize buttons and other options.

- Customize the sidebar to add, remove, and reorganize folders and other items.

Making changes like these helps you set up your computer so it works best for your particular needs.

This chapter takes a look at the things you can do to customize Finder windows and the desktop.

In This Chapter:

Setting View Options

You can customize Finder window and desktop views a number of ways:

- Change the settings for the default view for icon, list, column, and Cover Flow views.

- Change the settings for an individual window's view.

- Change the view for the desktop.

You do all this with the view options window for the active window or desktop.

The settings offered in the view options window vary depending on the window's current view settings. Here are some examples:

- **Icon view** settings include icon size, grid spacing, label text size and position, display options, arrangement, and background.

- **List view** settings include icon size, text size, columns, date format, and item size calculation.

- **Column view** settings include text size, icon appearance, and preview column.

- **Cover Flow** view options include icon size, text size, columns, date format, and item size calculation.

- **Desktop view** settings include icon size, label text size and position, display options, and arrangement.

Mac OS X remembers a window's view settings and uses them whenever you display the window. Any change you make in the view options window is automatically saved for use in the future.

TIP Chapter 4 discusses window views and how to switch from one view to another. That's also where you can find details about sorting window contents.

A Open the window you want to set options for. In this example, the Applications folder window is open and displayed in icon view.

B Choose Show View Options from the Finder's View menu.

C Here's the view options window for a window displayed in icon view.

D The Arrange By options for the Applications folder window. Options on this menu vary depending on what window is open.

Name
Application Category
Date Last Opened
Date Added
Size
Label
✓ None

E In this example, I've arranged the icons by Application Category and then sorted them by Date Last Opened.

✓ None
Snap to Grid
Name
Kind
Date Last Opened
Date Added
Date Modified
Date Created
Size
Label

F The options on the Sort By menu—and the availability of the menu itself—vary depending on what is selected in the Arrange By menu; in this case, it's None.

To set view options:

1. Open the window you want to set view options for **A**.

2. If necessary, switch to the view you want to customize.

3. Choose View > Show View Options **B**, or press Command-J.

   The view options window for that view appears **C**.

4. Set options as desired.

5. Click the window's close button or choose View > Hide View Options to dismiss the view options window.

TIP To open the view options window for the desktop, make sure no window is active before choosing View > **Show View Options**.

TIP The options in the view options window will change if you make a different window active. The view options window always displays options and settings for the currently active window.

To set icon view options:

In the view options window **C** for the icon view window you want to customize **A**, set options as desired:

- **Always open in icon view** sets the window so it always opens in icon view.

- **Browse in icon view** also displays the contents of a window's folders in icon view when they are opened. This option is only available when the Always open in icon view option above it is enabled.

- **Arrange By** **D** sorts and groups icons by the option you specify **E**.

- **Sort By** **F** sorts icons by the option you specify. In some instances, when the Arrange By option is set to something

continues on next page

other than None, the Sort By option is not available.

- **Icon size** enables you to use a slider to change the size of icons in the window , from 16 x 16 pixels to 512 x 512 pixels.

- **Grid spacing** enables you to use a slider to change the amount of space between each icon Ⓗ.

- **Text size** lets you change the size of text characters in the icon label ⒤. Options range from 10 to 16 points.

- **Label position** ⒥ enables you to set the position of an icon's label at the bottom (the default option) or to the right of the icon.

- **Show item info** ⒥ displays information about the item beneath its name.

- **Show icon preview** displays a document's preview, if available, in place of its standard icon.

- **Background** enables you to set the window's background:

Ⓖ The icons in Ⓐ are 48 pixels; here's the same window with the icons sized 128 pixels.

Ⓗ In this example, the icons are the same size as they are in Ⓐ, but the grid spacing is much tighter.

ⓘ Changing the text size also changes the grid spacing.

ⓙ This example from my Documents folder shows label position to the right and item info displayed. Like the other illustrations here, the icon preview option is enabled, too.

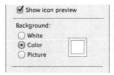

K When you select Color, a color well appears in the view options window.

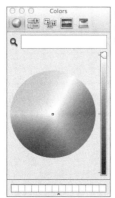

L Clicking the color well displays the Colors panel.

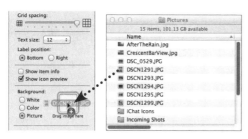

M Drag a picture file into the image well.

N The picture appears as the background for the window.

▸ **White** makes the background white, which is the default setting.

▸ **Color** enables you to select a background color for the window. If you select this option, click the color well that appears beside it **K** and use the Colors panel **L** (page 489) to select a color.

▸ **Picture** enables you to set a background picture for the window. If you select this option, you can drag an image file into the image well that appears beside it **M** to use that picture as a background image **N**. (You can change the picture by dragging a different picture into the image well; you can remove the picture by selecting one of the other two options.)

TIP Another way to resize the icons in a window is to drag the Icon size slider in the status bar (if displayed) left or right.

To set list or Cover Flow view options:

In the view options window  for the list view **P** or Cover Flow view window you want to customize, set options as desired:

- **Always open in list view** or **Always open in Cover Flow** sets the window so it always opens in list view or Cover Flow view.

- **Browse in list view** or **Browse in Cover Flow** also displays the contents of a window's folders in list view or Cover Flow view when they are opened. This option is only available when the option above it is enabled.

- **Arrange By** **D** sorts and groups icons by the option you specify **Q**.

- **Sort By** **R** sorts icons by the option you specify **Q**. In some instances, depending on the Arrange By setting, the Sort By option is not available.

- **Icon size** enables you to select from two different icon size options.

- **Text size** lets you change the size of text characters in the icon label. Options range from 10 to 16 points.

- **Show Columns** lets you toggle check boxes to specify which columns should appear.

- **Use relative dates** displays the date in relative terms (that is, using the words *today* and *yesterday*).

- **Calculate all sizes** displays the disk space occupied by items and the contents of folders in the list.

- **Show icon preview** shows a document preview for the icon, if available.

TIP Turning on the Calculate all sizes check box **Q** makes it possible to sort a list by size—even if it includes folders.

O The view options window for a window in list view. These options are virtually identical for a window in Cover Flow view.

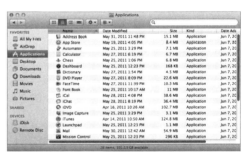

P The Applications window in list view.

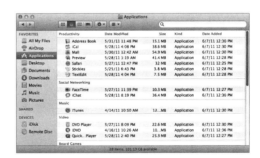

Q In this example, I arranged by Application Type and then sorted by name.

R The Sort By menu for list and Cover Flow views is slightly different from the one for icon view.

S The view options for a window in column view.

T A window in column view with default settings.

U In this example, I've arranged by Date Last Opened. The Sort By menu turns gray and can't be used.

To set column view options:

In the view options window **S** for the column view **T** window you want to customize, set options as desired:

- **Always open in column view** sets the window so it always opens in column view.

- **Browse in column view** also displays the contents of a window's folders in column view when they are opened. This option is only available when the option above it is enabled.

- **Arrange By D** sorts and groups icons by the option you specify **U**.

- **Sort By R** sorts icons by the option you specify. In some instances, depending on the Arrange By setting, the Sort By option is not available.

- **Show icons** shows file icons.

- **Show icon preview** shows a document preview for the icon, if available.

- **Show preview column** shows a preview for a selected item in the far right column **S U**.

To set desktop view options:

In the view options window  for the desktop, set options as desired:

- **Icon size** enables you to use a slider to change the size of icons in the win- dow **G**, from 16 x 16 pixels to 512 x 512 pixels.

- **Grid spacing** enables you to use a slider to change the amount of space between each icon.

- **Text size** lets you change the size of text characters in the icon label. Options range from 10 to 16 points.

- **Label position** enables you to set the position of an icon's label at the bottom (the default option) or to the right of the icon.

- **Show item info** displays information about the item beneath its name.

- **Show icon preview** displays a docu- ment's preview, if available, in place of its standard icon.

- **Sort By** **G** sorts icons by the option you specify.

TIP As you can see, these options are nearly identical to those for an icon view window **C**.

TIP You can set the desktop color or picture in the Desktop & Screen Saver preferences pane (page 480).

V You can also use the view options window to set options for the desktop.

To set view options as the default for all windows in icon, list, or Cover Flow view:

1. Use the view options window **C O** to set options for an icon, list, or Cover Flow view window.

2. Click the Use as Defaults button.

   The current options are set as defaults for that view.

A Choose Customize Toolbar from the View menu.

Customizing the Toolbar

The toolbar, which is discussed on page 33, can be customized to include buttons and icons for a variety of commands and items. You can also rearrange toolbar items to display them in any order you like.

TIP When you customize the toolbar, your changes affect the toolbar in all windows in which the toolbar is displayed.

TIP You must display the toolbar to customize it. To display the toolbar, choose View > **Show Toolbar**, or press **Option-Command-T**.

To customize the toolbar:

1. With any Finder window open and the toolbar displayed, choose View > Customize Toolbar **A**.

   The Customize Toolbar dialog appears **B**.

2. Make changes to the toolbar as follows:

   ▸ To add an item to the toolbar, drag it from the dialog to the position you want it to occupy on the toolbar **C**. When you release the item, it appears on the toolbar **D**.

   ▸ To remove an item from the toolbar, drag it off the toolbar **E**. When you release the item, it disappears in a puff of digital smoke and is removed from the toolbar **F**.

continues on next page

B The Customize Toolbar dialog.

C Drag a button from the Customize Toolbar dialog onto the toolbar.

D The button appears where you dragged it.

E Drag a button off the toolbar.

F When you release the button, it disappears.

▸ To rearrange the order of items on the toolbar, drag an item into the desired position **G**. When you release the item, it moves **H**.

3. To specify how items should appear on the toolbar, choose an option from the Show pop-up menu at the bottom of the window:

   ▸ **Icon & Text** displays both the icon and the icon's name **I**.

   ▸ **Icon Only** displays only the icon. This is the default setting.

   ▸ **Text Only** displays only the name of the icon **J**.

4. When you are finished making changes, click Done.

TIP You don't have to use the Customize Toolbar dialog to rearrange or remove toolbar items. Just hold down the Command key and drag the item you want to move to a new position or drag the item you want to remove off the toolbar.

TIP The toolbar includes spacers that you can move or remove like buttons. They appear on the toolbar as light gray boxes.

To restore the toolbar to its default settings:

1. With any Finder window displaying the toolbar open, choose View > Customize Toolbar **A**.

   The Customize Toolbar dialog appears **B**.

2. Drag the group of items in the box near the bottom of the window to the toolbar **K**.

   When you release it, the toolbar is reset to its default configuration **L**.

3. Click Done.

G To rearrange items, drag them into a new position on the toolbar.

H When you release an item, it moves.

I You can set the toolbar so it shows icons and text labels...

J ...or just text labels.

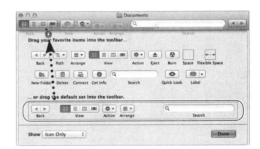

K To restore the toolbar to its default settings, drag the collection of tools at the bottom of the dialog onto the toolbar.

L When you release them, the toolbar is restored.

A When you position the pointer on the dividing line between the sidebar and the rest of the window, it turns into a line with two arrows.

B Drag the border of the sidebar to change its width.

Customizing the Sidebar

In addition to using Finder preferences (page 451) to specify what standard items should appear in the sidebar (page 35) you can customize the sidebar a number of other ways:

- Change the width of the sidebar to better display long item names.
- Add or remove folders, files, and other items in the bottom half of the sidebar.

TIP The sidebar only appears if the toolbar (page 33) is displayed.

To change the sidebar width:

1. Position the pointer on the divider between the sidebar and the rest of the Finder window.

   The pointer turns into a line with two arrows **A**.

2. Press the button down and drag.

   As you drag, the sidebar's width changes **B**.

3. When the sidebar is the desired width, release the button.

TIP Making the sidebar wider does not make the entire window wider. Instead, it just shifts the dividing point between the sidebar and the rest of the window.

To add a sidebar item:

Drag the icon for the item you want to add to the sidebar's Favorites area.

A blue line indicates where it will appear **C**. When you release the item, it appears on the sidebar **D**.

TIP The icon you drag can be the one that appears in the item's title bar.

TIP Adding an item to the sidebar does not move it from where it resides on disk. Instead, it creates a pointer to the original item and adds it to the sidebar.

TIP Be careful when adding an icon to the sidebar. If you drag the icon on top of a folder or disk icon on the sidebar, the icon will move into that folder or disk.

To remove a sidebar item:

Hold down the Command key and drag the item off the sidebar **E**.

When you release the item, it disappears in a puff of digital smoke and is removed from the sidebar.

TIP Removing an item from the sidebar does not delete it from disk. Instead, it removes the pointer to the original item from the sidebar.

TIP If you remove all the items under a sidebar heading, the heading disappears. It reappears if you add an item that belongs under that heading.

To rearrange sidebar items:

Drag the item you want to move into a new position on the sidebar.

Other items on the sidebar will shift to make room for it **F**. When you release the item, it moves.

C Drag an item's icon into the Favorites area of the sidebar.

D When you release the item, it appears where you dragged it.

E To remove an item from the sidebar, hold down Command and drag it off.

F To rearrange items, drag an item into a new position on the sidebar.

System Preferences Basics

One of the great things about Mac OS is the way it can be customized to look and work the way you want it to.

Many customization options can be set with the System Preferences application. That's where you'll find a variety of preferences panes, each containing settings for a part of Mac OS.

System Preferences panes are discussed in detail in the following chapters. This chapter provides an overview of System Preferences, with information about how they're organized and how you can access them. It also explains how you can lock preferences to prevent accidental or unauthorized changes to settings.

Getting Started with System Preferences

System Preferences panes are organized into five categories, four of which are included on a standard installation of Mac OS X :

- **Personal** preferences panes (Chapter 31) enable you to set options to customize various Mac OS X appearance and operation options for personal tastes. These preferences panes include:

  - General
  - Desktop & Screen Saver
  - Dock
  - Mission Control
  - Language & Text
  - Security & Privacy
  - Spotlight
  - Universal Access

- **Hardware** preferences panes (Chapter 32) control settings for various hardware devices. These preferences panes include:

  - CDs & DVDs
  - Displays
  - Energy Saver
  - Keyboard
  - Mouse
  - Trackpad
  - Print & Scan
  - Sound

- **Internet & Wireless** preferences panes (Chapter 33) enable you to set options related to Internet and network connections. These preferences panes include:

Ⓐ The System Preferences window for a standard installation of Mac OS X on a MacBook Air.

  - Mail, Contacts & Calendars
  - MobileMe
  - Network
  - Bluetooth
  - Sharing

- **System** preferences panes (Chapter 34) control various aspects of your computer's operation. These preferences panes include:

  - Users & Groups
  - Parental Controls
  - Date & Time
  - Software Update
  - Speech
  - Time Machine
  - Startup Disk

- **Other** preferences panes may be installed on your computer when you install various third-party software. They would appear in a fifth group at the bottom of the main System Preferences window and are not covered in this book.

B Choose System Preferences from the Apple menu.

C The System Preferences application icon.

System Preferences

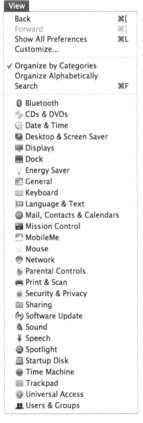

D System Preferences' View menu gives you access to all preferences panes.

To open System Preferences:

Use one of the following techniques:

- Choose Apple > System Preferences **B**.
- Open the System Preferences application icon **C** in the Applications folder window (page 147).
- Click the System Preferences icon in Launchpad (page 150).
- Click the System Preferences icon in the Dock (page 38).

The System Preferences window opens. It either displays all System Preferences pane icons **A** or the preferences pane you last used.

To open a specific preferences pane:

Use one of the following techniques:

- If all System Preferences pane icons are showing **A**, click the icon for the pane you want to display.
- Choose the name of the pane you want to display from the View menu **D**.

To show all preferences pane icons:

Use one of the following techniques:

- Choose View > Show All Preferences **D**, or press Command-L:
- Click the Show All button in the toolbar of the System Preferences window **A**.

To reorganize preferences panes:

Choose a command from the View menu:

- Organize by Categories displays all icons organized by category **A**.
- Organize Alphabetically displays all icons organized alphabetically by name **E**.

To find a preference pane by task or topic:

1. Enter a search word or phrase in the search box in the upper-right corner of the System Preferences window.

   Three things happen **F**:

   ▸ The window gets dark.

   ▸ Icons for related preferences panes are highlighted.

   ▸ A menu of possible topics appears.

2. Do one of the following:

   ▸ Select a topic from the menu.

   ▸ Click a highlighted icon.

   The appropriate preference pane opens.

To quit System Preferences:

Use one of the following techniques:

- Choose System Preferences > Quit System Preferences.
- Press Command-Q.
- Click the System Preferences window's close button.

TIP System Preferences is one of the Mac OS applications that automatically quits when all of its windows are closed.

E If you prefer, you can view preferences panes in alphabetical order.

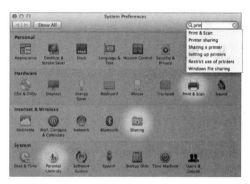

F You can search System Preferences to find the preferences pane you need to perform a task.

Ⓐ The Users & Groups preferences pane is locked by default.

Ⓑ A typical authentication dialog like this appears when you try to unlock a preferences pane.

Ⓒ The lock icon changes to an open padlock when a preferences pane is unlocked.

Locking & Unlocking Preference Settings

Many preferences panes include a lock button that enables you to lock the settings. Locking a preferences pane's settings prevent them from being changed accidentally or by users who do not have administrative privileges.

Some preferences panes—for example, Users & Groups **Ⓐ**—are locked by default. That means you need to unlock it with an administrator's account name and password to make changes.

To unlock a preferences pane:

1. Click the lock button at the bottom of a locked preferences pane window **Ⓐ**.

2. Enter an administrator's name and password in the authenticate dialog that appears **Ⓑ** and click Unlock.

    The button changes so that the icon looks like an unlocked padlock **Ⓒ**.

To lock a preferences pane:

Click the lock button at the bottom of a preferences pane window **Ⓒ**.

The button changes so that the icon looks like a locked padlock **Ⓐ**.

Customizing System Preferences

In OS X Lion, you can now customize the System Preference window so it only include the preferences panes you want to see. This can help simplify the interface by removing preferences panes you never use. Because all preference panes are listed on the View menu, you can still open any of them quickly—even if it doesn't appear in the main window. And, as you might imagine, you can always customize the window again to redisplay any that are hidden.

To customize the System Preferences window:

1. Choose View > Customize.

    The window's view changes to display check marks beside each preferences pane icon .

2. Toggle the check boxes to determine which preference panes appear.

3. Click Done.

    The System Preferences window displays only the preference pane icons that were checked when you customized it .

A Toggle the check boxes to determine which preferences pane icons should appear in the System Preferences window.

B In this example, I've hidden Language & Text, Universal Access, MobileMe, Parental Controls, and Time Machine.

Personal Preferences

Personal preferences panes enable you to configure the appearance and operation of Mac OS X to suit your needs. This chapter covers the following System Preferences panes:

- **Desktop & Screen Saver** sets the desktop picture and screen saver options.

- **Dock** configures the Dock.

- **General** controls general appearance, scrolling, and recent item options.

- **Language & Text** controls language, formatting, and input sources.

- **Mission Control** sets options for Mission Control, Exposé, and Spaces.

- **Security & Privacy** controls system-wide security options.

- **Spotlight** customizes the way searching works.

- **Universal Access** controls options of special interest to people with special access needs.

Need to learn the basics of System Preferences? Be sure to read Chapter 30.

Desktop & Screen Saver

The Desktop & Screen Saver preferences pane enables you to set the background color or picture for the Mac OS X desktop and configure a screen saver that appears when your computer is idle.

TIP Mac OS X's built-in screen saver doesn't really "save" anything. All it does is cover the normal screen display with graphics, providing an interesting visual when your computer is inactive.

TIP The Energy Saver preferences pane (page 509) offers more protection for LCD displays than Screen Saver.

To set the desktop picture:

1. In the Desktop & Screen Saver preferences pane, click the Desktop button to display its options **A**.

2. In the collections list on the left side of the window, select an image folder or collection.

   The images in the collection appear on the right side of the window.

3. Click the image you want to use.

   It appears in the image well above the collection list and the desktop's background picture changes **B**.

4. If desired, choose an option from the pop-up menu beside the image preview **C** to indicate how it should appear.

5. To change the picture periodically, turn on the Change picture check box and select a frequency option from the pop-up menu **D**. Turning on the Random order check box beneath this displays

A The Desktop options in the Desktop & Screen Saver preferences pane.

B In this example, I've selected an image of clouds from my Pictures folder.

C You can use this pop-up menu to tell Mac OS how to display the picture onscreen.

D You can set up your desktop picture to change automatically at a frequency you specify.

E If you don't like a translucent menu bar, you can make it opaque.

the images in the collection in random order.

6. To change the menu bar so it is opaque **E** rather than translucent **B**, turn off the Translucent menu bar check box.

TIP For best results, use pictures that are the same size or larger than your screen resolution. For example, if your screen resolution is set to 1024 x 768, the image should be at least this size. You can check or change your screen resolution in the Displays preferences pane (page 507).

TIP The collections list on the left side of the Desktop pane **A** includes photos installed with Mac OS X, as well as access to your Pictures folder, and your iPhoto library and albums (if iPhoto is installed).

TIP In step 2, you can click the + button at the bottom of the collections column and use the dialog that appears to locate and choose another folder that contains images.

TIP Although you can have your desktop display a virtual slide show by setting the picture changing frequency in step 5 to a low value like Every 5 seconds, you may find it distracting to have the background change that often. I know I would!

To configure the screen saver:

1. In the Desktop & Screen Saver preferences pane, click the Screen Saver button to display its options 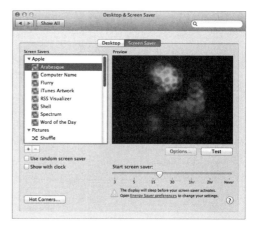.

2. In the Screen Savers list, select a screen saver module.

   The preview area changes accordingly.

3. To set options for the screen saver, click Options, make changes in the dialog that appears ⑤⑥, and click OK.

4. To see what the screen saver looks like on your screen, click Test.

   The screen goes black and the screen saver kicks in. To go back to work, move your mouse or move a finger across your trackpad.

5. To have the screen saver start automatically after a certain amount of idle time, drag the Start screen saver slider to the desired value.

6. To set "hot corners" that activate or deactivate the screen saver, click the Hot Corners button to display the Active Screen Corners dialog ⑦. Choose an option from each pop-up menu ⑧ to specify what should happen when you position the pointer in the corresponding corner. When you're finished, click OK to save your settings.

F The Screen Saver options of the Desktop & Screen Saver preferences pane.

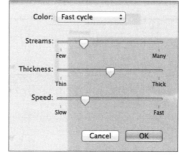

G Here's what the options look like for the Flurry screen saver.

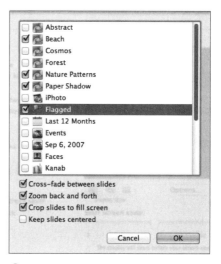

H Here's what the options look like for the Shuffle Pictures screen saver.

I Use this dialog to set trigger corners for the screen saver and other Mac OS X features. In this example, moving the pointer to the lower-right corner will activate the screen saver.

J Each pop-up menu in the Active Screen Corners dialog offers these options.

K You can use a pop-up menu at the bottom of the Screen Savers list to add other options.

TIP If you're not picky about what screen saver appears, you can turn on the Use random screen saver check box after step 1 and skip the remaining steps.

TIP In step 2, you can click the + button at the bottom of the Screen Savers list for additional options **K**. This makes it possible to create slide show screen savers based on a folder of pictures, a gallery on MobileMe, or an RSS feed. Or you can choose Browse Screen Savers to see screen savers available for download from Apple's website.

TIP In step 3, not all screen savers can be configured and the options that are available vary depending on the screen saver you selected in Step 3. **G** and **H** show two examples.

TIP To include a clock as part of the screen saver, turn on the Show with clock check box after step 3.

TIP In step 5, if Energy Saver (page 509) is configured for display sleep before the Start Screen Saver time, a warning will appear **F**. You'll need to either set the screen saver timing to a shorter period in the Desktop & Screen Saver preferences pane or set the display sleep time for a longer period in the Energy Saver preference pane for the screen saver to appear.

TIP Several of the screen saver modules are interactive. For example, pressing the D key while the Word of the Day screen saver is active opens the Dictionary application (page 265) to the currently displayed word.

TIP You can use the Active Screen Corners dialog to set up hot corners for Mission Control (page 295), Dashboard (Chapter 19), and Launchpad (page 150), too.

TIP In step 6, you can configure the hot corners any way you like. For example, you can set it up so every corner starts the screen saver.

Dock

The Dock preferences pane **A** enables you to set options that control the appearance and functionality of the Dock (page 38).

TIP You can learn how to further customize the Dock by adding, rearranging, or removing Dock icons on page 453.

TIP The Dock submenu under the Apple menu **B** offers easy access to some of the options found in the Dock preferences pane, as well as a handy way to open the preferences pane.

To set Dock preferences:

Set options as desired in the Dock preferences pane **A**:

- **Size** changes the size of the Dock and its icons. Drag the slider to resize.

- **Magnification** magnifies a Dock icon when you point to it **C**. Use the slider to specify how much magnification there should be.

- **Position on screen** lets you move the Dock to the left side, bottom, or right side of the screen. When positioned on the left or right, the Dock fits vertically down the screen **D**.

- **Minimize windows using** enables you to choose one of two special effects to use when minimizing a window to the Dock: Genie Effect or Scale Effect.

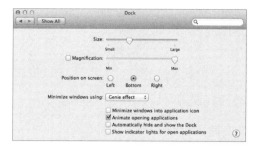

A The Dock preferences pane.

B The Dock submenu under the Apple menu offers several of the options found in the Dock preferences pane.

C With magnification enabled, pointing to a Dock icon enlarges it. This is especially useful if you have very small Dock icons.

D If you prefer, you can display the Dock vertically on one side of the screen.

E When you minimize windows into the Dock, you can access those windows from the application's Dock icon.

- **Minimize windows into application icon** makes an application's minimized windows accessible from the application's icon in the Dock **E**.

- **Animate opening applications** bounces an application's icon in the Dock as it opens.

- **Automatically hide and show the Dock** hides the Dock until you point to where it is hiding. This is a great way to regain screen real estate normally occupied by the Dock.

- **Show indicator lights for open applications** displays blue "bubbles" beneath Dock icons for applications that are open **F**. This option is new in OS X Lion; In previous versions of Mac OS X, the indicators could not be turned off.

TIP Another way to change the size of the Dock and its icons, is to drag the divider line up or down **G**.

F If you want to see which Dock icons represent applications that are open, enable the indicator lights.

G Another way to resize the Dock icons is to drag the divider.

General

The General preferences pane **A**, which was referred to as the Appearance preferences pane in previous versions of Mac OS X (and the General preferences pane a *very* long time ago), enables you to set options for color, scroll bar functionality, sidebar icon size, recent items, and text smoothing. These options help customize the Finder so it looks and works the way you prefer.

TIP You can learn more about customizing the Finder in Chapters 28 and 29.

To set General preferences:

In the General preferences pane **A**, set options as desired:

- **Appearance** sets the color for buttons, menus, and windows throughout your computer and its applications. Your options are Blue and Graphite.

- **Highlight Color** sets the highlight color for text in documents, fields, and lists. Choose an option from the pop-up menu **B**.

- **Show scroll bars** determines whether scroll bars should appear when not in use. You have three options:

  ▸ **Automatically based on input device** displays the scroll bars if you are using a mouse or other device that does not support Multi-Touch gestures.

  ▸ **When scrolling** displays scroll bars only when you are scrolling.

  ▸ **Always** displays scroll bars all the time.

  (This option is new in OS X Lion.)

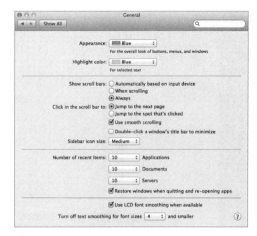

A The General preferences pane.

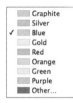

B Use this pop-up menu to choose a highlight color.

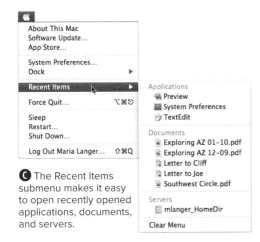

C The Recent Items submenu makes it easy to open recently opened applications, documents, and servers.

- **Click in the scroll bar to** determines what happens when you click in the scroll track of a scroll bar:

  - **Jump to the next page** scrolls to the next window or page of the document.

  - **Jump to the spot that's clicked** scrolls to the relative location in the document. For example, if you click in the scroll track two-thirds of the way between the top and bottom, you'll scroll two-thirds of the way through the document. This is the same as dragging the scroller to that position.

- **Use smooth scrolling** scrolls the contents of a window smoothly, without jumping.

- **Double-click a window's title bar to minimize** minimizes a window to the Dock (page 31) when you double-click its title bar.

- **Sidebar icon size** enables you to set the size of sidebar icons to small, medium (the default setting), or large. (This option is new in OS X Lion.)

- **Number of Recent Items** enables you to specify how many Applications, Documents, and Servers to consider "recent" when displaying recent applications, documents, and servers on the Recent Items submenu **C** (page 91). Options range from None to 50.

- **Restore windows when quitting and re-opening apps** enables the resume feature (page 154), which automatically reopens any document that was open when you quit an application the next time you open that application. (This option is new in OS X Lion.)

continues on next page

- **Use LCD font smoothing when available** determines how Mac OS X smooths text onscreen for LCD displays. This option varies depending on your computer model and display.

- **Turn off text smoothing for font sizes** enables you to choose a minimum font size for text smoothing. Text in the font size you set and smaller will not be smoothed. Your options range from 4 to 12.

TIP Font or text smoothing uses a process called *antialiasing* to make text more legible onscreen. Antialiasing creates gray pixels between black ones and white ones to eliminate sharp edges **D**.

TIP If you choose other from the Highlight Color pop-up menu **B**, you can use a standard Colors panel **E** to select any color supported by your computer. I explain how to use the Colors panel on the next page.

TIP You can clear the Recent Items submenu by choosing **Apple > Recent Items > Clear Menu C**.

12-point text with text smoothing turned on.

12-point text with text smoothing turned off.

D An example of text with text smoothing turned on (top) and off (bottom).

 In most cases, the Colors panel will display as a color wheel like this.

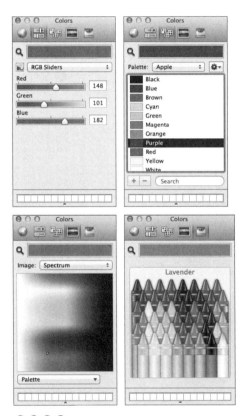

GGHⅠ The Colors panel can also appear as color sliders (top-left), color palettes (top-right), image palettes (bottom-left), and my personal favorite, crayons (bottom-right).

To use the Colors panel:

1. Click the icon along the top of the Colors panel to select one of the color models.

2. How you choose a color depends on the model you selected:

   ▸ **Color Wheel Ⓔ** displays a circle of color. Click inside the circle to choose a color. You can drag the vertical slider up or down to change the brightness.

   ▸ **Color Sliders Ⓕ** displays several sliders you can use to change color values. Start by selecting a slider group from the pop-up menu, and then move the sliders to create a color.

   ▸ **Color Palettes Ⓖ** displays clickable color samples. Choose a palette from the List pop-up menu, and then click the color you want.

   ▸ **Image Palettes Ⓗ** displays colors from an image. You can drag an image file onto the sample area and then click a color in the image to select it.

   ▸ **Crayons Ⓘ** displays different colored crayons. Click a crayon to choose its color.

   The color of the selected item changes immediately.

TIP You can use the color wells at the bottom of the Colors panel to store frequently used colors. Simply drag a color into an empty spot. Then, when you open the Colors panel, you can click a stored color to apply it.

Language & Text

The Language & Text preferences pane enables you to set options that control how Mac OS X works in an environment where U.S. English is not the primary language or multiple languages are used.

Language & Text preferences are broken down into four different categories: Language, Text, Formats, and Input Sources.

To set preferred language options:

1. In the Language & Text preferences pane, click the Language button .

2. To set the preferred order for languages to appear in application menus and dialogs, drag languages up or down in the Languages list **B**.

3. To set sort order for text in lists, choose an option from the Order for sorted lists pop-up menu.

TIP The changes you make to the Languages list in step 2 take effect in the Finder the next time you restart or log in. Changes take effect in applications the next time you open them.

TIP The Order for sorted list pop-up menu referred to in step 3 is very long and includes every language supported by Mac OS.

TIP You can edit the Languages list. Click the Edit List button in the Language pane **A**. In the dialog that appears **C**, toggle check boxes beside languages to specify which ones should appear in the list and click OK.

A The Language options in the Language & Text preferences pane.

B Drag a language to change its position in the preference order list.

C Toggle check boxes to specify which languages should appear in the list.

D The Text options in the Language & Text preferences pane.

E You can add a text substitution to the bottom of the list.

F Use this pop-up menu to choose the primary language for spelling checks in Apple applications.

G The Word Break pop-up menu.

H **I** The two Smart Quotes pop-up menus.

To set text substitution options:

1. In the Language & Text preferences pane, click the Text button **D**.

2. In the Symbol and Text Substitution list, toggle check boxes to enable the automatic substitutions you want.

3. To add a new substitution to the list, click the + button at the bottom of the list and, in the new line that appears **E** enter the text you want to replace as well as the text you want to replace it with.

4. Choose options from the pop-up menus on the right side of the preferences pane as desired:

   ▸ **Spelling** **F** is the language you want to use for spelling checks in your document.

   ▸ **Word Break** **G** determines how a word is selected when double-clicked. Choose your language style.

   ▸ **Smart Quotes** enables you to specify how quote characters should be displayed. Choose options for double quotes **H** and single quotes **I**.

TIP Text substitution controls automatic text substitution options available in several Apple applications, including TextEdit, iCal, and iMovie.

To set the date, time, & number formats:

1. In the Language & Text preferences pane, click the Formats button **J**.

2. Choose an option from the Region pop-up menu.

3. To customize the date or time format, click the Customize button in the appropriate area of the dialog. In the dialogs that appear **K** **L**, drag elements in the edit areas to set the formats and click OK.

4. Use the Calendar and First day of week pop-up menu to set additional calendar options as desired.

5. To customize the number format, click the Customize button in the Numbers area of the dialog, set options in the dialog that appears **M**, and click OK.

6. To change the currency format, choose an option from the Currency pop-up menu.

7. To change the measurement unit, choose an option from the Measurement Units pop-up menu.

TIP Changes in this pane affect how dates, times, and numbers are displayed throughout Mac OS X and applications.

TIP The sample dates, times, and numbers in the Formats pane **J** show the effect of your changes.

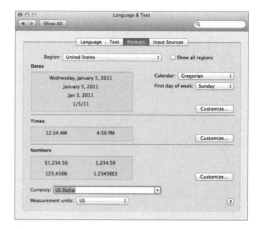

J The Formats options in the Language & Text preferences pane.

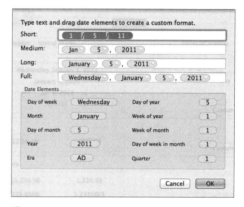

K Use this dialog to customize date formats.

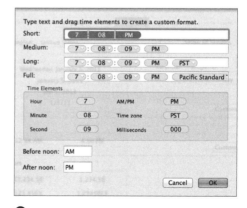

L Use this dialog to customize time formats.

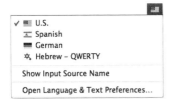

M Set number format options in this dialog.

N The Input Sources options of the Language & Text preferences pane.

O When you enable several languages, an Input menu with each language you selected appears on the menu bar.

To create & customize an input menu:

1. In the Language & Text preferences pane, click the Input Sources button **N**.

2. Turn on the check boxes beside each input method or keyboard layout you may want to use with Mac OS X. If more than one item is selected, an Input menu appears on the menu bar **O**.

3. Select one of the Input source options to determine whether you use the same input method in all documents or allow a different one for each document.

4. To toggle the display of the input menu, set the Show input menu in menu bar check box.

TIP To switch from one keyboard or input method to another, select an item from the Input menu **O** or press Option-Command-Spacebar to cycle through all options on the menu, one at a time.

TIP The Input menu may also automatically appear on the menu bar when you use the Special Characters command (page 320) in an application.

TIP Instructions for entering characters in complex languages such as Chinese is far beyond the scope of this book. If you need to use these features, you can find more information in Mac Help. Enter the search phrase *input method* to get started.

Mission Control

The Mission Control preferences pane  enables you to set general options and keyboard shortcuts for Mission Control (page 295), Exposé (page 297), Spaces (page 299), and Dashboard (Chapter 19) to customize the way these features work.

To set Mission Control preferences:

1. In the top part of the Mission Control preferences pane **A**, toggle check boxes to set options as desired:

   ▸ **Show Dashboard as a Space** creates a separate space for Dashboard.

   ▸ **Automatically rearrange spaces based on most recent use** places the most recently used spaces to the left of other spaces.

   ▸ **When switching to an application, switch to a space with open windows for the application** switches spaces when you switch to an application that has windows open in a space.

2. Under Keyboard and Mouse Shortcuts, use pop-up menus to choose keyboard keys **B** and mouse buttons **C** to activate various components of Mission Control and Dashboard.

TIP If you hold down the Shift, Control, Option, or Command key while displaying the keyboard shortcuts or mouse button pop-up menu, the menu changes to reflect the key(s) being held **D**.

TIP Clicking the Hot Corners button enables you to specify screen corners to invoke a Mission Control feature. You can learn more about setting hot corners on page 482.

A The Mission Control preferences pane.

B Use this menu to choose a keystroke to invoke a feature.

C Use this menu to choose a mouse button to invoke a feature.

D Holding down the Option and Command keys (for example) change the options available in the menu.

Security & Privacy

The Security & Privacy preferences pane includes four panels of options that you can use to enhance security on your Mac:

- **General** offers options for protecting your computer from unauthorized access, primarily in a work environment shared with other people.

- **FileVault** enables you to encrypt your hard disk's contents using Advanced Encryption Standard 128-bit (AES-128) encryption. This makes it virtually impossible for a hacker to access the files on your hard disk. Best of all, it's all done quickly and transparently—files are decrypted automatically when you log in and encrypted again when you log out.

- **Firewall** protects your computer from unauthorized access via a network or Internet connection by blocking your computer's networking ports from incoming traffic. You open only the ports you need to exchange information with various networking services. This helps prevent hackers from gaining access to your computer.

- **Privacy**, which is new in OS X Lion, enables you to set privacy options related to diagnostic and usage data and location services.

TIP You must have an administrator user name and password to make changes to Security & Privacy preference pane options.

TIP If your computer never connects to the Internet and is not part of a network, there's no benefit to using the firewall feature.

To set General security options:

1. In the Security & Privacy preferences pane, click the General button **A**.

2. If necessary, click the lock icon at the bottom of the window and enter an administrator name and password to unlock the preferences pane options.

3. Set options as desired:

   ▸ **Require password after sleep or screen saver begins** displays a login screen when you wake your computer or deactivate the screen saver (page 482). You can choose a time period from the pop-up menu, from immediately to 4 hours.

   ▸ **Disable automatic login** turns off the automatic login feature.

   ▸ **Require an administrator password to access system preferences with lock icons** prompts for an administrator password before allowing modification of a locked System Preferences pane (page 477).

   ▸ **Log out after *n* minutes of inactivity** automatically logs out (page 133) a user who has been inactive for the number of minutes you specify.

   ▸ **Show a message when the screen is locked** enables you to enter a message to display onscreen when the computer is locked.

   ▸ **Automatically update safe downloads list** gets periodic updates about malware from Apple.

   ▸ **Disable remote control infrared receiver** (not shown) prevents the computer from responding to a signal sent by an Apple remote control device. This option only appears on computers that support the Apple Remote.

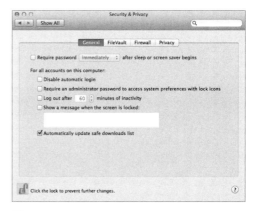

A The General options in the Security & Privacy preferences pane.

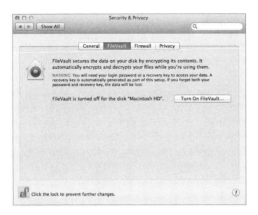

B Before enabling FileVault, the FileVault options look like this.

C Use this dialog to indicate who should have access to the encrypted files.

D Enter the password for each user who should be able to access the files.

E Write down the recovery key that appears.

To enable FileVault:

1. In the Security & Privacy preferences pane, click the FileVault button **B**.

2. If necessary, click the lock icon at the bottom of the window and enter an administrator name and password to unlock the preferences pane options.

3. Click Turn on FileVault.

4. A dialog listing all of the computer's users appears **C**. For each user you want to access the encrypted disk, click the Enable User button, enter the user's password in the dialog that appears **D**, and click OK.

5. Click Continue.

6. A dialog with a recovery key appears next **E**. Write down the key and put it in a safe place.

7. Click Continue.

8. Another dialog appears, offering to store the recovery key with Apple **F**. If you select this option, choose three questions and enter three corresponding answers in the dialog.

9. Click Continue.

continues on next page

F You can store the recovery key with Apple.

10. A dialog instructs you to click Restart to begin the encryption process **G**. Click Restart.

11. Your computer restarts and presents a login screen. Enter your password and press Return.

12. The FileVault pane of the Security & Privacy preferences pane opens again **H**. Wait while the disk is encrypted.

    When encryption is complete, a message in the FileVault panel tells you **I**.

TIP You can continue working with your computer while it encrypts your hard disk.

TIP When FileVault is enabled, you must log in each time you start or wake your computer.

To turn off FileVault:

1. In the Security & Privacy preferences pane, click the FileVault button **I**.

2. If necessary, click the lock icon at the bottom of the window and enter an administrator name and password to unlock the preferences pane options.

3. Click Turn Off FileVault.

4. A confirmation dialog appears **J**. Click Turn Off Encryption.

5. Wait while your computer decrypts your hard disk.

TIP You can continue working with your computer while it decrypts your hard disk.

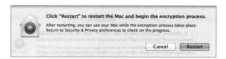

G Click Restart in this dialog to begin the encryption process.

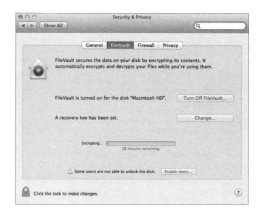

H When your computer restarts, encryption begins.

I When encryption is done, the FileVault panel should look something like this.

J Your Mac confirms that you really want to turn off FileVault.

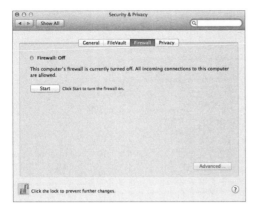

K The Firewall panel looks like this before the firewall feature is turned on.

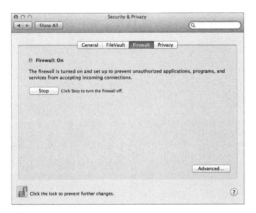

L Once the firewall is turned on, the Start button turns into a Stop button.

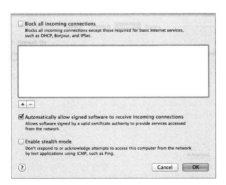

M You can set firewall options in this dialog.

To enable the firewall:

1. In the Security & Privacy preferences pane, click the Firewall button **K**.

2. If necessary, click the lock icon at the bottom of the window and enter an administrator name and password to unlock the preferences pane options.

3. Click the Start button.

   The window changes to indicate that the firewall is On and a Stop button appears **L**.

TIP To disable the firewall, click the Stop button in the Firewall panel **L**.

To set advanced firewall options:

1. In the Firewall panel of the Security & Privacy pane **L**, click Advanced.

2. Set options in the dialog that appears **M**:

   ▸ **Block all incoming connections** does not allow any outside connections to your computer.

   ▸ To limit incoming connections to specific services and applications click the + button and use the Open dialog that appears to add applications. The Block all incoming connections check box must be turned off.

   ▸ **Automatically allow signed software to receive incoming connections** allows connections for services with a valid certificate of authority.

   ▸ **Enable stealth mode** prevents your computer from responding to access attempts, making it appear as if your computer does not exist.

3. Click OK.

To set Privacy options:

1. In the Security & Privacy preferences pane, click the Privacy button 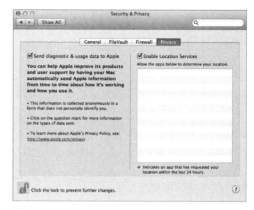.

2. If necessary, click the lock icon at the bottom of the window and enter an administrator name and password to unlock the preferences pane options.

3. Toggle check boxes to enable features as desired:

   ▸ **Send diagnostic & usage data to Apple** sends anonymous information to Apple about how you use your computer to help Apple improve its products.

   ▸ **Enable Location Services** allows applications that support Mac OS X's location services feature to access your location. Apps that use this feature will be listed beneath this check box.

N The Privacy options in the Security & Privacy preferences pane.

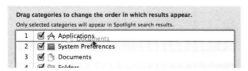

Spotlight

You can set options for the way Spotlight works and the results it shows in search results windows. You do this in the two panels of the Spotlight preferences pane:

- **Search Results** enables you to determine which categories of items should appear in search results and what order they should appear in.

- **Privacy** enables you to exclude specific folders or disks from searches.

To set Spotlight Search Results menu preferences:

1. In the Spotlight preferences pane, click the Search Results button **A**.

2. Toggle check boxes to specify which categories of search results should be displayed.

3. To change the order in which categories should appear in search results, drag a category to a new position in the list **B**.

TIP The changes you make in the Spotlight Search Results panel affect the Spotlight search menu **C** only—not the other search features of Mac OS X.

A Use the Search Results panel to specify which categories of items should appear in search results and what order they should appear in.

B Changing the order of search results is as easy as dragging categories around in a list.

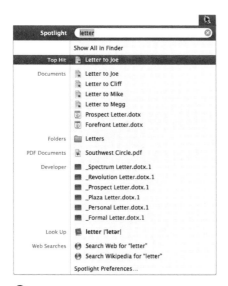

C Changes affect the Spotlight menu's search results.

To exclude locations from search:

1. In the Spotlight preferences pane, click the Privacy button **D**.

2. Do one of the following:
   - ▸ Click the + button beneath the list and use the dialog that appears **E** to add the folder or disk you want to exclude from searches.
   - ▸ Drag a folder or disk from a Finder window into the list area **F**.

   The item is added to the list **G**.

3. Repeat step 2 for each item you want to exclude from searches.

TIP To remove an item from the list **G**, select the item and click the − button at the bottom of the list. The item is removed and will be excluded from future searches.

TIP The Privacy panel settings affect all Mac OS X search features—not just the Spotlight menu.

D The Privacy options in the Spotlight preferences pane.

E Use an Open dialog like this to locate, select, and choose folders or disks to exclude.

G The folder is added to the list and will be excluded from searches.

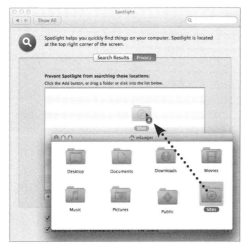

F Or drag a folder from the Finder into the list in the Spotlight preferences pane.

Pressing Command-Spacebar displays the Spotlight search menu.

Pressing Option-Command-Spacebar displays the searching window.

To set Spotlight keyboard shortcuts:

1. Display either panel of the Spotlight preferences pane A B.

2. Toggle the check boxes to enable or disable the two shortcuts:

   ▸ **Spotlight menu keyboard shortcut** displays the Spotlight menu H.

   ▸ **Spotlight window keyboard shortcut** displays the Searching window for the results of a Spotlight Search I.

3. To set a shortcut key, select an option from the drop-down list or select the list and press the keys you want to assign.

Universal Access

The Universal Access preferences pane enables you to set options for making your computer easier to use by people with special access needs.

Universal Access's features can be set in four different panels:

- **Seeing Ⓐ** enables you to set options for people with visual disabilities.

- **Hearing Ⓑ** allows you to set options for people with aural disabilities.

- **Keyboard Ⓒ** lets you set options for people who have difficulty using the keyboard.

- **Mouse & Trackpad Ⓓ** enables you to set options for people who have difficulty using the mouse.

A complete discussion of Universal Access is beyond the scope of this book. If you have a need to use these features, explore them on your own. You can click the Help (?) button in a panel to get detailed information about its options.

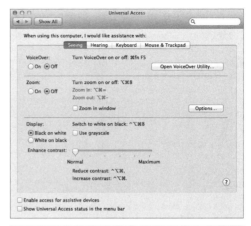

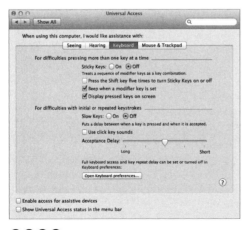

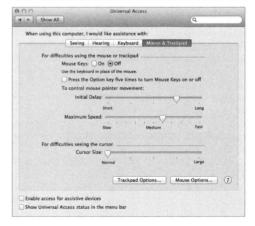

ⒶⒷⒸⒹ The Universal Access preferences pane is separated into four different panels of options: Seeing, Hearing, Keyboard, and Mouse & Trackpad.

32

Hardware Preferences

Hardware preferences panes enable you to configure the hardware components of your computer system. This chapter covers the following System Preferences panes:

- **CDs & DVDs** controls the way your optical drive works.

- **Displays** controls monitor settings, including resolution and color.

- **Energy Saver** controls energy consumption and schedules.

- **Keyboard** controls USB or Bluetooth keyboard operation and lets you customize keyboard shortcuts.

- **Mouse** controls USB or Bluetooth mouse operation.

- **Trackpad** controls built-in or Bluetooth trackpad options and operation.

- **Print & Scan** enables you to set up printers, scanners, and faxmodems.

- **Sound** controls sound input and output options, as well as alert sounds.

Need to learn the basics of System Preferences? Be sure to read Chapter 30.

CDs & DVDs

The CDs & DVDs preferences pane lets you specify what should happen when you insert a CD or DVD disc.

The options that appear vary depending on your computer's CD and DVD capabilities. The illustration here  shows how this preferences pane appears for a Mac-Book Air with a MacBook Air SuperDrive connected. This external drive, which is capable of reading and writing both CDs and DVDs, provides the same capabilities as the internal optical drive available in most recently released Macintosh models.

To specify what should happen when you insert a CD or DVD:

In the CDs & DVDs preferences pane **A**, choose an option from the pop-up menu beside each event that you want to set. The menus are basically the same; **B** and **C** show examples for a blank CD and a music CD. Your options are:

- **Ask what to do** displays a dialog **D** when you insert that type of disc. This enables you to tell your computer what to do on the fly, when a disc is inserted.

- **Open** *application name* always opens the specified application when you insert that type of disc.

- **Open other application** displays a dialog you can use to select the application that should open when you insert that type of disc.

- **Run script** displays a dialog you can use to select an AppleScript applet (page 373) that should open when you insert that type of disc.

- **Ignore** tells your computer not to do anything when you insert that type of disc.

A The CDs & DVDs preferences pane, as it appears for a Mac with a SuperDrive.

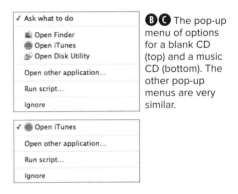

B C The pop-up menu of options for a blank CD (top) and a music CD (bottom). The other pop-up menus are very similar.

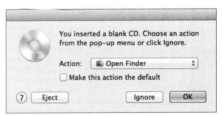

D Use this dialog to tell your computer what to do when you insert a disc.

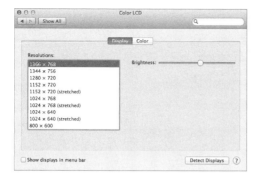

A The Display pane of the Displays preferences pane for an 11-inch MacBook Air.

B A MacBook Air display set to 1024 x 640...

C ...and the same display set to 1366 x 768.

D The Displays menu offers a quick way to switch among your favorite screen resolutions.

Displays

The Displays preferences pane enables you to set the resolution, colors, and other settings for your monitor. Settings are organized into panes; this section covers the Display and Color panes.

The options that are available in the Displays preferences pane vary depending on your computer and monitor. The options shown in this chapter are for an 11-inch MacBook Air.

To set basic display options:

1. In the Displays preferences pane, click the Display button **A**.

2. If your computer does not show a recently connected display, click the Detect Displays button to rescan for displays.

3. Set options as desired:
   - **Resolutions** control the number of pixels that appear on screen. The higher the resolution, the more pixels appear on screen. This makes the screen contents smaller but shows more **B C**.
   - **Show displays in menu bar** displays a menu of recently used display settings in the menu bar **D**.
   - **Brightness** lets you adjust the display's brightness by dragging a slider.
   - **Automatically adjust brightness** (not shown) adjusts brightness based on the brightness of your workspace. This option is only available on computers that support it.

TIP If you have multiple displays connected to your Mac, the Display pane will appear for each one.

To set display color options:

1. In the Displays preferences pane, click the Color button **E**.

2. To limit the selection of color profiles to just those designed to work with your display, turn on the Show profiles for this display only check box.

3. To use a predefined display, select one of the Display Profiles.

4. To get details for a selected display, click the Open Profile button to display a window with information **F**. You can click the window's close button to dismiss it when you're finished.

5. To calibrate your monitor, click the Calibrate button. This launches the Display Calibrator Assistant **G**, which steps you through the process of fine-tuning color options for your display.

TIP Color profiles and the Display Calibrator Assistant are advanced feature of Mac OS. They work with ColorSync (page 358) to display colors onscreen as they will appear when printed.

E The Color pane of the Displays preferences pane for an 11-inch MacBook Air.

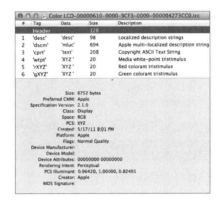

F The details of a color profile. (If you understand this, you qualify as a true Color Geek.)

G The first screen of the Display Calibrator Assistant.

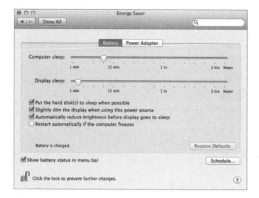

A The Energy Saver preferences pane on a MacBook Air. These are the settings for when on battery power...

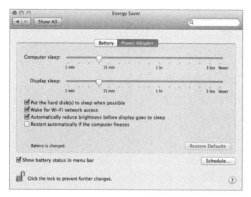

B ...and these are the settings for when plugged into a power adapter.

Energy Saver

The Energy Saver preference pane enables you to specify settings that can reduce the amount of power your computer uses when idle.

Energy Saver settings are especially important for laptop users running on battery power. Because of this, laptops have two panes of settings: one for Battery power **A** and one for when connected to a Power Adapter **B**.

The appearance of and options in the Energy Saver preferences pane vary depending on your computer. The illustrations here are for a MacBook Air.

To set Energy Saver options:

1. If necessary, in the Energy Saver preferences pane, click the button to select the power source you want to configure for: Battery **A** or Power Adapter **B**.

2. To set the amount of inactive time before the computer sleeps, drag the Computer sleep slider to the right or left. Dragging all the way to the right disables computer sleep.

3. To set the amount of inactive time before the display sleeps, drag the Display sleep to the left or right. (You cannot set display sleep for longer than computer sleep.) Dragging all the way to the right disables display sleep.

4. Toggle check boxes to set additional options as desired:

    ▸ **Put the hard disk(s) to sleep when possible** tells your computer to put the hard disk to sleep when it isn't needed.

continues on next page

- **Slightly dim the display when using this power source** reduces the brightness of the display when on battery power.

- **Wake for Wi-Fi network access** wakes the computer from computer sleep when it detects a Wake-on-LAN packet.

- **Automatically reduce brightness before display goes to sleep** dims the screen a short while before the display sleeps. You can use this as a sort of warning signal that the display will sleep shortly.

- **Start up automatically after a power failure** (not shown) automatically restarts the computer when power is restored after a power failure. This option only appears for desktop Macs.

- **Restart automatically after the computer freezes** automatically restarts the computer when it becomes responsive or had a kernel panic.

5. To display battery status on a laptop's menu bar **C**, turn on the Show battery status on the menu bar check box.

TIP To wake a sleeping display, press any key. A sleeping hard disk wakes automatically when it needs to.

TIP If your computer is being used as a server, it's important to turn on the Restart automatically check box. This ensures that the computer is running whenever possible.

TIP A kernel panic is a computer operating system "crash" that dims the screen and displays a multilanguage message telling you you'll need to restart.

TIP If you display the Battery Status menu **C**, you can use its Show submenu **D** to specify what information should appear in the menu bar: Icon Only, Time, or Percentage.

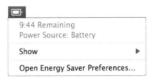

C The Battery Status menu offers a handy way to see how much power is left in your laptop's battery. (Gotta love the battery life in a MacBook Air, huh?)

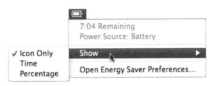

D Use the Show submenu on the Battery Status menu to specify what you want to show on the menu bar icon.

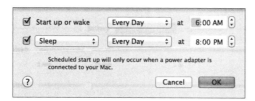

E Use this dialog to schedule automatic startup and shutdown days and times.

F Use this pop-up menu to specify the days of the week your computer should automatically start up or shut down.

G Use this pop-up menu to specify what it should do at shut down time.

H Your computer will give you a 10-minute warning before shutting down automatically.

To schedule start up & shut down:

1. In the Energy Saver preferences pane, click the Schedule button to display the schedule dialog **E**.

2. To set automatic startup, turn on the Start up or wake check box. Then choose an option from the pop-up menu **F** and enter a time beside it.

3. To set automatic sleep, restart, or shut down, turn on the second check box, choose options from the pop-up menus beside it **F G**, and enter a time beside them.

4. Click OK to save your settings.

TIP Your computer will give you a 10-minute warning for a scheduled shutdown. When the warning dialog appears **H**, you can choose to cancel the shutdown, shut down immediately, or just wrap up your work and let the computer shut down when it's ready.

TIP A laptop will not automatically start unless it is connected to a power adapter.

Keyboard

The Keyboard preferences pane enables you to customize the way the keyboard works. Options can be set in at least two panes:

- **Keyboard** enables you to set keyboard functionality options, such as key repeat rate.

- **Keyboard Shortcuts** enables you to view and assign shortcuts for application menu commands.

The appearance of the Keyboard preferences pane varies depending on the type of computer and keyboard you are using. The illustrations here are for a MacBook Air.

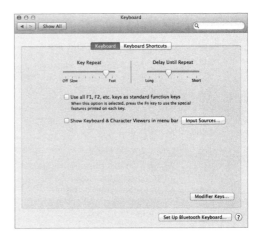

A The Keyboard options in the Keyboard preferences pane on a MacBook Air.

TIP To use a Bluetooth keyboard with your Mac, it must be paired (page 545).

To set keyboard options:

1. In the Keyboard preferences pane, click the Keyboard button **A**.

2. Set options as desired:

   ▸ **Key Repeat Rate** sets how fast a key repeats when held down. (Adjusting this is especially useful for heavy-handed typists.)

   ▸ **Delay Until Repeat** sets how long a key must be pressed before it starts to repeat.

3. Set additional options, if available, for a keyboard:

   ▸ **Use all F1, F2, etc. keys as standard function keys** takes away special functionality for these keys, such as brightness and volume control, and requires you to press the FN key with those keys for the same functionality.

B You can display this menu in the menu bar.

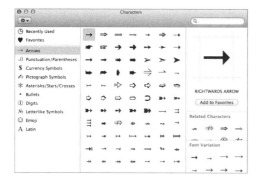

C Use the Character Viewer to insert a special character into a document with just a click.

D Use the Keyboard Viewer to enter characters by clicking a keyboard.

E You can use this dialog to change the behavior of modifier keys.

▸ **Illuminate keyboard in low light conditions** (not shown) turns on backlighting for your keyboard in low light conditions. (Keep in mind that this can reduce battery life.)

▸ **Turn off when computer is not used for** (not shown) lets you specify, with a slider, how long before keyboard lighting should be turned off when the computer is idle.

▸ **Show Keyboard & Character Viewers in menu bar** displays a menu **B**, which you can use to display the Character Viewer **C** and Keyboard Viewer **D** palettes. These palettes enable you to enter characters into Mac OS applications by clicking a palette button.

4. To change the behavior of modifier keys such as Command, Option, and Control, click the Modifier Keys button. In the dialog that appears **E**, use the pop-up menus to set the action you want each key to perform and click OK.

TIP Clicking the Input Sources button in the Keyboard pane displays the Input Sources pane of the Language & Text preferences pane (page 490).

TIP Why you'd want to change the behavior of modifier keys is beyond me. It would make a good April Fool's joke, though.

TIP If you have a Bluetooth keyboard paired and connected to your Mac, a battery level indicator will appear in the bottom-left corner of the Keyboard preferences pane.

To customize keyboard shortcuts:

1. In the Keyboard preferences pane, click the Keyboard Shortcuts button **F**.

2. In the list on the left side of the window, select the category or type of shortcut key you want to change.

3. To turn a shortcut on or off, toggle its check box in the list on the right side of the window.

4. To modify keyboard shortcuts in the list on the right side of the window, double-click the shortcut you want to change so it becomes selected **G** and then hold down the new keys to make the change **H**.

5. To set the way the Tab key highlights items in windows and dialogs, select one of the two options at the bottom of the preferences pane: Text boxes and lists only or All controls.

TIP You can also use the Keyboard Shortcuts pane **F** to learn about shortcuts available in the Finder and other applications that do not appear on menus. The ones listed under Keyboard & Text Input are especially interesting and you may find them useful.

TIP When you add a keyboard shortcut for a menu command, the shortcut appears on the menu **I**.

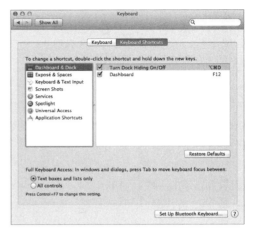

F The Keyboard Shortcuts options of the Keyboard preferences pane on a MacBook Air.

G To change a shortcut, double-click it...

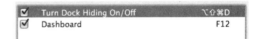

H ...and then press the desired keys.

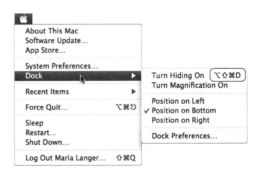

I Keyboard shortcuts you change or add for menu commands appear on the menus.

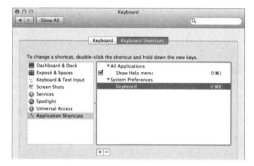

J In this example, I'm adding a shortcut to System Preferences that'll display the Keyboard preferences pane.

K The new shortcut appears in the list.

To add and remove application shortcuts:

1. In the Keyboard preferences pane, click the Keyboard Shortcuts button **F**.

2. In the list on the left side of the window, select Application Shortcuts.

3. Do the following:

   ▸ To add a shortcut, click the + button at the bottom of the list. Then set options in the dialog that appears **J** to specify the application, menu command, and keyboard shortcut you want to add. Click Add and the shortcut is added to the list **K**.

   ▸ To remove a shortcut, select the shortcut you want to add and click the – (minus) button at the bottom of the list. The shortcut is removed.

Mouse

The Mouse preferences pane enables you to set mouse functionality options, such as scroll speed and button assignment.

The appearance of the Mouse preferences pane varies depending on the type of mouse connected to your Macintosh. These illustrations show settings for a USB Apple Mouse **Ⓐ** and a Bluetooth Magic Mouse **Ⓑ**. If you have a different kind of mouse, you'll see different—but likely similar—options.

TIP To use a Bluetooth mouse with your Mac, it must be paired (page 545).

To set Mouse options:

1. Make sure your mouse is properly paired (if necessary) and connected to your Mac.

2. Open the Mouse preferences pane **Ⓐ Ⓑ**.

3. Toggle the check box at the top of the window to determine how content is scrolled. Turning this check box off sets scrolling to work as it did in Mac OS X 10.6 Snow Leopard or earlier. Leaving this check box on sets scrolling to work like an iPad or iPhone.

4. Use sliders at the top of the pane to set speed options:

   ▸ **Tracking** is the speed of the pointer movement on your screen.

   ▸ **Double-Click** is the amount of time between each click of a double-click.

   ▸ **Scrolling** is how scroll wheel or ball movements are translated to window scrolling.

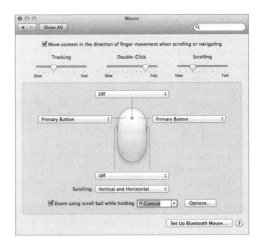

Ⓐ The Mouse preferences pane with a USB Apple Mouse connected.

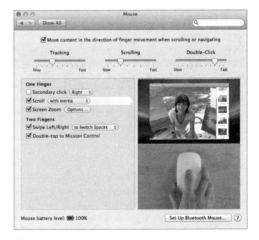

Ⓑ The Mouse preferences pane with a Magic Mouse connected.

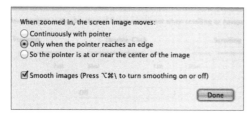

C Use a pop-up menu like this one to assign an action to each button.

D Use this pop-up menu to specify how the scroll ball should scroll.

E You can use this dialog to set additional options for zooming with your mouse.

5. If configuring an Apple Mouse, set these options **A**:

   ▸ Use pop-up menus **C** to assign actions to each mouse button.

   ▸ Select an option from the Scrolling pop-up menu **D** to determine how the scroll ball scrolls window contents.

   ▸ **Zoom using scroll ball while holding** enables you to zoom with the scroll ball while holding down a keyboard key. With this option enabled, you can click the Options button to display additional settings for zooming with the scroll ball **E**.

6. If configuring a Magic Mouse, toggle check boxes to enable the gestures you want to use **B**:

   Under **One finger:**

   ▸ **Secondary click** enables right-clicking (page 15) with one finger. If you enable this check box, use the menu to specify whether the secondary click will be done on the right or left side of the mouse.

   ▸ **Scroll** enables scrolling with one finger. Use the menu to specify whether you should scroll with or without inertia. With inertia scrolls faster when you swipe faster.

   ▸ **Screen Zoom** enables you to hold down a keyboard key and swipe with one finger to zoom. With this option enabled, you can click the Options button to display additional settings for zooming **E**.

continues on next page

Under **Two Fingers**:

▸ **Swipe Left/Right** enables you to swipe to the left or right with two fingers to either navigate pages or switch spaces. Choose your preference from the menu.

▸ **Double-tap to Mission Control** opens Mission Control (page 295) when you double-tap (or double-click) the mouse with two fingers.

TIP If you choose Other from any of the button pop-up menus ⓒ, you can assign that button to an application.

TIP You can learn more about the multi-touch gestures supported by your Magic Mouse by pointing to an option and watching the video demonstration in the window to the right ⓑ.

TIP If you have a Bluetooth mouse paired and connected to your Mac, a battery level indicator will appear in the bottom-left corner of the Mouse preferences pane ⓑ.

A The Trackpad preferences pane for a Multi-Touch trackpad.

Trackpad

The Trackpad preferences pane **A**, which is only available on computers with access to a trackpad, enables you to set trackpad functionality options, such as tracking speed and trackpad gestures.

The options that appear in the Trackpad preferences pane vary depending on the computer model and type of trackpad connected. The illustrations here show the options for the trackpad on a MacBook Air; the options are identical for recent Mac-Book Pro models, as well as Apple's Magic Trackpad. Older laptop models may not support all gesture options.

TIP To use a Bluetooth trackpad with your Mac, it must be paired (page 545).

To set trackpad options:

1. Open the Trackpad preferences pane **A**.

2. Toggle the check box at the top of the window to determine how content is scrolled. Turning this check box off sets scrolling to work as it did in Mac OS X 10.6 Snow Leopard or earlier. Leaving this check box on sets scrolling to work like an iPad or iPhone.

3. Use the sliders to set general speed options:

   ▸ **Tracking** is the speed of the pointer movement on your screen.

   ▸ **Scrolling** is how trackpad movements are translated to window scrolling.

   ▸ **Double-Click** is the amount of time between each click of a double-click.

continues on next page

4. Toggle check boxes to enable the gestures you want to use 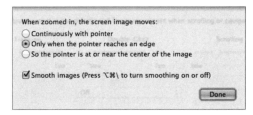:

Under **One Finger:**

- ▸ **Tap to Click** enables you to click with a light tap rather than pressing down hard enough to feel or hear a click.

- ▸ **Dragging** enables you to drag with one finger. To turn on this check box, the Tap to Click check box above it must be enabled. If you enable this option, you can use the pop-up menu to specify whether you want this feature to work with or without drag lock.

- ▸ **Secondary click** enables right-clicking (page 15) with one finger. If you enable this option, use the menu to specify whether the secondary click will be done on the bottom right or left corner of the trackpad.

Under **Two Fingers:**

- ▸ **Scroll** enables scrolling with two fingers. Use the menu to specify whether you should scroll with or without inertia. With inertia scrolls faster when you swipe faster.

- ▸ **Rotate** enables you to rotate images and other content by dragging in a rotating motion with two fingers.

- ▸ **Pinch Open & Close** enables you to zoom images and other content by pinching with two fingers.

- ▸ **Screen Zoom** enables you to hold down a keyboard key and pinch with two fingers to zoom the screen. With this option enabled, you can click the Options button to display additional settings for zooming **B**.

- ▸ **Secondary click** enables right-clicking (page 15) by clicking with two fingers.

When zoomed in, the screen image moves:
- ◯ Continuously with pointer
- ◉ Only when the pointer reaches an edge
- ◯ So the pointer is at or near the center of the image

☑ Smooth images (Press ⌥⌘\ to turn smoothing on or off)

[Done]

B You can use this dialog to set additional options for zooming with your trackpad.

Under **Three Fingers:**

▸ Swipe options enable you to use a pop-up menu to specify whether you want a three-finger swipe to navigate, open Mission Control and Spaces, or drag.

Under **Four Fingers:**

▸ **Swipe Up/Down** enables you to swipe with four fingers up or down to either open Mission Control or navigate pages. Choose an option from the pop-up menu.

▸ **Swipe Left/Right** enables you to swipe to the left or right with two fingers to either switch spaces or navigate pages. Choose an option from the pop-up menu.

▸ **Pinch for Launchpad, Spread for Desktop** enables you to use four fingers—or five; that's the only way I'm able to do it—to open Launchpad or view your desktop.

TIP You can learn more about the multi-touch gestures supported by your trackpad by pointing to an option and watching the video demonstration in the window to the right **Ⓐ**.

TIP If you have a Bluetooth trackpad paired and connected to your Mac, a battery level indicator will appear in the bottom-left corner of the Trackpad preferences pane.

Print & Scan

Before you can print from a Mac OS X application, you must make a printer accessible to Mac OS X. You do this with the Print & Scan preferences pane **A**.

Mac OS X is smart. If you connect a printer directly to your Mac and it has an appropriate driver installed, it automatically recognizes the printer and adds it to the Printers list.

However if Mac OS X does not recognize your printer or you want to use a printer accessible via a network (page 323), you may need to manually add the printer to the Print & Scan preferences pane.

The Print & Scan preferences pane enables you to perform the following tasks:

- Add printers, scanners, and faxmodems to the Printers list that your Mac consults when printing, scanning, or faxing.

- Set the default printer and paper size.

- Set printer options.

- Create printer pools (page 323) so your print jobs go to whatever networked printer is available when you're ready to print.

TIP You only have to add a printer if it does not already appear in the Printers list. This needs to be done only once; Mac OS will remember all printers that you add.

TIP You may have to unlock this preferences pane to set certain options in it. You can learn how on page 477.

TIP To set up printer sharing with the Sharing preferences pane, consult the section titled "To enable & configure printer sharing" on page 550.

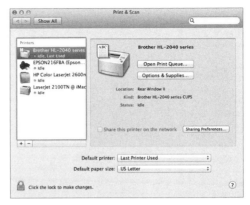

A The Print & Scan preferences pane with four printers added to the Printer list: a laser printer accessible via Time Capsule with Back to My Mac and a wide area network connection, a Wi-Fi inkjet printer accessible via local area network connection, a laser printer directly connected via USB, and a laser printer connected to another computer and shared over the local area network. This is not a typical setup, but it is possible.

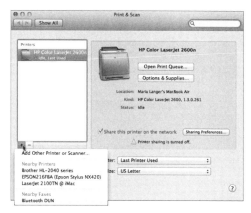

B In this example, my Mac automatically recognized and set up a printer that was directly connected to it via USB cable and found three other printers on my network.

C If driver software is not installed on your Mac, it may offer to get it for you.

D The printer is added to the list.

E In this example, all I did was plug in my printer—Mac OS offered to do the rest.

To add a printer that is listed by default:

1. If necessary, connect the printer you want to use with the computer and turn it on.

    If the printer appears in the Print & Scan preferences pane **A**, you're done. You can skip the remaining steps.

2. Click the + button beneath the Printers list in the Print & Scan preferences pane **A** to display a menu that lists the printers your computer "sees" locally or on a network you are connected to **B**.

3. Do one of the following:

    ▸ If the printer you want to add appears in the menu, select it.

    ▸ If the printer you want to add does not appear in the menu, skip the remaining steps and follow the instructions in the section titled "To add a printer that is not listed by default" on page 524.

4. If driver software is not installed on your computer, a dialog appears offering to get it from Apple **C**. Click Download & Install. Then wait while your computer connects to the Internet to download and install the software.

5. The printer is added to the list **D**.

TIP If you directly connect a printer to your Mac, it may offer to install the software and add the printer without even opening the Print & Scan preferences pane **E**.

TIP In step 3, if the printer you want to use does not appear in the list, double-check to make sure the printer is connected to your computer or network and turned on.

To add a printer that is not listed by default:

1. If you haven't already done so, follow steps 1 and 2 in the section titled "To add a printer that is listed by default" on page 523.

2. On the pop-up menu **B**, choose Add Other Printer or Scanner.

   The Add Printer dialog appears.

3. In the dialog's toolbar, click the button for the type of printer you want to add:

   ▸ **Default F** lists the printers your computer sees.

   ▸ **Fax G** lets you add an internal, external, or network fax modem.

   ▸ **IP H** enables you to add a printer at a specific IP address.

   ▸ **Windows I** lets you add a printer connected to a Windows computer or Windows network.

4. Set options in the bottom of the dialog for the printer type and location.

5. Click Add. The printer is added to the Printers list **A**.

TIP In step 3, it may be necessary to log in to a network to access certain types of network printers.

To delete a printer:

1. In the Printers list, select the printer you want to delete **A**.

2. Click the – button beneath the list.

3. Click Delete Printer in the confirmation dialog that appears.

   The printer is removed from the list.

TIP You cannot print to a printer that you have deleted unless you re-add it.

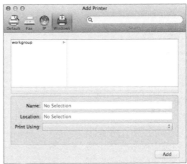

F G H I The Add Printer dialog for default printers, fax modems, IP printers, and Windows printers.

J Use this pop-up menu of printers to choose the one to use by default.

K The word *Default* appears beneath the name of the default printer in the Printers list.

L Use this pop-up menu to choose the printer's default paper size.

To set the default printer:

In the Print & Scan preferences pane, choose one of the printers from the Default Printer pop-up menu **J**.

The word Default appears in the Printers list beneath the name of the printer you chose **K**.

TIP The default printer is the one that is automatically chosen when you open the Print dialog (page 325).

TIP If you choose Last Printer Used from the Default Printer pop-up menu **J**, the last printer you used to print becomes the default printer. Thus, the default printer changes every time you choose a different printer for printing.

To set the default paper size:

1. In the Printers list, select the printer you want to set the default paper size for **A**.

2. Choose one of the paper sizes from the Default Paper Size pop-up menu **L**.

TIP The default paper size is the one that is automatically chosen when you open the Page Setup dialog (page 324).

To open a print queue:

1. In the Printers list, select the name of the printer queue you want to open **A**.

2. Click Open Print Queue.

   The print queue window opens, display-ing status and active print jobs.

TIP The print queue feature is illustrated and discussed in detail on page 335.

To configure a printer:

1. In the Printers list **Ⓐ**, select the printer you want to configure.

2. Click the Options & Supplies button.

3. Set options or review information in the three or four separate panes of the dialog that appears:

   ▸ **General Ⓜ** enables you to set the printer's name and location and provides additional information about the printer's location and driver.

   ▸ **Driver Ⓝ** enables you to set the printer driver and set printer-specific options (if available).

   ▸ **Supply Levels Ⓞ** enables you to see the ink or toner levels for printers that can communicate this information to your computer. (Only one of my printers can do this, so don't feel slighted if this pane comes up blank for you.)

   ▸ **Utilities Ⓟ** may give you access to additional installed utilities to work with your printer. This option is only available for some printers.

4. Click OK to save your settings.

TIP The options that appear in each pane of this dialog vary depending on printer type and model. It's not possible to show all configuration options for all printers. The instructions and illustrations here should be enough to get you started with your printer. Consult the manual that came with your printer for more information.

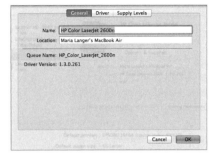

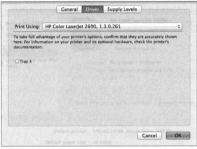

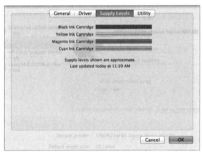

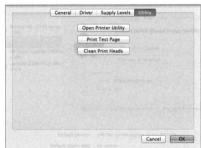

Ⓜ Ⓝ Ⓞ Ⓟ The Options & Supplies dialog's four possible panes. The first two are for a color HP LaserJet printer; the last two are for an all-in-one color Epson printer. Options vary widely depending on the printer.

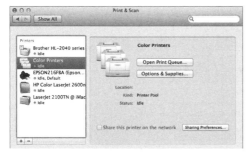

Q When you select multiple printers, the Create Printer Pool button appears in the Print & Scan dialog.

R A printer pool is added to the Printers list.

S Drag a printer from the Printers list to the desktop or a Finder window.

T A desktop printer is actually an alias file for a printer.

To create a printer pool:

1. In the Printer list, select the printers you want to include in the printer pool **Q**. To select more than one printer at a time, hold down the Command key while clicking the name of each one.

2. Click the Create Printer Pool button **Q**.

3. Enter a name for the printer pool in the Name box of the dialog that appears, and click OK.

   The printer pool you created appears in the Printer list window **R**.

TIP When you print to a printer pool, your computer automatically looks at each printer in the pool, in the order they are listed, and prints to the first one available.

To delete a printer pool:

1. In the Printers list, select the printer pool you want to delete **R**.

2. Click the − button beneath the list.

3. Click Delete Printer in the confirmation dialog that appears.

   The printer pool is removed from the list.

TIP Deleting a printer pool does not delete the printers it includes.

To create a desktop printer:

In the Print & Scan preferences pane, drag the icon for the printer you want to create a desktop printer for out of the window and onto the desktop **S**.

When you release the button, an alias icon (page 88) for the printer appears on the desktop **T**.

TIP Using desktop printers is covered on page 334.

To set up your computer to send & receive faxes:

1. Follow the instructions in the section titled "To add a printer that is listed by default" on page 523 to add a fax modem to the Print & Scan preferences pane.

2. In the Printers list, select a fax modem 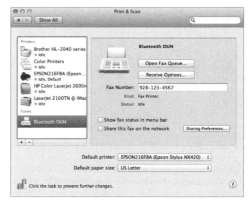.

3. Enter your fax number in the Fax Number box. This information will appear at the top of every fax you send.

4. To display a fax status menu 🅥, turn on the Show fax status in menu bar check box.

5. Click the Receive Options button to open the fax preferences dialog 🅦.

6. Turn on the check box marked Receive faxes on this computer.

7. Set other options as desired:

   ▸ **Answer after** is the number of rings before the computer answers the phone.

   ▸ **Save To** enables you to choose a folder in which faxes should be saved. The options are Faxes and Shared Faxes, but you can choose Other Folder and use the dialog that appears to choose a different folder.

   ▸ **Print To** tells your computer to print the fax on the printer you choose from the pop-up menu.

   ▸ **Email To** tells your computer to email a copy of the fax to the address you enter in the box.

8. Click OK.

TIP To receive faxes, your computer must be turned on and awake and its modem must be connected to a telephone line.

TIP Sending faxes is covered in on page 333.

🅤 Select a fax modem to set options for it.

🅥 You can add a Fax Status menu like this to the menu bar.

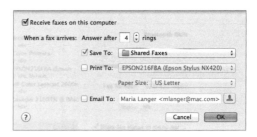

🅦 Use this dialog to set up your computer to receive faxes.

A The Sound Effects panel of the Sound preferences pane on a MacBook Air.

B You can display a Sound Volume menu in the menu bar.

Sound

The Sound preferences pane enables you to set options to control the system and alert sounds, output device, and input device. Sound settings can be changed in three panels:

- **Sound Effects** lets you set options for alert sounds and sound effects.

- **Output** allows you to set the output device and balance.

- **Input** enables you to set the input device and volume.

The options that appear in the Sound preferences pane vary depending on your computer and connected audio devices. The options shown here are for a MacBook Air.

To set system volume:

1. Display any panel of the Sound preferences pane **A**.

2. If necessary, on a Mac with only one audio port, select an option from the Use audio port for pop-up menu (not shown) to determine whether the audio port is used for Sound Input or Sound Output.

3. Set options in the bottom of the window:

   ▸ **Output volume** is the overall output volume for all sounds. Drag the slider to the left or right. Each time you move and release the slider, an alert sounds so you can hear a sample of your change.

   ▸ **Mute** keeps your computer quiet.

   ▸ **Show volume** in menu bar displays a sound volume menu in the menu bar **B**.

To set sound effects options:

1. In the Sound preferences pane, click the Sound Effects button Ⓐ.

2. To set the alert sound, select one of the options in the scrolling list. Each time you select a sound, it plays so you can hear what it sounds like.

3. Set other options as desired:

   ▸ **Play sound effects through** enables you to set the output device for alert and sound effect sounds. If you choose Selected sound output device, it will use whatever is set in the Output panel (page 531).

   ▸ **Alert volume** is the volume of alert sounds. Drag the slider to the left or right. Each time you move and release the slider, an alert sounds so you can hear a sample of your change.

   ▸ **Play user interface sound effects** plays sound effects for different system events, such as dragging an icon to the Trash or completing a copy operation.

   ▸ **Play feedback when volume is changed** enables you to hear the volume each time you change it.

TIP Alert volume depends partly on the system volume setting, which is discussed on page 529. An alert sound cannot be louder than the system sound.

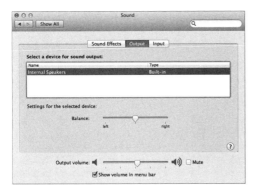

C The Output panel of the Sound preferences pane.

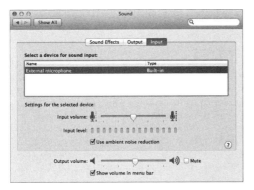

D The Input panel of the Sound preferences pane.

To set output device options:

1. In the Sound preferences pane, click the Output button **C**.

2. To set the output device, select one of the options in the scrolling list.

   The options that appear depend on the devices connected to your computer.

3. To set the speaker balance for the selected device, drag the Balance slider to the left or right. Each time you move and release the slider, an alert sounds so you can hear a sample of your change.

To set input device options:

1. In the Sound preferences pane, click the Input button **D**.

2. To set the input device, select one of the options in the scrolling list.

   The options that appear depend on the devices connected to your computer.

3. To set the input volume for the selected device, drag the Input volume slider to the left or right. The further to the right you drag the slider, the more sensitive the microphone will be. You can test this by watching the Input level bars as you speak or make sounds.

4. To filter out ambient sounds, turn on the Use ambient noise reduction check box. (This option is only available for some input devices.)

TIP Input device and volume are especially important if you plan to use Mac OS X's speech recognition features (page 569).

Internet & Wireless Preferences

Internet & Wireless preferences panes enable you to configure your Mac to take advantage of networking, sharing, and Internet-based services. This chapter covers the following System Preferences panes:

- **MobileMe** enables you to set up your computer to work with a MobileMe account.

- **Mail, Contacts, & Calendars** helps you configure a variety of Internet-based account services.

- **Network** enables you to fine-tune network connection settings.

- **Bluetooth** enables you to pair and manage Bluetooth devices.

- **Sharing** enables you to set up sharing services, including file sharing and printer sharing.

Need to learn the basics of System Preferences? Be sure to read Chapter 30.

In This Chapter:

Mail, Contacts & Calendar

The Mail, Contacts & Calendars preferences pane, which is new in OS X Lion, makes it easy to set up your Microsoft Exchange, MobileMe (page 536), Gmail, Yahoo!, AOL, and other accounts for use with Mail, iCal, iChat, and other applications. Adding an account to this preferences pane automatically sets up these accounts in the applications you specify, eliminating the need to set them up individually in each application.

TIP You must have an account with a service *before* you can set it up in the Mail, Contacts & Calendars preferences pane.

To add an account:

1. In the Mail, Contacts & Calendars preferences pane, select the Add Account item in the account list **A**.

2. On the right side of the window, click the button for the type of account you want to add.

   A dialog prompting you for information about that account appears **B**.

3. Enter required information for the account.

4. Click Set Up.

5. A dialog may appear with a list of applications **C**. Toggle the check boxes to select the applications you plan to use with that account.

6. Click Add Account.

   The account is added to the account list **D**.

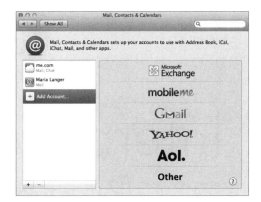

A The Mail, Contacts & Calendars preferences pane makes it easy to add accounts to Mac OS.

B Use the form that appears to enter information about the account you are adding.

C Toggle check boxes to indicate which applications you plan to use with that account.

D The account you added appears in the list.

E Use this dialog to make changes to an account's settings.

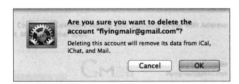

F Click OK in this dialog to delete the selected account.

To modify an account:

1. In the Mail, Contacts & Calendars preferences pane, select the account you want to modify **D**.

2. Do one or more of the following:
   - To stop using an account with an application, turn off the application's check box in the right side of the window.
   - To modify account settings, click the Details button on the right side of the window, make changes in the dialog that appears **E**, and click OK.

   Your changes are saved.

To remove an account:

1. In the Mail, Contacts & Calendars preferences pane, select the account you want to remove **D**.

2. Click the − button at the bottom of the account list.

3. In the confirmation dialog that appears **F**, click OK.

   The account is removed from the list.

TIP Deleting an account from the Mail, Contacts & Calendars preferences pane does not delete the account from the associated service. It just removes that service from your computer.

MobileMe

The MobileMe preferences pane enables you to set up your Mac to take advantage of the features of MobileMe, an Apple, Inc. service that offers subscribers a number of features that can work with Mac OS.

You use the MobileMe preferences pane to log your computer into MobileMe, set options for using the service, and monitor your account. Once you are logged in, there are four panes of options:

- **Account** provides information about your account.

- **Sync** offers options for using MobileMe to synchronize data between your computers.

- **iDisk** offers options for setting up your iDisk storage space.

- **Back to My Mac** controls the Back to My Mac feature.

TIP If you are not a MobileMe member, you can skip this part of the chapter; it does not apply to you.

TIP As this book went to press, Apple had announced a new service called iCloud, which would replace MobileMe and offer different features. MobileMe will be discontinued in June 2012.

To sign in to MobileMe:

1. In the MobileMe preferences pane , enter your member name and password in the appropriate boxes.

2. Click Sign In.

   Your Mac goes online to validate your password. It then displays the Account panel, which provides status information about your MobileMe account .

A Before you sign in to MobileMe, the MobileMe preferences pane looks like this.

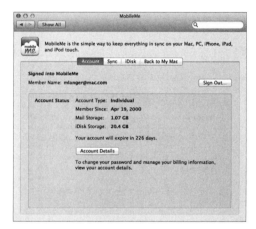

B Once you've signed in, you can access settings for your account.

TIP If, for some reason, you decide you don't want to be connected to MobileMe, you can click the Sign Out button in the Account panel of MobileMe preferences.

C The Sync panel of MobileMe preferences enables you to set options to sync data between your computers and MobileMe.

D Choose a sync frequency option from the pop-up menu.

E The Sync Status menu.

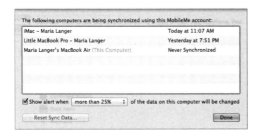

F This dialog lists all the computers being synchronized on your MobileMe account and enables you to reset sync data for any of them.

To set MobileMe Sync options:

1. In the MobileMe preferences pane, click the Sync button **C**.

2. If necessary, turn on the Synchronize with MobileMe check box.

3. Choose a frequency option from the pop-up menu **D**:
   - **Automatically** synchronizes each time you make a change.
   - **Every Hour**, **Every Day**, or **Every Week** synchronizes at that frequency.
   - **Manually** does not automatically synchronize at all; instead, you need to initiate a synchronization when you want it to occur.

4. Toggle check boxes in the list for each type of item you want to synchronize.

5. To display a Sync Status menu in the menu bar **E**, turn on the Show Sync status in menu bar check box.

6. To set advanced options for computers being synchronized, click the Advanced button. You can then use the dialog that appears **F** to set other options and click Done to save them.

TIP You can manually synchronize at any time by clicking the Sync Now button **C** or choosing Sync Now from the Sync Status menu **E**.

TIP If you're an iPhone or iPad user, you may prefer syncing your data via MobileMe instead of iTunes. With automatic synchronization enabled, changes are synced almost instantaneously to all of your devices, without having to deal with cables and plugging in.

To set iDisk options:

1. In the MobileMe preferences pane, click the iDisk button **G**.

2. To see how much disk space you're using on MobileMe, consult the iDisk Usage bar.

3. Set options in the iDisk Public Folder area:

   ▸ **Allow other to write files in your public folder** makes it possible for others to upload files to the Public folder of your iDisk space.

   ▸ **Password-protect your public folder** lets you assign a password to your iDisk public folder. If you enable this option, a dialog prompts you to enter the same password twice; do so and then click OK to save it.

4. To synchronize your iDisk with your Mac, click the Start button under iDisk Sync. This puts a copy of your iDisk on your computer so you can access your iDisk files at any time. If you enable this option, be sure to choose an Update option from the pop-up menu to specify whether the iDisk should be Automatically or Manually updated. You can also turn on the Always keep the most recent version of a file check box to automatically resolve any conflicts when synchronizing.

TIP If you use your iDisk public folder to exchange files with others, I highly recommend setting up a password. Otherwise, anyone with your MobileMe account name will be able to access the files in that folder.

TIP When you enable iDisk Sync, an icon for your iDisk appears in your Computer window **H** and may appear in the sidebar and on your Desktop. You can open and use this disk like any other disk.

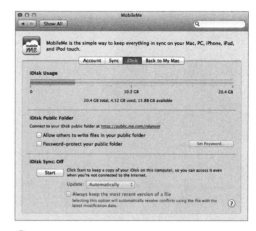

G The iDisk options in MobileMe preferences.

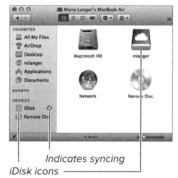

H An iDisk icon is added to your computer when you turn on iDisk Sync.

Indicates syncing iDisk icons

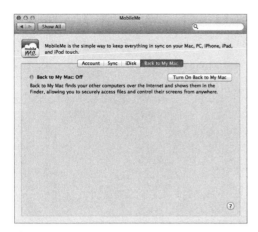

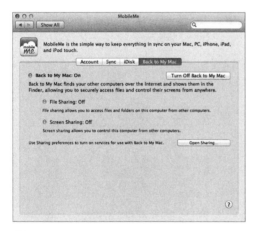

❶ The Back to My Mac panel before you turn on Back to My Mac.

❶ Once Back to My Mac is enabled, you can see which features are turned on and available for use.

❶ In this example, a Time Capsule has been set up for use with Back to My Mac.

To enable Back to My Mac:

1. In the MobileMe preferences pane, click the Back to My Mac button **❶**.

2. Click the Turn On Back to My Mac button.

Your Mac does a few things:

▸ It configures itself for Back to My Mac so other computers on your account can find it.

▸ It displays the current status of Back to My Mac features configured for your computer **❶**.

▸ It checks to see if there are any Back to My Mac servers available on your MobileMe account. If it finds any, it displays them in the Network window and in the sidebar under Shared **❶**.

3. Click the Open Sharing button, if desired, to use the Sharing preferences pane (page 546) to set up your computer for file sharing or screen sharing.

TIP Back to My Mac makes it possible to access any other computer enabled for Back to My Mac through your MobileMe account for file sharing and screen sharing.

TIP You must enable Back to My Mac as instructed here to see other computers on your MobileMe account with Back to My Mac enabled—even if you don't want to enable file or screen sharing on your computer.

Network

The Network preferences pane enables you to check, change, add, and remove network interfaces (page 378). In most cases, network connections are added automatically when you configure your computer to connect a network, but you can use the Network preferences pane to make changes to automatically added settings, if necessary.

You can also use the Network preferences pane to add and modify location settings. Locations are particularly useful if you travel with your computer and use different connection options at each destination.

TIP Each type of network interface has its own group of settings options. This section looks at the options for a Wi-Fi connection, which is the type of connection you're most likely to use. Options for other connection types are similar.

TIP A complete discussion of the advanced settings for a network interface is beyond the scope of this book. If you're not sure how to change a network setting, don't change it without assistance from someone who does know. Incorrectly setting an option could make it impossible for your computer to connect to the network or the Internet.

TIP Clicking the Help (?) button in the lower-left corner of the Advanced options dialog can help you learn more about advanced network settings.

A The Network preferences pane for a Wi-Fi connection.

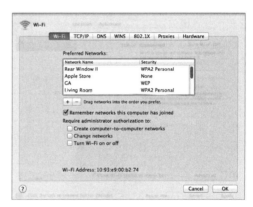

B The Wi-Fi options include preferred networks and some security settings.

C Use TCP/IP options to set the IP address.

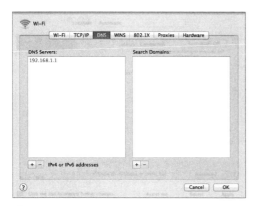

 You can specify DNS servers and search domains.

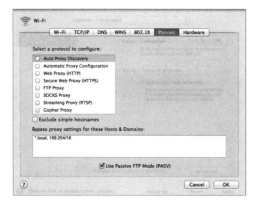

 Enable and configure proxies.

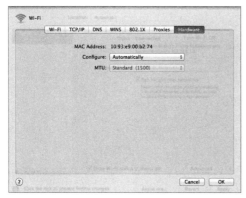

 The Hardware options provide your computer's MAC address and configuration options.

To check or modify Wi-Fi network settings:

1. In the Network preferences pane, select the Wi-Fi network connection you want to check or modify.

   Basic information appears on the right wide of the window Ⓐ.

2. To change the Wi-Fi network you're connected to, choose a different network from the Network Name pop-up menu. The menu includes all networks within range of your computer that your computer has connected to in the past. (You may be prompted to enter a password to connect.)

3. To check or modify advanced options, click Advanced. You can then change options in any of six screens:

   ▸ **Wi-Fi** Ⓑ lists your preferred networks and includes options for security your Wi-Fi settings.

   ▸ **TCP/IP** Ⓒ lets you configure your IP address and related options.

   ▸ **DNS** Ⓓ enables you to add DNS servers and search domains.

   ▸ **WINS** enables you to set Windows Internet Naming Service options.

   ▸ **802.1X** lets you add 802.1x profiles to your system.

   ▸ **Proxies** Ⓔ lets you enable and configure proxy protocols.

   ▸ **Hardware** Ⓕ displays the MAC address and configuration options for your computer's Wi-Fi device.

   Click OK to save your settings and dismiss the advanced settings dialog.

TIP Don't confuse Mac with MAC. A Mac is a computer. MAC is short for Media Access Control and is a unique device ID.

To save settings as a location:

1. Make changes as desired in the Network preferences pane.

2. Choose Edit Locations from the Location pop-up menu.

3. In the locations dialog that appears **G**, click the + button.

   A new location is added to the list with its name (Untitled) selected **H**.

4. Enter a new name for the location and press Return.

   The location is renamed.

5. Click Done.

   The current settings are saved as the location you specified.

To choose a location:

Use one of the following techniques:

- Choose the name of the location you want to use from the Locations submenu under the Apple menu **I**.

- In the Network preferences pane, choose the name of the location you want to use from the Location pop-up menu **J**.

TIP When you choose a different location, the settings in the Network preferences pane change to those associated with that location.

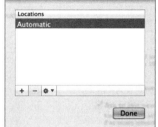

G The Locations dialog lists all locations you have created.

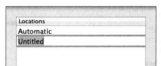

H A new location is added to the list.

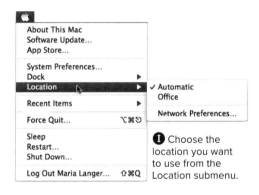

I Choose the location you want to use from the Location submenu.

J You could also choose a location from the Location pop-up menu in the Network preferences pane.

A The Bluetooth preferences pane with three devices paired, two of which are connected.

Bluetooth

You can use the Bluetooth preferences pane to do several things:

- Enable or disable Bluetooth on your computer.
- Set Bluetooth preferences.
- Add or remove Bluetooth devices.

This part of the chapter discusses all of these things.

To enable or disable Bluetooth:

Toggle check boxes at the top of the Bluetooth preferences pane **A**:

- **On** enables Bluetooth. Bluetooth must be enabled to connect to Bluetooth devices.
- **Discoverable** makes your computer "visible" to Bluetooth devices you might want to pair with.

TIP Bluetooth must be turned on to use Bluetooth sharing. You enable Bluetooth sharing in the Sharing preferences pane (page 552).

TIP Disabling Bluetooth can help conserve battery power on a laptop when you don't need a Bluetooth connection.

To set Bluetooth preferences:

1. In the Bluetooth preferences pane **A**, click Advanced to display advanced Bluetooth preferences **B**.

2. Toggle check boxes to set options as desired:

   ▸ **Open Bluetooth Setup Assistant at startup if no keyboard is detected** tells your computer to launch the Bluetooth Setup Assistant if no keyboard is connected; this assumes that you're going to set up a Bluetooth keyboard.

   ▸ **Open Bluetooth Setup Assistant at startup if no mouse or trackpad is detected** tells your computer to launch the Bluetooth Setup Assistant if no mouse or trackpad is connected; this assumes that you're going to set up a Bluetooth Input device.

   ▸ **Allow Bluetooth devices to wake this computer** makes it possible for a Bluetooth keyboard or mouse to wake the computer. This option is not supported by all computer models.

   ▸ **Reject incoming audio requests** prevents audio devices such as Bluetooth headphones from connecting to the computer.

   ▸ **Serial ports that devices use to connect to this computer** enables you to add serial port information for devices you will connect via Bluetooth. You normally will not need to make changes to this list unless instructed by a device's installation manual.

3. Click OK.

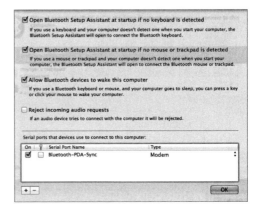

B Advanced Bluetooth preferences.

C Select the device you want to pair with.

D If a passkey appears, follow the instructions to enter it into the device.

E The paired device appears in the list of devices.

To pair a device:

1. In the Bluetooth preferences pane **A**, click the + button at the bottom of the list of devices.

   The Bluetooth Setup Assistant opens. It scans the area for Bluetooth devices and lists them **C**.

2. Select the device you want to pair with and click Continue.

3. If the device has an input method (for example, a cell phone or keyboard), the next screen displays a passkey and provides instructions **D**. Enter the passkey and press Return or click Continue.

4. A Conclusion screen appears next. To set up another device, click the Set Up Another Device button and follow steps 2 and 3 above. Otherwise, click Quit.

   The paired device appears in the Devices list in the Bluetooth preferences pane **E**.

TIP Some devices have predefined passkeys. If you aren't told the passkey for a pairing and need one, consult the device's manual for more information.

TIP If you're not prompted for a passkey at all, you can skip step 3.

TIP You can rename a Bluetooth device in the Bluetooth preferences pane **E**. Simply select the device and choose Rename from the Action pop-up menu beneath the list. Enter a new name for the device in the dialog that appears and click OK.

TIP You can set options for a Bluetooth keyboard, mouse, or trackpad in the Keyboard (page 512), Mouse (page 516), or Trackpad (page 519) preferences pane.

TIP To unpair a device, select it in the Devices list E and click the – button at the bottom of the list. Click Remove in the confirmation dialog that appears.

Sharing

To share files, printers, Internet connection, or other services with other network users, you must set options in the Sharing preferences pane . Sharing lets you name your computer, enable sharing for specific services, and control how other users can access your computer.

The Sharing preferences pane includes the following services:

- **DVD or CD Sharing** (not shown) enables other network users to use your computer's CD or DVD drive from their computer.

- **Screen Sharing** enables users of other computers to view and control your computer over the network. This is handy for providing support to novice users.

- **File Sharing** enables other network users to access files on your computer.

- **Printer Sharing** enables other network users to print or fax documents with your printers or fax modems.

- **Scanner Sharing** enables other network users to scan documents with your scanners.

- **Web Sharing** makes it possible for other network users to view Web pages stored on your computer.

- **Remote Login** enables other network users to access your computer using Secure Shell (SSH) and Unix.

- **Remote Management** enables other network users to operate your computer using Apple Remote Desktop, a software package available for an additional fee from Apple Inc.

A The Sharing preferences pane before any sharing services have been enabled. The options for File Sharing are shown here.

- **Remote Apple Events** makes it possible for other network computers to send Apple Events to your computer. Apple Events are scripting commands that perform specific tasks.

- **Xgrid Sharing** allows Xgrid controllers on the network to connect to your computer and distribute tasks for your computer to perform.

- **Internet Sharing** enables you to share an Internet connection with other network users.

- **Bluetooth Sharing** enables you to set options for how other computers can share files with your computer via Bluetooth.

To enable a sharing service, simply turn on its check box. You can then set options in the area to the right of the list. To disable a sharing service, turn off its check box.

This part of the chapter explains how to set sharing options for the following services: File Sharing, Printer Sharing, Internet Sharing, and Bluetooth Sharing. A discussion of the remaining sharing services is beyond the scope of this book.

CAUTION If your computer is on a large network, consult the system administrator before changing any sharing configuration options.

TIP Unless your computer is part of a big network and managed by a system administrator, it's extremely unlikely that you'll need to enable Remote Login, Remote Management, Remote Apple Events, or Xgrid Sharing. Leave these options turned off unless you know that you'll need to use them.

To set the computer's identity:

In the Sharing preferences pane Ⓐ, enter a name in the Computer Name text box Ⓑ.

TIP Your computer name is not the same as your hard disk name.

TIP If your computer is on a large network, give your computer a name that can easily distinguish it from others on the network. Ask your system administrator; there may be organization-wide computer naming conventions that you need to follow.

TIP If desired, you can change the identifier for your computer on the local subnet. Click the Edit button in the Sharing preferences pane Ⓐ and enter a new name in the dialog that appears Ⓒ. The name you enter cannot include spaces and must end in .local, which cannot be changed. Click OK.

To enable & configure file sharing:

1. In the Sharing preferences pane, turn on the File Sharing check box Ⓓ.

2. To specify folders to share, click the + button beneath the Shared Folders list. Then use the dialog that appears Ⓔ to locate and select the folder you want to share. Click Add to add it to the list of folders Ⓕ.

3. To specify users who can access a folder, select the folder you want to set access for and click the + button under the Users column. Then use the dialog that appears Ⓖ to select an existing account from Users & Groups or your Address Book. Or click the New Person button and use the New Person dialog Ⓗ to add a new user account. The additional user is added to the Users list Ⓘ. You'll need to repeat this step for each folder you want to add users for.

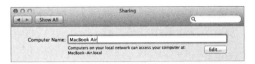

Ⓑ You can change your computer's network identity by entering a new name in the Computer Name box.

Ⓒ You can also set a custom name for your computer on the local subnet.

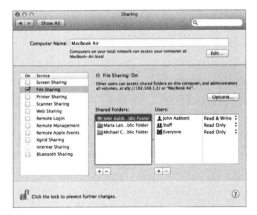

Ⓓ The Sharing preferences pane with File Sharing enabled.

Ⓔ Use this dialog to specify a folder to share.

⑥ The folder is added to the list of Shared folders.

⑥ Use a dialog like this to select an existing user or Address Book contact.

⑪ You could also create a new user account on the fly.

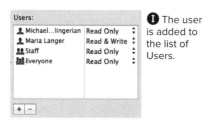

⑨ The user is added to the list of Users.

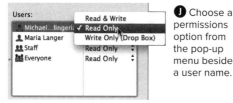

⑩ Choose a permissions option from the pop-up menu beside a user name.

4. To set permissions for a user, select the user name and choose an option from the pop-up menu that appears beside it **⑩**. Repeat this process for each user for each folder as desired.

5. To set more advanced options, click the Options button. Then set options in the dialog that appears **⑬** to enable specific connection methods, and click Done.

TIP By default, your Public folder is always set up to be shared.

TIP You can learn more about users, groups, and permissions on page 397. You set up users and groups in the Users & Groups preferences pane (page 579).

TIP To share files with Windows users, you must follow step 5 and enable SMB. Be sure to enable the Windows users' names in the bottom half of the dialog and enter their passwords when prompted.

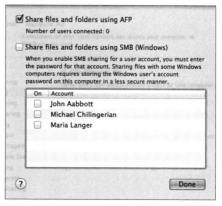

⑬ You can set additional options in this dialog.

To enable & configure printer sharing:

1. In the Sharing preferences pane, turn on the Printer Sharing check box 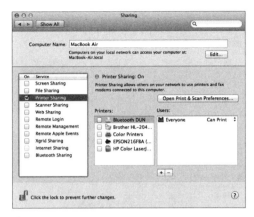.

2. In the Printers list, turn on the check box for each printer you want to share **M**.

3. To specify users who can share the printer, select the printer you want to set access for and click the + button under the Users column. Then use the dialog that appears **G** to select an existing account from Users & Groups or your Address Book. Or click the New Person button and use the New Person dialog **H** to add a new user account. The additional user is added to the Users list **N**. You'll need to repeat this step for each printer you want to add users for.

4. To prevent unlisted users from sharing a printer, make sure the permissions for the Everyone entry in the Users column is set to No Access **N**.

TIP You add printers in the Print & Scan preferences pane (page 522).

TIP You can learn more about using printers, including shared printers, in Chapter 22.

L The Sharing preferences pane with Printer Sharing enabled.

M Turn on the check box beside each printer you want to share.

N In this example, only one user can share the printer.

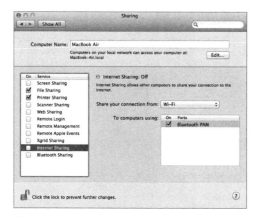

O You must set options on the right side of the window before enabling Internet sharing.

P A dialog like this warns you about the possible consequences of sharing an Internet connection.

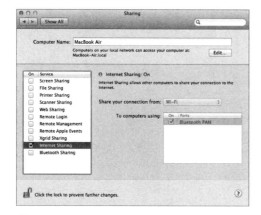

Q In this example, I'm sharing my Wi-Fi Internet connection with other users via Bluetooth.

To enable & configure Internet sharing:

1. In the Sharing preferences pane, select the Internet Sharing option in the Service list **O**.

2. Choose the source of your computer's Internet connection from the Share your connection from pop-up menu. This menu includes all network connections set up for your computer.

3. Turn on the check box for each port in the To computers using list to indicate how you want to distribute your Internet connection **O**.

4. Turn on the Internet Sharing check box in the Services list.

5. A confirmation dialog may appear **P**. Click Start.

    The Sharing preferences pane indicates that Internet sharing is enabled and how your preferences are set **Q**.

TIP To make changes to Internet Sharing options, you must first turn off the Internet Sharing check box in the Services list.

TIP Internet sharing enables you to share your existing Internet connection with another computer. If you do not have an Internet connection, you can use a connection shared by another network user. Use the Network preferences pane (page 540) to choose the interface on which the shared connection is available to you.

TIP When you share an Internet connection, the total connection throughput is divided among the active connections. So, for example, if two computers are actively sharing a 6 Mbps DSL connection with you, the average throughput of each connection will only be about 2 Mbps.

To enable & configure Bluetooth sharing:

1. In the Sharing preferences pane, turn on the check box for Bluetooth Sharing in the Service list 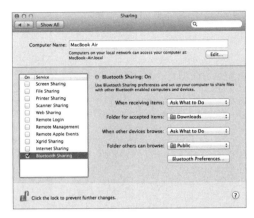.

2. Set options on the right side of the Sharing preferences pane:

    ▸ **When receiving items** lets you specify what your computer should do when receiving items from a Bluetooth device. Your options are Accept and Save, Accept and Open, Ask What to Do, and Never Allow.

    ▸ **Folder for accepted items** lets you select a folder to store items you receive from a Bluetooth device. Choose Other from this pop-up menu to use a dialog to select a folder other than Downloads.

    ▸ **When other devices browse** lets you specify what your computer should do when a Bluetooth device attempts to browse files on your disk. Your options are Always Allow, Ask What to Do, and Never Allow.

    ▸ **Folder others can browse** lets you choose the folder a Bluetooth device can browse. Choose Other from this pop-up menu to use a dialog to select a folder other than Public.

🅡 The Sharing preferences pane with Bluetooth sharing enabled.

System Preferences

System preferences panes enable you to configure the operation of Mac OS X to suit your needs. This chapter covers the following preferences panes:

- **Date & Time** enables you to set the date, time, time zone, and clock options.

- **Parental Controls** help you manage the way your children use the computer and Internet.

- **Software Update** manually or automatically downloads and installs Apple software updates.

- **Speech** enables you to set speech recognition and text to speech options.

- **Startup Disk** enables you to choose a startup disk for the next time you start your computer.

- **Time Machine** enables you to set up and configure OS X's backup feature.

- **Users & Groups** enables you to set up user accounts and groups for computer and network access.

Need to learn the basics of System Preferences? Be sure to read Chapter 30.

Date & Time

The Date & Time preferences pane includes three panes for setting the system time and clock options:

- **Date & Time** enables you to automatically or manually set the date and time.

- **Time Zone** enables you to set your time zone and specify whether daylight savings time is in effect.

- **Clock** enables you to set options for the appearance of the menu bar clock.

TIP To change the formats of dates and times throughout OS X, use the Language & Text preferences pane (page 492).

To set the date & time automatically:

1. In the Date & Time preferences pane, click the Date & Time button **A**.

2. If necessary, turn on the Set date and time automatically check box.

3. Choose the closest time server from the drop-down list **B**.

TIP With the network time server feature enabled, your computer will use its Internet connection to periodically get the date and time from a time server and update the system clock automatically. This ensures that your computer's clock is always correct.

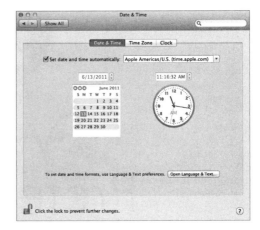

A The Date & Time options in the Date & Time preferences pane.

B Use this drop-down list to choose the time server closest to you.

C You can manually set the date and time by clicking, dragging, and entering values in the clock and calendar area.

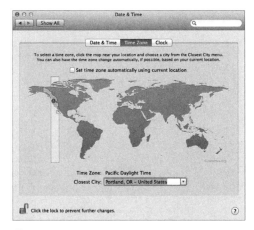

D The Time Zone options of the Date & Time preferences pane.

E If your computer can't figure out where it is, it tells you.

To set the date & time manually:

1. In the Date & Time preferences pane, click the Date & Time button **A**.

2. If necessary, turn off the Set date and time automatically check box.

3. Use any combination of the following techniques:

    ▸ Click the numbers you want to change in the date and time boxes and enter new values **C**.

    ▸ Click the calendar and clock images to set the correct values.

4. Click Save to save your settings.

To set the time zone automatically:

1. In the Date & Time preferences pane, click the Time Zone button **D**.

2. If necessary, turn on the Set time zone automatically using current location check box.

3. Wait while your computer attempts to determine your current location.

    One of two things happens:

    ▸ If your computer can determine your location, your time zone is set.

    ▸ If your computer cannot determine your location, it displays a message telling you so **E**. You'll need to set your time zone manually.

TIP An Internet connection is required to automatically set your time zone. This feature uses OS X's location services capabilities.

To set the time zone manually:

1. In the Date & Time preferences pane, click the Time Zone button **D**.

2. If necessary, turn off the Set time zone automatically using current location check box.

3. Click the map at your approximate location.

   A light gray bar indicates the time zone area **D**.

4. Choose the name of a city in your time zone from the Closest City drop-down list beneath the map **F**.

5. To toggle the daylight savings time setting, click the name of the time zone above the drop-down list.

TIP When manually setting the time zone, only those cities in or near the light gray bar on the map are listed in the drop-down list **F**. If a nearby city does not appear, make sure you clicked the correct area in the map.

TIP If you prefer, in step 4 you can type the name of a city in the text box. If it's included on the list, it'll appear in the box. Press Return to accept it.

TIP It's a good idea to choose the correct time zone, since Mac OS uses this information with the network time server (if utilized) and to properly change the clock for daylight saving time.

Portland, OR – United States
Portland, OR – United States
Redding, CA – United States
Reno, NV – United States
Richmond – Canada
Roseville, CA – United States
Sacramento, CA – United States
Salem, OR – United States
Seattle, WA – United States
Sparks, NV – United States
Spokane, WA – United States

F Although I clicked closest to Portland, I'm really closer to Seattle, which I can choose from this list.

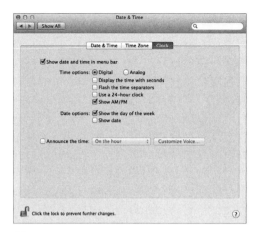

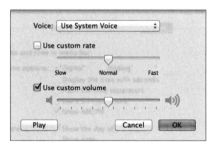

G The Clock options in the Date & Time preferences pane.

H I The far right end of the menu bar on my MacBook Air displaying the digital clock with settings in **G** (top) and the analog clock (bottom).

J If set your computer to announce the time, you can also set options for the voice it uses to do so.

To set clock options:

1. In the Date & Time preferences pane, click the Clock button **G**.

2. To enable the menu bar clock, turn on the Show date and time in menu bar check box.

3. Set Time options:

   ▸ **Digital** and **Analog** lets you choose between displaying the date and time with letters and numbers **H** or as an analog clock **I**. If you choose this Analog, the remaining Time and Date options turn gray; skip step 4.

   ▸ **Display the time with seconds** displays the seconds as part of the time.

   ▸ **Flash the time separators** blinks the colon(s) in the time every second.

   ▸ **Use a 24-hour clock** displays the time as a 24-hour (rather than 12-hour) clock.

   ▸ **Show AM/PM** displays AM or PM after the time.

4. Set Date options:

   ▸ **Show the day of the week** displays the three-letter abbreviation for the day of the week before the time.

   ▸ **Show date** displays the date before the time.

5. To instruct your computer to vocally announce the time periodically, turn on the Announce the time check box and choose a frequency option from the pop-up menu: On the hour, On the half hour, or On the quarter hour. You can also click the Customize Voice button and set voice options in the dialog that appears **J**.

TIP The menu bar clock is also a menu that displays the full date and time and offers options for changing the clock display.

Parental Controls

Parental controls enable you to limit an account's access to computer features. Designed to help parents protect their children from certain content and activities, it can also be used to limit a user to certain applications, activities, and usage times. In addition, it can keep a log of a user's activities for later review.

Parental controls are broken down into five groups of settings:

- **Apps** control what applications and tasks the user can access. It also allows you to enable Simple Finder, which is a greatly simplified version of the Finder for novice users. And it gives you access to logs so you can see what the user has been up to.

- **Web** enables you to control access to websites.

- **People** limits who the user can communicate with via email or iChat.

- **Time Limits** enables you to set the amount of time on weekdays and weekends the user can use the computer and to prevent the user from using the computer at certain times of the day or night.

- **Other** controls access to profanity in the Dictionary application and widget, printer administration, CD and DVD burning, and password changes.

This section explains how to activate parental controls for a user account. It also discusses the available settings you can assign to a user's account.

TIP The Parental Controls preferences pane is normally locked to prevent unauthorized changes. You can learn more about unlocking and locking preferences panes on page 477.

A The Parental Controls preference pane looks like this when it's disabled for a selected user account.

B Enabling parental controls for a user displays control options you can set for that account.

C The action pop-up menu in the Parental Controls preferences pane.

To enable parental controls for a user account:

1. In the Parental Controls preferences pane, select the user you want to enable parental controls for **A**.

2. Click the Enable Parental Controls button.

   Parental controls settings appear **B**.

TIP You cannot set parental controls for a user with administrator privileges.

TIP You can also enable parental controls by turning on the check box beside Enable Parental Controls in the user's account settings in the Users & Groups preferences pane (page 579).

TIP If parental controls settings for the user appear after step 1 **B**, parental controls are already enabled for that user.

TIP The Manage parental controls from another computer option in the Parental Controls preferences pane **B** enables a user on a networked computer running OS X 10.5 or later to log in to the computer and set parental control options. A parent might use this to manage controls on another computer used by her children. A discussion of this feature is beyond the scope of this book.

To disable parental controls for a user account:

1. In the Parental Controls preferences pane, select the user you want to disable parental controls for **B**.

2. Choose Turn off Parental Controls for "*User Name*" from the action pop-up menu at the bottom of the user list **C**.

To limit a user's access to applications & system functions:

1. In the Parental Controls preferences pane, select the name of the user you want to set access limitations for.

2. Click the Apps button .

3. To enable Simple Finder for the user, turn on the Use Simple Finder check box.

4. To limit the user's access to applications, turn on the Limit Applications check box. Then set application access options as desired:

   ▸ **Allow App Store Apps** lets you specify a maximum age rating for applications purchased from the App Store. Choose an option from the pop-up menu .

   ▸ **Allowed Apps** lets you specify which applications the user can access. Toggle check boxes in the list. You can click the disclosure triangle to the left of a category to display the individual applications within it. This option is only available if either the Use Simple Finder or Limit Applications check box is turned on.

5. To allow the user to add or remove Dock items for his account, turn on the Allow User to Modify the Dock check box. This option is not available if Simple Finder is enabled for the account.

TIP Simple Finder **E**, as the name suggests, is a highly simplified version of the Finder. Designed for users with little or no knowledge of computers, it offers a safe, highly controlled environment for kids and novices. If you want to try Simple Finder, create a new user with Simple Finder enabled, then log in as that user. If you've been using a Mac for more than a few years, I guarantee you'll go nuts in about five minutes. (I didn't even last two.)

D If you buy apps from the App Store, you can use a pop-up menu to limit access based on age rating.

E Simple Finder is just that: a simple version of the Finder.

F If a user tries to access an application he's not allowed to, he'll see this.

TIP If a user attempts to access an application he does not have access to, a dialog appears **F**. If the user clicks the Always Allow or Allow Once button, he'll need to enter an administrator's name and password to continue.

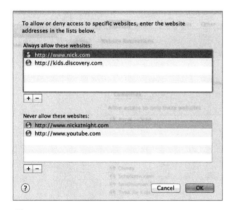

G Use the Web options to limit access to Web sites.

H In this example, I've listed two kid-friendly Web sites and two that might not be appropriate for young kids.

I Visiting a blocked site displays a message like this one.

To limit access to the Web:

1. In the Parental Controls preferences pane, select the name of the user you want to limit Web access for.

2. Click the Web button **G**.

3. Select one of the three website Restrictions options:

   ▸ **Allow unrestricted access to websites** does not apply restrictions.

   ▸ **Try to limit access to adult websites automatically** uses a built-in filter to prevent access to adult content websites. If you select this option, you can click the Customize button to create and maintain a list of websites the user can and can't access **H**. Just use the + and − buttons beneath each list to add or remove URLs.

   ▸ **Allow access to only these websites** displays a list of websites that the user can access. These are the only sites the user can access. Use the + and − buttons beneath the list to add or remove URLs.

TIP Customizing the content filter does not prevent access to content not listed in the dialog. For example, given the settings in **H**, if the user attempted to access my website (www.marialanger.com), he would not be stopped, since the site is not forbidden and has no objectionable content. (Well, at least I don't think so.)

TIP If a website is blocked, a message appears in the Web browser **I**. If the user clicks the Add Website button, he'll have to enter an administrator's password to view it.

To limit access to email & chat:

1. In the Parental Controls preferences pane, select the name of the user you want to set access limitations for.

2. Click the People button **J**.

3. Turn on the check box for the application you want to limit:

   ▸ **Limit Mail** restricts the addresses the user can exchange email with.

   ▸ **Limit iChat** restricts the instant messaging addresses the user can enter into a chat session with.

4. If you checked either of the options in step 3, build a list of the allowed email or instant messaging addresses in the Allowed Contacts list. Click the + button and use one or both of the following techniques to add people:

   ▸ Manually add the name, email address, and AIM account information for a person **K**. Then click Add.

   ▸ Click the disclosure triangle beside the Last Name field to displays a list of contacts in your Address Book **L** (Chapter 15). Then hold down the Command key and click the names of the people you want to allow. Click Add to add them.

5. To receive an email message from anyone not on the list who attempts to email the user, turn on the Send permission requests to check box and enter your email address in the box beside it. This makes it possible to see who is trying to send email to the user and what that email contains.

TIP Parental Controls for Mail and iChat are a good way to prevent your children from getting email from or chatting with people you don't know.

J Use the People options to limit communication to certain email and chat accounts.

K You can manually add accounts in a dialog like this one.

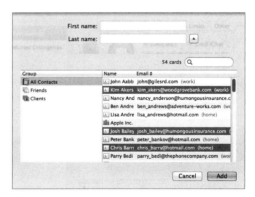

L You can also add accounts directly from your Address Book contacts list.

M You can set Time Limit options to limit the amount of time and time of day your child uses the computer.

To limit a user's time on the computer:

1. In the Parental Controls preferences pane, select the name of the user you want to set access limitations for.

2. Click the Time Limits button **M**.

3. Turn on the check boxes and set options for each of the times you want to limit:

   ▸ **Weekday time limits** limits the amount of time the user can spend on the computer on Monday through Friday.

   ▸ **Weekend time limits** limits the amount of time the user can spend on the computer on Saturdays and Sundays.

   ▸ **School nights** enables you to specify what times the computer can't be used on Sunday through Thursday nights.

   ▸ **Weekend** enables you to specify what times the computer can't be used on Friday and Saturday nights.

TIP Although this feature is designed to limit the time a child spends on a computer, I sometimes wish someone would set it for me!

To set other control options:

1. In the Parental Controls preferences pane, select the name of the user you want to set access limitations for.

2. Click the Other button .

3. Toggle check boxes to set other control options:

   ▸ **Hide profanity in Dictionary** hides "bad words" in OS X's Dictionary application and widget.

   ▸ **Limit printer administration** prevents the user from changing printer settings, adding printers, or removing printers.

   ▸ **Limit CD and DVD burning** prevents the user from copying data, music, or other material to disc in the Finder.

   ▸ **Disable changing the password** prevents the user from changing his password.

TIP The Hide profanity in Dictionary check box setting does not affect non-Apple application dictionaries, like the one that comes with Microsoft Word.

N The Other options in the Parental Controls preferences pane.

O Here's an example of the Websites Visited log.

To review access logs for a user:

1. In the Parental Controls preferences pane, select the name of the user you want to view logs for.

2. Click the Apps **B**, Web **G**, or People **J** button.

3. Click the Logs button to display the logs dialog **O**.

4. In the Log Collections column, click the name of the Log you want to view.

5. Choose a time period from the Show activity for pop-up menu. The options range from Today to All.

6. Choose an option from the Group by pop-up menu to specify how the log should be arranged. The options that appear vary based on what you selected in step 4.

7. View log details in the Logs column. You can click disclosure triangles to display more information about items.

8. To open an item in the log, select it and click the Open button at the bottom of the window.

9. To allow or restrict a site, application, or contact, select the item in the log and click the Restrict or Allow button at the bottom of the window. (The button that appears varies based on what is selected.)

TIP Although it might seem sneaky, it's a good idea to review this information periodically to see what your children have been doing with the computer.

Software Update

The Software Update preferences pane enables you to configure the software update feature of OS X. This feature checks Apple's servers for updates to your Apple software and, if it finds updates, it can download and install them.

To set automatic update options:

1. In the Software Update preferences pane, click Scheduled Check **A**.

2. Turn on the Check for updates check box.

3. Use the pop-up menu to specify how often your computer should check for updates: Daily, Weekly, or Monthly.

4. To automatically download important updates without asking you, turn on the check box labeled Download important updates automatically.

TIP When your computer checks for updates and finds one, it displays a window **B**. Follow the instructions in the section titled "To install updates" to install the updates.

To manually check for updates:

1. In the Scheduled Check panel of the Software Update preferences pane **A**, click Check Now.

    Your computer uses its Internet connection to check for updates **C**.

2. When the check is complete, one of two things happens:

    ▶ If updates are available, a Software Update window appears **B**. Follow the instructions in the section titled "To install updates."

    ▶ If no updates are available, a dialog tells you **D**. Click Quit.

A The Scheduled Checks options of the Software Update preferences pane.

B When Software Update finds updates, it displays a dialog like this.

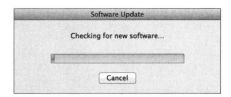

C Software Update displays a progress dialog like this as it checks for updates.

D If no updates are available, Software Update tells you.

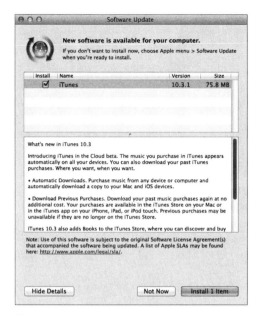

⑤ You can learn more about available updates and begin to install them in this dialog.

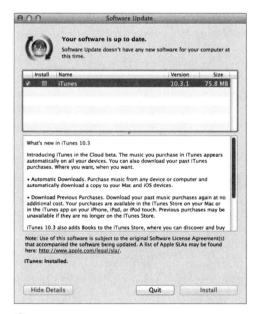

⑥ After an update is installed, Software Update often checks again for more updates. In this example, it installed an update, then checked for more updates but didn't find any.

To install updates:

1. In the Software Update window **⑧**, click the Show Details button.

2. The window expands to display a list of available updates **⑤**. You have two options:

   ▸ **Not Now** temporarily ignores the updates and dismisses the dialog. You'll be reminded about the updates the next time Software Update runs. Skip the remaining steps.

   ▸ **Install *n* item(s)** installs the items checked off in the list. Before clicking this button be sure to deselect any items you don't want to install.

3. If a License Agreement window appears, read the license agreement (or at least pretend to) and click Agree.

4. If an authentication dialog appears, enter an administrator name and password and click OK.

5. If you'll need to restart your computer after installing the software, a dialog tells you. Click Restart.

6. Wait while your computer downloads (if necessary) and installs the update from Apple's server.

7. When Software Update is finished installing software, one of two things happens:

   ▸ If a restart is necessary, your computer restarts. In many cases, Software Update will run again after restart to check for updates.

   ▸ Software Update runs again to check for updates. If it finds any, repeat these steps. Otherwise, it tells you the software is up to date **⑥**. Click Quit.

continues on next page

TIP You can continue working with your Mac as updates are downloaded and installed.

TIP You can learn about an update before you install it by selecting it in the top half of the **Software Update** window. A description appears in the bottom half of the window ⓔ.

TIP If you don't install a listed update, it will appear in the **Software Update** window ⓔ again the next time you check for updates. To remove it from the list without installing it, select it and choose **Update > Ignore Update** and then click **OK** in the confirmation dialog that appears.

TIP To view a log of installed updates, click the **Installed Software** button in the **Software Update** preferences pane ⓖ.

ⓖ Clicking the Installed Software button displays a list of updates you've installed.

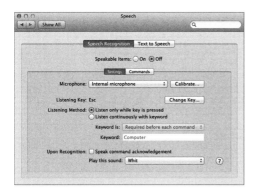

A The Speech Recognition Options in the Speech preferences pane.

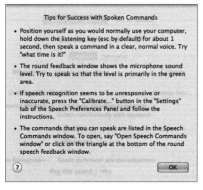

B When you turn on Speakable Items, a dialog like this might appear.

 C The Feedback window appears when Speakable Items is enabled.

Speech

Mac OS X's Speech preferences pane includes two groups of options:

- **Speech Recognition** lets you enable and configure speech recognition features.

- **Text to Speech** allows you to set the default system voice and enable and configure talking alerts and other spoken items.

In this section, I explain how to set up and use these features.

TIP Speech recognition requires a sound input device, such as a built-in or external microphone or FaceTime camera.

TIP The speech recognition feature works best in a relatively quiet work environment.

To enable & configure speech recognition:

1. In the Speech preferences pane, click the Speech Recognition button **A**.

2. Select the On radio button.

3. A dialog may appear with instructions for using Spoken Commands **B**. Read the contents of the dialog and click Continue to dismiss it.

   The round Feedback window appears **C**.

4. If necessary, click the Settings button to display its options.

5. Set options as desired:

   ▸ **Microphone** is your sound input device.

   ▸ **Listening Key** is the keyboard key you must press to either listen to spoken commands or toggle listening

   continues on next page

on or off. By default, the key is Esc. To change the key, click the Change Key button, enter a new key in the dialog that appears ⑩, and click OK.

▸ **Listening Method** enables you to select how you want your Mac to listen for commands. **Listen only while key is pressed** requires you to press the listening key to listen. **Listen continuously with keyword** tells the computer to listen all the time. If you select this option, you can choose an option from the Keyword is pop-up menu ⑭ and enter a keyword for your computer to recognize commands.

▸ **Upon Recognition** tells your computer how to acknowledge that it has heard a command. **Speak command acknowledgement** tells your computer to repeat the command. **Play this sound** enables you to choose a sound for acknowledgement.

6. Click the Commands button to display its options ⑮.

7. Turn on the check box beside each command set you want your computer to recognize.

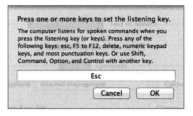

⑩ You can use this dialog to change the key you need to press to enable listening.

> Optional before commands
> ✓ Required before each command
> Required 15 seconds after last command
> Required 30 seconds after last command

⑭ Set the timing for using a keyword.

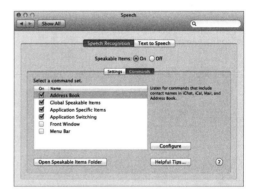

⑮ The Commands options for Speech Recognition lists command sets you can work with.

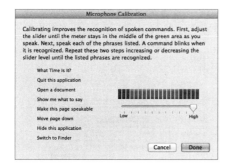

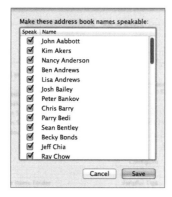

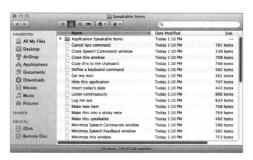

G You can fine-tune your microphone's settings with the Microphone Calibration dialog.

H Some command sets, like the one for Address Book, can be configured.

I Clicking the Speakable Items button opens the Speakable Items folder inside your Library folder.

TIP An external microphone—especially one on a headset—will work more reliably than a built-in microphone, such as the one on the front of the computer.

TIP Clicking the Calibrate button in the Settings pane **A** displays a dialog you can use to test and adjust microphone volume **G**.

TIP For best results, either set the Listening method to Listen only while key is pressed or require the computer name before each spoken command. Otherwise, your computer could interpret background noise and conversations as commands.

TIP The description of a command set appears in the Commands pane when you select the command set in the list **F**.

TIP You can set options for some command sets. Select the command set in the Commands pane **F** and click the Configure button. A dialog appears with options you can set **H**.

TIP Clicking the Open Speakable Items Folder button in the Commands pane **F** opens a Finder window that includes all Speakable Items commands OS X can recognize **I**.

TIP Each user has his or her own Speakable Items folder, which can be found at /Users/username/Library/Speech/Speakable Items.

To use Speakable Items:

Use one of the following techniques to issue voice commands:

- If your computer is configured to listen with a listening key, hold down the listening key and speak the command you want your computer to perform.

- If your computer is configured to listen continuously, speak the command you want your computer to perform. If the keyword is required before or after the command, be sure to include it.

One of two things happens:

- If your computer understands the command, it will acknowledge it with voice and/or sound and the command will appear above the Feedback window . The command is executed (if possible).

- If your computer did not understand the command, nothing happens. Wait a moment and try again.

TIP The Speakable Items folder **I** contains preprogrammed Speakable Items. Each file corresponds to a command. Say the file name to issue the command.

TIP The Application Speakable Items folder inside the Speakable Items folder **K** contains Speakable Items commands that work in specific applications.

TIP If it is not possible to execute a command, nothing will happen after the command appears above the Feedback window. For example, if you use the "Empty the Trash" command and there's nothing in the Trash, nothing will happen.

 J The Feedback window confirms when a command has been understood.

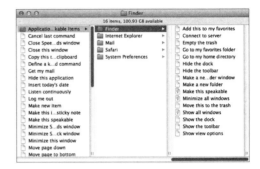

K Speakable items for specific applications are organized by folder.

 L When a response is necessary, it appears beneath the Feedback window.

TIP If the command you issued results in feedback (for example, the "What Time Is It?" command) and you set up speech recognition to speak feedback, your computer displays **L** and speaks the results of the command.

TIP To add a Speakable Item, use Apple-Script Editor (page 373) to create a script for the command. Save the script as a compiled script in the appropriate location in the Speakable Items folder. Be sure to name the script with the words you want to use to issue the command.

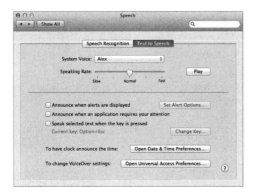

M The Text to Speech options in the Speech preferences pane.

N Choose a voice from this menu.

O Set options for speaking alerts.

P Use this menu to choose a phrase that should be spoken before alert text.

Q You can set a different keystroke for speaking selected text.

To set Text to Speech options:

1. In the Speech preferences pane, click the Text to Speech button **M**.

2. Select one of the voices in the System Voice list **N**.

3. To change the speed at which the voice speaks, use the Speaking Rate slider.

4. To test the settings, click the Play button.

5. To speak alerts, turn on the Announce when alerts are displayed check box. Then click the Set Alert Options button, set options in the dialog that appears **O**, and click OK:

   ▸ **Voice** enables you to choose the System Voice or another voice.

   ▸ **Phrase** **P** is text that should be spoken before the alert.

   ▸ **Delay** is the amount of time that should elapse between when the dialog appears and the alert is spoken. Use the slider to set the delay.

6. To get a verbal alert when an application needs your attention, turn on the Announce when application requires your attention check box. (Normally, the icon for an application needing attention bounces in the Dock.)

7. To have your computer speak selected text, turn on the Speak selected text when the key is pressed check box. The default keystroke is Options-Esc, but you can change the keystroke by clicking the Set Key button and using the dialog that appears **O** to set a new one.

continues on next page

TIP You can list additional voices by choosing Customize from the Voices menu **N**. This displays a dialog you can use to check off the voices you want on the menu **R**. This list includes many for languages other than English.

TIP The settings you make in the Text to Speech pane affect any application that can speak text.

TIP In step 5, you can choose Edit Phrase List from the Phrase pop-up menu **P** to display the Alert Phrases dialog **S**. Click the Add or Remove buttons to add a new phrase or remove a selected one. When you're finished, click OK to save your changes.

TIP To speak the time, click the Open Date & Time Preferences button. This displays the Clock options of Date & Time preferences pane (page 557) so you can set options

TIP To change VoiceOver settings, click the Open Universal Access Preferences button. This displays the Seeing options of the Universal Access preferences pane (page 504) so you can set options.

R OS X Lion includes dozens of voices for many different languages. Toggle check boxes to add or remove them from the Voices menu.

S You can add your own alert phrases if you don't like the ones that are part of OS X.

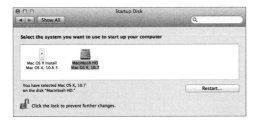

Ⓐ The Startup Disk preferences pane on my
MacBook Air with the USB Reinstall Drive plugged
in. Note that because this computer does not
have a FireWire port there is not Target Disk Mode
option.

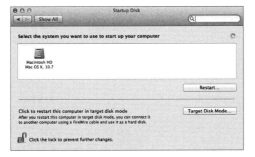

Ⓑ My MacBook Pro does have a FireWire port,
so the Target Disk Mode button appears in the
Startup Disk preferences pane.

Startup Disk

The Startup Disk preferences pane **Ⓐ**
enables you to select a startup disk and, if
desired, restart your computer. You might
find this helpful if you want to start your
computer under Windows using Boot
Camp (page 356) or from a bootable CD or
DVD disc, such as a Mac OS installer disc.

OS X's Target Disk Mode feature, which is
supported by some Mac models, makes
it possible for your computer's hard
disk to be used as an external hard disk
when connected to another computer via
FireWire cable. If your computer supports
it, you can enable this option in the Startup
Disk preferences pane **Ⓑ**.

TIP To decide "on the fly" which startup disk
to use, hold down the Option key at startup
to display icons for each startup disk. Click
the disk you want and then press Return to
complete the startup process from the disk
you selected.

TIP Holding down the C key while restarting
your computer with a bootable disc inserted
usually starts the computer from the System
folder on that disc.

TIP A discussion of the Network Startup
feature, which works with Mac OS X Server
and its NetBoot service, is beyond the scope
of this book.

To select a startup disk:

1. Display the Startup Disk preferences pane Ⓐ.

2. Click the icon for the startup disk you want to use.

3. Do one of the following:

   ▸ To immediately restart your computer, click the Restart button. The startup disk you selected in step 2 will be used to start the computer.

   ▸ Quit System Preferences. The next time you start the computer, the startup disk you selected in step 2 (if available) will be used to start the computer.

To use target disk mode:

1. Use a FireWire cable to connect your computer to another computer.

2. In the Startup Disk preferences pane Ⓑ, click Target Disk Mode.

3. Read the information in the dialog sheet that appears.

4. Click Restart.

TIP **When you're finished using your computer in target disk mode, press its power button.**

A The Time Machine preferences pane, with Time Machine already enabled.

B Use this dialog to set Time Machine backup options.

C Use this dialog to select disks, folders, or individual items to exclude from the backup.

Time Machine

The Time Machine preferences pane allows you to enable and configure Time Machine (page 125), OS X's built-in backup and restore feature.

This section explains how to set Time Machine options.

To set Time Machine options:

1. If necessary, follow the instructions on page 127 to enable Time Machine for external backups.

2. In the Time Machine preferences pane **A** click the Options button.

   A dialog with a list of items that should not be included in the backup, as well as one or more option check boxes, appears **B**.

3. To exclude an item from backup, click the + button and use the dialog that appears to locate and select the disk or folder you want to exclude **C**. Then click Exclude.

   The item is added to the list of items that will not be backed up **D**. Repeat this process for each item you want to exclude from the backup.

continues on next page

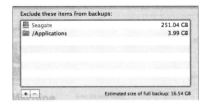

D Items you exclude appear in the list.

4. Toggle check boxes to set other options as desired:

▶ **Back up while on battery power** tells your laptop to create a Time Machine backup while not plugged in.

▶ **Notify after old backups are deleted** displays a warning when your backup disk is full and old backups need to be deleted to make room for new ones.

▶ **Lock documents after last edit** prevents applications that support Auto Save from overwriting Time Machine backups with new versions. If you enable this option, choose a time from the pop-up menu; your options range from 1 day to 1 year.

5. Click Save.

TIP You may have to unlock the Time Machine preferences pane (page 477) before you can make changes to it.

TIP If you change your mind and want to start backing up an item you have previously excluded, in the list of items to exclude **D**, select the item you want to start backing up and click the – button at the bottom of the list. The item is removed from the list and will be backed up from that point forward.

A The Users & Groups preferences pane with two user accounts configured.

Users & Groups

To take advantage of the multiple users features of OS X you need to set up user accounts.

The Mac OS X Setup Assistant, which is discussed in Chapter 1, does part of the setup for you. Immediately after you install Mac OS X, the Setup Assistant prompts you for information to set up the Admin user account.

If you are your computer's only user, you're finished setting up users. But if additional people—coworkers, friends, or family members—will be using your computer, it's in your best interest to set up a separate user account for each one. You can then specify what each user is allowed to do on the computer. You do all this with the Users & Groups preferences pane **A**.

This part of the chapter explains how to add, modify, set capabilities for, and delete user accounts. It also tells you how to use the Users & Groups preferences pane to modify settings for your own account and to set up Login Options and Login Items.

TIP You must unlock the Users & Groups preferences pane (page 477) before you can make changes to it. If you are the person who set up the computer, you are the administrator and can use your own name and password to unlock the preferences pane and make changes.

To activate the guest user account:

1. In the list of users on the left side of the Users & Groups preferences pane, select Guest User **B**.

2. Set options on the right side of the window to specify how guests can access the computer:

   ▶ **Allow guests to log in to this computer** enables the Guest User account for login. This makes it possible for a guest user to access your computer's applications and temporarily store files in a Guest user folder on your hard disk.

   ▶ **Enable Parental Controls** turns on the Parental Controls feature to limit access for the Guest User account. If you turn on this check box, you can click the Open Parental Controls button to set options in the Parental Controls preferences pane (page 558).

   ▶ **Allow guests to connect to shared folders** enables guest users to login to your computer via a network connection to access the contents of shared folders (page 400).

B Select the Guest User account to set options.

TIP Files created or saved to a Guest User account user folder are deleted when the guest logs out. If you expect a user to regularly login to your computer, you might find it more convenient to set up a regular account for that user.

TIP The guest account cannot be used to log in to your computer from a remote location.

TIP You can disable guest access to your computer by turning off both check boxes for the guest account in the Accounts preferences window **B**.

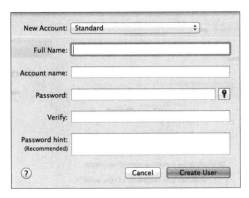

C Use this dialog to set options for a new user account.

D The New Account pop-up menu offers five different options.

To add a new user:

1. In the Users & Groups preferences pane **A**, click the + button at the bottom of the accounts list to display a blank new user dialog **C**.

2. Choose the type of account you want to create from the New Account pop-up menu **D**:

   ▸ **Administrator** is an account that has full administrative access over the computer.

   CAUTION Only give Administrator privileges to individuals you trust and who have a good understanding of how OS X works. An Administrator has access to the entire computer and can make changes that lock you out or prevent the computer from working properly.

   ▸ **Standard** is a normal user account with regular privileges.

   ▸ **Managed with Parental Controls** is an account with limited access and privileges, as set up with parental controls (page 558).

   ▸ **Sharing Only** is an account for file sharing only. A user with this kind of account cannot log in to your computer to access its applications.

   ▸ **Group** is a collection of multiple users. If you choose this option, follow the instructions in the section titled "To create a group" on page 582.

3. Enter information for the user account in each field:

   ▸ **Full Name** is the user's full name.

   ▸ **Account name** is the account name for the user. This name, which is often a shorter variation of the user's full name, should be in lowercase characters and should not include spaces.

continues on next page

▶ **Password** and **Verify** is the user's password, entered the same in both fields. The password should be at least six characters long.

▶ **Password hint** is a hint to help the user remember the password.

4. Click Create User.

Two things happen:

▶ The new account appears in the list of accounts on the left side of the Users & Groups preferences pane **E**.

▶ A folder for the new user appears in the Users folder on your hard disk **F**.

TIP In step 3, you can use the Password Assistant to generate a random password. Click the key button beside the Password box to display the Password Assistant **G**, choose an option from the Type pop-up menu, drag the slider to modify the password length, and consider the password that appears in the Suggestion box.

TIP After step 4, a dialog may appear, asking if you want to turn off automatic login **H**. Click the button for the option you prefer.

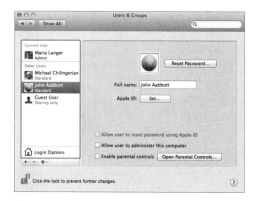

E The new user's account appears in the Users & Groups preferences pane.

F A home folder for the user account appears in the Users folder.

G The Password Assistant can help you create a secure password.

H When you add a user, you may be prompted to turn off or keep automatic login.

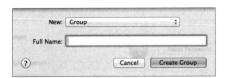

I There's just one option for creating a new group.

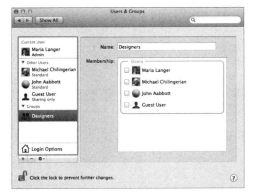

J A new group appears at the bottom of the users list.

K Toggle check boxes to indicate who is part of the group.

To create a group:

1. In the Users & Groups preferences pane **A**, click the + button at the bottom of the accounts list to display a blank new user dialog **C**.

2. From the New Account pop-up menu **D**, choose Group.

   The dialog collapses to offer just one field **I**.

3. Enter a name for the group in the Full Name field.

4. Click Create Group.

   The new Group appears in the List on the left side of the Users & Groups preferences pane **J**.

5. With the group selected, toggle check boxes in the Membership area on the right side of the preferences pane **K** to indicate which users are part of the group.

TIP You can change the accounts in a group at any time. Just open the Users & Groups preferences pane and repeat step 5.

TIP Groups are used to assign permissions to files and folders, as discussed on page 399.

To modify an existing user's settings:

1. In the accounts list of the Users & Groups preferences pane, select the name of the account you want to modify **E**.

2. Make changes as desired on the left side of the window:

   ▸ **Reset Password** displays a dialog you can use to change the user's password **L**. Enter a new password twice and change the password hint, if necessary. Then click Reset Password.

   ▸ **Full Name** is the user's name.

   ▸ **Apple ID** is the user's Apple ID. Click the Set button to display a dialog **M**, enter the Apple ID, and click OK.

   ▸ **Allow user to reset password using Apple ID** makes it possible for a user to reset his password by logging in with his Apple ID.

   ▸ **Allow user to administer this computer** gives the user administrator privileges.

   ▸ **Enable parental controls** lets you limit the user's access based on options in the parental controls feature (page 558).

TIP You cannot modify a user's account settings while he is logged in using fast user switching (page 134).

L Use this dialog to change a password.

M Enter a user's Apple ID in this dialog.

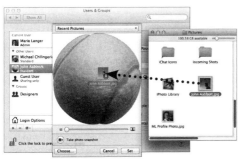

N Choose one of the images that are part of OS X.

O You can also drag a picture from the Finder into the image dialog.

P Drag the image and slider to frame it the way you like.

To change a user's picture:

1. In the Users & Groups preferences pane, select the name of the user you want to change the picture for **E**.

2. Click the picture well to display a menu of pictures **N**.

3. Do one of the following:
   ▸ Choose a new picture.
   ▸ Choose Edit Picture to display an image dialog. Then drag the icon for an image from a Finder window into the image area **O**. You can drag the image into position and drag the slider to zoom the image in or out to frame it **P**. Then click Set.

4. The picture changes to the image you selected or inserted **Q**.

TIP If your computer has a FaceTime camera, you could also click the Take photo snapshot button at the bottom of the image dialog **P** to take a photo for the profile picture.

TIP A user's picture appears in his Address Book card, the Login screen, and as his default iChat picture.

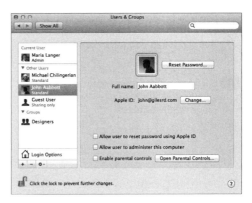

Q The new image appears in the Users & Groups preferences pane for the user.

To specify login items:

1. In the Users & Groups preferences pane, select the name of the account you logged in with. Normally, this will be your account, but if you want to set login items for another user, you must log in with that user's account.

2. Click the Login Items button to display its options **R**.

3. To add a login item, use one of the following techniques:

   ▸ Drag its icon from a Finder window to the list **S**.

   ▸ Click the + button at the bottom of the list and use the dialog that appears **T** to locate and select the item. Then click Add.

   The item you dragged or selected appears in the list **U**.

4. To remove a login item, select it in the list and then click the – button at the bottom of the list. The item is removed.

5. To automatically hide an item when it launches, turn on the Hide check box beside it in the list.

TIP Login items are applications, documents, folders, or other items that are automatically opened when you log in or start up the computer.

TIP Each user can change his own login items, unless his account has Parental Controls (page 558) enabled.

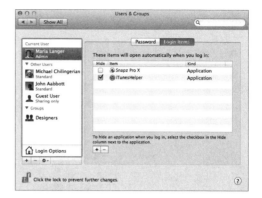

R The Login Items for my account.

S You can add a login item by dragging it into the list.

T You can also use a dialog like this to locate, select, and add an item.

U The item appears in the list.

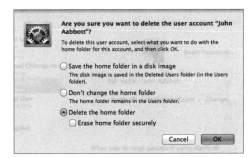

V Use this dialog to specify what should happen to the user's home folder when you delete his account.

To delete a user's account:

1. In the Users & Groups preferences pane, select the name of the user you want to delete **E**.

2. Click the – button at the bottom of the accounts list.

3. A dialog with three options for dealing with the user's Home folder appears **V**:

   ▸ **Save the home folder in a disk image** saves the contents of the user's Home folder in a disk image file in the Deleted Users folder. The file can be opened, if necessary, to extract files.

   ▸ **Do not change the home folder** leaves the Home folder in the Users folder, without making any changes.

   ▸ **Delete the home folder** removes the user's Home folder from the hard disk. If you select this option, you can toggle the **Erase home folder securely** check box to completely remove all data in the Home folder in a way that makes it unrecoverable.

   CAUTION If you delete a user's Home folder, all the files within it are also deleted.

4. Click OK to delete the user.

   TIP When you delete a user's account, he can no longer log in to the computer and access his files.

To set Login Options:

1. In the Users & Groups preferences pane, click the Login Options button at the bottom of the accounts list.

    Login options appear on the right side of the window .

2. Set options as desired:

    ▸ **Automatic login** enables you to choose a user account for the computer to automatically log in to when you start the computer. To disable this feature, choose Off.

    ▸ **Display login window as** lets you select how the Login window (page 133) should appear: as a list of users or as blank fields for user name and password.

    ▸ **Show the Restart, Sleep, and Shut Down buttons** displays these buttons in the login window, making it possible to do any of these things without logging in to the computer.

    ▸ **Show input menu in login window** displays the input menu (page 493), which can be used to choose a different keyboard layout for logging in and using the computer.

    ▸ **Show password hints** displays a password hint in the login window (page 133) if the user has unsuccessfully attempted to log in three times.

    ▸ **Show fast user switching menu as** enables the fast user switching feature (page 134). Use the pop-up menu to determine what should display on the far right end of the menu bar: Full Name, Short Name, or Icon.

    ▸ **Use VoiceOver in the login window** activates the VoiceOver feature (page 371) to speak each item in the login window as a user points to it.

W You can set Login Options in the Users & Groups preferences pane.

▸ **Network Account Server** enables you to join or edit connection information for a network account server. This is an advanced feature of Mac OS X that is beyond the scope of this book.

TIP With the automatic login feature enabled, the login window (page 133) will not appear when you start the computer.

TIP The login window option to display **Name and password** is more secure than a **List of users** because it requires unauthorized users to know both a valid user name and the corresponding password.

References

In This Part

Menus & Keyboard Shortcuts

This appendix illustrates all of Mac OS X's Finder menus and provides a list of corresponding keyboard shortcuts.

To use a keyboard shortcut, hold down the modifier key (usually Command) while pressing the keyboard key for the command.

Menus and keyboard commands are discussed in detail in Chapter 2.

Apple Menu

Option-Command-D	Dock > Turn Hiding On/Off
Option-Command-Esc	Force Quit
Option-Command- Media Eject	Sleep
Shift-Command-Q	Log Out

Finder Menu

Command-,	Preferences
Shift-Command-Delete	Empty Trash
Command-H	Hide Finder
Option-Command-H	Hide Others

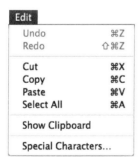

File Menu

Command-N	New Finder Window
Shift-Command-N	New Folder
Control-Command-N	New Folder with Selection
Option-Command-N	New Smart Folder
Command-O	Open
Option-Command-O	Open and Close Window
Control-Command-O	Open in New Window
Command-W	Close Window
Option-Command-W	Close All
Command-I	Get Info
Option-Command-I	Show Inspector
Control-Command-I	Get Summary Info
Command-D	Duplicate
Command-L	Make Alias
Command-Y	Quick Look
Option-Command-Y	Slideshow
Command-R	Show Original
Command-T	Add to Sidebar
Shift-Command-T	Add to Dock
Command-Delete	Move to Trash
Command-E	Eject
Command-F	Find

Edit Menu

Command-Z	Undo
Shift-Command-Z	Redo
Command-X	Cut
Command-C	Copy
Command-V	Paste
Command-A	Select All
Option-Command-A	Deselect All

View Menu

Command-1	as Icons
Command-2	as List
Command-3	as Columns
Command-4	as Cover Flow
Option-Command-1	Clean Up By > Name
Option-Command-2	Clean Up By > Kind
Option-Command-5	Clean Up By > Date Modified
Option-Command-6	Clean Up By > Label
Option-Command-7	Clean Up By > Name
Control-Command-1	Arrange By > Name
Control-Command-2	Arrange By > Kind
Control-Command-3	Arrange By > Date Last Opened
Control-Command-4	Arrange By > Date Added
Control-Command-5	Arrange By > Date Modified
Control-Command-6	Arrange By > Size
Control-Command-7	Arrange By > Label
Control-Command-0	Arrange By > None
Control-Option-Command-0	Sort By > None
Control-Option-Command-1	Sort By > Name
Control-Option-Command-2	Sort By > Kind
Control-Option-Command-3	Sort By > Date Last Opened
Control-Option-Command-4	Sort By > Date Added
Control-Option-Command-5	Sort By > Date Modified
Control-Option-Command-6	Sort By > Size
Control-Option-Command-7	Sort By > Label

View

✓ as Icons ⌘1
as List ⌘2
as Columns ⌘3
as Cover Flow ⌘4

Clean Up Selection
Clean Up By ▶
Arrange By ▶

Show Path Bar
Hide Status Bar ⌘/
Hide Sidebar ⌥⌘S

Hide Toolbar ⌥⌘T
Customize Toolbar…

Show View Options ⌘J

Command-/	Show/Hide Status Bar
Option-Command-S	Show/Hide Sidebar
Option-Command-T	Show/Hide Toolbar
Command-J	Show/Hide View Options

Go Menu

Go	
Back	⌘[
Forward	⌘]
Enclosing Folder	⌘↑
🖥 All My Files	⇧⌘F
📄 Documents	⇧⌘O
🖼 Desktop	⇧⌘D
⬇ Downloads	⌥⌘L
🏠 Home	⇧⌘H
💻 Computer	⇧⌘C
📡 AirDrop	⇧⌘R
🌐 Network	⇧⌘K
📀 iDisk	▶
🅰 Applications	⇧⌘A
✂ Utilities	⇧⌘U
Recent Folders	▶
Go to Folder...	⇧⌘G
Connect to Server...	⌘K

Command-[	Back
Command-]	Forward
Command-Up Arrow	Enclosing Folder
Shift-Command- Up Arrow	Select Startup Disk on Desktop
Option-Command- Up Arrow	Enclosing Folder
Control-Command- Up Arrow	Enclosing Folder in New Window
Shift-Command-F	All My Files
Shift-Command-O	Documents
Shift-Command-D	Desktop
Option-Command-L	Downloads
Shift-Command-H	Home
Shift-Command-C	Computer
Shift-Command-R	AirDrop
Shift-Command-K	Network
Shift-Command-I	iDisk > My iDisk
Shift-Command-A	Applications
Shift-Command-U	Utilities
Shift-Command-G	Go to Folder
Command-K	Connect to Server

Window Menu

Command-M	Minimize
Option-Command-M	Minimize All
Command-`	Cycle Through Windows

Help Menu

Shift-Command-/	Display Mac Help menu

Index

networking, 397
smart, 215
guest user accounts, 580

H

Hard Disk name option (New Finder window), 449
hard disks, 112
  disconnecting, 117
  mount external, 115
  unmounting, 116
  window, 42
hardware preferences, 475
  CDs & DVDs pane, 506
  Displays pane, 507–508
  Energy Saver pane, 509–511
  Keyboard pane, 512–515
  Mouse pane, 516–518
  Print & Scan pane, 522–528
  Sound pane, 530–531
  Trackpad pane, 519–521
Hardware screen, 541
Hearing panel (Universal Access preferences pane), 504
Help, 73–80
Help Center, 73–79
Help Center window, 79
Help menu, 79, 171, 596
Help Tags, 73–74
HFS (hierarchical filing system), 42
Hide Sidebar command (View menu), 35
Hide Status Bar command (View menu), 37
Hide Toolbar command (View menu), 34
Hide/Show command, 160
hiding
  applications, 162
  path bar, 45
  profanity, 564
  sidebar, 35
  status bar, 37
  toolbars, 34

hierarchical filing system (HFS), 42
Highlight Color option (General preferences pane), 486
Home command (Go menu), 46
Home folders, 42, 135
hotspots (Wi-Fi), 416

I

iCal, 143, 219
  creating calendar events, 426
  creating calendars, 232–233
  events, 223–228
  launching, 220
  reminders, 229–231
  sharing calendars, 234–238
  widgets, 289
  window, 221–222
iChat, 144, 427–433
  accounts, 428
  adding buddies, 429
  opening, 428
  removing buddies, 429
  text chats, 430, 432
  video chats, 431, 433
Icon view settings (Finder windows), 462–465
icons
  Finder, 12, 21–26
  Launchpad, 457
  menu bar, 459
  names, 48
  views, 58–60
identity (computer), setting, 548
iDisk command (Go menu), 46–47
iDisk options
  MobileMe, 538
  New Finder window, 449
iDisk storage, opening from Finder, 443
Ignore option (CDs and DVDs pane), 506
Image Capture, 144, 267–270
Image Palettes model, 489

M

N

O

sidebar
    customizing, 471–472
    preferences, 451
Sidebar icon size option (General preferences pane), 487
Sidebar option (Finder's Preferences window), 448
sidebars, 27, 35–36
Sign In dialog, 179
Sign Out command (Store menu), 179
signing into MobileMe, 536
Sites folders, 135
size, desktop pictures, 481
Size option (Dock preferences pane), 484
Ski Report, widgets, 289
Sleep command (Apple menu), 40
sleeping, 39–40
sleeping display, waking, 510
slide shows, screen savers, 483
slider controls, 173
Slightly dim the display when using this power source option (Energy Saver), 510
smart folders, 49, 106–108
smart groups, 215
Smart Quotes option (Language & Text preferences pane), 491
Snow Leopard, latest version update, 5
software
    automatic updates, 566
    updates, installing, 567–568
Software Update preferences pane, 566–568
solid state drive (SSD), 112
sorting
    contact cards, 211
    versus arranging, 70
    window content, 61, 72
sound effects, 530
Sound preferences pane, 530–531
sound volume, 529
Spaces, 299–301

Speakable Items folder, 572
Special Characters command (Edit menu), 320
special effects, 273
speech options, text, 573
Speech preferences pane, 569–574
speech recognition
    configuring, 569–570
    enabling, 569–570
spell check, 197–199
Spelling and Grammar dialog, 172
Spelling option (Language & Text preferences pane), 491
Spotlight, 501–503
Spotlight Comments (Info window), 95
Spotlight menu, searching files, 100–101
Spotlight preferences pane, 100, 495–500
Spotlight Search Results menu, setting preferences, 501
spring-open folders. See spring-loaded folders
SSD (solid state drive), 112
stack folders, customizing, 455
Stacks, 292–294
standard menus, applications, 159
    application menu, 160–162
    dialogs, 172–174
    Edit menu, 170
    File menu, 163–169
    Help menu, 171
    Window menu, 171
Standard option (Users & Groups preferences pane), 581
Start up automatically after a power failure option (Energy Saver), 510
starting
    Energy Saver, 511
    iChat text chats, 430
    iChat video chats, 431
Startup Disk preferences pane, 575–576
startup disks, selecting, 576
status bars, 27, 37

Network pane, 540–542

Sharing pane, 546–552

Word 2007 format, 201

Word Break option (Language & Text preferences pane), 491

word wrap, 187

World Clock widgets, 290

X

Xgrid Sharing option (Sharing preferences pane), 547

Y

Your account name option (New Finder window), 449

Z

zoom button, 27

Zoom command (Window menu), 171

Zoom using scroll ball while holding option (Mouse preferences pane), 517

zooming, windows, 31

VISUAL QUICKSTART GUIDE

Visual QuickStart Guides, designed in an attractive tutorial and reference format, are the quickest, easiest, and most thorough way to learn applications, tasks, and technologies. The Visual QuickStart Guides are the smart choice—they guide the learner with a friendly and supportive approach. The visual presentation (with copious screenshots) and focused discussions by topic and tasks make learning a breeze and take you to exactly what you want to learn.

CSS3:
Visual QuickStart Guide
ISBN: 9780321719638
456 pages, $29.99
September 2010

Drupal 7:
Visual QuickStart Guide
ISBN: 9780321619211
264 pages, $29.99
December 2010

PHP for the Web:
Visual QuickStart Guide
ISBN: 9780321733450
528 pages, $39.99
March 2011

Photoshop CS5 for
Windows and Macintosh:
Visual QuickStart Guide
Elaine Weinmann and
Peter Lourekas
ISBN: 9780321701534
456 pages, $34.99
June 2010

Photoshop Lightroom 3:
Visual QuickStart Guide
Nolan Hester
ISBN: 9780321713100
288 pages, $29.99
June 2010

Dreamweaver CS5 for
Windows and Macintosh:
Visual QuickStart Guide
Tom Negrino and
Dori Smith
ISBN: 9780321703576
552 pages, $29.99
June 2010

Illustrator CS5 for
Windows and Macintosh:
Visual QuickStart Guide
Elaine Weinmann and
Peter Lourekas
ISBN: 9780321706614
464 pages, $34.99
August 2010

Flash Professional CS5 for
Windows and Macintosh:
Visual QuickStart Guide
Katherine Ulrich
ISBN: 9780321704467
600 pages, $34.99
July 2010

InDesign CS5 for
Macintosh and Windows:
Visual QuickStart Guide
Sandee Cohen
ISBN: 9780321705204
576 pages, $29.99
August 2010

www.peachpit.com/vqs